amond Jenness was born in New Zealand in 1886, and came to
nada in 1913 as an ethnologist. He retired from the Federal Service
1947 after over thirty years of study of the ethnology of Canada's
lians and Eskimos.

e *Indians of Canada*, first published in 1932, remains the most com-
hensive work available on Canada's Indians. Part One includes
pters on languages, economic conditions, food resources, hunting
I fishing, dress and adornment, dwellings, travel and transportation,
de and commerce, social and political organization, social life,
gion, folklore and traditions, and drama, music, and art. The second
t of the work describes the tribes in different groupings: the
gratory tribes of the eastern woodlands, the agricultural tribes of the
tern woodlands, the plains tribes, tribes of the Pacific coast, of the
rdillera, and the Mackenzie and Yukon River basins, and finally the
kimo.

DIAMOND JENNESS

The Indians of Canada

SEVENTH EDITION

Published by
UNIVERSITY OF TORONTO PRESS, TORONTO AND BUFFALO
in association with the
NATIONAL MUSEUM OF MAN, NATIONAL MUSEUMS OF CANADA
and
PUBLISHING CENTRE, SUPPLY AND SERVICES
Ottawa, Canada

Originally published in 1932 as Bulletin 65, Anthropological Series No. 15,
of the National Museum of Canada
Second edition 1934
Third edition 1955
Fourth edition 1958
Fifth edition 1960
Sixth edition 1963
Reprinted 1967, 1972
Seventh edition 1977
Reprinted 1980, 1982, 1984, 1986, 1989, 1993, 1996

Canadian Cataloguing in Publication Data

Jenness, Diamond, 1886-1969.
  The Indians of Canada

  'Originally published in 1932 as Bulletin 65,
  Anthropological series no. 15, of the National
  Museum of Canada.'

  Includes index.
  ISBN 0-8020-2286-3 bd.   ISBN 0-8020-6326-8 pa.

  1. Indians of North America — Canada. I. National
  Museum of Man. II. National Museums of Canada.
  III. Title. IV. Series: National Museum of Canada.
  Bulletin — National Museum of Canada ; no. 65.
  V. Series: Anthropological series ; no. 15.

E78.C2J4 1977   971'.004'97   C77-001582-4

FOREWORD

The telegraph read: 'Will you join the Stefansson Arctic Expedition and study Eskimos for three years. Reply collect.' It was signed 'Edward Sapir.' Young Diamond Jenness had never heard of Edward Sapir in the spring of 1913 nor of Vilhaljmur Stefansson — nor had he ever thought of work in Arctic Canada, then still a distant and little known wilderness. He had just completed his first anthropological field work, a year in the Goodenough Islands off the southeast coast of New Guinea and was at home in Wellington, New Zealand, recovering from yellow fever and working on his field notes. He learned that Edward Sapir was the chief of the anthropology staff of the Victoria Memorial Museum in Ottawa and that Stefansson was a widely acclaimed Arctic explorer. A month later he joined the expedition assembling in Victoria, BC, and sailed north that summer. Thus began the Canadian career of Canada's most distinguished anthropologist and one of the world's most respected Eskimologists.

Born in Wellington, New Zealand, Jenness received his BA in Honours Classics there from Victoria University College and, as an outstanding student, gained entry to Balliol College, Oxford, where in 1908 he began a three-year course in Classics. There he met Marius Barbeau, a young French-Canadian who went on to become the father of Canadian folk culture studies. They both took the two-year course in anthropology, at the time a relatively new field of study, and received diplomas in anthropology under Dr R.R. Marett in 1910. Barbeau returned to Canada to join Ottawa's new museum anthropology staff, then being recruited by Sapir. Jenness completed the third year of his classics and late in 1911 joined his brother-in-law, the Reverend A. Ballantyne, at his jungle mission. He spent exactly a year among those tropic mountain islands with the Papuans and, with Ballantyne, wrote *The Northern D'Entrecasteaux*, published in 1920.

Diamond Jenness' research and publications span 58 years from the Papuan jungle of 1911 until 1969, when he died quietly on 29 November, a clear sunny early winter day in the Ottawa Valley. Here he and Eileen Jenness had lived since their marriage in 1919 and had raised three sons — and it was here, in the National Museum of Canada, that Jenness produced that long list of admired books and brilliant papers that comprise an enduring record of his scholarship.

But all this and more were in the future in the summer of 1913, when Stefansson took the *Karluk*, *Alaska*, and *Mary Sacks* north to sail around Alaska to Arctic Canada. Jenness was in the *Karluk*, which became trapped in the unusually heavy early autumn ice off the north Alaskan coast. Stefansson took him on a six-man hunting party, luckily, for the *Karluk* very soon after that was carried away and crushed, and most of her people died during the winter of 1913-14. The very few exhausted survivors were rescued from Wrangell Island the following summer. Among the dead were Henri Beauchat, the expedition's other anthropologist, like Jenness recommended to Stefansson for the expedition by Marius Barbeau, their old friend of graduate student days.

Jenness consequently took on all the anthropological research of the Canadian Arctic expedition of 1913-18. He spent that first winter on the bleak north Alaskan shore rather than with the Copper Eskimo of Coronation Gulf as he had planned. And so one may imagine him as a young man, recently recovered from yellow fever, sledding eastward along the coast to spend the winter building up a supply of fish for the expedition members who were to follow later and, in the process, learning the hard lessons of a hard land while undertaking his first Arctic research in learning a new language. He met these diverse challenges so well that some 45 years later, he could report them in his somber and eloquent *Dawn in Arctic Alaska*. Despite this brutal beginning in a strange, remorseless environment, Jenness emerged with a brilliant record of achievement.

In the summer of 1914, Dr Rudolph Anderson, with one Eskimo hunter, Jenness, and three other scientists, sailed from Camden Bay, Alaska, to Barter Island where Jenness excavated old house ruins. Then their little schooner took them, as the Southern Party of the Canadian Arctic Expedition, to Bernard Harbour at the western end of Coronation Gulf on the Canadian Arctic coast. There Jenness helped to build a hut for the group, established contact with the Copper Eskimo, and began his varied work with them. His research covered general ethnology, material culture, mythology, physical anthropology, ethnomusicology, and linguistics.

In the early spring of 1915, Jenness was adopted by Ikpukhuak and Higilak and moved with his Eskimo parents north across Dolphin and Union Strait to Victoria Island. Under their tutelage, he learned, in still greater detail, how to live as a traditional Copper Eskimo, for these people still were scarcely touched by southern influence. In this work he was a pioneer of the participant-observer method, a field technique later to become standard in the developing discipline of ethnology. Probably its significance escaped him as he ate fish, fish, and more fish.

In the autumn of 1915, back at Bernard Harbour on the mainland Arctic coast, the Southern Party learned of the outbreak of war the previous August. When the summer of 1916 brought open water, the party's members sailed south. After three years in the Arctic, Jenness arrived at last in Ottawa in September and met Sapir, the National Museum's chief anthropologist, who had telegraphed him in New Zealand. After a winter in the Museum sorting his data and meeting again with Barbeau, Jenness went overseas in 1917 as a gunner in the Canadian field artillery.

He returned to Ottawa in 1919, married Eileen, and launched into an incredibly productive phase of analysis, writing, publishing, further field research, and additional museum duties. The resulting flood of papers and monographs include his masterly volumes on the Copper Eskimo, notably *The Life of the Copper Eskimo* (1923) and *Songs of the Copper Eskimos* (1925) with Helen H. Roberts. Also during this phase he completed *The People of the Twilight* (1928), probably the best single book ever published on an Eskimo people.

With all that work, Jenness also continued field research. He spent two months in 1922 among the Sarcee of southern Alberta learning from older people the traditional life of that tribe. Then he wintered in 1923-4 with the Carrier Indians on the Skeena River in the northern interior of British Columbia. Next came an arduous nine-month trip wandering among the Sekani of northern British Columbia. In 1926, he undertook archaeological work at Cape Prince of Wales and Little Diomede Island at the western tip of Alaska. From this work, he discovered and defined the Old Bering Sea culture, a most important contribution to Alaskan prehistory and Eskimo origins.

Although claiming not to be an archaeologist, Jenness had already, in 1925, defined the Dorset culture of Arctic Canada. His discovery of this culture was one of the most brilliant feats of scientific induction in the history of American archaeology. A collection of artifacts dug up by Eskimos at Cape Dorset or on Mansel Island had been sent to the Museum by the Royal Canadian Mounted Police. On examining the material, Jenness saw that it was a mixture of modern and prehistoric Thule artifacts along with others that appeared previously unknown and strange. The latter, consisting of small, delicate harpoon heads and other artifacts of ivory, bone, and stone, he interpreted as belonging to a new and distinctive phase of Eskimo culture, the Cape Dorset, which in his view had preceded the prehistoric Thule culture in the eastern Arctic. On the basis of this small collection of second-hand material, he not only defined the main characteristics of the new culture, but postulated its age, its geographic distribution, and the basic economy of its people. Therkel Mathiassen, the distinguished Danish archaeologist who had excavated at numerous localities in the Canadian Arctic a few years earlier, had found Dorset artifacts at several of his sites but had regarded them as local and specialized types of the Thule culture. Jenness' theory was strongly resisted, but later investigations have completely supported his earlier analysis.

Also in 1926, Jenness became Chief Anthropologist in the National Museum of Canada. Thus he became responsible for the Museum's work in ethnology, physical anthropology, and archaeology, in research, display, collecting, and other museum activities. Nevertheless he was back in the field in 1927, devoting two months to the archaeological pursuit of the extinct and still poorly-known Beothuk of Newfoundland. Again, in 1929, Jenness found the time and funds for two months of ethnographic field studies with the Ojibway at Parry Sound, Ontario. Finally, despite the Museum's poverty during the depression, he visited the Coast Salish in 1935.

These later field projects no longer brought isolation, hunger, exhausting trips, and risk of death. They did contribute to that continuing flow of publications despite the demands of lectures, committee work, and administrative duties. During this time he completed the present work, his monumental *Indians of Canada* (1932), the first comprehensive presentation of Canadian aborigines. Now a classic, it continues to be simply the best of its kind.

And so much more. In 1929 he represented Canada at the Fourth Pacific Science Congress, and in Vancouver in 1933 chaired the Anthropological Section of the Fifth Pacific Science Congress. For the latter, Jenness organized and edited *The American Aborigines; their Origin and Antiquity* (1933), one of the basic syntheses on American prehistory. The ten contributors to the volume included some of the foremost anthropologists of the time: Franz Boas, Roland B. Dixon, E.A. Hooton, N.C. Nelson, Herbert J. Spinden, Clark Wissler. Jenness' own contribution, 'The Problem of the Eskimo,' is one of the most valuable and the one that probably has best stood the test of time. In it he showed the special talent he so often displayed of being able to survey a wide scene, analyse its complexities, contradictions, and difficulties, and, with convincing logic, come up with what turned out to be the right solution. In 1938, he was Canada's official delegate to the International Congress of Anthropological and Ethnological Sciences in Copenhagen. His exceptional stature as an anthropologist and the high personal regard he had earned in his profession are reflected in his being elected president of the Society for American Archaeology in 1937, vice-president of Section H (Anthropology) of the American

Association for the Advancement of Science in 1938, and president of the American Anthropological Association in 1939. Also during the years between the wars he developed the antiquities legislation that has been so important for the protection of archaeological resources in the Northwest Territories.

With the outbreak of the second world war, Jenness joined the Dependents Allowance Board and then, in 1940, became Deputy-Director of Intelligence for the Royal Canadian Air Force. In 1943, he became Chief of the Inter-Service Topographical Section. Afterward, he organized the Geographical Bureau and was its Director until his retirement in 1947. Thousands passing through Coral Harbour or Frobisher Bay are unaware of the influence that Jenness' wartime recommendations have had on the course of their travels in the Canadian Arctic since that time.

With his retirement, the Jennesses travelled widely. He continued his research and writing, lectured, and advised scores of scholars, especially younger ones who could depend on his rare combination of kindness and brilliance. After living in Cyprus and echoing his Balliol College studies, he published *The Economics of Cyprus, A Survey to 1914* (1962). Between 1962 and 1968, the Arctic Institute of North America published his admirable five volumes on Eskimo administration in Alaska, Canada, and Greenland. These monographs reflect his durable and compassionate concern for Canadian Indians and Eskimos and in them one can find much of the advice that he, for so many decades, provided the Canadian Government.

Diamond Jenness was an Honorary Fellow of the Royal Danish Geographical Society, an Honorary Member of the Royal Society of New Zealand, a Fellow of the Royal Society of Canada, an Honorary Associate of the Arctic Institute of North America, and a member of the American Ethnological Society. In 1962 he received the Massey Medal of the Royal Canadian Geographical Society, of which he was also a Fellow. He received honorary degrees from the University of New Zealand, Waterloo University, Carleton University, the University of Saskatchewan, and McGill University. Finally, this quiet man was appointed a Companion of the Order of Canada, his country's highest honour. As winter passed in March 1970, the Governor General, the Right Honourable Roland Michener, awarded the insignia of the Order to Mrs Jenness on behalf of her late husband for his 'services in the field of anthropology, particularly in connection with the Indian and Eskimo population of Canada.' In western Victoria Island in Arctic Canada, where he had done much of his pioneer work, stretches a vast, rolling tundra plain; the Canadian Government has named it the Diamond Jenness Peninsula.

Diamond Jenness was patient, sentient, and an extremely modest man, yet courageous, aggressive, and resourceful in fighting for any cause he felt worthwhile. His generosity and consideration for his younger colleagues were boundless. He had great strength of character, a rugged integrity, and tenacity of purpose, traits that were the more admirable because of the selfless ends toward which they were always directed. Generosity, courage, integrity — one senses that these were the essential traits of character that endeared him to his Eskimo and Indian friends and insured the success of his work among them. Such qualities, even more than his professional eminence and admirable public services, cause all of us to cherish the memory of this exceptional man.

William E. Taylor, Jr
Director,
National Museum of Man
Ottawa, Canada
July 1977

THE INDIANS OF CANADA

A Sioux Indian. (*Painting by Paul Coze.*)

THE INDIANS
OF CANADA

BY

DIAMOND JENNESS

ISSUED UNDER THE AUTHORITY OF THE
SECRETARY OF STATE

NATIONAL MUSEUM OF CANADA
BULLETIN 65
ANTHROPOLOGICAL SERIES No. 15

CONTENTS

Part I

CHAPTER I   PAGE

INTRODUCTION..   1

CHAPTER II

LANGUAGES...   17

CHAPTER III

ECONOMIC CONDITIONS.....................................   28

CHAPTER IV

FOOD RESOURCES..   40

CHAPTER V

HUNTING AND FISHING.....................................   53

CHAPTER VI

DRESS AND ADORNMENT....................................   67

CHAPTER VII

DWELLINGS...   84

CHAPTER VIII

TRAVEL AND TRANSPORTATION, TRADE AND COMMERCE   100

CHAPTER IX

SOCIAL AND POLITICAL ORGANIZATION—PRIMITIVE MIGRATORY TRIBES   118

CHAPTER X

SOCIAL AND POLITICAL ORGANIZATION—IROQUOIANS AND PACIFIC
    COAST TRIBES...   133

CHAPTER XI

SOCIAL LIFE..   149

CHAPTER XII

RELIGION..   167

CHAPTER XIII

PAGE

FOLK-LORE AND TRADITIONS 185

CHAPTER XIV

ORATORY AND DRAMA, MUSIC AND ART 200

CHAPTER XV

ARCHÆOLOGICAL REMAINS 216

CHAPTER XVI

WHO ARE THE INDIANS? 233

CHAPTER XVII

INTERACTION OF INDIANS AND WHITES 249

Part II

CHAPTER XVIII

MIGRATORY TRIBES OF THE EASTERN WOODLANDS 265

    Beothuk 265

    Micmac 267

    Malecite 270

    Montagnais and Naskapi 270

    Algonkin 274

    Ojibwa 277

    Cree 283

CHAPTER XIX

AGRICULTURAL TRIBES OF THE EASTERN WOODLANDS 288

    Huron 289

    Tobacco Nation and Neutrals 300

    Iroquois 300

CHAPTER XX

PLAINS' TRIBES 308

    Assiniboine 308

    Plains' Cree 316

    Blackfoot 317

    Sarcee 324

    Gros-Ventre and Sioux 326

CHAPTER XXI

PAGE

TRIBES OF THE PACIFIC COAST 327
Tlinkit... 328
Haida.. 331
Tsimshian.. 335
Bella Coola.. 339
Kwakiutl... 342
Nootka... 345
Coast Salish... 347

CHAPTER XXII

TRIBES OF THE CORDILLERA 351
Interior Salish.. 351
Kootenay... 358
Chilcotin.. 361
Carrier.. 363
Tsetsaut... 369
Tahltan.. 370
Tagish... 376

CHAPTER XXIII

TRIBES OF THE MACKENZIE AND YUKON RIVER BASINS........... 377
Sekani... 377
Beaver... 382
Chipewyan.. 385
Yellowknife.. 388
Slave.. 389
Dogrib... 392
Hare... 394
Nahani... 396
Kutchin.. 399

CHAPTER XXIV

THE ESKIMO... 405

INDEX.. 423

Illustrations

Part I

A Sioux Indian. Painting by Paul Coze..............................*Frontispiece*

A Kootenay chief, a typical Indian of the plains, although his home lies west of the Rocky mountains (Photo by James Teit)............................. 3

A Tahltan hunter, typical of the Indians of northern Canada (Photo by James Teit)... 5

A typical Eskimo of Hudson bay (Photo by A. P. Low)......................... 7

Major physical divisions of Canada (by D. A. Nichols)....................... 10

Cultural areas of Canada... 11

A Kwakiutl woman of Vancouver island, representative of the Indians of the Pacific coast. Tight ligatures in infancy have unnaturally elongated her head (Photo by G. M. Dawson).. 13

Cree-Ojibwa village of bark lodges. Painting by Verner, in the Public Archives of Canada.. 18

Interior of an Iroquois long-house (reproduced, through the courtesy of A. C. Parker, Municipal Museum, Rochester, from a painting by R. J. Tucker)............ 23

Indian methods of making fire: *a*, lumps of iron pyrites; *b*, a fire-plough; *c*, a hand-drill; *d*, a pump-drill.. 29

Eskimo archers of Coronation gulf. Their bow had an extreme range of only 125 yards and an effective range of from 30 to 40 (Photo by Sir G. Hubert Wilkins) 31

An Eskimo of the Mackenzie River delta using a bow-drill for piercing bone (Photo by J. R. Cox).. 35

Some basic aboriginal stone tools: knife, adze, hammer, drill, and scraper...... 37

Carrier Indian woman dressing a moose hide with a stone-bladed scraper (Photo by Harlan I. Smith)... 39

Corn cultivation among the Hurons (from Lafitau, J. F.: Moeurs des Sauvages Amériquains, vol. 2, p. 155, Paris, 1724).................................. 41

Modern Ojibwa Indians harvesting wild rice in the same manner as their forefathers (Photo by F. W. Waugh)... 42

Red elderberries drying in the sun, Bella Coola (Photo by Harlan I. Smith)...... 44

Smoke-houses of the Tsimshian Indians, for drying salmon, Kitkargas, B.C. (Photo by C. M. Barbeau).. 47

Salmon caches of the Coast Salish Indians, Fraser river, B.C. (Photo by R. Maynard)... 50

A buffalo pound (from Franklin, J.: "Narrative of a Journey to the Shores of the Polar Sea," p. 113, London, 1823)... 55

Plains' Indian running a buffalo (reproduced, through the courtesy of the Public Archives of Canada, from a painting by George Catlin)..................... 57

Coronation Gulf Eskimos spearing salmon trout (Photo by D. Jenness).......... 62

Fishtraps of the Tsimshian Indians, at Kitkargas, B.C. (Photo by C. M. Barbeau). 64

A salmon-weir on the Cowichan river, B.C. (Photo by Gentile)................. 66

Coast Salish woman weaving a blanket of dog hair and mountain-goat wool; another woman spinning the wool; in the foreground a shorn dog (reproduced, through the courtesy of the Royal Ontario Museum of Archæology, from a painting by Paul Kane).. 68

Man, woman, and child of the Nootka tribe, west coast of Vancouver island (reproduced, through the courtesy of the Public Archives of Canada, from Atlas para el viage de las goletas sutil y Mexicana al reconocimiento del estrecho de Juan de Fuca en 1792, publicado en 1802)................................. 69

An Indian of the plains, in the modified costume of the late nineteenth century (Photo by Canadian National Railways)..................................... 71

Illustrations—*Continued*

PAGE

An Eskimo and his wife, Coronation gulf (Photo by D. Jenness)............... 74

Tsimshian Indian wearing a wooden head-dress inlaid with abalone shell, and a woven "chilkat" blanket of goat's wool and cedar bark (Photo by National Museum of Canada).. 77

Interior Salish girl, with her hair specially braided to mark the termination of her adolescence (Photo by James Teit)....................................... 81

Two types of Ojibwa birch-bark lodges (Photo by T. C. Weston)............... 88

Typical tipis of the plains, formerly of buffalo-hide, now of cloth (Photo by Harlan I. Smith).. 91

Plan of an Interior Salish semi-subterranean house (reproduced from Teit, J. A.: "The Thompson Indians of British Columbia", Memoirs of the American Museum of Natural History, vol. 2; Jesup Expedition to the North Pacific, vol. I, p. 193, New York, 1900)....................................... 92

Plank houses of the Coast Salish at Victoria, B.C. Potlatch in progress in the foreground (Photo by R. Maynard)...................................... 93

Haida Indian village at Skidegate, Queen Charlotte islands, B.C. (Photo by G. M. Dawson).. 96

An Eskimo snow hut with a window of ice. The owner's poles and harpoons are planted in the walls, and his sled, upturned and raised on snow blocks, faces the entrance (Photo by D. Jenness)................................... 98

The horse travois of the plains (Photo by Canadian National Railways)......... 103

A small Bella Coola dug out, "spoon" type, for river use (Photo by Harlan I. Smith) 104

A small Nootka dug out, for coast use (Photo by N. K. Luxton)............... 105

Types of Canadian canoes (reproduced from Waugh, F. W.: "Canadian Aboriginal Canoes," The Canadian Field-Naturalist, vol. XXXIII, May, 1919, p. 25)...106, 107

Ojibwa Indians in a birch-bark canoe (reproduced, through the courtesy of the Public Archives of Canada, from a painting by Krieghoff)................. 109

A Kutchin chief with ornaments of dentalium shells (reproduced from Richardson, Sir J.: "Arctic Searching Expedition, A Journal of a Boat Voyage through Rupert's Land and the Arctic Sea", vol. I, Pl. VII, London, 1851).......... 115

Winter migration of an Eskimo community, Coronation gulf (Photo by D. Jenness) 119

Summer migration of an Eskimo community, Coronation gulf (Photo by K. G. Chipman).. 122

Cree camp at Oxford House (Photo by R. Bell)............................. 126

Blackfoot on the watch (Photo by Canadian National Railways)............... 130

The wampum circle with its fifty pendant strings, one for each sachem, that was entrusted to the Mohawk nation at the foundation of the Confederacy of the Five Nations. The X-ray photograph of some of the beads reveals how they were drilled from both ends (Photo by National Museum of Canada)........ 136

Interior of a Coast Salish lodge at Esquimalt, B.C. (reproduced, through the courtesy of the Royal Ontario Museum of Archæology, from a painting by Paul Kane).. 140

A Haida woman, with nose-ring and labret (Photo by R. Maynard)............. 143

"A feast given at Nootka by Chief Macuina (Maquinna) to celebrate his daughter's coming-of-age" (reproduced, through the courtesy of the Public Archives of Canada, from Atlas para el viage de las goletas sutil y Mexicana al reconocimiento del estrecho de Juan de Fuca en 1792, publicado en 1802)............ 146

Tsimshian baby in its wooden cradle (Photo by D. Jenness)................... 150

Interior Salish woman with baby in cradle (Photo by James Teit)............... 151

Tent, of fir-boughs and rushes, for the seclusion of an Interior Salish adolescent girl (Photo by James Teit)...................................... 153

Interior Salish girl wearing the fir-boughs and goat's wool blanket that signify her adolescence (Photo by James Teit)....................................... 155

Coast Salish woman weaving a blanket from the wool of the wild mountain goat (Photo by Harlan I. Smith)... 157

Illustrations—*Continued*

PAGE

Blackfoot (Blood) burial scaffold.. 164

Effigies of two men in a canoe, made of twigs by a Nootka Indian and secluded in the forest to give success in sealing (Photo by G. A. Cox)................. 172

Sarcee medicine-pipe bundle resting on a horse travois outside the owner's tipi; the head-dress associated with the bundle is covered beneath the blanket (Photo by D. Jenness).. 177

Tlinkit medicine-man and his incantations (reproduced from an old illustration, source unknown)... 179

Dance of Haida (?) Indians at Esquimalt, B.C. (reproduced, through the courtesy of the Royal Ontario Museum of Archæology, from a painting by Paul Kane)... 181

A Kwakiutl house with legendary figures painted on its front (Photo by G. M. Dawson).. 182

Bella Coola Indian dramatizing the supernatural being Echo (Photo by Harlan I. Smith).. 186

"Legend of the burning buffalo grass", a ceremony held by the Blackfoot at the first full moon in June (Photo by Canadian National Railways)........... 190

Bella Coola Indian wearing the "Thunder" mask (Photo by Harlan I. Smith).... 196

Actors in the "Cannibal" dance, Bella Coola (Photo by Harlan I. Smith)........ 202

A Coronation Gulf Eskimo with his drum (Photo by Sir G. Hubert Wilkins)...... 205

An Eskimo song... 207

Typical designs in the art of the Canadian aborigines (prepared by D. Leechman). 208

A painted wall-board that was used as a sliding partition in a Tsimshian initiation ceremony. The design is supposed to represent a woodpecker (Photo by National Museum of Canada)... 211

Coiled baskets of the Thompson River Indians (Photo by National Museum of Canada)... 213

Petroglyph near the Bella Coola river, four miles from the village of Bella Coola (Photo by Harlan I. Smith).. 218

Shell-heap or kitchen-midden near the mouth of the Fraser river, B.C., showing the stumps of the trees that grew above it after its formation. Much of the heap has been removed (Photo by Harlan I. Smith)........................ 221

The two types of Indians, one broad-headed, the other narrow-headed, found in British Columbia shell-heaps. The latter type seems absent from the present Indian population of the coast... 227

Soapstone cliff at Fleur-de-Lys, Newfoundland, where Eskimo (?) quarried out their pots in pre-European times (Photo by D. Jenness).................... 231

A Chukchee woman and her children, northeast Siberia. Except for their clothes they are hardly distinguishable from Canadian Indians (Photo by Captain J. Bernard)... 234

Sun temple at Chitzen Itza, showing the high development of architecture among the Maya Indians of Central America (Photo by courtesy of Peabody Museum, Harvard University)... 237

Chukchee from the Siberian coast approaching Little Diomede island, Bering strait, on their way to Alaska (Photo by D. Jenness)........................... 244

"The old graveyards are small, but the new ones large and overflowing." A Haida graveyard in 1919. Marble slabs sculptured by white men have replaced the old memorial columns of wood (Photo by Harlan I. Smith)............. 252

A typical fur-trading post, with its Indian cabins and church, Macleod Lake, B.C., in the territory of the Sekani (Photo by D. Jenness)...................... 257

The transformation of the Indian. A Chilcotin cowboy (Photo by Harlan I. Smith) 262

Illustrations—*Continued*

Part II

	PAGE
Approximate distribution of the eastern Algonkian tribes in 1525	266
A Micmac woman (Photo by Frank Speck)	267
Camp of a Naskapi family (Photo by F. W. Waugh)	271
Algonkins in aboriginal dress (reproduced from "Works of Samuel de Champlain, edited by H. P. Biggar", vol. 3, p. 44, The Champlain Society, Toronto, 1929)	275
Ojibwa Indians in front of their birch-bark lodge (Photo by T. C. Weston)	278
Ojibwa Indian women in a birch-bark canoe (Photo by F. W. Waugh)	282
A Cree Indian (Painting by Paul Coze. Reproduction rights reserved by the artist)	284
Hurons in aboriginal dress (reproduced from "Works of Samuel de Champlain, edited by H. P. Biggar", vol. 3, p. 135, The Champlain Society, Toronto, 1929)	289
Approximate distribution of Iroquoian tribes about 1525	290
Hurons and French attacking a palisaded Onondaga village (reproduced from "Works of Samuel de Champlain, edited by H. P. Biggar," vol. 3, p. 135, The Champlain Society, Toronto, 1929)	291
Hurons gambling with cherry-stones (reproduced from Lafitau, Moeurs des Sauvages Amériquains, vol. 2, p. 341, Paris, 1724)	294
Huron feast of the dead (reproduced from Lafitau, Moeurs des Sauvages Amériquains, vol. 2, p. 457, Paris, 1724)	297
Model of an Iroquois "long-house" of bark, in the Rochester Municipal Museum (Photo by courtesy of A. C. Parker)	301
Masks worn by members of the False Face Society	303
Approximate distribution of the plains' tribes in 1725	309
Two Assiniboine Indians running a buffalo, from a painting by Paul Kane (Photo by courtesy of the Royal Ontario Museum of Archæology)	311
Tipi of a Blood Indian medicine-man, with his medicine-bundle suspended outdoors (Photo by G. Anderton)	318
A Blood Indian girl (Photo by courtesy of Canadian National Railways)	321
Blackfoot crossing the Elbow river, Alberta (Photo by courtesy of Canadian National Railways)	323
A Sarcee chief inside his tipi (Photo by D. Jenness)	325
A Sioux Indian (Painting by Paul Coze. Reproduction rights reserved by the artist)	326
Approximate distribution of Pacific Coast tribes in 1725	329
Skedans, a Haida Indian village on the Queen Charlotte islands (Photo by G. M. Dawson)	332
A Tsimshian maiden wearing a Chilkat blanket and carved head-dress	336
A Tsimshian Indian (Painting by Paul Coze. Reproduction rights reserved by the artist)	337
A Kwakiutl woman (Photo by G. M. Dawson)	338
Koskimo, a Kwakiutl village on Quatsino sound, B.C. (Photo by G. M. Dawson)	343
Interior of a Nootka house (reproduced from "Cook's Third Voyage," London, 1785, Plate 42)	345
Coast Salish dug-outs at Victoria, B.C. (Photo by R. Maynard)	348
Grave monument of the Coast Salish (Photo by Harlan I. Smith)	349
Approximate distribution of Cordilleran tribes in 1725	352
Chiefs of the Thompson River Indians (Photo by James Teit)	353
Winter underground house of the Thompson River Indians (Photo by courtesy of the American Museum of Natural History)	354
Interior Salish girl, wearing a feather head-dress and a blanket woven from the wool of the wild mountain goat (Photo by James Teit)	356

Illustrations—*Concluded*

PAGE

Summer tent of Shuswap Indians at Kamloops (Photo by courtesy of the American Museum of Natural History)... 357

A Kootenay chief (Photo by James Teit)....................................... 360

Summer camp of a Carrier family (Photo by Harlan I. Smith).................. 365

A Tahltan fishing village (Photo by James Teit)............................. 371

A Tahltan sweat-house (Photo by James Teit)................................. 375

Approximate distribution of Mackenzie River and Yukon tribes in 1725......... 378

A Sekani hut of poles and spruce bark (Photo by D. Jenness).................. 380

A Chipewyan Indian (Painting by Paul Coze. Reproduction rights reserved by the artist)... 385

A Chipewyan camp near Churchill, Hudson bay (Photo by R. Bell)............. 387

Salmon-weir of the Kutchin Indians, Upper Yukon river (Photo by W. E. Cockfield)... 397

Kutchin chiefs (reproduced from Richardson, Sir John: "Arctic Searching Expedition, London, 1851", vol. 1, Pl. III)..................................... 400

A Kutchin dance (reproduced from Richardson, Sir John: "Arctic Searching Expedition, London, 1851," vol. 1, Pl. IX)................................. 403

Approximate distribution of the Eskimo in 1525............................. 406

The fuel-gatherer of a Copper Eskimo family (Photo by D. Jenness)........... 407

A Labrador Eskimo hunter in his kayak (Photo by F. Johansen)................ 410

A village of snow-huts (Photo by D. Jenness)................................ 413

Eskimo travelling by sled and dog-team (Photo by J. J. O'Neill)............. 416

Copper Eskimo woman and child (Photo by J. R. Cox)........................ 419

THE INDIANS OF CANADA

PART I

CHAPTER I

INTRODUCTION

When Samuel Champlain in 1603 sailed up the St. Lawrence river and agreed to support the Algonkian Indians at Tadoussac against the aggression of the Iroquois, he could not foresee that the petty strife between those two apparently insignificant hordes of " savages " would one day decide the fate of New France and of the vast territory that stretched for an unknown distance to the west. At the time no other choice lay open to him. The migratory Algonkians and their allies, the Hurons, controlled most of the territory which he hoped to explore, possessed the best means—birch-bark canoes and snow-shoes—of travelling through that territory, and supplied the furs from which he hoped to finance his explorations. Of the Iroquois to the southward he knew little except that they practised agriculture, built permanent or semi-permanent villages, and were far less rich in the furs which at that time seemed to be the most important of the country's natural resources. Had Champlain, like his predecessor Cartier, encountered first the Iroquois on the St. Lawrence river and discovered their military strength and genius for political organization, France might to-day be the dominant power in North America. But fate decreed that the hostility of a few thousand Indians should check the expansion of the new colony and determine the course of history.

When the Dominion was discovered, its inhabitants, if we may trust one of our foremost authorities,[1] numbered only about 220,000; yet they roamed over all the territory from the Atlantic to the Pacific, and from the Great Lakes to the Arctic coast. There was only one section of the country (apart from the mountain peaks and some islands in the Arctic archipelago) to which perhaps no tribe laid claim, namely, a tract of a few hundred square miles in the foothills

[1] Mooney, J.: " Aboriginal Population of America": Smith. Misc. Coll.. vol. 80, No. 7, p. 33 (Washington, 1928). The present population, largely of mixed blood, is roughly 110,000.

1

of the Rocky mountains between the headwaters of the Saskatchewan and Athabaska rivers. A quarter of a million people cannot effectively occupy an area of nearly four million square miles, and there were doubtless many districts seldom or never trodden by the foot of man, just as there are to-day. But it is important to remember that almost every part of the country was claimed by one or other of the numerous tribes of Indians, and that the Europeans who came to colonize it were usurpers in the eyes of the aborigines, except so far as they received rights to their land from the aborigines themselves.

The name Indian which we use to designate the aborigines of America owes its origin to Columbus, who believed that his voyage had brought him by a new route to Asiatic India. Since Columbus' day it has been applied to all the aborigines of the New World, except the Eskimo in the far north, who received a special designation owing to their singular appearance and unusual mode of life. Yet in Canada alone there existed over fifty tribes, each of which spoke a separate language or dialect and possessed its own peculiar manners and customs. There was no common designation for the whole country, no single name for all its inhabitants. Is there any justification, then, other than a purely geographical one, for entitling all the aborigines Indians, with the implication that they belong to one common stock?

Disregarding the Eskimo for the moment, let us consider what are the physical characteristics of the Indians of Canada. We notice, first, some remarkable uniformities throughout the entire country. Everywhere the colour of the skin is some shade of brown, varying from a yellowish to a reddish tinge; it is never a distinct red, however, so that the term "Red" Indian is really a misnomer. The hair of the head is lank, black, and fairly abundant; but hair is generally sparse on other parts of the person. The eyes, which range in colour from medium to dark brown, are often somewhat oblique, and the so-called "mongolian fold" occurs fairly frequently, especially in children. The face is wider and rather more prognathic than among Europeans, and the chest is somewhat full; but the body and limbs are well-proportioned, even if the hands and feet are often not as large as in the white race.

Underlying these general uniformities, however, we notice a considerable diversity in appearance as we pass from east to west,

41202

A Kootenay chief, a typical Indian of the plains, although his home lies west of the Rocky mountains. *(Photo by James Teit.)*

and from north to south. The Indians east of the Rocky mountains are generally of medium height, with here and there, particularly among the Iroquois, a tendency to tallness; but in British Columbia most of the natives are of short stature. The Indians of the Mackenzie basin, and most of the tribes in British Columbia, have round heads (i.e. are brachycephalic), whereas the Indians of the prairies and of eastern Canada are either medium-headed (mesocephalic) or, more rarely, long-headed (dolichocephalic). Even the breadth of the face varies considerably, although it is nearly always greater than among Europeans; and the shape and height of the nose differ widely from tribe to tribe, even from individual to individual.

Are these differences weighty enough to counterbalance the resemblances we listed previously? Do they preclude the possibility that all the various tribes in the Dominion have sprung from one common stock? At the present time no criteria for classifying the numerous varieties of mankind have met with universal acceptance. Earlier writers usually selected the colour of the skin as their guide, and divided mankind into three principal races, the white, the yellow, and the black. A few, like Keane, then subdivided the whites into dark and light, and added a brown race to include the Polynesians, and a coppery red the inhabitants of America. Skin colour, however, appears to be too unstable a characteristic to serve as a major criterion, so that most authorities now adopt in its place the colour and shape of the hair, or else the shape of the head (i.e., the ratio of its length to its breadth), and employ skin and eye colour, breadth of face, stature, and other features as secondary criteria only. How far any of these features have become fixed, how far they may still vary with the environment, and the variations become heritable, is as yet uncertain. Stature, indeed, seems to be more variable than headform; and even head-form, if the results of recent investigations are confirmed, undergoes modification when a population is subjected to prolonged famine or migrates to a country where the climate and economic environment differ from those of its old home.[1] Temperature and humidity, again, have probably played a large part in regulating the size of the nasal aperture, and consequently the shape of the entire nose; for, generally speaking, tropical man has

[1] *Cf.* Boas, F.: "Changes in Bodily Form of Descendants of Immigrants"; The Immigration Commission, Sen. Doc. No. 208 (Washington, 1910); *also* Ivanovsky, A.: "Physical Modifications of the Population of Russia under Famine"; Am. Jour. of Phys. Anth., vol. vi, pp. 331-353 (October, 1923).

33083

A Tahltan hunter, typical of the Indians of northern Canada
(Photo by James Teit.)

a flatter and wider nose than dwellers in the temperate zones, and the Eskimo, who has lived for countless centuries in an arctic or sub-arctic region, possesses the narrowest nose of any people.[1] It is quite possible, therefore, that some of the differences displayed by our Indians are merely the result of differences in their present and past environments; and when we consider the remarkable uniformity in the colour of their skin, the colour of their eyes, and the colour and shape of their hair, three of the most important characteristics, we can hardly escape the conclusion that all the Indian tribes of Canada are at least partly derived from a single racial stock.

The Eskimo of the Arctic and sub-Arctic coast-line diverges considerably from the other aborigines. His skin is lighter in colour, verging towards a yellowish white, his head longer and often keel-shaped, the face wider and flatter, the eyes more often and more markedly oblique, and the nasal aperture unusually small. The cranial capacity slightly exceeds that of the average European, whereas the capacity of Indian skulls is slightly less. It is quite possible, however, that both the skin colour and the smallness of the nose are due to the climatic conditions; and the shape of the head probably depends in large measure on the development of the temporal muscles, which in turn depends on the diet.[2] The Eskimo may well have inherited some of the same racial elements as the Indians, but may have deviated so greatly, owing to his peculiar environment, that he now forms a distinct sub-type.

On anatomical grounds, then, we may divide the aborigines of Canada into two groups, Indians and Eskimo, thus confirming the current usage of those names. How shall we classify them further? Shall we group them by their political divisions, by their languages, or, finally, by the types of culture that prevailed in different parts of the country, that is to say, by cultural areas?

In most parts of the world the political unit among primitive peoples has been the tribe, which may be defined as a body of people bound together by a common culture and a common language, and

---

[1] Cf. Thomson, A., and Buxton, L. H. D.: " Man's Nasal Index in Relation to Certain Climatic Conditions"; Jour. Roy. Anth. Inst., vol. iii, pp. 92-122 (1923).

[2] Thomson, A.: " Consideration of Some of the More Important Factors Concerned in the Production of Man's Cranial Form "; Ibid., vol. xxxiii (1903). Hrdlicka, A.: " Contribution to the Anthropology of the Central and Smith Sound Eskimo "; Anth. Papers, Am. Mus. Nat. Hist., vol. v, pt. II (1910). Knowles, F. H. S.: " The Glenoid Fossa in the Skull of the Eskimo"; Geol. Surv., Canada, Mus. Bull. No. 9 (Ottawa, 1915).

A typical Eskimo of Hudson bay. *(Photo by A. P. Low.)*

acting in concert towards all neighbouring peoples. The tribe often contained numerous subdivisions—the bands of migratory peoples, the villages of the more settled—and each of these subdivisions had its own leader or chief; but there was generally a head chief governing and unifying the entire tribe, with authority over all the subdivisions. Wherever these conditions held, the most natural procedure in describing the aborigines of a country is to consider one by one the individual tribes. In Canada, however, the tribe was seldom so definite an organization. Head chiefs were rare, for as a rule bands or villages were politically independent of their neighbours, to whom they were bound only by ties of kinship and common interest. The remoter bands often diverged considerably in dialect, and so readily assimilated the customs of alien peoples around them that they lost all feeling of political unity with their distant relatives and sometimes became openly hostile. Furthermore, in the widespread migrations that occurred shortly before Europeans penetrated into the interior, many bands became entirely separated from their kinsmen and established themselves in new and remote hunting-grounds. It thus becomes impossible in many cases to determine the limits of tribal units, or indeed of any political unit larger than the band; and the bands were too small, and too numerous, to provide a satisfactory basis of classification.

Even less satisfactory for a detailed description of the aborigines is a classification by languages, although it may prove of great value in reconstructing their history. Such a classification would compel us to join together widely-separated tribes that differed in every other way, and to separate neighbouring tribes that differed only in speech. Thus the Micmac Indians of Nova Scotia and the Blackfoot of the prairies spoke dialects of the same tongue, but were separated by two thousand miles, and lived entirely different lives, in ignorance of each other's existence. Conversely, the Haida Indians of the Queen Charlotte islands resembled their neighbours, the Tsimshian of the Skeena and Nass River basins, in everything except language, which was unlike and unrelated.

A division according to cultural areas holds out more promise than either linguistic or tribal divisions, because the cultural areas closely corresponded to the physiographic which in large measure determined them. The upland portions of Ontario and Quebec—the

Laurentian Shield—together with the very similar Maritime Provinces and Newfoundland, harboured numerous small bands of Indians all of whom spoke dialects of a common tongue, subsisted solely on fish and game, and migrated from place to place along the waterways in birch-bark canoes during the summer months, and with toboggans and dog-teams during the winter. Agricultural peoples, organized into more or less settled communities, occupied the fertile lowland of Ontario between the Great Lakes and its continuation along the St. Lawrence valley south of the Laurentian Shield. Westward, on the prairies, were migratory hunting tribes again, but there the chase centred around the buffalo, elk, and antelope instead of the caribou, moose, and rabbit; fishing disappeared; conical skin tents replaced the birch-bark wigwam; and instead of heavily-laden canoes or toboggans threading their way up the rivers, the dogs dragged on poles— "travois"—over the treeless plains, whatever the Indians could not carry on their own backs. The Pacific coast was another region of settled habitations. There the natives clustered into villages of plank houses near the mouths of salmon rivers, or in bays frequented by seals, otters, and other sea-mammals. Society was divided into grades according to hereditary rank; life was enriched by many elaborate festivals, and art, particularly the painting and carving of enormous boards and poles of cedar, flourished in every community. The inhabitants of the plateau region between the Rockies and the coast were for the most part immigrants from across the mountains, who either preserved their old customs and institutions with such modifications as their new environment suggested, or adopted part of the culture of the coast tribes with whom they came into contact. The Kootenay, for example, used to recross the Rockies every summer to hunt the buffalo with other plains' tribes, whereas the Tahltan Indians of the Stikine river, in the north of British Columbia, took over the clan organization and religious rites of the Tlinkit Indians at its mouth, but preserved their old language and maintained a certain measure of contact with their kinsmen across the divide. The great basin of the Mackenzie river supported a scanty population that resembled in many respects the migratory tribes of eastern Canada, but was even more primitive because of the more limited resources of its territory, and its isolation from centres of more advanced culture. Finally, the Arctic and sub-Arctic shores main-

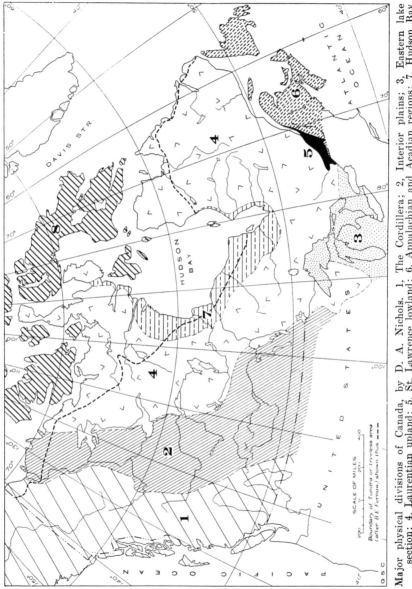

Major physical divisions of Canada, by D. A. Nichols. 1, The Cordillera; 2, Interior plains; 3, Eastern lake section; 4, Laurentian upland; 5, St. Lawrence lowland; 6, Appalachian and Acadian regions; 7, Hudson Bay lowland; 8, Arctic archipelago.

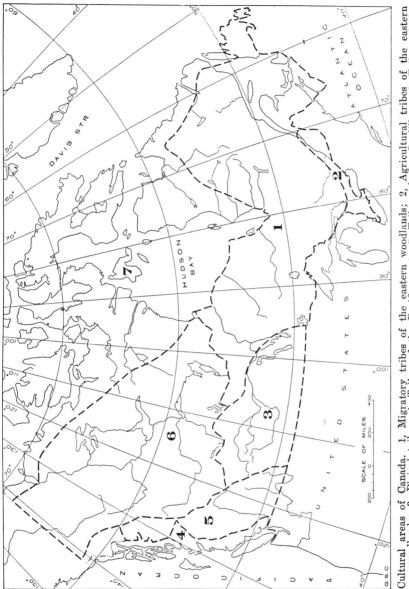

Cultural areas of Canada. 1, Migratory tribes of the eastern woodlands; 2, Agricultural tribes of the eastern woodlands; 3, Plains' tribes; 4, Tribes of the Pacific coast; 5, Tribes of the Cordillera; 6, Tribes of the Mackenzie and Yukon River basins; 7, The Eskimo.

tained the Eskimo tribes, who differed in appearance, language, and mode of life from all other tribes on the American continent.

This is the classification we shall adopt in this book, a classification based primarily on culture areas, which were themselves largely determined by the physiography of the country. But in discussing each culture area in turn, we shall find it most convenient to subdivide according to cleavages of tribe and language, so that in the end we shall be adopting all three bases of classification. The scheme in brief is as follows:

(1) *Migratory Tribes of the Eastern Woodlands.* This group comprises the Micmac Indians of Nova Scotia; the Malecite of New Brunswick and the neighbouring parts of Quebec south of the St. Lawrence river; the Montagnais of eastern Quebec and their near kinsmen the Naskapi in the eastern half of the Labrador peninsula; the Algonkins between Ottawa river and the St. Maurice; the Ojibwa of northern Ontario; the Cree from about the middle of the Labrador peninsula westward to the prairies; and, finally, the extinct Beothuk Indians of Newfoundland.

(2) *Agricultural Tribes of the Eastern Woodlands.* In this group are the Iroquois-speaking peoples, viz., the Five Nations of the Iroquois (Seneca, Oneida, Onondaga, Cayuga, and Mohawk), the Hurons, and the now extinct Tobacco and Neutral tribes of Niagara peninsula.

(3) *Plains' Tribes.* The three divisions of the Blackfoot (Blackfoot proper, Piegan, and Blood), the Sarcee, the Assiniboine or Stonies, and a branch of the Cree.

(4) *Tribes of the Pacific Coast.* The Tlinkit Indians in southeastern Alaska, who encroached on what is now British Columbia; the Tsimshian of the Nass and Skeena rivers; the Haida of the Queen Charlotte islands; the Bella Coola of Dean channel, North Bentinck arm, and the Bella Coola river; the Kwakiutl from Douglas channel to Bute inlet on the mainland (except for the portion controlled by the Bella Coola), and in the northeast corner of Vancouver island; the Nootka on the west coast of the same island; and finally, the Salishan-speaking Indians at the southern end of Vancouver island and around the mouth of the Fraser river.

(5) *Tribes of the Cordillera.* The interior Salishan-speaking peoples of the Fraser river; the Kootenay; the Chilcotin of the Chilko River district; the Carriers along the line of the transcontinental railway running to Prince Rupert; the extinct Tsetsaut tribe at the head of Portland canal; the Tahltan on the Stikine river; and the Tagish of Marsh and Tagish lakes.

716

A Kwakiutl woman of Vancouver island, representative of the Indians of the Pacific coast. Tight ligatures in infancy have unnaturally elongated her head. *(Photo by G. M. Dawson.)*

(6) *Tribes of the Mackenzie and Yukon River Basins.* The Sekani at the head of the Peace river; the Beaver lower down its course; the Chipewyan who roamed between Hudson bay, Athabaska river, and Great Slave lake;[1] the Yellowknives northeast of Great Slave lake; the Dogribs between Great Slave and Great Bear lakes; the Slaves on the Mackenzie river from Great Slave lake almost to

---

[1] The Caribou-Eaters seem to have been a subdivision of the Chipewyan, not distinct enough to rank as a separate tribe.

Norman; the Hare from Norman to the ramparts of the Mackenzie river; the little-known Nahani tribes of the Rocky mountains from the upper Liard river north to the headwaters of the Keele and Stewart; and the rather confused Kutchin tribes of the Peel, Porcupine, and upper Yukon rivers.

(7) *The Eskimos* along the Arctic coast, and around the shores of Hudson bay and the Labrador peninsula.

There were numerous disturbances of population between Jacques Cartier's visit to the St. Lawrence river in 1535 and the confinement of many tribes to reserves in the latter half of the nineteenth century. Some tribes disappeared altogether during the interval, others expanded or moved away to new territories. We are not certain, indeed, of the exact location of every western and northern tribe even as late as 1725, for much of Canada was still entirely unknown.

The eleven languages current in Canada were distributed very unevenly, two of them, Algonkian and Athapaskan,[1] covering nine-tenths of the territory outside the shores of the Arctic, where Eskimo held sway. Physiography again played its part in determining the distribution of the languages, but to a less marked extent than in the case of the culture areas. Thus the two culture areas in the eastern woodlands would have coincided with the two linguistic areas, Algonkian and Iroquoian, if the Algonkian had not extended also into the prairies.[2] The Athapaskan tongue occupied the whole of the Mackenzie River basin, but it also had an offshoot, Sarcee, into the prairies, besides being strongly represented in the plateau regions of British Columbia. Five languages, Tlinkit, Haida, Tsimshian, Salishan, and Wakashan (Kwakiutl-Nootka), contended for possession of the British Columbia coast-line, and an Athapaskan dialect, Tsetsaut, touched the sea at the head of Portland canal, so that this single physiographic and cultural area nurtured a remarkable diversity of speech. Two other languages, Kootenay and Siouan, mark the invasion, shortly before the historical

---

[1] Names of linguistic stocks, when derived from tribal names, are sometimes distinguished by the suffix -*an*, as Algonkin, Algonkian; Sioux, Siouan; but linguists have not been consistent in this respect, Haida, for example, meaning either the tribe or the language.

[2] The affiliations of the old Beothukan language of Newfoundland are uncertain. Latham concluded that it was related to Algonkian, but Gatschet, who had a fuller aquaintance with Algonkian, and a larger Beothukan vocabulary at his disposal, believed that it was an independent language. By 1725, Micmac hunters from Nova Scotia who spoke an Algonkian dialect were overrunning the island, although the Beothuks survived for another hundred years.

period, of some small bands from the United States, where the majority of their kinsmen still survive.

This invasion of alien tribes into what is now Canada reminds us that the political boundaries of the Dominion had no existence before the nineteenth century, and bear little or no relation to any boundaries based on either physiographic or ethnological considerations. The 141st meridian and the 49th parallel of latitude were purely arbitrary lines that cut through cultural, linguistic, and even tribal areas, placing half the Blackfoot Indians, for example, under the flag of the United States and the other half under the British. We cannot logically separate the Eskimo of our Arctic coast-line from the Eskimo of Greenland and Alaska; or the Iroquoian tribes of Ontario from their kinsmen in the state of New York. From a broad viewpoint, therefore, all the cultural areas outlined above, with the exception of the Mackenzie River region, extend beyond the frontiers of the Dominion. Canada's present political boundaries are equally useless for linguistic purposes, since even the Athapaskan dialects of the Mackenzie basin have sister dialects in Alaska and in the western and southwestern parts of the United States. It is not possible, therefore, to study our aborigines thoroughly without studying also the tribes on the remainder of the continent. Nevertheless, we can describe their principal traits without great difficulty, merely glancing now and then at neighbouring regions to fill in small gaps in our picture.

It might seem natural, after this preliminary survey of the field, to proceed with a detailed description of each culture area and of the various tribes that inhabited it. Yet such a course would involve us in endless difficulties. We need, first of all, a clear vision of the economic background which formed the basis of tribal life, a knowledge of the resources the Indians possessed and of those they lacked. So many thousands of years have elapsed since agriculture and iron became known in Europe, since the horse, the ox, and the sheep were domesticated, since man discovered the principle of the wheel, that it is hard for us to conceive of life without these things. Furthermore, no civilized country to-day relies entirely upon its own resources. Canada, for example, imports many important products from abroad—steel from the United States, sugar from the West Indies, and cloth from England; and to be cut off, as the Indians were, from trade with other continents, and with other parts of the same continent, would uproot the foundations of its daily life. In the first days of colonization even the poorest immigrants from France brought with them firearms to shoot the game, steel axes to build and furnish their log cabins, and ploughshares to break up the soil. The Indian had none of these implements at his command. What resources, then, did he possess that enabled him to support his family, and survive?

Clearly, we must first examine the economic environment of the Indians. It will scarcely profit us, even then, to describe each separate tribe. For all the tribes had many elements in common, some derived, it may be, from a common heritage in the distant past, others evolved at a later period during their residence in America before the dawn of history. Thus every tribe was founded on groups of families closely united by ties of kinship; religion was always some form of animism where protecting spirits were believed to guide man's course and to assist him in life's crises; each community practised blood-revenge, and each marked by some rite the change from childhood to manhood. Rather than repeat all these for every tribe, it will be better to paint them in broad outline for the whole country, that is to say, to give a general sketch of the social, political, and religious life of the Indians considered *en masse,* merely noting here and there the more important differences.

The languages spoken by the aborigines fall somewhat outside this scheme, but we may readily describe them in an introductory chapter which will also help the reader to remember the main tribal divisions.

CHAPTER II

LANGUAGES

The highway of the St. Lawrence and Ottawa rivers, connecting with the Great Lakes, inevitably attracted the early settlers towards the vast expanse of the interior continental plain; and the Nelson river, flowing into Hudson bay, though of lesser importance, beckoned the early traders in the same direction. These rivers are neither unnavigable like the Fraser in British Columbia, nor do they rise in a high range of mountains that blocks man's passage into the interior. Between their headwaters and the Atlantic they embrace a wooded upland stamped with a network of lakes and rivers, a stretch of country uniform in character from the boundaries of the prairies to New Brunswick and the Labrador main, except for a small area of fertile lowland in southeastern Ontario and the neighbouring portion of Quebec.

The linguistic features of this region closely correspond to the geographic, being indeed partly determined by them. Only one language, the Algonkian, prevailed from the Atlantic to the prairies, except that some time before history opened a colony of Indians speaking another tongue, Iroquoian, occupied part of the lowland of southeastern Ontario. The voyageur from Montreal, who journeyed westward up the Ottawa river to the Great Lakes, lake Winnipeg, and the Churchill river, encountered no tribes that did not speak the same tongue as the Indians from around his own home who were manning his canoe; and the same tongue served him if he pushed northward from the St. Lawrence river to James bay. Even after he passed the low watershed where the rivers flowing to the Atlantic took their rise, he often had occasion to use one of the dialects of this same Algonkian language, the Cree, whether he followed the course of the Mackenzie river northward to the Arctic ocean, or, turning westward, ascended its tributary, the Peace, to the Rocky mountains; for some of the Crees, leaving their old homes in northern Ontario and northern Manitoba shortly after the establishment of the first trading-posts on Hudson bay, blazed a trail into the far interior that the fur-traders followed later.

The early travellers who pushed westward from the settlements on the lower St. Lawrence river seem hardly to have realized how great an asset to their explorations was this far-flung currency of the Algonkian tongue; but Sir Alexander Mackenzie repeatedly mentions the aid he received from the equally wide distribution of Athapaskan, another of the Indian languages. It carried him from Great Slave lake to the Arctic ocean, and from the same lake again through the Peace and Upper Fraser River areas almost to the Pacific coast. It was on the frontiers of this language that he encountered the greatest obstacles to his explorations—on the Fraser river near Alexandria, where the Athapaskan-speaking Carriers and Chilcotins adjoined Shuswap Indians who spoke the totally different Salishan tongue, and on the Bella Coola river and inlet, where another dialect of the Salishan language held sway. Everywhere else throughout Mackenzie's long journeys his Chipewyan interpreters from Great Slave lake could make themselves understood with little difficulty, and obtain valuable advance information concerning routes and portages.

Eleven linguistic stocks were current in Canada, most of them subdivided into numerous dialects. No less than six were confined to British Columbia. There the Tlinkit language of southern Alaska abutted on the Tsimshian of the Nass and Skeena rivers and confronted the Haida of the Queen Charlotte islands. Vancouver island was the home of the Wakashan tongue, separated into two dialects so divergent that they constituted almost distinct languages, the Nootka on the west coast and the Kwakiutl on the east. The tribes at the southern end of the island, and on the Fraser river as far up as Alexandria, used the Salishan language, other dialects of which prevailed at Dean and Burke channels and in the Okanagan valley. The Kootenay Indians possessed a language of their own, and throughout the northern interior of British Columbia invading tribes from across the mountains introduced the Athapaskan tongue. British Columbia, therefore, like the Pacific coast of the United States, was a babel of conflicting tongues, suggesting that it had been a cul-de-sac from which neither invaded nor invader could escape. In pre-European times contact between the tribes was so frequently hostile that no one language gained the ascendancy; but during the more peaceful era that succeeded the first

Cree-Ojibwa village of bark lodges. *(Painting by Verner in the Public Archives of Canada.)*

colonization by white men a degraded form of the Chinookan language spoken in the state of Washington became the usual medium of intercourse between the different tribes, like the jargon of broken English current in many parts of the South Seas.

On the prairies another linguistic stock appeared, Siouan, spoken by the Assiniboines or Stonies who entered Canada from the south, probably around 1600. The Blackfoot, Blood, and Piegan Indians spoke an Algonkian dialect, as did also those Cree who migrated to the plains after the introduction of firearms. The Sarcee, who now live on a reserve near Calgary, are the remnant of a once powerful tribe that moved down from the north a few centuries ago. Though assimilated to the Blackfoot in all their customs they still preserve their Athapaskan tongue.

The Iroquoian language of southeastern Ontario was not confined to the historic Five (later Six) Nations, but was shared by them with the Huron, the Tobacco, and the Neutral nations which they displaced or destroyed. Elsewhere in eastern Canada Algonkian dialects prevailed; one of them, Cree, extended far into the northwest during early historical times, penetrating the great block of territory held by the Athapaskan tongue. The Eskimo language reigned exclusively along the Arctic and sub-Arctic coast-line outside the shores of James bay.

The number of distinct languages in Canada raises the question whether they may not all be derived from a single source, even if they have changed so greatly that we cannot to-day detect their relationship. We know that every language changes in vocabulary, pronunciation, and even grammar. Many words in the English Bible, and in Shakespeare, are now obsolete; others, though still used, are pronounced differently; and grammatical forms that were formerly correct are no longer so. These changes still continue, although the spread of education, and the printing press, with their tendency to standardize spelling, often mask and sometimes perhaps retard them; for in spite of such checks all the Dominions of the British Empire are slowly developing distinctive dialects. The languages of the Indians have undoubtedly changed in the same way, though since the aborigines evolved no form of writing (except a crude picture-writing) we have no ancient documents with which to compare their present-day speech and are less able to gauge the rates of change. That all languages do not change at the same rate we can see from the examples of Greek and English, since modern Greek differs less from the Greek spoken a thousand years ago than modern English from the Anglo-Saxon of 900 A.D. In America, Eskimo and Athapaskan seem more resistant to change than some of the other languages, e.g., Algonkian and Salishan; for in Algonkian and Salishan the dialects diverge rather widely from one another, whereas an Eskimo of the Mackenzie River delta can readily converse with a Labrador Eskimo, and a Chipewyan Indian of Great Slave lake with a Carrier of British Columbia, although their tribes have been separated for an untold number of centuries. Philologists, who must work with the languages as spoken to-day, have discovered no kinship among any of the eleven Canadian tongues, unless perhaps between Haida, Tlinkit, and Athapaskan, which Sapir would group together under the name of Nadene.[1] He has never published entirely satisfactory proof of their kinship, however, so that some other authorities still consider them separate languages, and attribute certain undoubted resemblances between them to mutual contact and borrowing rather than to common descent. One or two philologists have also ventured the opinion that Eskimo and Algonkian may be related to one another, but have put forward no evidence in support of their view.[2] In spite, then, of all the researches of the last half century, we are still unable to trace to a common source any two of the eleven languages current among our Canadian aborigines.

Looking farther afield, we find that seven of the Canadian languages, Athapaskan, Salishan, Wakashan, Kootenayan, Siouan, Iroquoian, and Algonkian, are spoken also in the United States; while Eskimo ranges from Greenland in the east to the Asiatic shore of Bering strait in the west. Certain writers, extending their view to the Old World, have claimed kinship between Eskimo and Finnish,[3] and between Nadene (Athapaskan and related tongues) and the Sinitic (Tibeto-Chinese-Siamese) group of eastern Asia. In no case,

---

[1] The Na-Dene Languages, a preliminary report; Am. Anth., vol. xvii, pp. 354 ff.

[2] Sapir even speculates on an early " Algonkian-Wakashan " root language from which have sprung Algonkian, Beothuk (?), Wakashan, Salish, and Kootenay. Sapir, E.: " Central and North American Languages"; Encyclopedia Britannica, 14th ed., vol. 5, p. 139.

[3] Sauvageot, A.: Esquimalt et Ouralien, Journal de la Société des Américanistes de Paris, N.S. tome xvi, pp. 279-316.

however, has full and convincing proof been provided, and our present knowledge does not warrant us in asserting genetic relationship between any of the Canadian languages and any language outside North America.

The question may perhaps be asked whether the close physical resemblances between the aborigines, their apparent derivation from a single racial stock, does not also imply a common origin for all their languages. If we assume, with most authorities, a single origin for all the present varieties of the human race, we must also assume a single origin for its multiple varieties of speech. The term " distinct language," or " distinct linguistic stock," is, therefore, a purely relative one, meaning no more than that a certain language or linguistic stock, while derived from the same ultimate source as other languages in the far-distant past, has yet diverged so widely from them that no kinship is now discernible. It is quite possible that if the languages of the Canadian aborigines had been recorded phonetically three or four thousand years ago, we could discover resemblances among them that would reduce the number of separate stocks. Yet even this is doubtful, for the human race is certainly a hundred times older than four thousand years, and our Indians may have been descended from many different bands of immigrants that spoke different languages before they entered America.

Here a word of caution is necessary concerning two errors that occur very frequently even in scientific books. It is often assumed that language and physical type are co-ordinate, that tribes or peoples who speak dialects of the same language are *ipso facto* of the same racial stock. A moment's reflection will show how misleading this assumption can be. The United States is inhabited at the present time by people of widely different physical types, ranging from the fair, blond-haired descendants of Scandinavian immigrants to the blackest negroes; yet all alike employ the English language. Conversely, there is often a close resemblance in physical appearance between peoples whose languages seem to have no connexion with one another, as for example, between the Pacific Coast tribes of Canada and some Mongolian peoples of northeastern Asia. So the numerous tribes that now speak Algonkian dialects may have diverse origins; whereas the multiplicity of languages on the Pacific coast, where the Indians differ so little in outward appearance, really obscures the presence of one fundamental racial stock.

The same distinction holds between language and culture as between language and race. Beneath the diversity of the Pacific Coast languages there is the closest resemblance in customs and mode of life. The Sarcee, though but recently separated from their kinsmen of the Mackenzie River valley, have yet so assimilated themselves to the Blackfoot that they can be distinguished only by language. On the other hand, the scattered bands that use the Cree dialect of Algonkian differ widely in culture according as they have come into contact with the Athapaskan-speaking tribes of the Mackenzie river, the plains' tribes, or the Indians of eastern Canada. Similarly, in the world at large, peoples of very different cultures often employ the English tongue, and contrariwise a generalized European culture has permeated among many peoples who make use of diverse languages. Race, culture, and language, then, are distinct features, no one of which affords a certain guide to the others. Each can change independently, so that similarity of physical type may conceal radical differences of culture or of language; and community of language, or of culture, may indicate no more than close contact between two peoples of different racial stock.

We must guard, also, against another widely-spread error of a somewhat different nature. Simplicity of culture does *not* entail a simple language. The most primitive Indians in Canada, those of the Mackenzie River valley, possessed the most complex language; and English or French appears comparatively simple beside the intricacies of Eskimo.

Indian languages seem especially complex to a European because the words are often strangely difficult to pronounce. Theoretically, the number of sounds that can be produced by the organs of human speech is almost unlimited; in practice, each language (or dialect) unconsciously makes its own selection of from fifteen to forty. The Indian languages have selected many sounds that are foreign to European ears. Thus most of them draw a different line of demarcation between the voiced and voiceless stops, which we write in English *k* and *g, t* and *d, p* and *b.* It is as though in each of these groups there were four sounds, represented in the first group by *kh, k, kg,* and *g,* where *k* and *g* are pronounced as in English, *kh* denotes a *k* uttered with great stress and a noticeable emission of breath, and *kg* a sound intermediate between *k* and *g.* Certain Indian languages will then have chosen the first and third of these sounds, *kh* and *kg,* whereas English has chosen *k* and *g.* Many go even further; they glottalize the *kh* i.e., close the glottis during its formation so as to produce a peculiar clicking sound, and they add a velar *k,* pronounced far back in the throat, that is very characteristic of Semitic tongues, but unknown in western Europe.

76024

Interior of an Iroquois long-house. (Reproduced through the courtesy of A. C. Parker, Municipal Museum, Rochester, from a painting by R. J. Tucker.)

Another difficulty for Europeans lies in the grammatical structures of Indian languages, which are based on unfamiliar principles. Often there are very few parts of speech, some languages possessing no adverbs, prepositions, or conjunctions. The verb and noun may be imperfectly distinguished, the pronoun subordinated to the verb, and the intransitive verb assume the function of an adjective. Gender based on sex appears in the coast dialects of the Salishan tongue, but only in pronominal forms; and the Iroquoian dialects separate nouns into masculine and non-masculine. Elsewhere, the nearest approach to gender is the distinction between animate and inanimate objects in the Algonkian language and in one of the dialects of Siouan. Number is treated in a variety of ways. In Eskimo there is a differentiation between " one," " two," and " many," i.e., a dual number as in ancient Greek; but very frequently a distinction between the collective and the distributive, between " all " and " each," or between " some " and " many," takes the place of singular and plural. Again, instead of a sharp distinction between present, past, and future time, tense may be based on such categories as the " beginning " or " duration " of an action, its " momentary " or " continuous " character, or on the " transition " from one state to another. These and other differences have probably deterred many philologists from studying the Indian languages, and help to explain our imperfect knowledge of some of them to-day.

However much they may vary in structure one from another, nearly all the Canadian languages possess one feature in common, the elaborate employment of affixes preceding and following the stem. Infixes are rare—only Siouan and Nootka make use of them —but most languages employ both prefixes and suffixes. In Eskimo there is only one prefix, a syllable *ta* used with certain pronominal place stems; but there are something like three hundred suffixes which may be combined with one another in bewildering variety to produce words of ten, fifteen, and even twenty syllables. These suffixes (together with prefixes in other languages) supply the need of several parts of speech and permit a whole sentence to be embraced within a single word. Thus, from the word *igdlo:* " house," a West Greenland Eskimo can produce the following and many other forms:[1]

igdlorssuaq: a large house;

igdlorssualiorpoq: he builds a large house;

igdlorssualiorfik: the place where a large house is being built;

igdlorssualiorfilik: one who has a place where a large house is being built;

igdlorssualiortugssarsiumavoq: he wants to find a man who can build a large house.

Numerous affixes of this nature, easily combined with one another, give the Indian languages great flexibility and enable them to overcome many deficiencies in their vocabularies. It has often

[1] Taken from Rink, H.: " The Eskimo Tribes"; Meddelelser om Grønland, vol. xi, p. 48 (Copenhagen, 1887).

been thought that because an Indian distinguishes perhaps only three or four colours, and possesses few abstract nouns, his vocabulary is very limited. Nothing could be further from the truth. If he distinguishes few colours it is because fine discrimination in colour has no value in his life. He will differentiate, in matters that are important to him, where Europeans may make no distinction. Thus Eskimo has one term for falling snow, another for granular snow, a third for a snow-drift, and several others; whereas English possesses but the one word "snow," and must employ descriptive phrases to separate its varieties or manifestations. It is true that the vocabularies of Indian languages are small when compared with European dictionaries, even if we eliminate from the latter all derivative forms and count only the stem words. Thus the latest dictionary of the Eskimo dialect of West Greenland,[1] one of the best known American languages, contains less than two thousand six hundred stem words. At least half of these words, however, are in everyday use, whereas European dictionaries are filled with scientific, technical, poetical, and semi-obsolete words that are never employed in ordinary conversation and are known to comparatively few individuals. The vocabulary of an uneducated English peasant, it is often stated, rarely exceeds seven hundred words, which is no more than that of an Eskimo.

In addition, the Indian, like the European peasant, talks concretely, his vocabulary being more suitable for descriptive narrative than for the expression of abstract ideas. Abstract terms are indeed rare, although they could readily have been developed by the use of appropriate affixes. That they were not so developed we may ascribe, perhaps, to the primitive economic conditions and to the absence of a leisured class devoted to intellectual pursuits. There were Indian philosophers who pondered deeply and spent much time in silent meditation; but they seldom revealed their thoughts to others or sought the stimulus and discipline that come from open discussion and debate. So their meditations tended to revolve around concrete things and their languages reflected the concreteness of their thoughts.

In their chants and religious ceremonies the Indians employed many words, archaic or descriptive, that were not current in ordinary

[1] Schultz-Lorentzen, *Den Gronlandske Ordbog.* (Kobnhavn, 1926.)

conversation. Sometimes they preserved, too, archaic grammatical forms, like the use of "thou" in the English churches. More strange to Europeans were the slight differences in speech between men and women, that appeared in a few languages. These were sometimes mere differences of vocabulary, certain words being used by women only; but in Siouan and in the Eskimo dialect of Baffin island there were also slight differences in grammatical forms.

The most musical of all the Indian languages was Algonkian, owing to its richness in vowel sounds and its avoidance of the harsher consonants. It had a fondness for whispered syllables, *h* and a voiceless *w* (like *wh* in *while*) occurring very commonly as terminations; glottal stops between vowels, though not uncommon, were never stressed, and there were few of the glottalized consonants (i.e., consonants pronounced with a momentary stopping of the breath) that were so frequent in other Indian languages. In striking contrast was the exceeding harshness of the Salishan dialects of British Columbia, which not only abounded in harsh consonants like *k* and *g*, frequently glottalized, but combined two and often three consonants, for example, *klm* and *pts* (with perhaps the *k* and the *p* glottalized), which in European languages would be separated by vowels. The Athapaskan dialects were less harsh than the Salishan, but more difficult and elusive on account of the complexity of the prefixes and suffixes, the vagueness of the stems, the numerous vowel and consonantal changes, and the use of tonal systems that varied from one tribe to another. Athapaskan was perhaps the most difficult of all the Indian tongues, nearly every one of which would seem difficult if compared with French or German among European languages.

The presence of many distinct languages in Canada seems to have proved no great barrier to tribal contacts, to the spread of cultural elements, or even to the formation of political alliances between groups of different speech. Thus a more or less uniform culture prevailed all along the Pacific coast, despite the diversity of languages in that region. The Sarcee and the Cree, both immigrants to the plains, preserved their respective languages when they adopted the culture of the older plains' tribes. In the east, the Hurons allied themselves with their Algonkian neighbours against their own kinsmen, the Iroquois proper. Nearly every tribe, indeed, absorbed through marriage or warfare a few members of some neighbouring tribe; and trading relations, however limited their scope, fostered the growth of a restricted bilingualism. New arts and new appliances easily overrode linguistic boundaries; and even social and religious institutions and ideas overflowed them with considerable freedom, as shown by the penetration far into the interior of the phratric systems of the Pacific coast,[1] and the occurrence of sun-dance and medicine-bundle ceremonies in every prairie tribe. Indian traditions tell us that in Canada, as in Europe, differences of speech often engendered misunderstandings and distrust resulting in quarrels and even wars; but warfare itself is a form of intertribal contact that leads to many cultural exchanges. It would seem, therefore, that the multiplicity of languages was neither the principal, nor even an important, factor in promoting the inequality of progress among the aborigines in different areas, the primitiveness of some groups, and the relatively high level of culture attained by others. This inequality arose rather from the varying economic conditions, the difficulties of travel and transportation, and the self-sustaining character of each tribal unit that rendered it virtually independent of its neighbours.

---

[1] *See* p. 148, note.

CHAPTER III

ECONOMIC CONDITIONS

The difference between the immediate resources of a country and its potential resources is the measure of the limitations in man's knowledge. Statisticians calculate for us the value of Canada's minerals, its waterpowers, lumber, agricultural and pastoral land, fisheries, and fur-bearing animals; and their figures soar with every increase in our knowledge, whether it be the production of an earlier-ripening wheat or the invention of a cheaper process for refining low-grade ores. Just as we have no right to despise the early French-Canadian settlers because they did not realize the power that lay buried in the Nova Scotia coal-fields, or in the waterfalls on the Saguenay river, so they in turn were not justified in scorning, as many did, the Indian tribes because they made even less use of the potential resources. For the Indians, isolated in a remote corner of the New World, had lagged behind in the march of progress, whereas the colonists inherited all the knowledge and experience that had resulted from the successive civilizations in the Old. If the settlers who came over during the first fifty years of colonization had themselves remained isolated during the next two hundred years, in all probability they would either have perished or have fallen back into a condition not much better than that of the " sauvages " around them.[1]

Let us consider, for a moment, some of the advantages the colonists possessed. They imported with them the seeds of various grains and vegetables, such as wheat, oats, rye, barley, potatoes, and turnips, and they possessed the knowledge of their cultivation. They knew how to irrigate and to fertilize the land, how to rotate their crops. They brought steel axes and saws to clear the ground, ploughs and oxen to break up the soil, scythes to cut the grain, and vehicles to gather in the harvest. Cows, sheep, goats, and poultry provided them both meat and clothing. The newcomers could anchor themselves to any fertile plot of ground, certain that with reasonable industry

---

[1] The early Norse colonies in Greenland, established before the time of firearms, relied on Europe for iron, timber, and domestic animals for breeding. They disappeared within little more than a century after importations ceased and they had to fall back, like the Eskimo, on the resources of their local environment.

they could wrest from its few square rods sufficient food to keep
starvation from their doors. They could erect substantial buildings
of brick or stone, since the same soil that provided their sustenance
would provide sustenance also for their children's children; and they
could concentrate their homes as a single community, facing the river
that linked them during the summer with the motherland.

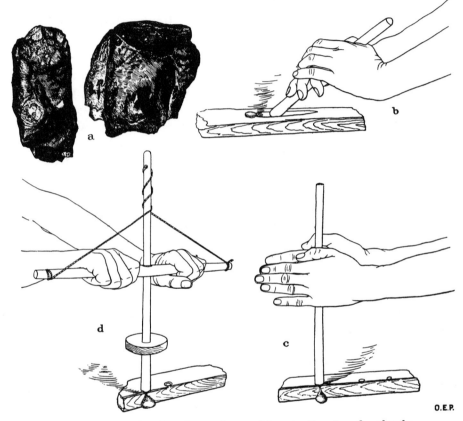

Indian methods of making fire: a, lumps of iron pyrites; b, a fire-plough;
c, a hand-drill; d, a pump-drill.

The Indians lacked every one of these things. Their only domesticated animal was the dog, which was useful for transportation and
hunting, but of little value for either food or clothing.[1] The Iroquoian
tribes, who had learned in the south how to grow maize, beans,

[1] The Iroquoian and other tribes frequently ate the dog when meat was scarce; the Ojibwa, some
plains' and some Pacific coast tribes also ate it on ceremonial occasions; but it was never an important
article of diet. The Eskimo of southeast Baffin island, according to the historian of Frobisher's voyage,
raised a small breed of dogs solely for eating, and a larger breed for drawing the sleds; but apparently
this small breed quickly became extinct, for there is no further reference to it in the literature (Allen,
G. M.: "Dogs of the American Aborigines"; Bull. Mus. of Com. Zool., vol. lxiii, p. 492 (Cambridge,
Mass., 1920)). The use of dogs' wool in clothing by the Coast Salish Indians is noticed on p. 68.

squashes, and sunflowers, introduced their cultivation into south-eastern Ontario and the St. Lawrence valley, whence they spread into New Brunswick. But the Indian methods of cultivation were exceedingly primitive. Their stone axes barely bit into hard maple or birch trees that were not first charred by fire, so that they depended mainly on burning for the clearing of their land. Long digging-sticks or hoes fitted with blades of shell supplied the place of ploughs; the ripened ears of corn were gathered by hand and transported in baskets by the women to the husking shed. No tribe understood the rotation of crops or indeed possessed the means to rotate them, and but few made any attempt to fertilize the soil. Consequently when their plots became exhausted within ten or twelve years, the community moved away to new but unbroken ground.[1] Under such conditions the Indians could supply their daily needs only by combining agriculture with fishing, hunting, and the gathering of wild fruits, seasonal occupations that necessitated frequent migrations and temporary disbandments of the communities. So even the Iroquoian tribes were unable to establish really permanent villages and towns where easier living conditions and greater leisure might foster inventions and the growth of knowledge. Outside the lowlands of eastern Canada there was no agriculture, and the exigencies of a life dependent on fish and game kept the tribes in constant motion. It is true that semi-permanent villages existed on the Pacific coast, where the aborigines subsisted mainly on the marine fauna, shellfish, salmon, and sea-mammals; but even there migrations to new fishing grounds were not infrequent, and there were also seasonal movements to gather berries, or to hunt bears, goats, and other game.

The French-Canadian settler enjoyed another great advantage in the knowledge and possession of metals, especially of iron and steel. Unaided, he could build in seven days a log cabin far superior to any bark lodge of the eastern Indians, a cabin as enduring and comfortable as the plank houses on which a dozen or twenty Pacific coast natives, the most skilful carpenters in North America, laboured industriously for months with their crude stone tools.[2] His steel ax

---

[1] The exhaustion of the fuel supply around a village, and the labour of carrying firewood from a distance without wheeled vehicles or transport animals, were also common causes for the abandonment of otherwise favourable sites. *See* p. 84 f.

[2] " The felling of trees, as practised by them, is a slow and most tedious process, three of them being generally from two to three days in cutting down a large one." " The Adventures and Sufferings of John R. Jewitt"; Edinburgh, 1824. p. 94. *Cf.* Henry and Thompson: " New Light on the Early History of the Greater Northwest "; edited by Elliott. Coues, vol. ii; p. 724 (New York, 1897). The Iroquoians often spent three or four years deforesting new land for cornfields before they moved their villages (Lafitau: Moeurs des Sauvages Amériquains, vol. II, p. 109 (Paris, 1724)).

lightened the labour of gathering firewood, and, in conjunction with a saw, knife, nails, and hammer, enabled him to furnish his home with such conveniences as chairs and tables, that were beyond the reach of the aborigines, to whom the making of a single board was a heavy task. Sheet-iron stoves were not yet invented, but with mortar and brick (or stone) the European settler could build a chimney that permitted him to enjoy the open fire of the Indians without the smoke that often made their dwellings almost uninhabitable. His copper cooking-pot was not fragile like their pottery

51166

Eskimo archers of Coronation gulf. Their bow had an extreme range of only 125 yards and an effective range of from 30 to 40. *(Photo by Sir G. Hubert Wilkins.)*

vessels, or perishable like the wooden boxes, the birch-bark kettles, and the bags of buffalo-hide, in which the tribes who lacked pottery cooked their meat with the aid of hot stones. Lanterns and candlesticks of metal helped to illumine his home during the long nights of winter, extending the working hours, while the Indians were crouching in semi-darkness around their lodge fires. Steel knives rendered easy the cutting of wood and meat, steel awls and needles facilitated sewing and the working of hides and leather.

Finally, iron and gunpowder gave him the muzzle-loading gun, which was infinitely more effective for war and the chase than the Indian's bow and arrow. Gun, steel hatchet, and steel knife, these three things by themselves gave the French-Canadian an immeasurable advantage, as we can see from their effect on the Indian tribes that first acquired them. Thus a handful of Micmac who crossed from Nova Scotia to Newfoundland early in the eighteenth century quickly exterminated with their muzzle-loading guns the unhappy Beothuk, whose feeble bows and arrows gave no chance of effective resistance. The Iroquois, equipped with hatchets and guns by the Dutch colonists in Pennsylvania, easily drove the Huron tribes from their homeland around lake Simcoe; and the previously insignificant Cree marched northwest from the hinterland of James bay, and raided the whole valley of the Mackenzie river, driving before them the unfortunate tribes that had been too remote from Hudson bay to secure firearms from the early trading posts.[1]

No tribe in the New World, again, not even the highly civilized Maya and Inca peoples of Central America and Peru, was acquainted with the practical applications of the wheel,[2] which the French-Canadian settler turned to many uses. The carriage wheel gave him rapid and easy transportation; the water-wheel ground his corn; the windmill pumped his water; the spinning-wheel twisted his yarn; the potter's wheel facilitated the shaping of his household vessels; and the pulley increased his capacity for moving heavy weights. The Indian relied on man-power alone. He ground his corn with a pestle and mortar, twisted by hand the little yarn he made, and fashioned his pottery either by building it up in short strips (coiling), or by the still cruder process of hollowing out the stationary mass by hand.[3]

We should not forget, also, one other great difference between the French-Canadian immigrant and the Indian whom he dispossessed. During the first two hundred years of colonization the

[1] *Cf.* also Kelsey's description of the Cree attacking the Blackfoot: "Their enemies, many whom they cannot rout. But now of late they hunt their enemies. And with our English guns do make y'm flie." The Kelsey Papers, with an introduction by Arthur G. Doughty and Chester Martin, Published by the Public Archives of Canada and the Public Record Office of North Ireland, Ottawa, 1929, p. 3 f.

[2] Many tribes used a wooden hoop in games.

[3] Although few immigrants were scholars, writing yet preserved for them the ancient lore and transmitted a knowledge of new discoveries. Probably many Indian inventions failed to take root because they could be imparted only orally.

settler, however industrious and resourceful, was dependent economically on the Old World. Each year the ships that sailed from France brought him fresh cargoes of firearms and ammunition, supplies of metal, and even clothing and food. No doubt he often raised all his own food supplies, his wife clothed him with the pelts from his hunting and the wool from their sheep and goats. Yet every year, or every second year, he needed to replenish his supply of powder and lead, to purchase a new knife, a new ax, or new cooking utensils. Furthermore, the vessels that lay at anchor off Quebec or Louisburg were a visible sign of his connexion with a powerful motherland that would surely come to his aid in times of stress or danger. The Indian had no motherland save the country over which he roamed. The tribes that surrounded him were economically no more advanced than his own, and he neither knew of, nor could communicate with, the great centres of civilization beyond. He was merely one of a community, small in numbers and self-dependent, that looked no farther than its own borders for the fulfilment of all its needs. His raw materials, his tools and his weapons, everything indeed that he possessed, came as the fruit of his own labour from the resources of his own narrow domain.[1]

What, then, were the resources on which he relied? How far in the scale of civilization had he progressed? And by what means did he procure life's three basic necessities, food, clothing, and shelter.

When man first invented tools, some time in the late Pliocene or early Pleistocene, he took the first step forward on the long road to civilization. The Indian had passed far beyond those early stages in man's ascent that have been uncovered in the glacial drifts of the Old World—beyond the palæolithic or Old Stone epoch into a neolithic age, when stones were not only chipped but polished, agriculture had arisen, and pottery had made its appearance. Many tribes even made tools and ornaments of native copper; but since they treated it simply as a malleable stone, and possessed no knowledge of its smelting, they were still far removed from a true metal age. Tools of stone still formed the basis of all their material culture, and they were no farther advanced economically than the inhabitants of England two thousand years before Christ.

---

[1] Cf. Chacun mesnage (among the Hurons) faict de luymesme ce qui luy est convenable et necessaire, soit à couder, à filler, faire des pots de terre, et toute autre ouvrage et action de mestier qui leur faict besoin. Sagard, T. G.: " Histoire du Canada"; ii, p. 324 (Paris, 1866).

The primary tool of the Canadian Indians was a stone-bladed knife[1] set in a handle of wood, bone, or, among the Eskimo, ivory. Its shape varied greatly according to its exact purpose, and according to the fashions of different tribes; and it was made from many different varieties of stone, igneous and sedimentary, that called for different processes of manufacture. Whatever its shape and material the knife was the Indian's indispensable tool. An early explorer relates of the Dogrib Indians on the lower Mackenzie river that a man, carrying in his hand nothing except a knife, could march alone into the wilderness and secure everything he needed. Hearne, who travelled with the Chipewyans after they had been trading for many years with the fur posts on Hudson bay, placed the needs of that tribe a little higher. " The real wants of these people," he says, " are few and easily supplied; a hatchet, an ice-chisel, a file, and a knife, are all that is required to enable them, with a little industry, to procure a comfortable livelihood."[2] Yet the same author describes[3] how his party chanced on the well-furnished camp of a western Dogrib woman, a fugitive from the Cree, who had lived in solitude for seven months: " Five or six inches of an iron hoop, made into a knife, and the shank of an arrow-head of iron, which served her for an awl, were all the metals this poor woman had with her when she eloped; and with these implements she had made herself complete snow-shoes, and several other useful articles." Fifty years earlier the blade of her knife would have been, not iron, but stone, native copper, or the tooth of an animal, probably of a beaver.

Next to the knife in importance was the stone adze or ax, some tribes attaching their blades both vertically and transversely, some transversely only. With this implement, which also varied greatly in shape and material, the Indian cleared his land, made planks and poles for his house, his toboggan, and his sled, hollowed his dug-out canoe, and secured all the wood that he required for household utensils, tools, and weapons. Naturally he could not obtain with stone, however hard, either the strength or the keen-

---

[1] It is worth remarking that very few stone tools have been discovered in the basin of the Mackenzie river. Crude stone axes were apparently not uncommon in this region, but many if not most knives had blades of beaver teeth, caribou antler, or among the Yellowknives, Chipewyans, and some of the Dogribs, native copper. On the Pacific coast the Indians often used knives of shell. Nevertheless, the statement made above applies generally throughout the Dominion.

[2] Hearne, Samuel: " A Journey from Prince of Wales Fort in Hudson's Bay to the Northern Ocean"; Edited by J. B. Tyrrell, p. 123, The Champlain Society (Toronto, 1911).

[3] Ibid., p. 265.

ness of edge that more civilized peoples secured with metal; steel knives and hatchets were, therefore, the trade goods most in demand during the early days of colonization, reaching many parts of the country long before the first white explorers.[1]

39674

An Eskimo of the Mackenzie River delta using a bow-drill for piercing bone. *(Photo by J. R. Cox.)*

Closely allied to stone knives, and often distinguishable from them only by the handles or shafts in which they were mounted, were saws, drills, daggers, and two-edged points for spears, harpoons, and arrows. Gouges and chisels, on the other hand, closely resem-

[1] Sproat says that the Nootka Indians of Vancouver island did not make stone tools, and that although a few stone adzes were current among them, these were obtained from northern tribes: " The blade of their adze was a mussel-shell, of their knife, bone, and of their chisels elk-horn " (Sproat, G. M.: " Scenes and Studies of Savage Life"; Appendix, p. 316 (London, 1868)). Yet Meares expressly states that the Nootka built their canoes with utensils of stone made by themselves, which can only mean stone adzes (Meares, J.: " Voyage to the North-West Coast of America"; p. 262 (London, 1790)).

bled adze and ax blades; and there were combination tools, an adze or ax at one end and a gouge at the other. Any rounded stone served on occasion as a hammer, but the aborigines often expended much time and energy in making carefully-shaped pestles, hammers, and maceheads, from basalt and other hard rocks. They had special stone implements, also, for scraping skins, and for smoothing the wooden shafts of arrows and spears.

In manufacturing these tools and weapons, with others of less importance which it is unnecessary to enumerate, the Indians employed many different varieties of stone, and made use of several distinct processes. Hard, igneous rocks like granite and diorite, which had a rather loose, crystalline texture and made convenient hammers, adzes, and chisels, they generally pounded and pecked into shape with other stones; but nephrite, which was most valuable for adzes and drills, and slate, which served for arrow and spear-points and for knives, they sawed with a thin stone blade, often of shale, sometimes adding water and sand to the slowly forming groove. Glassy stones, such as flint, quartz, jasper, and obsidian, they chipped into form with bone or antler mallets, and produced a keen, saw-like edge by breaking off tiny flakes with bone pencils. These glassy stones were seldom polished, but others were ground and sharpened on gritty sandstones, and in the Eskimo area their edges were rendered keener by means of whetstones derived from hard nephrite. To perforate their stone implements the Indians employed two methods; large holes they pecked out with a pointed stone, small ones they drilled, using for the purpose a point of flint or nephrite set in a stem of wood or bone. A few minerals were so soft that they could be quarried and shaped with the ordinary hammer, adze, and knife. It was thus that the Indians fashioned their copper, which replaced stone in many tools among the Ontario Indians and among the Indians and Eskimo east and northeast of Great Bear lake. Thus, too, they fashioned argillite and soapstone, which served for pipes, lamps, vessels, and miscellaneous implements and ornaments, although useless for tools or weapons.

Stone tools, particularly the ax, adze, knife, and drill, gave the Indians a mastery over animal and vegetable products. They carved from bone, or from the similar substances, ivory, horn, and antler, numerous implements of everyday use, as mattocks, spearheads, spoons, combs, awls, and needles; and they made ornaments of hali- otis, dentalium, clam, and other shells. It was the possession of stone tools that made these articles possible, even though the natives some- times used a beaver or fox tooth for graving antler and bone, and employed hunting knives made of bone or antler instead of stone. Similarly, it was with stone knives, and stone and bone scrapers, that they dressed and tailored the skins that provided them with both tents and clothing.

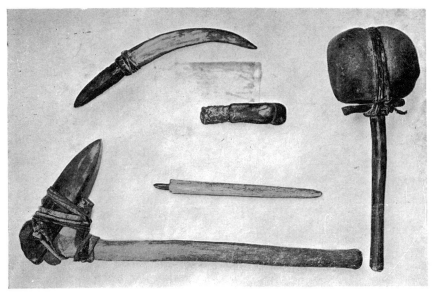

73464

Some basic aboriginal stone tools; knife, adze, hammer, drill, and scraper.

The stone knife and the stone adze were equally indispensable for all wood-work. The Indians utilized both the hard and the soft timbers in which the Dominion abounded. From the giant cotton- wood, cedar, and elm, they carved dug-outs that often exceeded fifty and even sixty feet in length; and from the bark of the birch, spruce, and elm, they made lighter canoes eminently fitted for travelling along the swift rivers. The rather soft, straight-grained cedar, which can be split so readily into long planks, even with wooden or antler wedges and stone mauls, furnished the Pacific Coast natives with large, comfortable dwellings capable of housing several families. Other planks from the same cedar, bent with steam and either pegged or sewn together with spruce roots, gave them roomy chests and boxes for cooking their meat and fish and for storing their household effects. Tough, elastic woods like yew, ash, hickory, and maple, made excellent bows and clubs, as well as handles for adzes, spears, and knives. Even the northern Indians and the Eskimo had the willow, spruce, and in some places birch, all woods that can be applied to many uses. Many of these trees, particularly the elm, willow, and spruce, had long, tough roots that the Indians could employ as thread and twine even to the extent of making fish-nets; willow and spruce roots, indeed, were favourite materials for basketry. Certain barks were valuable. Spruce- and birch-bark covered the frames not only of canoes but of dwellings, and from birch-bark the Indians made buckets and other utensils. Cedar bark shredded too readily for canoe coverings, and was very inflammable as a roofing; but, like the bark of the basswood, it was beaten into cloth, woven into baskets and mats, and twisted into cord and ropes.

Stone tools, therefore, were the foundation of the whole fabric of economic life, and their manufacture had an essential place in the education of every Indian. Many natives acquired remarkable skill in the chipping of flint and quartz, and some of their arrowheads, knife-blades, and animal figures rival the best work of the pre-historic Egyptians. Chipped implements, however, call for skill rather than time or labour, whereas the quarrying of hard rocks, and their pecking and grinding into polished adzes and pestles, embellished occasionally with realistic figures, required not only skill, but days and weeks of patient toil.[1] Since the value of an object is largely proportional to the labour expended on its manu-facture and the difficulty of replacing it, an indispensable tool like the stone adze was worth as much to the Indian as a steel ax to the woodsman or trapper who lives far removed from the outposts of civilization.

Neither chipped nor polished stone implements, however, are as efficient as steel tools for cutting wood and bone; and the making of a wooden bowl, a horn spoon, or any of the implements and utensils necessary for the home, involved an amount of labour that Europeans, accustomed to machine-made products, would consider

---

[1] Lafitau greatly exaggerates, however, when he says " Often a savage's whole lifetime hardly suffices (for the manufacture of a stone adze)"; op. cit., ii, 110.

altogether out of proportion to the results achieved. It is true that time had little value for the Indian, that his only clock was the sun, his only calendar the seasons with their changing supplies of fruit, fish, and game. Nevertheless, the slow, tedious manufacture

56902

Carrier Indian woman dressing a moosehide with a stone-bladed scraper.
(Photo by Harlan I. Smith.)

of tools and household effects during the hours that could be spared from fishing and hunting greatly restricted his leisure for other pursuits, and powerfully strengthened all the other cogs that checked the wheel of progress.[1]

---

[1] *Cf.* Meares, John: Op. cit., p. 262.

CHAPTER IV

FOOD RESOURCES

The basis of all modern civilization rests on agriculture, especially the cultivation of cereals, for without wheat, or a substitute cereal, the vast majority of the human race would perish within a few weeks. Old World archæologists have traced back the cradle of civilization to two great river valleys, the Nile and the Euphrates, one or other of which saw the first domestication of wheat and barley four or five millenia before the Christian era. The Old World, for some reason not at present understood, possessed a greater wealth of seed grasses than the New; it gave man not only wheat and barley, but oats, rye, millet, and rice. The only cereals indigenous to America were maize and wild rice (*Zizania* sp.). The latter was never domesticated, although the Indians used it extensively for food; but long before the Christian era maize had become the staff of life for numerous tribes living in the southern parts of North America, and was slowly spreading northward. We do not know when it reached Canada, nor how, except that it was probably introduced by Iroquoian tribes moving northeastward out of the valley of the Ohio river. In Cartier's time offshoots from these tribes occupied the broad peninsula between lakes Huron, Ontario, and Erie, together with a narrow fringe of land along the St. Lawrence river as far east as Quebec; and the cultivation of maize had spread from them to some adjacent Algonkian tribes, the Malecite of Quebec south of the St. Lawrence, some Algonkins on the Ottawa river, the Ottawa of Georgian bay, and the Missisauga on the north shore of lake Huron. Further extension northward was not possible, for although maize can be grown for fodder within the highlands of Ontario and Quebec, no variety that man has yet produced will ripen sufficiently for grain. Modern methods of cultivating it, indeed, hardly differ from the original Indian method, and some of our best known varieties were grown in America centuries before the coming of the white man.

Although the Iroquoian tribes subsisted very largely on maize, they raised also beans and squashes, the latter in separate gardens, but the beans in the maize fields, where the long grain-stalks supported the growing vines. In the same fields they often planted the sunflower, which yielded an oil esteemed by the Indians of Virginia for making bread and soup, but by the Iroquois mainly as an ointment. The growing of tobacco, which was far more widely spread. does not concern us here, since it has no value as a food. Maize, beans, and squashes, cultivated during the summer months, maintained these Indians throughout the winter, the squashes being preserved in underground caches lined with bark and covered with earth, the corn and beans in similar caches, in specially built granaries, or, most often perhaps, in large bark chests retained inside the dwelling-

Corn cultivation among the Hurons. *(From Lafitau, J. F.: Moeurs des Sauvages Amériquains, vol. 2, p. 155, Paris, 1724.)*

houses.[1] So greatly did the Iroquoians depend on agriculture that it actually determined the sites of their villages, which always lay close to fertile land, in places well adapted for defence.[2] The cornfields around their villages covered an amazing area when we consider the primitive tools the Indians possessed. An old writer tells us that in 1677 the Onondaga, who mustered at that time about three hundred and fifty fighting men, built their village on a large hill, cleared the land, and planted cornfields for two miles on either side.[3] Ten years

[1] *See* references quoted by Waugh, F. W.: " Iroquois Foods and Food Preparation"; Geol. Surv., Canada, Mem. 86, p. 42 (Ottawa, 1916).
[2] Beauchamp, W. M.: " Aboriginal Population of New York"; New York State Mus. Bull. No. 32, p. 23 (New York, 1900).
[3] Stites, S. H.: " Economics of the Iroquois"; Bryn Mawr College Mons., vol. 1, No. 3, p. 25, footnote (Bryn Mawr, 1905).

later, when Frontenac attacked the same tribe, he spent three days in destroying the growing corn, which extended from a league and a half to two leagues from its fort. Agriculture, indeed, was at once the strength and the weakness of the Iroquoian tribes. It permitted them to congregate in large, semi-permanent villages, assured them of an adequate supply of food for every season of the year, and even gave them a surplus stock to barter with neighbours, or to carry on the war-trail. But it likewise exposed them to the danger of a sudden invasion which could inflict a disaster almost as serious as a crushing defeat by destroying the crops that supplied their winter sustenance.

Although wild rice was plentiful in the territory of the Iroquoians they seem to have made no use of it, probably owing to the abundance of maize. It is strange that the Micmac of New Brunswick, where it

45758

Modern Ojibwa Indians harvesting wild rice in the same manner as their forefathers. *(Photo by F. W. Waugh.)*

was equally common, should have neglected it also; for the Ojibwa north and west of lake Superior gathered it in large quantities, and the Assiniboine a little farther west even sowed it occasionally, although they made no further progress in its cultivation.[1] The

---

[1] "Indian Tribes of the Upper Mississippi and the Great Lakes Regions"; edited by E. H. Blair, I, 103 f. (Cleveland, 1911). The Ojibwa of Georgian bay state that their forefathers used to throw into the water a few seeds of the wild rice, wrapped in mud, to supply new plants for the succeeding year. It may have been a similar custom that gave birth to agriculture in the Old World.

early explorer, Thompson, gives a good description of its harvesting among the Ojibwa. " The wild rice," he says, " is fully ripe in the early part of September. The natives lay thin birch rind all over the bottom of the canoe, a man lightly clothed, or naked, places himself in the middle of the canoe, and with a hand on each side, seizes the stalks and knocks the ears of rice against the inside of the canoe, into which the rice falls, and thus he continues until the canoe is full of rice; on coming ashore the women assist in unloading. A canoe may hold from ten to twelve bushels. He smokes his pipe, sings a song; and returns to collect another canoe load. And so plentiful is the rice, an industrious man may fill his canoe three times in a day. Scaffolds are prepared about six feet from the ground, made of small sticks covered with long grass; on this the rice is laid, and gentle clear fires kept underneath by the women, and turned until the rice is fully dried. The quantity is no more than the scaffolds can dry, as the rice is better on the stalk than on the ground. The rice when dried is pounded in a mortar made of a piece of hollow oak with a pestle of the same until the husk comes off. It is then put up in bags made of rushes and secured against animals."[1]

Rice was but one of many wild plants that the Indians employed to give variety to their diet, and to tide them over seasons of scarcity. The tribes of British Columbia ate several species of seaweed, the camas root (*Quamasia*, a plant closely related to the hyacinth, which when steamed made a kind of sweetish bread), elderberries, gooseberries, soapberries, huckleberries, salal-berries, currants, crabapples, and many other roots and fruits that the women gathered during the summer and stored away for the winter months. A common dish, not restricted to times of famine, was the inner bark of the hemlock dried in cakes. The plains' Indians had the wild turnip, wild cherries, and service-berries. Their favourite food, next to fresh meat, was a variety of pemmican made of meat and fat that was dried, pounded, and mixed with crushed service-berries or wild cherries. Nuts—the hickory, chestnut, butternut, and acorn—were more prominent than fruits in the diet of the Iroquoians, although they gathered raspberries, strawberries, and cranberries. They also

---

[1] *David Thompson's Narrative;* edited by J. B. Tyrrell, p. 275, The Champlain Society (Toronto, 1916).

collected the sap of the maple for its sugar, but did not value it as highly as some of the Algonkian tribes. The Ojibwa of lake Superior, for example, stored it away in quantity for the lean months of winter.[1] Nut-trees, and the maple disappeared north of the low-lands of eastern Canada, and fruits and berries became gradually scarcer. The Cree and the Indians of the Mackenzie River basin gathered crowberries, cranberries, and a few other varieties; in times of scarcity they sometimes subsisted on reindeer moss; but the supply of these articles was generally so scanty that it did not affect the regular diet. Speaking broadly, it would appear that roots and wild fruits formed a considerable portion of the food supply in British Columbia, diminished in value eastward, and in the northern parts of Canada ceased to possess any real importance.

50203

Red elderberries drying in the sun, Bella Coola. *(Photo by Harlan I. Smith.)*

In spite of the wild fruits that they collected, and the vast quantity of maize, beans, and squashes they harvested, neither the Iroquoian tribes nor their neighbours could live on vegetable products alone. Meat, or fish, seems to be a physiological necessity in cold climates, and in the absence of domesticated animals or of wool-

---

[1] *Ibid*, p. 286. The Indians solidified the sap in several ways. They boiled it in clay pots directly over the fire, and in vessels of birch-bark by means of hot stones; they froze it in shallow basins and threw away the ice; and they poured it slowly over a sheet of birch-bark placed in warm sunlight or near a fire, when it hardened to the consistency of treacle and finally crystallized.

len goods the Indians required the furs of the wild animals to protect them from the rigorous winter. The Hurons used their surplus maize to purchase furs from the Ottawa; but generally the men of the agricultural tribes left the tillage of the fields to the women in order that they might spend the summer in fishing, and the winter in hunting the moose. Fish and game, even though they were perhaps not as plentiful in their territories as in other parts of the Dominion, effectively reinforced the products of the soil, and by ensuring a certain livelihood at every season of the year, placed the agricultural tribes in a far more favourable position economically than the tribes that, knowing no agriculture, lived by fishing and the chase alone.

Fortunately for the non-agricultural tribes, no country in the world possessed a richer land and sea fauna than Canada in the days preceding its discovery. The coasts of both the Pacific and the Atlantic oceans teemed with salmon of various species that annually migrated up the rivers to their spawning-grounds. So densely did they mass in certain years that many fish were pushed high and dry upon the banks. Both oceans, too, abounded in shell-fish, and in halibut and cod, while of sea-mammals there were seals, whales, and walruses on the Atlantic coast, seals, whales, sea-lions, and sea-otters on the Pacific. Even the ice-strewn waters of the Arctic, where the Eskimo fished and hunted, had its seals, whales, and walruses, its cod and its salmon-trout, the last often reaching a weight of eleven and sometimes fourteen pounds. The interior lakes contained white-fish and sturgeon, lake-trout, salmon-trout, pike, pickerel, and other species of lesser economic value. Equally abundant was the land fauna. Bears, deer, and rabbits (or hares) were common everywhere. The moose, the woodland caribou, and the porcupine tenanted the eastern forested area; huge herds of bison and of antelope roamed the plains; the mountains of the west sheltered sheep and goats, elk wandered in their foothills and mountain caribou grazed on the plateaux between the various ranges; moose and deer haunted the Pacific coast; and throughout the northland of Canada east of the Mackenzie river there were small bands of musk-oxen, and herds of caribou so immense that no man could estimate their numbers. Innumerable wild-fowl, too, made the Dominion their breeding-ground, and ducks, geese, swans, grouse, and ptarmigan all contributed their quota to the food resources of the aborigines. Starvation might seem hardly possible in a land that teemed with so many forms of life.

Unhappily this was not the case. The density of game was by no means the same in all regions. In northern Ontario and Quebec, for example, the animals were so scattered that sometimes even the best hunters failed to keep starvation from their homes.[1] Many of the fish, animals, and birds appeared at certain seasons only. The buffalo of the plains, and the caribou of the barren grounds, moved northward every spring to new grazing-grounds, and southward again in the autumn, not always following the same routes. In the autumn, too, most of the birds flew southward to winter in warmer climes. The salmon, which seldom entered the rivers before June, completed their migrations about September, and the cod and halibut fluctuated from one month to another. At certain seasons some animals, like the caribou during their spring migration, were too lean to possess much food value. Thompson found the salmon spawning on the upper Columbia river so poor that they were scarcely edible, and his party preferred horse flesh.[2] Moreover, game was difficult to track in certain months. In winter moose could be run down on snow-shoes and speared with a lance, bears could be attacked in their dens; but it was not easy to approach either of these animals in summer or to kill them with a stone or bone-pointed arrow. Similarly, beaver were captured most readily in the late autumn when the ice was still thin, and rabbits and hares were snared in the winter when their runways were visible in the snow.[3]

The seasonal character of the food supply and the habits of the fish and animals greatly affected the daily life of the Indians. They compelled the various bands to move from one fishing or hunting ground to another as soon as the first began to slacken in its yield. These endless migrations evoked adaptations in dwellings and household furniture, and the invention of appliances like tumplines and

---

[1] Cf. Thompson, D.: Op. cit., pp. 76-77. " The Works of Samuel de Champlain"; edited by H. P. Biggar, vol. ii, p. 46, The Champlain Society (Toronto, 1925).

[2] Ibid., p. 377.

[3] It is interesting to note that some of the fur-bearing animals now most highly esteemed were of little value in pre-European days. The fox, marten, mink, lynx, and land-otter added nothing to the food supply, and their furs, though sometimes used for clothing, were either inferior to other furs for everyday use, or regarded as luxuries rather than necessities. Lescarbot says that the Micmac scorned even the beaver, and made hats of its fur only after the coming of the French. Lescarbot, Marc: " The History of New France"; edited by W. L. Grant, iii, p. 117, The Champlain Society (Toronto, 1907).

toboggans to aid in transport. Then the periodic scarcity of fish and game necessitated methods for preserving the supplies accumulated in seasons of abundance. Finally, the movements of the salmon in large shoals, and of the buffalo and caribou in herds, favoured cooperative rather than individual effort, and influenced not only the methods of fishing and hunting, but even the social organization of the Indian communities.

49490

Smoke-houses of the Tsimshian Indians, for drying salmon, Kitkargas, B.C.
(Photo by C. M. Barbeau.)

No tribe in Canada escaped these seasonal movements in quest of food, although there was considerable variation in the frequency and times of the movements. The Eskimo of the Arctic regularly marched inland at the end of spring to hunt caribou or to fish in the lakes, and as regularly marched back to the coast at the beginning of winter to track out the seals on the sea ice. Almost reversing these movements, the Micmac of the Maritime Provinces, and the Bella Coola, Tsimshian, Carrier, and other tribes of British Columbia, hunted moose and various land animals during the winter, and settled on the coast or along the rivers during the summer to trap the migrating salmon. The Chipewyan east of the Mackenzie river followed the caribou, season by season, impounding them in the woods when the snow lay deep on the ground, and pursuing them out into the barren grounds at the approach of spring; while the Hare on the lower Mackenzie river, whose country contained few caribou, snared the Arctic hare during the winter months (whence their name), and wandered from one fishing place to another during the summer. The Algonkian and Iroquoian tribes of eastern Canada, like the Micmac, had their summer fishing grounds and their winter territories for hunting moose. Henry and Thompson's description of the Piegan will serve for all the plains' tribes: " The buffalo regulates their movements over this vast extent of prairie throughout the year, as they must keep near these animals to obtain food. In summer they are obliged to assemble in large camps of from one hundred to two hundred tents, the better to defend themselves from enemies. In winter, when there is not so much danger, they disperse in small camps of ten to twenty tents, make pounds for buffalo, and hunt wolves and foxes."[1] Vancouver island contained no land animals of economic importance except the elk and the black-tailed deer, which were not plentiful enough to justify prolonged and systematic hunting on the part of a whole tribe. Yet even the Nootka Indians on the west coast of the island migrated seasonably, spending the period from March to August on the outer coast gathering shell-fish, hunting whales, and fishing for halibut and cod, then paddling back in September to the heads of the fiords to trap the ascending salmon and to pass the winter in shelter.[2]

Often as they moved their camps, however, very few tribes could escape periods of intense privation at times when game was scarce and the climatic or weather conditions unfavourable. The Eskimo secured very little fresh food in the season from November to Christmas, when the caribou had disappeared inland and the sea ice was not firm enough to resist a heavy gale. After the new year a succession of blizzards that prevented the hunters from finding the breathing holes of the seals often brought starvation into every home. The eastern Algonkians prospered when the winter was stormy and they could easily run down the moose in the deep snow; but they starved when the snowfall was light. A Cree Indian came to Thompson one December after a spell of calm weather and begged him to

[1] Henry and Thompson: Op. cit., vol. ii, pp. 723-4.
[2] Jewitt: Op. cit., pp. 116, 145. In Barclay sound, about 1860, the Nootka reversed these seasonal movements; they spent the summer inland and the winter on the coast (Sproat: Op. cit. p. 38).

stir up a gale. " I spent the autumn and early part of the winter,"
he said, " working on beaver houses, it is hard work, and only gives
meat while we are working; when the snow was well on the ground
I left off to hunt moose deer, but the winds were weak and unsteady;
my women had to snare hares, my little boy, with his bow killed a
few grouse, which kept us alive until the long calm came. I waited
a little, then in the evening I took my rattle and tambour and sung
to the Great Spirit and the Manito of the Winds; the next morning
I did the same, and took out of my medicine bag sweet smelling
herbs and laid them on a small fire to the Manito. I smoked and
sung to him for a wind, but he shut his ears and would not listen to
me; for three days I did the same; but he kept his ears shut. I
became afraid that he was angry with me; I left my tent and came
to you."[1]

For many other tribes the lean season was the early spring, when
the melting snow encumbered land travelling, the birds and animals
had not yet returned, and ice still bound the lakes and rivers. The
late autumn and early winter would have been equally lean had not
every family accumulated a reserve of provisions during the summer.
The agricultural peoples of eastern Canada, indeed, generally harvested enough maize and other produce to last them until the next
crop ripened, so that they rarely suffered from want of food. The
Indians along the Pacific coast were equally secure, for when fish
and game failed they could gather unlimited quantities of clams on
the sandy beaches outside their doors, or within a few miles of their
homes; moreover, their country contained an unusual abundance of
wild fruits and edible roots, which the women gathered in quantity
and stored away in boxes for winter use. It was on the prairie
tribes, and on those in the more northern sections of the country
where the resources were fewer and the climate more severe, that
the lean seasons pressed most heavily. Many writers have accused
those tribes of wastefulness and improvidence because when buffalo
and caribou were plentiful they often took only the tongues and
hides of the carcasses, leaving the meat for the birds and foxes.
Certainly they were wasteful at that season, and had no conception
of the conservation of game;[2] but then no conservation was neces-

[1] Thompson, D.: Op. cit., p. 124; cf. p. 309.
[2] Since the early fur-trading days the Indians have carefully conserved the beaver, always leaving
a pair to propagate on each stream. One of their chief grievances at the present time is the neglect
of this precaution by transitory white trappers and the consequent extermination of the beaver in
many districts.

sary as long as they lacked firearms, for the natural increase of each species more than balanced the destruction wrought by spears and arrows. The Indians were not improvident, however, for every tribe carefully dried during the summer months all the meat and fish that its migratory existence permitted it to conserve and to store away in safety.[1] The natives were very skilful in making caches both

20500

Salmon caches of the Coast Salish Indians, Fraser river, B.C. *(Photo by R. Maynard.)*

on the ground and in trees; but it was almost impossible to construct a cache that was impregnable against the attacks of foxes, wolverines, and bears alike. Many an Indian family starved to death when the meat it had so carefully stored way in the summer fell booty to the crafty wolverine.[2] Pounding the dried meat into pemmican, as was done by most tribes, had obvious advantages; it gave them the same food, but in a compressed form easier to carry with them in their wanderings. The natives did not dry the meat and fish secured in

[1] *Cf.* Works of Samuel de Champlain; Op. cit., vol. ii, p. 45. Many Eskimo tribes dry and store away the bodies of all the trout and salmon they capture during the summer, and dine on the heads only. The dogs live miserably at this season on bones and broth.

[2] The writer has helped to bury three caribou carcasses under stones that two men could hardly lift; and since even these could be dislodged by a wolverine, they were covered with a thick layer of snow that was converted into solid ice by the addition of water. Two weeks later a wolverine, unable to break through the ice, tunnelled under the cache and devoured all the meat, leaving only a few scraps of hide to show what we had buried.

the autumn, but allowed them to freeze. At this season of the year, when a thin sheet of ice covered the lakes, the Eskimo often sank his caribou carcasses into shallow ponds, where no bears or foxes could disturb them before he recovered them a few weeks later and carried them away on his sled. The low temperature of the water apparently prevented the growth of bacteria, so that the meat remained perfectly fresh and wholesome.

Frequent famines, and the hardships and accidents incidental to a migratory existence devoted to hunting and fishing, must have shortened the average span of life and caused a high rate of mortality among all classes of the population, adults and children alike. The infant death-rate was appalling, partly through ignorance of some of the most elementary principles in child welfare, partly also through lack of proper food. The total absence of milk, except what the mother herself could provide, and the absence of cereals among all but the agricultural tribes, lengthened the period of lactation, because no infant under the age of three years could assimilate a diet solely of meat and fish; and prolonged lactation affected the fertility of the women, making the average family small, although the Indians were naturally as fecund as Europeans.[1] Social factors also helped to reduce the population, particularly the blood-feud, which was prevalent nearly everywhere, and the frequent wars between neighbouring peoples. In warfare many tribes spared no one, but massacred their enemies without regard to age or sex.[2] The Indians of the British Columbia coast enslaved men, women, and children, but even this practice checked the normal increase of the population, since marriage with slaves was considered discreditable. The Iroquoian system[3] of adopting young captive women into the tribe and marrying them to the warriors was really based on a sound economic principle, and aided not a little in maintaining the strength of that warlike nation throughout a large part of its history.

In spite of the social factors, however, the most important checks on natural increase undoubtedly arose from the character and uncer-

---

[1]Carega has tried to prove that the Eskimo were physiologically less fecund than Europeans, partly because of inbreeding, partly because their vitality was impaired by frequent periods of malnutrition or starvation. Carega, G.: Alcuni dati demografici sugli Esquimesi, Metron, vol vii, No. 3, pp. 52-111 (Rome, 1928). His arguments seem hardly convincing, although they may hold good for one or two isolated communities.

[2]For a well-known historical instance, the massacre of an Eskimo band by the Chipewyans, See Hearne: Op. cit., ch. vi.

[3]Practised occasionally by the plains' Indians also.

tainty of the food supply. These operated both directly and indirectly, their indirect effects being perhaps the more far-reaching. The hardships of the never-ending food quest fell heaviest on the weaklings, who were often deliberately abandoned when they could no longer keep pace with the wanderings of the main tribe. In seasons of famine women were the first to suffer, and their loss seriously diminished the number of the next generation.[1] Their lives were full of drudgery at all times and their status very inferior,[2] so that they often sought to escape the added burdens of maternity, especially in seasons of want, by the twin practices of pre-natal abortion and infanticide. " The hardships the women suffer, induce them, too often to let the female infants die, as soon as born; and they look upon it as an act of kindness to them. And when any of us spoke to a woman who had thus acted, the common answer was: ' She wished her mother had done the same to herself!' "[3] As late as 1916, during a rather severe winter, five Eskimo mothers around the western end of Coronation gulf, where the total population did not exceed four hundred, destroyed their babies within an hour of delivery. As the Indians generally hesitated to sacrifice their male offspring, who would be the hunters of the community, their constant destruction of girl babies seriously affected the balance of the sexes. High infant mortality, female infanticide, and famines, all due in the main to the economic conditions, kept the hunting tribes down to a marginal level so that many of them barely escaped extinction.[4] The two regions where food was most abundant, southeastern Ontario and the coast of British Columbia, were precisely the two regions that were most densely inhabited.

---

[1] " It was frequently their lot to be left without a single morsel." Hearne: Op. cit., p. 130.

[2] Even among the Iroquois the women occupied an inferior position, and endured many hardships, although they enjoyed greater privileges and exercised more influence politically than the women of other tribes except perhaps the Eskimo; cf. Weld, Isaac: " Travels Through the States of North America," pp. 377-412 (London, 1799). For the Maritime tribes See " Jesuit Relations"; edited by R. G. Thwaites, vol. iii, p. 101 (Cleveland, 1896-1901); and for a representative plains' tribe, the Assiniboine, See the Kelsey Papers, pp. 21 f. . It is perhaps unnecessary to add that the women accepted this inferior status without question, and generally found as much contentment in life as their sisters in more favoured communities.

[3] Thompson: Op. cit., p. 130. Cf. Mackenzie, Alexander: " Voyages from Montreal through the Continent of North America to the Frozen and Pacific Oceans in 1789 and 1793", pp. xcvii f (London, 1801).

[4] " Abortions were frequent and infant mortality such that hardly one in thirty survives." " Jesuit Relations"; edited by R. G. Thwaites, vol. i, p. 257. Cf. Hardisty, W. L.: "Notes on the Loucheux Indians"; Smithsonian Rept., 1866, p. 312.

CHAPTER V

HUNTING AND FISHING

A migratory, outdoor life, wherein man pits his wits against the habits and instincts of the game on which he preys, inevitably develops a close perception of the phenomena of nature, and calls for many ingenious methods of obtaining the daily supply of food. The Indians were keen naturalists within the limitations of their interests. They knew the life-histories of the animals they hunted, the different stages of their growth, their seasonal movements and hibernation haunts, and the various foods they sought for sustenance. Difficulties of observation naturally prevented them from gaining as complete a knowledge of the habits of the fish, but they recognized every stage of the salmon from the egg to the adult, and the Nootka of Vancouver island artificially stocked their rivers by transporting salmon ova from one stream to another.[1] Nor were the Indians less observant of the flora of their territories, noting not only the edible plants, and those that were useful for tools, weapons, and various household appliances, but many inconspicuous varieties that apparently served no useful purpose whatever. Their interest in their environment, and eagerness to experiment, led to their discovering the medical properties of many plants, and Indian simples gained a deservedly high repute among the early colonists.[2] Several of them, indeed, have found a place in our pharmacopœia, and others fail to appear there only because modern science has found better sources elsewhere for the same remedies.

Nowhere was the Indian's keenness of observation more displayed than in fishing and hunting. Few Europeans have equalled them in these pursuits, except when superior equipment has given them an initial advantage; for the aborigines employed practically every method that was known to the white man, and others that were unknown. All tribes were not equally proficient in both pursuits; some excelled in hunting, others in fishing; and there were poor hunters, and poor fishermen, in every community. The Cree, who

---

[1] So, at least, states Sproat: Op. cit., p. 220, note.
[2] The tribes in the basin of Mackenzie river, and the Eskimo, lacked the herbal remedies so common elsewhere, partly, no doubt, on account of the more restricted flora in their territories.

were among the most skilful hunters on the continent, regarded
fishing as an occupation worthy only of women, and scorned their
Chipewyan neighbours, who were keener fishermen but less proficient
in hunting moose and caribou. Generally speaking, however, the
average Indian, whatever his tribe, possessed more ability in both
pursuits than the average white man, because from his earliest childhood he was trained to give the closest attention and study to every
outdoor phenomenon.

Among all the methods of securing game, the still-hunt offers
perhaps the greatest scope for individual skill. To the experienced
Indian a turned leaf, a broken twig, a slight scraping of a tree,
a faint track in the moss, each told a story. In the treeless Arctic
the Eskimo who sighted a caribou tested the direction of the air-
current by tossing up a shred of down or fur, or by moistening his
finger to discover which side felt the cooler; then, if the topography
of the ground prevented him from approaching his quarry under
cover, he would wait in hiding for several hours, or he would imitate
its actions and gait, and boldly advancing into the open, lure it within
range of his arrows.[1] Similarly, the prairie Indian often masked
himself under a buffalo hide and approached the buffalo herds unsus-
pected. Many of the natives could imitate the calls of various birds
and animals; and the " moose-call " of the Algonkian tribes, usually
performed with a roll of birch-bark, has been passed on to Europeans.
The explorer Thompson, himself no mean hunter, pays tribute to the
skill of one of his Cree. " An Indian came to hunt for us," he says,
" and on looking about thought the ground good for moose, and told
us to make no noise; he was told no noise would be made except the
falling of the trees, this he said the moose did not mind; when he
returned, he told us he had seen the place a doe moose had been
feeding in the beginning of May; in two days more he had unravelled
her feeding places to the beginning of September. One evening he
remarked to us, that he had been so near to her that he could proceed
no nearer, unless it blew a gale of wind, when this took place he set

---

[1] Jenness, D.: " The Life of the Copper Eskimo"; Report of the Canadian Arctic Expedition, 1913-1918, vol. xii, pt. A, p. 146 (Ottawa, 1923). For the same practice among the Hare and Dogrib,
Petitot, E.: "Exploration de la région du Grand Lac des Ours," p. 385 (Paris, 1893); Wentzel, W. F.
Letters to the Hon. Roderic McKenzie, 1807-1824, in Masson, L. F.: " Les Bourgeois de la Compagnie
du Nord-Ouest," première série, p. 82, Quebec, 1889; and Franklin, John: " Narrative of a Journey
to the Shores of the Polar Sea," p. 244 (London, 1823).

off early, and shot the moose deer. This took place in the very early part of October."[1]

Most Indian tribes employed dogs for bringing to bay their game, especially moose, bear, and caribou; they then attacked the quarry with spears rather than with bows and arrows, which often failed to take effect. The Eskimo dog was strong and hardy, and, though not a match for the Arctic wolf, fierce enough to check the progress of a polar bear; but the dogs possessed by the Indians were in general small and ill-nourished.[2]

A buffalo pound. *(From Franklin, J.: "Narrative of a Journey to the Shores of the Polar Sea," p. 113, London, 1823.)*

Until the natives obtained firearms, however, and even after they secured flintlock guns that required reloading after each shot, the still-hunt, whether with or without dogs, was less effective against animals that wandered in herds, such as the deer, caribou, musk-oxen, and buffalo, than the community hunt in which a large body of men participated, often aided by women and children. This community

[1] Thompson: Op. cit., p. 97.
[2] *Cf.* Richardson, Sir John: "Arctic Searching Expedition"; vol. ii, p. 30 (London, 1851): " When the fur traders first penetrated to the Elk river the Athabascans (i.e. Chipewyan) had only a small breed of dogs useful for the chase, but unfitted for draught; and the women did the laborious work of dragging the sledges. Now the cultivation of a stouter race of dogs has in some respects ameliorated the lot of the females."

hunt corresponded in many ways to the "beating" of tigers and leopards in the Asiatic jungles, and the rounding up of ostriches by the Bushmen of South Africa. It was indeed an ancient method, successfully employed by men of the Old Stone Age in Europe, thousands of years before the Christian era, in hunting the wild reindeer, mammoths, and other animals that in those days migrated back and forth across the Carpathian mountains. The Salish Indians of the Columbia river practised it in a very simple form; they merely surrounded a herd of antelope on a plain and shot down a small proportion before the remainder broke through the circle and escaped.[1] The plains' Indians, the Iroquoians and other eastern woodland tribes, and the Indians of the Mackenzie River basin adopted a more complex method; they drove or lured the buffalo, caribou, or deer into some kind of trap, usually an enclosed pound, and shot down entire herds. The old explorer Henry has left an excellent description of the buffalo hunts, which he witnessed among the Assiniboine.

"It is supposed that these people (the Assiniboine) are the most expert and dexterous nation of the plains in constructing pounds, and in driving buffalo into them. The pounds are of different dimensions, according to the number of tents in one camp. The common size is from 60 to 100 paces or yards in circumference, and about five feet in height. Trees are cut down, laid upon one another, and interwoven with branches and green twigs; small openings are left to admit the dogs to feed upon the carcasses of the bulls, which are generally left as useless. This enclosure is commonly made between two hummocks on the declivity or at the foot of rising ground. The entrance is about ten paces wide, and always fronts the plains. On each side of this entrance commences a thick range of fascines, the two ranges spreading asunder as they extend, to the distance of 100 yards, beyond which openings are left at intervals; but the fascines soon become more thinly planted and continue to spread apart to the right and left, until each range has been extended about 300 yards from the pound. The labor is then diminished by only placing at

---

[1] Thompson: Op. cit., p. 476. *Cf.* Kelsey's description of the buffalo hunt among the Assiniboine at the end of the seventeenth century, before they were acquainted with horses. "Now ye manner of hunting these beasts on ye barren ground is when they see a great parcel of them together they surround them wth men wch done they gather themselves into a smaller compass keeping ye beast still in ye middle and so shooting ym till they break out at some place or other and so get away from ym." The Kelsey Papers, p. 13.

intervals three or four cross-sticks, in imitation of a dog or other animal (sometimes called 'dead men'); these extend on the plain for about two miles, and double rows of them are planted in several other directions to a still greater distance. Young men are usually sent out to collect and bring in the buffalo—a tedious task which requires great patience, for the herd must be started by slow degrees. This is done by setting fire to dung or grass. Three young men will bring in a herd of several hundred from a great distance.

Plains' Indian running a buffalo. *(Reproduced, through the courtesy of the Public Archives of Canada, from a painting by George Catlin.)*

When the wind is aft it is most favorable, as they can then direct the buffalo with great ease. Having come in sight of the ranges, they generally drive the herd faster, until it begins to enter the ranges, where a swift-footed person has been stationed with a buffalo robe over his head, to imitate that animal; but sometimes a horse performs this business. When he sees buffaloes approaching, he moves slowly toward the pound until they appear to follow him; then he sets off at full speed, imitating a buffalo as well as he can, with the herd after him. The young men in the rear now discover themselves, and drive the herd on with all possible speed. There is always a sentinel on some elevated spot to notify the camp when the buffalo appear; and this intelligence is no sooner given than every man, woman, and child runs to the ranges that lead to the pound, to prevent the buffalo from taking a wrong direction. There they lie down between fascines and cross-sticks, and if the buffalo attempt to break through, the people wave their robes, which causes the herd to keep on, or turn to the opposite side, where other persons do the same. When the buffalo have been thus directed to the entrance of the pound, the Indian who leads them rushes into it and out at the other side, either by jumping over the inclosure or creeping through an opening left for that purpose. The buffalo tumble in pell-mell at his heels, almost exhausted, but keep moving around the inclosure from east to west, and never in a direction against the sun. What appeared extraordinary to me, on those occasions, was that when word was given to the camp of the near approach of the buffalo, the dogs would skulk away from the pound, and not approach until the herd entered. Many buffaloes break their legs, and some their necks, in jumping into the pound, as the descent is generally six or eight feet and stumps are left standing there. The buffalo being caught, the men assemble at the inclosure, armed with bows and arrows; every arrow has a particular mark of the owner, and they fly until the whole herd is killed."[1]

Buffalo were occasionally driven over precipices instead of into a pound; and their bones may still be recovered in large numbers from certain ravines on the prairies.[2] The northern Indians, who saw no buffalo, but who impounded caribou during the winter months, often set hedges and snares inside their enclosures, which were built only of saplings and brush. In summer they adopted the same methods as the Eskimo, forcing the caribou into lakes and rivers to spear them from canoes, or else driving them against a line of archers concealed in shallow pits.[3] The Nootka Indians similarly drove the

---

[1] Henry and Thompson: Op. cit., vol. ii, p. 517. *Cf.* "Life, Letters and Travels of Father Pierre-Jean de Smet"; edited by Chittenden, H. M., and Richardson, A. T., vol. iii, pp. 1027 ff (New York, 1905); and, for buffalo drives among the Cree, Franklin, J.: "Narrative of a Journey to the Shores of the Polar Sea," p. 112 f (London, 1823); and Hind. H. Y.: North-West Territory Reports of Progress, together with a preliminary and general report on the Assiniboine and Saskatchewan exploring expedition, pp. 55-56 (Toronto, 1859).

[2] At the close of the late war (in 1919 and 1920) the Sarcee Indians near Calgary gathered and sold for fertilizer all the buffalo bones that lay at the bottom of a narrow ravine on their reserve.

[3] Mackenzie: Op. cit., p. cxxv; Hearne: Op. cit., pp. 120-309; Jenness: Op. cit., pp. 148 ff.

black-tailed deer into bays and fiords,[1] and the Algonkian Indians speared the moose as it swam from one bank or headland to another.

Steel traps for the capture of fur-bearing game originated, of course, with Europeans, but the natives in every part of the Dominion had long employed both dead-falls and snares, the former mainly for carnivorous animals, the latter for herbivorous. Dead-falls, operated by some kind of trigger, were especially common in British Columbia, where the Carrier Indians alone constructed at least four varieties.[2] Most of the Athapaskan tribes in the north depended largely on snares for the capture of caribou and moose, and everywhere this was the accepted method for small animals like rabbits, hares, and marmots, and for birds like grouse and ptarmigan. Both snares and dead-falls required the exercise of much ingenuity and woodcraft, and all the Indians were skilful trappers centuries before there were any trading posts where their furs could find a market.

The hunting of the sea-mammals that frequented the coasts required not only ingenuity but courage. However uncertain the weather the Nootka Indians of Vancouver island fearlessly put to sea in their dug-out canoes, during the months of April and May, to attack the mighty whale, which with one blow of its tail could break to pieces their largest vessel. The whaling equipment of this and other west coast tribes closely resembled that of the Eskimo, which was adopted by Europeans until superseded by the modern whaling-gun. Meares describes it thus: " The harpoons which they use to strike the whale or any other sea-animal, except the otter, are contrived with no common skill. The shaft is from eighteen to twenty-eight feet in length; at the end whereof is fixed a large piece of bone, cut in notches, which being spliced to the shaft, serves as a secure hold for the harpoon, which is fastened to it with thongs. The harpoon is of an oval form, and rendered extremely sharp at the sides as well as the point—it is made out of a large muscle-shell, and is fixed into another piece of bone, about three inches long, and to which a line is fastened made of the sinews of certain beasts, of several fathoms in length; this is again attached to the shaft; so that when the fish is pierced, the shaft floats on the water by means of seal-skins filled with wind, or the ventilated bladders of fish, which

---

[1] Sproat: Op. cit., p. 145.
[2] Morice. A. G.: " Notes on the Western Dénés"; Trans. Canadian Inst., vol. iv, p. 95 ff (1892-3).

are securely attached to it. The chief himself is the principal harpooner, and is the first that strikes the whale. He is attended by several canoes of the same size as his own, filled with people armed with harpoons, to be employed as occasion may require. When the huge fish feels the smart of the first weapon, he instantly dives, and carries the shaft with all its bladders along with him. The boats immediately follow his wake, and as he rises, continue to fix their weapons in him, till he finds it impossible for him to sink, from the number of floating buoys which are now attached to his body. The whale then drowns, and is towed to shore with great noise and rejoicings."[1]

Almost as strenuous as whaling was the sea-otter hunting of the Pacific Coast Indians. For this pursuit four men, equipped with light harpoons and with bows and arrows, set out in two very light canoes. If they found an otter sleeping on the surface of the water, they harpooned it and dragged it to one of the boats, where it fought savagely with its claws and teeth, sometimes inflicting serious wounds. Usually it sighted their approach and dived. The two canoes then followed in its course, separating in order that one or the other might be within bow-shot when it rose for breath; but the otter was swift and cunning, so that the pursuit often lasted several hours before it was killed or finally made good its escape.[2]

The same Indians lured seals within range of their arrows by wearing wooden masks, covering their bodies with branches, and imitating the actions of a seal basking among the rocks.[3] Sea-lions, which were less timid and more frequently came ashore, they attacked with clubs; the Haida Indians killed large numbers of these animals during their spring excursions to the west coast of the Queen Charlotte islands. But the most skilful hunters of sea-mammals were the Eskimo. Like the Pacific Coast Indians they harpooned the whale, the seal, and also the walrus from their boats during the summer months. The whale and the walrus disappeared in the autumn, but the seal at that season broke small holes in the slowly-forming ice and kept these breathing-places open all winter. Drifting snow soon rendered the holes invisible, but the dogs could scent them out,

[1] Meares: Op. cit., pp. 259-260.
[2] Ibid., p. 260.
[3] Ibid., p. 261. Several tribes in British Columbia used the same tactics for catching geese and swans. The hunter covered his head with a goose or swan skin, swam out into the middle of a flock and pulled the birds under water.

and the Eskimo himself often discovered them by probing every suspicious outline on the surface of the snow. Over such a breathing-hole he waited, sometimes for hours, until the seal either rose and was harpooned, or the long winter darkness drove the hunter home to his snow hut. When the winter finally ended, and the seal came out of its hole to bask in the warm spring sun, he adopted still another method. Harpoon in hand, he crawled cautiously toward it, imitating its own motions with his dark, fur-clad form. If it gazed at him in suspicion he stopped and lay motionless, or slowly moved his head from side to side and gently scratched the ice with a special pair of claws. Thus, little by little, he approached his quarry and, with a sudden cast of his harpoon, transfixed the startled animal before it had time to dive into its hole.

All these methods of hunting the sea mammals were merely adaptations of still more ancient methods of hunting animals on land, and of capturing fish in the sea, lakes, and rivers;[1] for the aborigines were as skilful in fishing as in hunting, and employed as great a variety of methods. Only the Indians of the prairies, where lakes were absent and the muddy rivers were poorly stocked with fish—and those of inferior quality only—paid little attention to fishing, trusting to the larger resources of game and wild fruits. Elsewhere in Canada the fish-hook and the fish-spear, the net, trap, and weir, were as indispensable at certain seasons as the bow and arrow; and dried fish was a staple food in nearly every community during the first two months of winter.

The Indians were well acquainted with the barb, which they used on spears and harpoons; but they generally avoided it on fish-hooks,[2] which in consequence served only for jigging or trolling. Their bait was either some part of a fish—the eye, or the skin from the belly—or else a piece of bright bone, ivory, or even stone, often coloured, and, among the Eskimo and Kutchin, carved to imitate a fish. The Indians of the Atlantic and Pacific shores jigged from canoes in the bays and gulfs, catching mainly cod, halibut, and salmon; whereas the northern Indians and the Eskimo used their

---

[1] Compare, e.g., the use of nets for capturing seals under the ice, a practice formerly widespread among Eskimo tribes, and still in vogue in the Mackenzie delta and in Alaska. The Greenland Eskimo often employ another well-known fishing method; they drop a lure through a hole in the ice and harpoon the seal as it approaches the bait. Porsild, M. P.: "The Material Culture of the Eskimo in West Greenland"; Meddelelser om Grønland, li, p. 133 (Copenhagen, 1915).

[2] A few fish-hooks with true barbs have been found on old Iroquoian sites.

canoes for trolling, and jigged through the ice of the lakes for white-fish, trout, and salmon trout.[1] For set lines the natives used a gorge—a short pencil of bone or hardened wood sharpened at both ends and inserted inside a piece of meat or fish, with the line attached to the middle. The eastern Indians captured large numbers of sturgeon, salmon, and eels with torches and spears. "Two men go

37080

Coronation Gulf Eskimo spearing salmon trout. *(Photo by D. Jenness.)*

together in a canoe at night; the one sits in the stern and paddles and the other stands with a spear over a flambeau (of birch bark) placed in the head of the canoe. The fish, attracted by the light, come in numbers around the canoe, and the spearman then takes the opportunity of striking them."[2] Some tribes in British Columbia similarly speared (or clubbed) by night the salmon that were migrat-

---

[1] The Eskimo caught also a few rock-cod through cracks in the sea ice during the autumn and spring.

[2] Weld, I.: "Travels through the States of North America"; p. 295 (London, 1799). *Cf.* Thompson: Op. cit., pp. 267-8, and "The Jesuit Relations" and Allied Documents; edited by Thwaites, R. G.: vol. vi, p. 311 (Cleveland, 1897). The Micmac of Nova Scotia, and the Bella Coola and neighbouring tribes of British Columbia, caught geese, ducks, and brant in the same way, the former employing clubs instead of spears, the latter using a net, shaped among the Bella Coola like a lacrosse stick. Denys, N.: "Description and Natural History of the Coasts of North America (Acadia)"; edited by Ganong, W. J.: p. 435, The Champlain Society (Toronto, 1908); McIlwraith, T. F.: MS., The Social Organization of the Bella Coola"; Nat. Mus., Canada; Boas, F.: "The Kwakiutl, Vancouver Island"; Am. Mus. Nat. Hist., Mem. 8. Jesup Expedition vol. v, p. 515. Jewitt: Op. cit., p. 188.

ing up the rivers. By day they often adopted a method common among the Indians and Eskimo of northern Canada; they set lures, such as a bear's tooth, at holes in the ice and speared the fish that approached the bait.

Several tribes employed for hooking salmon a one-pronged, or more often multi-pronged, gaff that might rather be termed a rake. A modification of the instrument—a pole generally about ten feet long armed with a row of bone spikes for two feet from one end— served the Nootka for both herring and oolakan; drawn through a shoal of herring it nearly always impaled three or four fish.[1] Special contrivances of this kind were not uncommon in Canada, for the Indians were quick to conceive or borrow new ideas in all matters that related to fishing and hunting.

Despite their variety, all these methods yielded but a small toll of fish compared with the number caught with nets, traps, and weirs. It is a curious fact that the Eskimo, who employed a kind of square seine for capturing seals, never adopted the same method for fish until about the time of the discovery of America, when it was introduced from Siberian tribes into Alaska and spread eastward as far as the Mackenzie delta. The northern, eastern, and west coast Indians all used the seine, the two first setting it under the ice during the winter as is often done to-day. The eastern Indians and those of British Columbia had also bag-nets and dip-nets, which they usually employed in conjunction with weirs. The material of these nets varied considerably; the Pacific Coast Indians generally used nettle, their inland neighbours hemp, the eastern Indians nettle or hemp, northern natives willow-root or caribou thongs, and the Eskimo willow-root or baleen.

Of weirs Nature herself provided many, which the Indians turned to full advantage. Certain rocky canyons, like that at Hagwilget on the Bulkley river, in northern British Columbia, left only a few narrow openings for the passage of the migrating salmon; there the natives planted their basket-traps, and plied their nets and spears in the swirling water below them. On the sea-coast, again, the receding tide often left a few fish stranded in pools among the rocks. These natural weirs probably suggested the construction of artificial ones in suitable places. The Kwakiutl and Salish Indians on the east coast of Van-

---

[1] Cf. Hearne: Op. cit., p. 265. Sproat: Op. cit. p. 224. Jewitt: O. cit., p. 143. Meares: Op. cit.. p. 265, exaggerates the length of the instrument.

couver island built dams of stones in the shape of large horseshoes, along the banks of tidal rivers, to impound the salmon when the tide went out;[1] and in the Arctic the Eskimo laid straight, stone dams across streams that the salmon trout ascended, leaving small openings in the lower rows, but completely closing the uppermost.[2] The Indians of eastern and western Canada had fences of piles and brush,

49489

Fishtraps of the Tsimshian Indians, at Kitkargas, B.C. *(Photo by C. M. Barbeau.)*

many of them so elaborate and extensive that their construction required the combined labour of an entire community. These log weirs provided many tribes in British Columbia with two-thirds of the yearly food supply, so that their destruction by floods or enemies was a terrible disaster. Sir Alexander Mackenzie, who examined one on the upper reaches of the Bella Coola river during his memorable

---

[1] Boas, F.: Op. cit., p. **465** f.
[2] Jenness, D.: Op. cit., p. **155** f.

journey overland, describes it thus: " Salmon is so abundant in this river, that these people have a constant and plentiful supply of that excellent fish. To take them with more facility, they had, with great labour, formed an embankment or weir across the river for the purpose of placing their fishing machines, which they disposed both above and below it. I expressed my wish to visit this extraordinary work, but these people are so superstitious, that they would not allow me a nearer examination than I could obtain by viewing it from the bank. The river is about fifty yards in breadth, and by observing a man fish with a dipping net, I judged it to be about ten feet deep at the foot of the fall. The weir is a work of great labour, and contrived with considerable ingenuity. It was near four feet above the level of the water, at the time I saw it, and nearly the height of the bank on which I stood to examine it. The stream is stopped nearly two-thirds by it. It is constructed by fixing small trees in the bed of the river in a slanting position (which could be practicable only when the water is much lower than I saw it), with the thick part downwards; over these is laid a bed of gravel, on which is placed a range of lesser trees, and so on alternately, till the work is brought to its proper height. Beneath it the machines are placed, into which the salmon fall when they attempt to leap over. On either side there is a large frame of timber-work six feet above the level of the upper water, in which passages are left for the salmon leading directly into the machines, which are taken up at pleasure. At the foot of the fall dipping nets are also successfully employed."[1]

Whatever its construction, whether of timber, brush, or stones, the community weir, like the buffalo or caribou pound, was a powerful factor in welding the different families of Indians into a single, social unit. Every man contributed his labour to the building and mainten-ance of the weir or pound, and every man was entitled to his share of the booty. The master of a buffalo pound apportioned the meat equally among all the tents except his own, which nevertheless received the largest share through the gifts offered by each household in payment of his services. At the weirs each man retained whatever fish he caught, but allowed no family to remain in want. The Indians realized that every man had his days of ill-luck when the animals and

---

[1] Mackenzie: Op. cit., p. 320-1. *Cf.* Fraser, Simon: "Journal of a Voyage from the Rocky Mountains to the Pacific Coast, 1808," in Masson: Op. cit., series i, p. 220.

fish seemed to elude his weapons; that accidents and sickness attacked the strongest and ablest hunter, making him dependent for a time on his fellow-men; and they insisted on an equitable division of food, permitting no one to hoard it while his companions starved. They did not accept real communism, which would have destroyed all competition, all stimulus to individual enterprise. Rather. they placed a

73459

A salmon-weir on the Cowichan river, B.C. *(Photo by Gentile.)*

high premium on skill in hunting, ranking it with prowess in war. But the vicissitudes of their migratory life, the necessity for close co-operation in order to provide the daily needs, produced a freer distribution of wealth, especially of food, and prevented those extremes of poverty on the one hand, and riches on the other, which are so apparent in more civilized countries.

CHAPTER VI

DRESS AND ADORNMENT

The fur-bearing animals which the Indian hunted for his daily food provided him also with the clothing he required to withstand the rigours of a continental climate in a country of rather high latitudes. He might have survived without clothing on the Pacific coast, where the warm Japanese current, sweeping southward from the Aleutian islands and the Alaskan gulf, kept the temperature within moderate limits at every season of the year; but nowhere else in Canada could he have lived through a single winter without warm garments to shield his body and limbs. He knew neither cotton nor linen, which in any case cannot give adequate protection in zero and sub-zero temperatures, and he had never domesticated the wild sheep or the wild goat of the Rocky mountains, the buffalo of the plains, or the musk-ox of the Arctic and sub-Arctic tundra, all animals provided with long coats of wool. The amount of wool yielded by the buffalo and the musk-ox is indeed small compared with the yield from the sheep and goat, and their domestication might have produced little change in the Indian's clothing (which already included the dressed hides with their wool), although it would have furnished him an ample supply of meat. But the domestication of the sheep and goat would surely have stimulated the art of weaving, already familiar to most tribes, and have made woollen garments the everyday dress west of the Rocky mountains, if not to the east of those ranges. The Tlinkit Indians of southern Alaska and the Tsimshian of the Skeena and Nass rivers did actually weave the wool of the wild mountain goat into blankets, which were traded all down the coast of British Columbia. But the wool was so difficult to procure that they generally mixed it with strands of cedar bark, or, less often perhaps, with narrow strips of sea-otter skin;[1] and the manufacture of a single blanket, with its intricate and often beautiful patterns, entailed so much labour that only the most influential natives could aspire to its possession, and then for ceremonial purposes only. The Salish tribes, particularly those near the mouth of the Fraser, made

---

[1] *Cf.* Milet-Moreau, M.L.A.: "Voyage de la Pérouse"; tome second, p. 233 (Paris, 1798).

cruder blankets of goats' wool mingled with dogs' hair[1] and feathers, but their supply of the wool was even more restricted than that of the northern tribes. This scarcity of wool forced the west coast natives to have recourse either to dressed skins, like other Indians, or to a very different material, the bark of the yellow cedar, which they wove into blankets on a primitive frame, and bordered with goat yarn or strips of sea-otter skin.[2] Some Salish Indians living in the dry belt of the Fraser River area, where cedar was lacking, used sagebrush instead of cedar bark; and others wove blankets from

Coast Salish woman weaving a blanket of dog hair and mountain-goat wool; another woman spinning the wool; in the foreground a shorn dog. *(Reproduced, through the courtesy of the Royal Ontario Museum of Archæology, from a painting by Paul Kane.)*

strips of rabbit furs, like the Indians throughout the basin of the upper Mackenzie and in the northern parts of Ontario and Quebec. But these woven garments of bast and fur were more akin to mats

---

[1] For this purpose they raised a special breed of dogs, now extinct apparently, but described by the early navigator Vancouver: " The dogs belonging to this tribe of Indians were numerous, and much resembled those of Pomerania, though in general somewhat larger. They were all shorn as close to the skin as sheep are in England; and so compact were their fleeces, that large portions could be lifted up by a corner without causing any separation. They were composed of a mixture of a coarse kind of wool, with very fine, long hair, capable of being spun into yarn." Vancouver, George: " A Voyage of Discovery to the North Pacific Ocean, and Round the World"; vol. i, p. 266 (London, 1798). *Cf.* Allen, G. M.: " Dogs of the American Aborigines"; Bull. Mus. Com. Zool., vol. lxiii, No. 9, p. 469 ff (Cambridge, Mass., 1920).

[2] Mackenzie (Op. cit., pp. 322-338) says that the Bella Coola interwove the skin with the cedar bark, but no specimen of this kind seems to have been preserved.

and bags than to true textiles like the goats' wool blanket, which was manufactured from spun yarn.

The natives of the Pacific coast not only used different materials, but evolved a different style of clothing from that prevailing, with certain variations, over the rest of Canada. In summer the men frequently wore nothing at all, and both in summer and in winter men and women nearly always went barefoot, except among tribes like the Bella Coola, Tsimshian, and Tlinkit, who were in close contact with the interior natives and consequently often adopted the moccasin.[1] The typical garment for everyday wear was an oblong cloak of skin

Man, woman, and child of the Nootka tribe, west coast of Vancouver island. *(Reproduced, through the courtesy of the Public Archives of Canada, from Atlas para el viage de las goletas sutil y Mexicana al reconocimiento del estrecho de Juan de Fuca en 1792, publicado en 1802.)*

or cedar bark[2] that passed under the left arm and tied over the right shoulder, with a girdle encircling the waist. The men's cloaks fell to the knees in front, and a little below them behind; the women extended it to reach the ankles,[3] and in some tribes tied over or under it[4] a short apron that stretched from the waist to the knees. In

---

[1] It is sometimes stated that the Pacific Coast tribes *always* went barefoot; but Cook says of the Nootka that "a few have a kind of skin stockings, which reach half-way up the thigh." Cook, James: "A Voyage to the Pacific Ocean"; vol. ii, p. 368 (London, 1785).

[2] Skin was more general among the northern tribes, cedar bark among the southern.

[3] Among the Bella Coola the cloak worn by both sexes had apparently the same length, reaching a little below the knees in front and to the heels behind. Mackenzie: Op. cit., pp. 322-371.

[4] The Haida women tied it over the cloak or dress, the Bella Coola apparently under. Dixon, G.: "A Voyage Round the World"; p. 239 (London, 1789). Mackenzie: Op. cit., p. 323.

rainy weather, or when travelling by sea, both sexes threw over this cloak a short cape, generally of cedar bark, that slipped over the head like a poncho; and the men, sometimes also the women, wore a curious conical hat of woven cedar bark or spruce root, often adorned with conventionalized designs of fish and animals. There were mittens for winter use, and loose robes of sea-otter and other skins to wrap about the shoulders over the other garments, as occasion required. The sea-otter cloaks and robes, restricted by some tribes (e.g. the Nootka) to men, aroused a keen competition among Russian, Spanish, and English traders during the last quarter of the eighteenth century, and the heavy demand for the raw skins of the animal speedily brought about its virtual extinction.

Outside the area of the Pacific coast clothing consisted entirely of dressed skins, completely tailored among the Eskimo and some adjacent tribes, partly tailored among the remainder. The dressing and cooking of meat and the dressing and sewing of skins were indeed the principal occupations of the women all over the country, who matched their skill with the needle against their husbands' skill in hunting.[1] There were no professional tailors; the man supplied all the skins his family required, and his wife manufactured them into clothing. The sewing outfit was very primitive; a knife of stone (more rarely of native copper) to cut out the skins, a bodkin to punch the holes, a bone needle with thread of twisted sinew from the back or leg of some animal, and, among the Eskimo, a thimble of bone or skin to protect the finger. There were, of course, no steel needles or manufacturer's thread, no scissors, and no sewing machine. The women did not even use patterns to guide them in their tailoring, but cut and trimmed and sewed according to designs in their own minds, following methods and styles which they had learned in childhood.[2]

These methods and styles differed only in minor details. Speaking broadly, the men's costume consisted of a shirt that fell to the thighs, a breech-cloth,[3] long leggings, and moccasins, with the addition of a robe, mittens, and sometimes a cap in cold weather. Women dressed in much the same way, except that they converted the shirt

---

[1] Iroquois women also performed most of the work in the maize fields.

[2] The designs woven by the Tlinkit women on the goats' wool blankets, however, were copied from drawings made on boards by the men.

[3] Some of the interior tribes of British Columbia did not adopt the breech-cloth until post-European times.

73460

An Indian of the plains, in the modified costume of the late nineteenth century.
(Photo by Canadian National Railways.)

into a flowing gown by extending it to the knees or ankles, and so could wear shorter leggings and dispense with the breech-cloth. For fuller details we may cite Mackenzie's description of the Cree costume: " Their dress is at once simple and commodious. It consists of tight leggins, reaching near the hip: a strip of cloth or leather, called assian, about a foot wide, and five feet long, whose ends are drawn inwards and hang behind and before, over a belt tied to the former garment, and cinctured with a broad strip of parchment fastened with thongs behind; and a cap for the head, consisting of a piece of fur, or small skin, with the brush of the animal as a suspended ornament; a kind of robe is thrown occasionally over the whole of the dress, and serves both night and day. These articles, with the addition of shoes and mittens, constitute the variety of their apparel. The materials vary according to the season, and consist of dressed moosekin, beaver prepared with the fur, or European woollens. The leather is neatly painted, and fancifully worked in some parts with porcupine quills, and moose-deer hair; the shirts and leggins are also adorned with fringe and tassels, nor are the shoes and mittens without somewhat of appropriate decoration, and worked with a considerable degree of skill and taste. These habiliments are put on, however, as fancy or convenience suggests; and they will sometimes proceed to the chase in the severest frost, covered only with the slightest of them. . . . The female dress is formed of the same materials as those of the other sex, but of a different make and arrangement. Their shoes are commonly plain, and their leggins gartered beneath the knee. The coat, or body covering, falls down to the middle of the leg, and is fastened over the shoulders with cords, a flap or cape turning down about eight inches, both before and behind, and agreeably ornamented with quill-work and fringe; the bottom is also fringed, and fancifully painted as high as the knee. As it is very loose, it is enclosed round the waist with a stiff belt, decorated with tassels, and fastened behind. The arms are covered to the wrist, with detached sleeves, which are sewed as far as the bend of the arm; from thence they are drawn up to the neck, and the corners of them fall down behind, as low as the waist. The cap, when they wear one, consists of a certain quantity of leather or cloth, sewed at one end, by which means it is kept on the head, and, hanging down the back is fastened to the belt, as well as under the chin. The upper garment is a robe like that worn by the men."[1]

Some of the variations in this costume undoubtedly arose from the varying climatic conditions. Although the extremes of temperature at Edmonton, let us say, and in the Mackenzie delta, are much alike, the mean temperatures week by week, and month by month, differ greatly owing to the differences in latitude and the relative positions of the two places in regard to land and water areas, with consequent differences in the prevailing winds and atmospheric humidity. So, during the summer the men of the prairie tribes often wore only a breech-cloth and moccasins, using the robe for ceremonial occasions and for a covering during the night; and their shirts were hairless and sleeveless both in summer and in winter, the arms and head being protected by the robe alone. In eastern Canada, too, the natives went lightly clad in summer. The Iroquois, like the plains' tribes, covered their heads with their robes in wintry weather and drew separate sleeves over their arms; their women divided the dress into two parts, a blouse and a skirt, as did many plains' tribes in the United States. The Micmac and Malecite of the Maritime Provinces wore caps, but often their summer costume was simply a breech-cloth and moccasins for the men, and a dress and moccasins for the women. A warmer and fuller dress was necessary in the northern regions. There the Indians used furred shirts fitted with permanent sleeves, and wore a double layer of garments during the winter months, with the fur of the inner layer against the body. The Eskimo, and some adjacent tribes who followed their example, like the Naskapi of the Labrador peninsula, attached the cap to the shirt, making a kind of capote, and substituted fur trousers and fur stockings for the breech-cloth and leggings. The Mackenzie Delta Eskimo, and their enemies the Kutchin, joined trousers and stockings into one garment, but the eastern Eskimo kept them separate. The Slave and neighbouring tribes on the Mackenzie retained the breech-cloth (or a leather tassel that served the same purpose), but generally united the leggings with the moccasins. Notwithstanding these local differences, there was clearly a general similarity in the costume of all the aborigines outside of the Pacific coast; and although climate was not the only factor in

---

[1] Mackenzie: Op. cit., pp. xciii ff.

producing the tribal variations, it was certainly one of the most important.

The actual furs that made up this costume naturally depended on the local fauna. Furs from the deer family were the most general, on account of their size, warmth, lightness, and the ease with which

36913

An Eskimo and his wife, Coronation gulf. *(Photo by D. Jenness.)*

they could be procured. The eastern Indians commonly dressed in moose skin, the northern Indians and the Eskimo in caribou fur, the prairie tribes in antelope hide, and the Indians of the Cordillera region in the skins of all three animals, according to the locality. Since these hides quickly lose their fur with dampness, the southern Indians generally dehaired them before making them up into garments. In the north, where rain fell comparatively seldom and the winters were longer and more severe, the natives retained the fur on their caribou hides, but wore their oldest garments during the summer months, or, if Eskimo, substituted clothing of seal or polar-bear fur, which sustains no harm from moisture. No less than seven prime caribou hides were necessary to clothe a single Eskimo, three moose skins to clothe the more scantily-clad Indian of eastern Canada; so that although the natives hunted these animals for their meat as well as for their fur, failure to kill a sufficient number at the proper seasons often forced them to supplement the supply of furs from other sources. Buffalo, musk-ox, bear, and elk hides were so stiff and heavy that they were generally avoided for clothing and adopted only for blankets and bedding;[1] but the beaver, marmot, squirrel, and rabbit (or hare) all provided serviceable furs that were widely used throughout the country. Some British Columbia tribes made robes of fisher and marten fur, but restricted them to persons of rank, since the animals were neither very plentiful nor easily trapped. Garments of fox, wolf, or wolverine skin were rare, but several tribes in the north of Canada used those furs for trimming.

Despite all the discoveries of modern science, skin still provides the best protection against the zero and sub-zero temperatures of a Canadian winter. It has serious disadvantages, however, during the summer months. As that keen explorer, David Thompson, remarked, " Leather does very well in dry weather, but in wet weather, or heavy rains it is very uncomfortable, and as is frequently the case on a march, cannot be dried for a few days; it thus injures the constitution and brings on premature decay. Of this the natives appear sensible, for all those that have it in their power, buy woollen clothing."[2] In the sentences preceding this passage he says, speaking of the Piegan Indians, "The grown-up population of these people appears to be about three men to every five women, and yet the births appear in favour of the boys. The few that are killed in battle will not account for this, and the deficiency may be reckoned to the want of woollen or cotton clothing." We may perhaps hesitate to accept Thompson's explanation of the disproportion between the sexes in this particular tribe, but we can hardly doubt that unsuitable clothing during a

---

[1] The thickness of buffalo, bear, and moose hides led to their use in warfare as coats of mail.
[2] Thompson: Op. cit., p. 352 f.

portion of the year did cause considerable hardship, and operated in no slight degree to increase the death rate.

Many primitive peoples, especially in warm and temperate countries, have regarded clothing more as a method of adornment than as a covering required by modesty, or for protection against the climatic conditions. Several writers have, therefore, ascribed its origin to a natural tendency of man to decorate his person. Whether this theory be true or not, the Indians of Canada certainly did not neglect its æsthetic possibilities. Men generally adorned themselves more than women, a phenomenon common enough among primitive people, if contrary to civilized usage.[1] Even the everyday dress normally had decorative fringes, and for ceremonial occasions the Indians wore exceedingly elaborate costumes. The most distinctive features were, probably, feather head-dresses, and a kind of embroidery of dyed and undyed porcupine quills, goose quills, or moose hair. Neither of these forms of decoration extended to the Pacific or Arctic oceans, although the feather head-dress had a wide vogue over the two Americas, and quill work reached far down into the United States. Robes painted with realistic scenes depicting incidents in the lives of the wearers, usually war exploits or dreams, were peculiar to the plains' tribes; the paintings on the robes of the eastern Indians sometimes represented crests or clan emblems, like the Scottish tartans. The Eskimo and some adjacent tribes in the north produced pleasing effects by insertion of differently coloured furs, or by striped bands of dyed and undyed skin; and a dancing head-dress characteristic of certain Eskimo groups was a cap of variegated fur or leather surmounted by a loon's bill. Peculiar to the Pacific coast were the painted hats already mentioned, and the beautifully patterned blankets of goat's wool mingled with cedar bark.

Hunting peoples naturally tend to adorn themselves with trophies of the chase. The Eskimo attached bear teeth and bear claws to their clothing, several Indian tribes wore bear-claw necklaces, and some Pacific Coast natives used bear-claw head-dresses on ceremonial occasions. The Slaves and Dogribs of the Mackenzie basin delighted in head-bands of leather embroidered with porcupine quills, and embellished with animal claws and the white

---

[1] The reasons are often obscure; sometimes they appear to be associated with the status of women and the division of labour.

35989

Tsimshian Indian wearing a wooden head-dress inlaid with abalone shell, and a woven "chilkat" blanket of goat's wool and cedar bark. *(Photo by National Museum of Canada.)*

skins of the ermine. The plains' Indians wore bracelets of antelope teeth, the Carrier of northern British Columbia attached the claws and teeth of both the caribou and the beaver to their clothing, and wore necklaces of split and dyed antler, while their neighbours, the Tsimshian, and other coastal tribes, sewed fringes of jingling caribou claws or puffin bills to their dancing aprons. The Eskimo, again, and some tribes on the Pacific coast, greatly esteemed the white ermine skins; the former often suspended ten or a dozen from a single coat, while the Haida and Tsimshian of the Pacific coast wore them behind like a train, attached to an elaborate head-dress. Both Eskimo and Indians sometimes loaded the dress with objects of the most varied character, from curiously shaped stones to woodpecker's heads; but the majority of such pendants carried some religious meaning, and so ranked less as ornaments than as charms.

Of ornaments not attached to the clothing the commonest were necklets and bracelets, which prevailed among every tribe except the Eskimo; the Eskimo were so completely enveloped in fur clothing that they had little space for detached ornaments except ear pendants, and, in the western Arctic, labrets. Anklets were most common on the Pacific coast, and labrets were restricted to the northern tribes of that region and to the western Arctic. Very few plains' or northern Indians wore ear or nose pendants,[1] although these were fashionable in both eastern and western Canada. Instead of nose pendants, the Nootka of Vancouver island sometimes passed through the septum long shell pins ("sprit-sails," as Jewitt humorously called them), like some tribes in Melanesia. Every region, indeed, gave a stamp of individuality to its ornaments. The British Columbia Indians esteemed most highly their ornaments of native copper and dentalia shells, which passed in barter from tribe to tribe, the copper southward, and the dentalia shells north; but as the scarcity of these objects placed them beyond the reach of all but the most influential natives, the majority substituted bands of painted leather, or ornaments of dyed and undyed cedar bark.[2] Copper was more plentiful in eastern Canada, and, therefore, less highly esteemed. Although frequently used for bracelets and other orna-

---

[1] *Cf.* Franklin, J.: " Narrative of a Second Expedition to the Shores of the Polar Sea"; p. 28, London, 1828.

[2] Some tribes, e.g. the Tsimshian and the Bella Coola, restricted dyed bark ornaments to members of certain secret societies; others, like the Haida, placed no restrictions on their use.

ments it was supplanted in popular esteem by disks and beads of shell, which were manufactured by coastal tribes from the Maritime Provinces southward and traded far into the interior. In the sixteenth century two varieties of beads prevailed in eastern Canada, a white, and a violet or purple. The white typified to the Iroquois and some adjacent tribes, peace, prosperity, and good-will; the purple, war, disaster, and death. Besides their ornamental and symbolic uses they had a definite exchange value, and became a regular currency among all the Indians east of the Mississippi river in the United States, and of the Great Lakes in Canada.

Tattooing as a means of decoration prevailed throughout the northern parts of Canada, and among all the tribes of the Pacific coast; it was rarely practised by the plains' Indians, and in eastern Canada by a few tribes only, the Iroquoians of Ontario, the Naskapi, and the Cree. The usual method was to pass an awl under the skin and draw through the puncture a thread of sinew covered with charcoal or soot. The Haida (who used a red pigment also), the Tahltan, and probably other west coast tribes employed a puncturing process closely resembling that of the Iroquoian tribes of Ontario;[1] whereas the Naskapi of the Labrador peninsula rubbed the pigment into small incisions made with a piece of flint.[2] The first two processes are clearly described by Franklin: " Tattooing is almost universal among the Crees. The women are in general content with having one or two lines drawn from the corners of the mouth towards the angles of the lower jaw; but some of the men have their bodies covered with a great variety of lines and figures. It seems to be considered by most rather as a proof of courage than an ornament, the operation being very painful, and, if the figures are numerous and intricate, lasting three days. The lines on the face are formed by dexterously running an awl under the cuticle, and then drawing a cord, dipped in charcoal and water, through the canal thus formed. The punctures on the body are formed by needles of various sizes set in a frame.[3] A number of hawk bells attached to this frame serve by their noise to cover the suppressed groans of the sufferer, and, probably for the same reason, the process is accompanied by

---

[1] Dawson, G. M.: " Report on the Queen Charlotte Islands"; Geol. Surv., Canada, Rept. of Prog. 1878-79, pt. B, p. 108 (Montreal, 1880). Teit, J.: Unpublished Notes. " Jesuit Relations ", vol. i, p. 279.
[2] Hind, H. Y.: "Explorations in the Interior of the Labrador Peninsula"; vol. ii, p. 97 f (London, 1863).
[3] The Tahltan and the Iroquois made the punctures singly by tapping a bone awl with a light mallet.

singing. An indelible stain is produced by rubbing a little finely-powdered willow-charcoal into the punctures. A half-breed, whose arm I amputated, declared that tattooing was not only the more painful operation of the two, but rendered infinitely more difficult to bear by its tediousness, having lasted in his case three days."[1]

Eskimo women always tattooed their faces, sometimes also their limbs; but the men rarely marked their persons and then only with one or two short bars. Among the Indians, men practised this form of decoration more than women. The designs varied greatly, following to some extent the art patterns of each region. Natives of the Pacific coast often tattooed their clan crests in the conventional form typical of the art of that area.[2] East of the Rockies three or four lines radiating from the lower lip to the chin were universal from the Cree northward, and the other designs consisted mainly of straight lines either parallel, radiating, or forked. The Iroquoians, like the Assiniboine, "impressed upon the skin fixed and permanent representations of birds or animals, such as a snake, an eagle, or a toad."[3]

More widely spread than tattooing was face and body painting, practised by all the tribes in Canada except the Eskimo. The aborigines had at their command a variety of colours derived from both vegetable and mineral sources. The Piegan, for example, had ten colours: "a dark red, nearly a Spanish brown; a red, inclining to pale vermilion; a deep yellow; a light yellow; a dark blue; a light or sky-coloured blue; a shining and glossy lead colour; a green; a white; and charcoal."[4] There were no colours or patterns distinctive of the tribal units, but on the plains various organizations that corresponded roughly with our fraternities or lodges had each its special style of face-painting, and both in that region and among the eastern Indians distinctive patterns indicated valour in battle, or were associated with certain religious beliefs. It is rather curious that the Indians east of the Rocky mountains should have exercised more care and taste in face and body painting than the Indians on the coast of British Columbia, where painting on wood and other

---

[1] Franklin, J.: "A Journey to the Shores of the Polar Sea," p. 71 (London, 1823).
[2] Dawson: Loc. cit. Morice, A. G.: "Notes on the Western Dénés"; Trans. Can. Inst., vol. iv, p. 182 (Toronto, 1895). Teit, J.: Unpublished Notes.
[3] "Jesuit Relations," vol. i, p. 279; vol. lxvi, p. 109.
[4] Henry and Thompson: Op. cit., vol. ii, p. 731. *Cf.* "Jesuit Relations," vol. lxx, p. 95 (1747-64): "Vermilion, white, green, yellow, and black. . . on a single savage face are seen united all these different colours."

materials attained its highest development. Black was used for mourning in certain tribes, and bright red was a favourite colour everywhere; the Beothuk of Newfoundland gained the special designation of "Red Indians" from their custom of smearing their

27059

Interior Salish girl, with her hair specially braided to mark the termination of her adolescence. *(Photo by James Teit.)*

persons, clothing, and implements with red ochre. Many tribes rubbed grease over the face and hands as a protection against sunburn and flies, and some mixed vegetable compounds with the grease. Probably paint was nearly as effective as grease, although its primary purpose was certainly not protection, but adornment.

The aborigines of the Dominion never indulged in the elaborate coiffures that characterize so many African peoples. Women generally divided the hair into two braids that fell over the shoulders; occasionally they left it unbraided, or bound it into a single pigtail down the back. Men allowed themselves more liberty. On the Pacific coast the majority, unless they were medicine-men, cut it short; on the plains they sometimes shaved it off around the sides, but always left the scalp-lock, a long braid that depended from the crown. Among the eastern Indians each man followed his own inclination. Thus we read in the Jesuit Relations: "some shave the hair, others cultivate it; some have half the head bare, others the back of the head; the hair of some is raised up on their heads, that of others hangs down scantily upon each temple."[1] Here and there in this region certain styles became fashionable for a time, and were adopted by the majority of a tribe or community. In the early days of colonization one tribe wore upstanding locks "like the bristles of a wild boar", whence the French-Canadians nicknamed the people Hurons, the "bristly savages."[2] The Eskimo in the north allowed the hair to grow loose, or cut it short, according to their fancy; their women usually wore it in two braids, but those of the Mackenzie delta preferred a tonsure for their husbands, and, for themselves, a top-knot, which was rarely seen elsewhere in the Dominion. Every tribe anointed the hair with liberal quantities of grease or oil.[3] The plains' Indians made brushes of twigs or bundles of porcupine quills. Other natives used combs of wood, bone, or ivory; but the most usual comb was the fingers. East of the Rockies no costume was quite complete that did not include a few feathers stuck at jaunty angles in the hair.

Contact with Europeans quickly revolutionized both dress and ornament among the aborigines. Styles changed, woollen and cotton goods partly replaced fur and leather, and some of the old furs ceased to be used for clothing, but found their way to the white man's markets. Beads and silk embroidery gradually replaced embroidery of porcupine quills and moose hair, metal ornaments superseded ornaments of shell. The aborigines followed European

---

[1] "Jesuit Relations," vol. i, p. 281 (1610-1613).
[2] *Ibid.*, vol. xxxviii, p. 249 (1652-1653).
[3] The Kutchin of the upper Yukon plastered so much grease and ochre on their hair that their heads leaned forward with the weight.

styles of wearing the hair, and abandoned both tattooing and face-painting. As the contact increased they discarded their old dress entirely and adopted the costume of the new possessors of the soil. Now only the Eskimo of the north still retain their ancient winter garb with little change, because the white man cannot as yet furnish another costume that offers more protection against the climatic conditions.

CHAPTER VII

DWELLINGS

With primitive as with civilized peoples, the centre of social life is the home; but just as the home of an Italian peasant differs greatly from that of a Norwegian, so the homes of the Canadian aborigines varied greatly one from another, in shape and in size, in the materials of which they were constructed, in their internal arrangements, and in the number of families that occupied them. Climatic, physiographic, and biological conditions all played a part in producing these variations; but cultural and historical influences were equally active, so that a type of dwelling that seemed to be peculiarly the product of one environment occasionally extended beyond the bounds of that environment into another where it appeared less suitable.

All the aborigines of Canada, even the agricultural Iroquoians, were to a greater or less extent migratory. The prairie and northern Indians roamed almost continuously in search of game, and several years often elapsed before they revisited exactly the same localities. In these circumstances they required either portable dwellings, or dwellings that could be erected in an hour or two from the materials that nature supplied around them. The eastern Algonkians, who seldom lingered in one spot more than a few weeks, had much the same needs. One might have expected more substantial dwellings from the Iroquoians, who were tied down by agriculture to a more sedentary life. Their dwellings were indeed larger than those of other tribes east of the Rocky mountains, but not more durable, for even they practically deserted their villages for three or four months each year in order to fish and hunt, to work on distant farms, or to trade with their neighbours.[1] Moreover, "when there was no longer sufficient wood for their fires, or when the land, long tilled, produced scanty crops",[2] they abandoned their villages entirely and erected new homes in another locality. Any dwelling that provided tolerable

---

[1] " Jesuit Relations," vol. x, p. 53: " Summer here (among the Hurons) is a very inconvenient season for instructing the savages. Their trading expeditions and the farms take everyone away, men, women, and children, almost no one remains in the villages."
[2] Ibid., xi, p. 7.

shelter for ten or fifteen years would satisfy their needs; to expend time and labour on buildings that would outlast this period was useless. Conditions were different on the Pacific coast. There the natives made seasonal migrations indeed, but the greater part of the year they lived in fixed localities, which they occupied generation after generation, unless dislodged by wars or other calamities.[1] On this coast, then, we find not only rude shelters of brush or mats, but permanent houses of solid lumber intended to last a man's whole lifetime. Similarly, in the Arctic and around the shores of the Labrador peninsula, the Eskimo had fixed sealing grounds to which they returned after each summer's fishing and hunting inland; and in those places, in prehistoric times at least, they erected permanent homes, of driftwood in the Mackenzie delta, of stone and bones of whale in the eastern Arctic where driftwood was scarce or lacking.[2]

It was not only the constant migrations that prevented the construction of durable buildings, whether in brick or in stone, comparable with those that survive in the Old World, or in the jungles of Central America. The use of brick was unknown to the aborigines, although many tribes made crude pottery from the local clay; and the rocks that predominated throughout the Dominion were too hard for the individual Indian to hew into shape with a stone ax and a stone hammer. It is true that the megalithic monuments scattered from western Europe to Polynesia were erected for the most part before the age of iron, and that many of these monuments are constructed of hard, igneous rocks. It is true also that the Indians of Central America and Peru often incorporated hard rocks in their temples and fortifications, and that they utilized only stone tools to quarry and dress them. But the peoples who executed these works seem to have been populous agricultural communities with strong, centralized governments that had considerable resources of labour at their command. There were no communities in Canada that had reached this level of development, not even the maize-growing Iroquoians. The Eskimo who erected the stone huts in the

---

[1] The climate is milder on the Pacific coast, the forests heavier, and the villages were generally less populous than those of the Iroquoians in Ontario. Hence there was never any scarcity of fuel. In the interior of British Columbia, however, the Carrier Indians moved their winter settlements yearly, or at frequent intervals, owing to the exhaustion of wood in the vicinity. Morice, A. G.: "Notes on the Northern Dénés"; Trans. Can. Inst., vol. iv, p. 184 (Toronto, 1892).

[2] Nootka hunters occasionally built shelters of stone in the mountains of Vancouver island, when outside the timber (Sproat: Op. cit., p. 241); but no traces of these shelters are known.

eastern Arctic worked singly, or perhaps two or three together. They used undressed boulders only, such as lay ready to their hands; and they laid them one on top of another without mortar, as does the farmer who builds a stone fence around his meadow. This crude method of construction did not permit them to utilize even their knowledge of the dome, so conspicuously displayed in their snow huts; or to erect dwellings of larger size than could be spanned by the rib of a whale, or by the short logs of driftwood that occasionally floated up on their shores.[1]

Encampments or village sites naturally lay close to supplies of fuel and fresh water. Canada is pre-eminently a land of lakes and rivers, so that the problem of water supply was seldom serious. Neither did fuel present any difficulties in the forested areas which comprise more than half the country; but on the treeless prairies the Indians often resorted to buffalo chips during the summer months, and spent the winter in groves on the outskirts of the plains.[2] Other factors that determined the choice of sites were the facilities for fishing or for gathering shell-fish, the abundance of game in the vicinity, the proximity of a hill or dominant point (like a promontory on a waterway) from which to scour the landscape, shelter from the prevailing cold winds, security from a sudden attack, the character of the soil and the location in reference to routes of trade and travel. When the Beothuk Indians of Newfoundland moved out to the coast during the summer months they preferred to camp in small, sheltered bays that had freshwater streams at their heads and gravel or sandy beaches that offered good landing-places for the birch-bark canoes. In the interior of the island the campsites of this extinct tribe appear most numerous at river and lake crossings formerly frequented by the caribou, or on promontories that afford a wide view up and down the lakes. The tribes of eastern Canada preferred sandy soil to clay or loam on account of the better drainage. In the Maritime Provinces one may find remains of settlements near clam beds, on rivers which the salmon ascended, and at the

[1] The Handbook of American Indians North of Mexico, article, "Architecture" (Bull. 30, Bur. Am. Eth., Washington, 1907) states that the aborigines of North America knew neither the off-set span of stone nor the key-stone arch. This is not altogether accurate in respect to the Eskimo, for in at least one stone structure they applied, albeit very crudely, the off-set span (Jenness, D.: Op. cit.. p. 57), and the dome of their snow-hut was really a development of the arch.

[2] The Eskimo of the Arctic, whose homes lay beyond the limit of trees, combined the fuel problem with the food quest, using the train-oil of sea mammals, and the fat of bears and caribou, for both heat and light. During the brief season when the snow had melted from the land they kindled open-air fires of heather and dwarf willow.

entrances and exits of lakes on the main waterways. Tadoussac was frequented by the Indians long before Champlain's time because it was a strategic point at the junction of two waterways, the St. Lawrence and the Saguenay, and because cod were abundant in the adjacent sea. Hochelaga (Montreal) was another strategic point at the foot of the Lachine rapids, the meeting-point of trade-routes down the Ottawa and St. Lawrence rivers; the fertile land below mount Royal was eminently suited for the cultivation of maize, and the summit of the hill offered a wide view up and down the river.[1] An early Jesuit missionary, Lafitau, makes a very pertinent remark on sites like Hochelaga that were occupied by Iroquoian tribes: " They locate them, as far as possible, in the centre of fertile soil on a small rise that gives them a view of the surrounding landscape— this to prevent surprise—and on the bank of a stream which, if possible, winds around the place, adding a kind of natural moat to the fortifications which art can supply to a site already well defended by nature."[2] The prairie Indians, when following the buffalo during the summer months, camped near fords in the rivers, in hollow valleys near commanding hill-tops, and on the hill-tops themselves; while in British Columbia the aborigines built their houses near good fishing-grounds or clam-beds and on the rivers that the salmon ascended—especially near the mouths of these rivers, at their exits from the lakes, and at rapids and canyons in their courses where obstructions in the channels facilitated the use of weirs and fish-traps.[3]

Let us now consider the various regions more in detail. The typical dwelling in eastern Canada was the lodge or wigwam, which consisted of a framework of poles covered with rolls of bark, rushes. or skin. For winter most tribes preferred a conical form that could be erected in about an hour. " The women go to the woods and bring back some poles which are stuck into the ground in a circle around the fire, and at the top are interlaced, in the form of a pyramid, so that they come together directly over the fire, for there is the chimney.

---

[1] For similar reasons one would expect to find the remains of prehistoric settlements at Ottawa, where the Rideau and Ottawa rivers join. Some Indian implements have been found in the vicinity, mainly around lake Deschênes and on the north shore of the river below the Chaudière falls, but very few traces of any village site. *See* Twenty-ninth Ann. Arch. Rept., 1917, being part of Appendix to the Report of the Minister of Education, Ontario, pp. 78-85 (Toronto, 1917).
[2] Lafitau, J. F.: Moeurs des Sauvages Amériquains, vol. ii, p. 3 (Paris, 1724).
[3] Sproat says of Nootka villages: " The village sites are generally well chosen, and, though not selected for any other reason than nearness to firewood and water, and safety against a surprise, are often beautiful." But fish abounded in every fiord occupied by the Nootka on the west coast of Vancouver island. *Cf.* Dawson, G. M.: Geol. Surv., Canada, Rept. of Prog. 1878-79, pt. B, p. 116.

Upon the poles they throw some skins, matting, or bark. At the foot of the poles, under the skins, they put their baggage. All the space around the fire is strewn with leaves of the fir tree, so they will not feel the dampness of the ground; over these leaves are often thrown some mats, or sealskins as soft as velvet; upon this they stretch themselves around the fire with their heads resting upon their baggage."[1] A lodge of this kind could accommodate up to fifteen persons. To increase its warmth the Indians often cleared away the snow on the floor and hollowed out the soil to a depth of six inches or a foot, so that the dwelling was partly underground.[2]

594

Two types of Ojibwa birch-bark lodges. *(Photo by T. C. Weston.)*

Most of these eastern tribes built rectangular lodges in summer, because they were larger and more airy than the conical form. Each housed from two to four families; but the lodges of the Iroquois, who used the rectangular form winter and summer alike, often held as many as twenty. Champlain describes some of these "long houses" that he visited in the Huron country, in southeastern Ontario: " Their cabins are a kind of arbour or bower, covered with bark, approximately fifty or sixty yards long by twelve wide, with a passage ten or twelve feet broad down the middle from one end to the other. Along each side runs a bench four feet above the ground, where the inmates sleep in summer to avoid the innumerable fleas. In winter they sleep close to the fire on mats, underneath the benches where it

1 "Jesuit Relations," vol. iii, p. 77.
2 LeClerq, Chrétien: " New Relations of Gaspesia," edited by W. F. Ganong, p. 100 f, The Champlain Society (Toronto, 1910). *Cf.* Skinner, A.: " Notes on Eastern Cree and Northern Saulteaux"; Anthropological Papers, Am. Mus. Nat. Hist., vol. ix, pt. I, p. 13 (New York, 1911).

is warmer; and they fill the hut with a supply of dry wood to burn at that season. A space is left at one end of the cabin for storing their maize, which they place in large bark barrels in the middle of the floor; and boards suspended overhead preserve their clothing, food, and other things from the numerous mice. There will be a dozen fires to each cabin, making two dozen families. The smoke circulates at will, causing much eye trouble, to which the natives are so subject that many become blind in their old age. For there is no window in the cabin, and no opening except a place in the roof where the smoke finds an outlet."[1]

The Ojibwa and the Cree had still a third form of lodge, one shaped like a dome or beehive, for the willow poles that formed its frame were arched over until both ends entered the ground. The largest of these lodges were ten or twelve feet in diameter by eight or ten feet high. The Kutchin Indians of the Yukon River basin lived in skin tents of exactly the same form. Elsewhere in Canada the dome-shaped lodge was not a dwelling, but a sudatory or sweat-house, for which purpose the Indians employ it even today from the Atlantic to British Columbia.[2]

All the three types of lodges described above were essentially portable; the natives could strike camp and move away within a few minutes.[3] Naturally, they transported only the coverings of the dwellings—whether bark, skin, or rush mats—since they could procure new poles at every halting-place. Each kind of covering had its advantages and disadvantages. Skin was wind-proof, non-inflammable, and easily rolled into a bundle; but when soaked with rain it could not be dried under twenty-four hours. Bark was rain-proof, but it became brittle in cold weather and required warming before it could be either rolled or unrolled. Rush-mats, if skilfully made, also shed the rain, and made warm lodges in winter, but they were heavier and bulkier to transport than rolls of bark.[4] Then there were various kinds of bark from which to choose. Most of the tribes in eastern Canada used birch-bark, which they could strip from the tree in large rolls. The Iroquoians, whose territory contained few

---

[1] "Oeuvres de Champlain," par C. H. Laverdière; vol. 4, p. 74 (562) (Quebec, 1870).
[2] These sweat-houses, however, are small, rarely exceeding 6 feet in diameter.
[3] Cf. The Works of Samuel de Champlain, edited by H. P. Biggar, vol. i, p. 104, The Champlain Society (Toronto, 1922).
[4] Cf. Henry and Thompson: Op. cit., vol. i, p. 133. Thompson: Op. cit., pp. 117, 247. "Jesuit Relations," vol. viii, p. 105.

large birch trees, substituted cedar bark; but it was so inflammable that many preferred the bark of the elm or ash. This could not be transported as easily as birch-bark, but the Iroquoians had not the same need for portable dwellings as the Algonkians, because they occupied the same village sites for several years in succession. They did, in fact, carry birch-bark on some of their hunting and fishing excursions; but more often they simply constructed rude shelters of brush, bark, skin, or anything else that lay ready to their hands. Summarizing for eastern Canada as a whole, we may say that the northern tribes, the Cree, Naskapi, and certain bands of the Montagnais, used mainly skin coverings both winter and summer; the Indians of southern Quebec and of the Maritime Provinces used birch-bark; the Iroquoian tribes used the bark of cedar, ash, elm, or spruce; and the Ojibwa, with some of their Algonkian neighbours, adopted birch-bark for summer lodges and rush mats for winter.

The plains' area was the home of the tipi, a tent of buffalo hide stretched around a conical framework formed by fourteen to eighteen long poles, whose points radiated like a funnel above the peak.[1] Two projecting "ears" near the top, on the outside, served as cowls for the smoke-holes, each being adjusted by a pole in accordance with the direction of the wind. The doorway, which could be closed with a small flap, was a narrow aperture in the face of the tent; the fireplace was in the centre, and beyond it, facing the door, sat the head of the household. Sometimes an inner curtain of hide three or four feet high was suspended behind him to cover half the back wall. The furniture was meagre; two or three tall tripods that supported triangular back-rests of parallel twigs; some fur robes for bedding at their base; one or two leather bags containing clothing, and a few household tools and utensils. An average tipi of the Blackfoot Indians had a floor diameter of fourteen feet.

Apart from the "ears," there was little difference between this plains' tipi and the conical tent of the eastern Indians already mentioned, which often had a covering of skins. Tents of the same type, without ears and with coverings of either skin or brush, prevailed throughout much of the Mackenzie basin, although a few tribes in this area, notably the Hare and the Slave, generally

---

[1] The tops of three, or, in some tribes, four, poles, were first lashed together and set up like a tripod; the remaining poles were then spaced evenly between them, resting against the forked apex.

passed the winter in rectangular or A-shaped cabins covered with brush and snow.[1] West of the Rockies we meet with more substantial dwellings. The Tahltan, Sekani, and some bands of the Carrier, all of whom were immigrants from the Mackenzie basin, retained the skin and bough shelters of their earlier home, or constructed crude, gable-roofed huts sheathed with birch-bark; but

34574

Typical tipis of the plains, formerly of buffalo-hide, now of cloth.
(Photo by Harlan I. Smith.)

other Carrier bands and the interior Salish tribes to the southward built strong log cabins, so completely underground that they could be entered only by ladders leading down through the rectangular smoke-holes.

The adjoining plan[2] explains the construction of these underground cabins better than a long description. They accommodated

---

[1] Wentzel and Keith in Masson: Op. cit., i, 90, ii, 121. The Slaves rarely or never visited the Barren Grounds to hunt caribou, and seldom secured enough skins to provide both clothing and coverings for their tents.
[2] *See also* the illustration on p. 354.

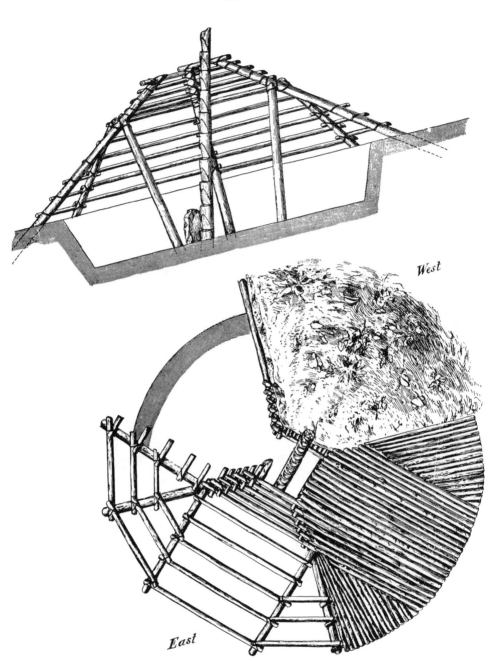

West

East

Plan of an Interior Salish semi-subterranean house. *(Reproduced from Teit J. A.: "The Thompson Indians of British Columbia," Memoirs of the American Museum of Natural History, vol. 2; Jesup Expedition to the North Pacific, vol. I, p. 193, New York, 1900.)*

from fifteen to thirty persons, but had two disadvantages; first, water seeped in occasionally from the ground outside and no amount of lining with cedar bark could make the walls quite impermeable; secondly, no one could enter over the earth-covered roof without showering dirt on the inmates below. The houses were so warm that the natives occupied them in winter only, moving out at the beginning of spring into conical or rectangular lodges, covered with bark or brush, that closely resembled those of eastern Canada.

The coast Indians of British Columbia, who differed in costume from all other tribes in Canada, differed also in their houses. The cedar trees that furnished so much of their dress, fur-

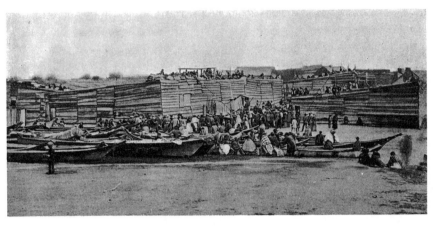

20535

Plank houses of the Coast Salish at Victoria, B.C. Potlatch in progress in the foreground.
(Photo by R. Maynard.)

nished also beams and planks of solid timber, from which the Salish tribes around the straits of Georgia and Juan de Fuca, and the Nootka on the west coast of Vancouver island, built oblong dwellings of amazing size, several hundred feet long in some cases by fifty or sixty feet wide. Structurally they contained two parts, an inner frame and a detachable outer shell. The frame comprised two rows of oblong posts arranged parallel to each other at an interval equal to the breadth of the house, but with the posts of the front row slightly higher, or lower,[1] than those of the back. Each opposite pair supported a rafter, and the rafters supported a gently sloping roof of

---

[1] The Nootka apparently made the front of the house lower, the Coast Salish, the back. There seems to have been much variety in house forms all along the Pacific coast, even in a single village.

planks, some of which, at least, could be moved at will to let out the smoke. The shell, which was carried away each spring to line a house frame in some other locality, consisted of long planks laid horizontally on edge one above the other, resting against the house posts on one face and lashed to a few slender poles on the other. A gap between the ends of two or four planks in the front of the house served as a door, and other gaps, irregularly spaced, were windows, often covered with mats to exclude the rain. Theoretically, the house contained as many families as there were posts, if we omit two of the end posts, for the normal space assigned to a family was the section between two posts, from the wall to the middle of the house, where its fire was shared by the family on the opposite side. Each section had a low sleeping bench, and usually a mat curtain or a plank to mark its limits. As Cook aptly remarked, "The whole might be compared to a long stable, with a double range of stalls, and a broad passage in the middle." "Their furniture", he continues, "consists chiefly of a great number of chests and boxes of all sizes, which are generally piled upon each other, close to the sides or ends of the house; and contain their spare garments, skins, masks, and other things which they set a value upon."[1]

The Nootka Indians (or perhaps only their chiefs) had also another type of house, built after the manner of the houses of the Kwakiutl and the northern tribes. Its frame was square rather than oblong, and the roof was gabled, not shaped like a penthouse. The planks of the shell seem to have been arranged horizontally, as in the other type of house, not perpendicularly, after the usual custom of the Kwakiutl and Haida Indians.[2] The roof beams were often of enormous size, and the pillars supporting them carved with fantastic figures. Weird paintings on the outside of the front wall, and sometimes a gigantic totem-pole planted at the entrance, or a little aloof, increased the savage dignity of the structure, which greatly impressed the early voyagers. "On entering the house," writes Meares, "we were absolutely astonished at the vast area it enclosed. It contained a large square, boarded up close on all sides to the height of twenty feet, with planks of an uncommon breadth

---

[1] Cook: Op. cit., vol. ii, p. 315 f. *Cf.* the description of a Coast Salish house 640 feet long near the mouth of the Fraser river, in the Journal of Simon Fraser, Masson: Op. cit., ser. i, p. 197 f.
[2] Jewitt: Op. cit., p. 69. The prevailing arrangement among the Tsimshian and Tlinkit was horizontal.

and length. Three enormous trees, rudely carved and painted, formed the rafters, which were supported at the ends and in the middle by gigantic images, carved out of huge blocks of timber. The same kind of broad planks covered the whole to keep out the rain; but they were so placed as to be removed at pleasure, either to receive the air and light, or let out the smoke. In the middle of this spacious room were several fires. . . . The trees that supported the roof were of a size which would render the mast of a first-rate man of war diminutive, on a comparison with them. . . The door by which we entered this extraordinary fabric was the mouth of one of these huge images, which, large as it may be supposed, was not disproportioned to the other features of this monstrous visage. We ascended by a few steps on the outside, and after passing this extraordinary kind of portal, descended down the chin into the house, where we found new matter for astonishment in the number of men, women, and children, who composed the family of the chief; which consisted of at least eight hundred persons. These were divided into groups, according to their respective offices, which had their distinct places assigned them. The whole of the building was surrounded by a bench, about two feet from the ground, on which the various inhabitants sat, eat, and slept."[1]

Not all the gabled houses of the Pacific Coast Indians were as large as that visited by Meares, which belonged to a principal chief of the Nootka. Kwakiutl houses normally held only four families, one in each corner.[2] There were other variations, too, at different points along the coast, particularly among the Haida of the Queen Charlotte islands, who often hollowed out the floor and used the underground level as an extra story.[3] Some houses, again, had two or three tiers of benches around the walls, after the manner of an amphitheatre.

The most remarkable feature about all these West Coast houses was the extraordinary labour and patience required to fell and dress the trees, carve the posts, and split off and dress the planks, with no other tools than adzes and chisels of stone or shell, and wedges

---

[1] Meares: Op. cit., pp. 138-139. He perhaps exaggerates; the 800 probably gathered for the ceremony.

[2] Boas, F.: "The Houses of the Kwakiutl Indians, British Columbia"; Proc. United States Nat. Mus., vol. xi, 1888, p. 200 (Washington, 1889).

[3] Marchand, Etienne: "A Voyage Round the World"; translated by C.-P. Claret Fleurieu, vol. i, p. 400 (London, 1801).

of wood or antler.[1] We cannot but admire, too, the engineering skill of the Indians, who possessed no machinery of any kind to move the gigantic tree trunks, not even the simple pulley. To place a roof-beam in position they levered it up a sloping log whose end rested on top of the pillar; and to erect a house-post or totem-pole they planked one side of the excavation, bevelled off the other side, and raised the top of the pole with levers and supporting crib-work

255

Haida Indian village at Skidegate, Queen Charlotte islands, B.C.
(Photo by G. M. Dawson.)

until the butt slid gently into its hole. Such undertakings naturally called for the co-operation of several men, sometimes of a whole community; and the completion of a house was an occasion for great festivities. Unfortunately, not one of these dwellings survived to the twentieth century, and very few ruins remain to show us the details of their construction.

---

[1] The Indians generally smoothed their posts and planks with shark-skin or the horse-tailed (equisetum) rush; but often they retained the adze marks as a decorative feature. The adzing of a tree trunk readily produced a kind of fluting up and down the stem, as may be seen on some of the totem-poles. Mr. P. A. Taverner, of the National Museum of Canada, suggests that a similar practice in the Old World may have been the forerunner of the Doric pillar, which undoubtedly had a prototype in wood.

Stranger than any of the dwellings erected by the Indian tribes of Canada was the Eskimo snow hut, a striking example of how admirably man sometimes adapts himself to his environment. Its origin is lost in antiquity; possibly it developed out of the beehive tent of willows covered with skins,[1] through the substitution of snow blocks for the envelope of soft, loose snow and the subsequent discovery that the snow blocks could be made to stand alone. The snow hut possesses several peculiar features. It resembles, superficially, a dome of stone constructed without mortar; but since blocks of snow adhere more tightly to each other than blocks of stone, the roof can be arched in at a steeper angle. The Eskimo builds spirally from within, trimming each block as he places it in position; like a stonemason, he generally avoids overlying joints, although this precaution is not essential for ultimate stability. After the key block has been inserted the hut is tightly sealed and a lamp kindled inside. The heated air, having no exit, begins to melt the face of the snow, which rapidly congeals again on the admission of cold air from the outside. Thus each snow block is firmly cemented to its neighbours and converted to ice on its inner face. Occupation for a few days then gradually changes the interior of the blocks, so that the structure is no longer a snow house, but a house of ice. The transformation gives it remarkable stability; ·a man may stand on its summit without causing its collapse, and half the house can be demolished without destroying the other half. Consequently, by building a series of intersecting domes and omitting, or opening up, the common segments, an Eskimo can enlarge a small, circular hut, capable of housing only one or two families, into a community dwelling of three, four, and even five rooms that will house fifteen or twenty people.

Glance, for a moment, at the interior of an ordinary, single-room snow hut. You pass with bowed head along a narrow, roofed passage of snow blocks until you arrive at the doorway, a hole at your feet which you traverse on hands and knees. You rise to your feet. On the right (or left), two feet above the floor, is the lamp, a saucer-shaped vessel of stone filled with burning seal-oil, and with

[1] The Eskimo of northern Alaska, who cannot build a circular snow hut, still use this tent, but replace the skins with canvas. On the coast they occasionally cover a rectangular frame of drift-wood with canvas, and line the walls and roof with snow-blocks; in such a dwelling they will pass a whole winter. For a night's shelter, again, they sometimes build small, rectangular snow huts, so narrow that the roof can be spanned by single blocks.

a stone cooking pot suspended above it. Behind the lamp are some bags containing meat and blubber; in front of it, a wooden table bearing, perhaps, a knife and a ladle. A low platform covered with skins occupies fully half the floor space; there, side by side, with their heads facing the door, the inmates sleep in bags or robes of caribou fur. If you stand at the edge of this platform, exactly in the centre of the hut, you can place both hands on the ceiling and almost touch the wall on either side. A thermometer, three feet from the lamp, will register one or two degrees below the freezing point of water, quite a comfortable temperature if you are enveloped, like the Eskimo, in soft, warm garments of caribou fur. Only your feet become slowly chilled on the snow floor, unless you find a seat on the sleeping platform and draw them up into safety.

37018

An Eskimo snow-hut with a window of ice. The owner's poles and harpoons are planted in the walls, and his sled upturned and raised on snow blocks, faces the entrance. *(Photo by D. Jenness.)*

The snow hut is essentially the product of a treeless zone where the unbroken force of the wind so compacts the surface of the snow that it can be carved into building blocks. For many centuries it has been the ordinary winter dwelling of all the Eskimo tribes of the Dominion east of the Mackenzie delta, the stone huts mentioned a little earlier in this chapter standing deserted and in ruins. In the delta itself, and in Alaska, driftwood was generally so plentiful along the coast that the Eskimo could build underground houses of logs similar in many respects to those inhabited by the Salish Indians of British Columbia. Every tribe of Eskimo moved at spring into rectangular or conical tents of skin that differed only in minor details from the tents of the Indians to the southward.

None of the dwellings of the Canadian aborigines, not even the imposing houses of the British Columbia Indians, could compare in comfort with the homes of mediaeval Europe, still less with our homes of to-day. The Indians had no conception of hygiene; they seldom washed, unless for ceremonial reasons, and their homes were squalid and often filthy. Rotting meat and fish strewed the floors and ground outside; dogs, mice, and parasites of every kind shared the interior with its human inmates. Cooking utensils were invariably unclean; "the more they are covered with thick grease, so much the better are they."[1] The ventilation was inadequate; smoke pervaded every corner, despite the hole in the roof, so that many natives incurred serious eye troubles, especially in their advancing years. Even the snow hut of the Eskimo, which was so fresh and clean when first erected, and which escaped the smoke through the substitution of a lamp for the open fire, became dingy within two or three days, its walls discoloured inside and out, its floor sodden with dripping meat and blubber, and its atmosphere tainted with the smell of burning seal-oil. Tribes that continually moved their camps had cleaner homes, but were no less unclean in their habits and persons. Privacy in home life was unknown; a fellow tribesman could enter any dwelling without ceremony, even though it were occupied by a single family. The natives often performed most of their tasks, and ate their meals, outside their houses, if the weather permitted; and their dwellings were not so much homes in our conception of that term, as indispensable shelters against the elements.

---

[1] " Jesuit Relations," vol. i, p. 285.

CHAPTER VIII

TRAVEL AND TRANSPORTATION, TRADE AND COMMERCE

The character and extent of a country's roads mirror with some clearness its civilization and prosperity. The Romans, who were the greatest road-builders of antiquity, linked together their " provinces " with broad, well-graded highways that excite the admiration of our professional civil engineers. In South America, a thousand years later, the Peruvians constructed a splendid series of roads in the mountainous Andean region to unite the scattered towns and villages that acknowledged the rule of the Incas in Cuzco, although, unlike the Romans, who possessed wheeled vehicles, they made their roads too narrow and steep to meet our present-day needs. Both Rome and Peru, however, were the seats of mighty empires that could command unlimited resources of man-power for the construction of great public works. In Canada the largest political unit was the tribe,[1] which was too small numerically, too self-contained, and in most places too migratory to demand or require specially built highways for communication and transport, particularly when there were no vehicles save sleds and toboggans to drive over them, and no pack animal except the dog. So from east to west, and north to south, throughout the whole Dominion, there was not a single mile of road before the coming of Europeans, nothing except a few narrow trails[2] that led past rapids and canyons, or through forest, plain, or upland from one valley or lake to another, trails that were often so overgrown with brush or lichens that they could hardly be distinguished from those of the bison and deer. War parties, indeed, commonly followed the tracks of these animals, or travelled along stream beds where their footsteps left no imprints; and in times of peace the natives generally avoided the soft, low ground and dense undergrowth where twigs and briers scratched their bare limbs and rent their clothing, avoided also the stony ground that cut their feet

---

[1] The Iroquoian Confederacy of the Five Nations (Mohawk, Oneida, Onondaga, Cayuga, and Seneca) bore the seed of empire in its composition, but the seed never germinated. Each tribe (or nation) within the confederacy retained its independence in everything except war, and in some cases even in war. In any case this Iroquoian Confederacy was post-European, and, therefore, later than the period we are here considering.

[2] Seldom more than 18 inches wide in the eastern regions. Handbook of American Indians North of Mexico, Article: " Trails and Trade Routes"; Bur. Am. Ethn. Bull. 30 (Washington, 1910).

or wore out their moccasins, and traversed the dry upland, where the hard soil preserved few traces of their passage. The treeless prairies, and the plains of the Arctic and sub-Arctic, offered so few obstacles that definite paths were needless. In other regions the numerous fiords and the network of rivers and lakes navigable for long distances by canoe rendered much land travel unnecessary. Not only was there an absence of roads in the Dominion, but an absence of bridges also, apart from an occasional tree spanning some narrow stream. The Indians merely forded such rivers as lay in their line of march, or crossed them in hastily built rafts and canoes.

Travel necessarily varied with the seasons, except on the coast of British Columbia where the climate remained mild throughout the year. In summer the Indians either carried their possessions in canoes from one camping ground to another, or transformed themselves into beasts of burden and packed their property on their backs. The Kwakiutl and other west coast tribes used special baskets for this purpose; elsewhere the natives simply rolled their goods into bundles, or lashed them inside large hides. Light burdens they suspended from a single tump-line that passed across the forehead; with heavier loads they often added a second strap that crossed the chest and arms a little below the shoulders. When the snow lay deep on the ground and the lakes and rivers were fast bound with ice, many of the natives abandoned the back pack for the toboggan or sled; but the change was not complete, and back packs were common in winter also. An early Jesuit missionary thus describes the winter marches of a Montagnais band: " They begin by having breakfast, if there is any; for sometimes they depart without breakfasting, continue on their way without dining, and go to bed without supping. Each one arranges his own baggage as best he can; and the women strike the cabin, to remove the ice and snow from the bark, which they roll up in a bundle. The baggage being packed, they throw it upon their backs or loins in long bundles, which they hold with a cord that passes over their foreheads, beneath which they place a piece of bark so that it will not hurt them. When everyone is loaded, they mount their snow-shoes, which are bound to the feet so that they will not sink into the snow; and then they march over plain and mountain, making the little ones go on ahead, who start early, and often do not arrive until quite late. These little ones have their load, or their sledge, to accustom them early to fatigue; and they try to stimulate them to see who will carry or drag the most." [1]

Snow-shoes, the dog-sled, the toboggan, and the bark canoe (the last as a model for our cedar and basswood canoes), all these the Canadian aborigines have contributed to our civilization. Snow-shoes for winter travel were almost universal outside of the Pacific and Arctic coasts.[2] They varied in shape from tribe to tribe, the Cree and some of their neighbours preferring broad oval forms, whereas the northern and Cordillera Indians made them narrower and more pointed. Since the webbing of an ordinary snow-shoe becomes matted with slush when the temperature rises above the freezing point, the Indians of Little Whale river, on the east coast of Hudson bay, occasionally made a form without webbing by joining together two pieces of board.[3] These wooden shoes suggest skis, but they were flat in front, not upturned, and being also too broad and short to glide over the surface of the snow, needed to be lifted at every step like the ordinary snow-shoe. The true ski was not known in America, although the toboggan may perhaps be considered a double or multiple ski adapted for transport.

The sled was restricted to the Eskimo, and to neighbouring tribes like the Kutchin who followed their example. The usual form had no handle-bars, but consisted merely of two heavy wooden runners bound together by crossbars of wood or bone. The runners were shod with bone plates or with frozen turf (sometimes both), which were coated with water or blood before each day's march to produce an icy film that offered little friction against the snow.

Eastern and northern Canada substituted the toboggan for the sled, but the plains' and British Columbia natives had neither. It is true that both the plains' and the Cordillera Indians, like other tribes, occasionally used a large hide after the manner of a toboggan, lashing their goods inside it to be dragged by women or dogs; but they never made the real toboggan of long, slender planks, lashed side by side and turned up at the front, that was the typical vehicle

---

1 "Jesuit Relations," vol. vii, pp. 109-111.
2 They were used, however, by the Eskimo from Mackenzie River delta westward.
3 Turner, L. M.: "Ethnology of the Ungava District, Hudson Bay Territory"; Eleventh Ann. Rept., Bur. Am. Ethn., 1889-90, p. 312 (Washington, 1894). Even to-day the Algonkins on some of the rivers tributary to the Ottawa use a wooden snow-shoe, made from a single board cut to the shape of the ordinary webbed shoe.

for winter transport among the Mackenzie River tribes and the Algonkians and Iroquoians of the eastern woodlands. In its place the plains' Indians substituted a peculiar contrivance called a travois, which doubtless originated from the custom, still common among the Eskimos, of fastening the tent-poles to the packs of the dogs. The travois consisted of two long poles lashed one on each side of the dog, and supporting a bag-net behind it for the reception of small articles. When dogs were replaced by horses in later years, the Blackfoot, Sarcee, and Assiniboine transported in these peculiar vehicles not

73458
The horse travois of the plains. *(Photo by Canadian National Railways.)*

only their tents and other possessions but even women and children. The dog travois of pre-European times, however, was small and low, capable of bearing not more than thirty-five or fifty pounds.

The travois provided transport for both winter and summer, sleds and toboggans for winter only. The Eskimo raised a special breed of sled-dog, a rather large animal with pointed ears and a bushy tail curled backward. The Indians had several breeds, none quite as large as the Eskimo dog; indeed, one of the commonest varieties in the Mackenzie basin was little bigger than a fox. A dog of average size cannot carry more than fifty pounds on its back, or drag on a sled or toboggan more than a hundred; and before the introduction of firearms few families could provide food for more than one or two animals. Consequently the main burden of transportation fell upon the people themselves, particularly on the women,

50178

A small Bella Coola dugout, "spoon" type, for river use. *(Photo by Harlan I. Smith.)*

since their husbands had oftentimes to wander away to the chase or guard the caravan against enemies.[1] Even among the Eskimos, who had little to fear from enemies, the women hauled on the sleds with the men, and in summer carried the greater part of the camp equipment.

Canoes greatly lightened the burden of summer transportation in all regions except the prairies and certain parts of the Arctic and sub-Arctic. There were two main types, a dugout and a canoe covered with bark or skin. The dugout prevailed all along the Pacific coast, but elsewhere in Canada only among some Iroquoian tribes,[2] whose territory, being near the southern limit of the birch, seldom provided satisfactory material for a bark-covered canoe. The Iroquoian dugouts were miserable vessels, little more than logs of pine rudely hollowed and pointed at bow and stern. So heavy were they, so

---

[1] None of the tribes in the basin of the Mackenzie river used dogs for dragging the tobaggans except the Chipewyans, and they rarely. Hearne: Op. cit., p. 310.

[2] Perhaps also among some of the southern Ojibwa near the International Boundary.

easily water-logged, and so ill-adapted for portaging from one lake or river to another, that these tribes frequently purchased birch-bark canoes from their Algonkian neighbours, or constructed canoes of elm bark after the same pattern.

Almost equally crude were some of the river dugouts of British Columbia, which were made of cottonwood, with rounded ends and a gunwale level from bow to stern. Portages were seldom possible in this region on account of the precipitous mountains, and the rivers themselves were swifter and shallower, as a rule, than those in Iroquoian territory. Hence these river dugouts in the west were longer and narrower than the Iroquoian to prevent excessive swinging in the eddies and currents; and they were propelled by poles more often than by paddles. The sea canoe of the Pacific coast, made of cedar instead of cottonwood, was broader than the river canoe,

58502

A small Nootka dugout, for coast use. *(Photo by N. K. Luxton.)*

and much more carefully constructed. Although keelless, like all the craft in the New World, it was so buoyant and seaworthy that the Nootka often paddled out of sight of land off the stormy west coast of Vancouver island, and the Haida of the Queen Charlotte islands, in the early days of European settlement, made frequent voyages to Victoria, a distance of three hundred miles. These sea canoes varied greatly in size. Some held two persons only, others, sixty or seventy feet long with a beam of seven or eight feet, carried a crew of fifty, although it was only on Queen Charlotte islands that the cedar grew large enough to make a dugout of such magnitude. There was considerable variation, also, in shape. The canoes of the northern tribes had rounded bottoms, and curved gently upward and forward in both bow and stern, whereas the canoes of the Nootka and other southern tribes had flat bottoms, and high, almost vertical sterns. All alike,

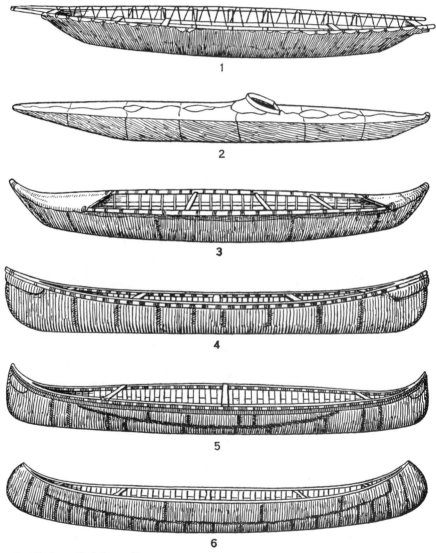

1, Alaskan *Umiak;* 2, Labrador *Kayak;* 3, Dogrib; 4, Malecite; 5, Algonkin; 6, Montagnais.

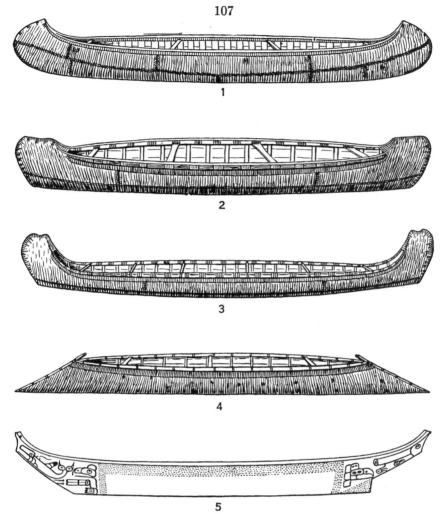

1, Ojibwa; 2, Chipewyan; 3, Slave; 4, Interior Salish; 5, Haida. *(Reproduced from Waugh, F. W.: "Canadian Aboriginal Canoes," The Canadian Field-Naturalist, vol. xxxiii, May, 1919, p. 25.)*

however, had one serious defect; the free-grained cedar was apt to split with the pounding of the waves and cause the craft to swamp. To prevent this some of the early missionaries taught the Indians to strengthen the larger boats with ribs,[1] but the device failed to meet with general acceptance.

Bark-covered canoes had a much wider range than dugouts, for they prevailed not only in eastern Canada, but throughout the basin

[1] Crosby, T.: "Up and down the North Pacific Coast by Canoe and Mission Ship," p. 123 (Toronto, n.d).

of the Mackenzie and the Cordillera region of British Columbia. Birch bark was the commonest covering, and the most satisfactory; but even the Algonkian tribes of eastern Canada, who made the finest of all bark canoes, sometimes used other materials, spruce bark, elm bark, and moose hide. Spruce bark was more general than birch bark in the Cordilleras and in the Mackenzie basin, probably on account of the scarcity of large birch trees in those regions. Bark canoes varied somewhat from tribe to tribe, in the amount of curvature at bow and stern, in the decking of the ends, and in a few other details, but the methods of construction, and the general shape, were much the same everywhere. The three most divergent types were the Beothuk canoe, in which the gunwale curved sharply upward in the middle as well as at the ends; the Dogrib canoe, which had small, narrow ribs, widely-separated floor or side strips extending from end to end, and extensive decking at bow and stern;[1] and the Kootenay-Salish canoe of the southern interior of British Columbia, which was often made of pine instead of birch bark, and ran out to a point under water at either end like the bark canoes on the Amur river in eastern Siberia.[2]

The extreme lightness of the birch-bark canoe more than compensated for its frailty, for one man could carry it on his shoulders over several miles of portage. Although cranky, and easily capsized if handled unskilfully, it answered the slightest pressure from the paddle, thus allowing instant changes of direction when running rapids. Moreover, even a seriously damaged canoe could be repaired within a few hours with no other materials than a strip or two of birch bark, a few threads of spruce root to sew them on, and a little spruce gum to cover the seams. The birch-bark canoe was, therefore, an admirable craft for regions abounding in lakes and rivers that were separated only by low watersheds. It was immediately adopted by the early fur-traders, and played a most important part in the exploration and opening up of the Dominion. For almost a century it carried European trade goods from the Atlantic ocean and Hudson bay to the Arctic, across the prairies to the Rocky mountains, and through the mountains to the plateau region in the interior of British

---

[1] In the last two features it slightly resembled the Eskimo kayak. Its form, however, may be post-European (See footnote, p. 383).

[2] For fuller details See Waugh, F. W.: "Canadian Aboriginal Canoes"; The Canadian Field-Naturalist, vol. xxxiii, No. 2 (May, 1919). Mason, O. T.: "Pointed Bark Canoes of the Kutenai and Amur"; Ann. Rept. Smithsonian Inst., U.S. Nat. Mus., 1899, pp. 525-537 (Washington, 1901).

Columbia. And to-day its derivative, the cedar or basswood canoe, still carries out the same rôle by conveying prospectors, surveyors, and explorers into regions far beyond the reach of our railways and gasoline launches.

Ojibwa Indians in a birch-bark canoe. *(Reproduced, through the courtesy of the Public Archives of Canada, from a painting by Krieghoff.)*

Birch bark does not readily strip from the tree until early summer, and the construction of an ordinary canoe required the combined labour of a man and woman for about two weeks. In the early spring, therefore, when the Indians of the Maritime Provinces wished to convey their winter catch of furs down to the coast, they often covered a crude canoe-frame with moose hides instead of bark, and discarded the frame when they reached their destination.[1] An obscure band of Nahani Indians living at the head of Keele river west of Great Bear lake makes use of similar boats to visit Norman each summer, and after selling the moose hides at the trading-post, returns to the mountains on foot. The Eskimo, who lived in a treeless region beyond the limits of the birch, spruce, and pine, used nothing except skin to cover their craft, preferably the skin of the large bearded seal, *Erignathus barbatus.* Their boats were of two kinds, the *umiak,* a large, open, travelling vessel something like a whaleboat, that was

---

[1] For similar reasons the Ojibwa often used an elm-bark canoe, which would last two or three years and could be made by one man in a day.

propelled by oars and steered with a paddle; and the *kayak,* a narrow, one-man, hunting craft not unlike a racing shell, but propelled with a double-bladed paddle. The kayak was completely decked except for the manhole a little behind the middle, but, notwithstanding its decking, it was as light and portable as a birch-bark canoe. It was cranky, too, like the racing shell, yet remarkably seaworthy in the hands of a skilful paddler, for an oiled jacket drawn tight about his neck above, and around the manhole below, prevented any water from penetrating the interior; and even if the vessel did overturn the submerged occupant could often right it again with a single strong sweep of the paddle.[1]

The Eskimo were the only people in Canada who used the oar, for even the Pacific Coast natives employed paddles to propel their immense dugouts. Keels were an invention of the Old World that never reached pre-Columbian America. As for sails, it is open to doubt whether they were known north of Mexico before the first navigators appeared on the coasts, although both Indians and Eskimo freely employed them a few years afterward.[2]

Facilities for travel and transport naturally exerted a considerable influence on trade and commerce. In the absence of wheeled vehicles and of large pack animals like the camel and the horse, the most convenient trade routes were the waterways, where the aborigines could transport their property in canoes. Trade flourished, therefore, in eastern Canada, where there were innumerable rivers navigable for long distances, and agricultural peoples with an assured food supply (in times of peace at least) contiguous to more migratory peoples ready to barter the products of the chase. It flourished, too, in the fiord region of the Pacific coast, where the geographical conditions made the sea the natural highway, the giant cedars permitted the construction of large ocean-going canoes, and the mild climate and abundant food supply invited travel for adventure and profit. Elsewhere in Canada the struggle for existence was so hard, and transport so difficult, that trade was sporadic and limited. Tribes like the plains' and northern Indians, who moved continually to new hunting-grounds with all their possessions, could not accumulate more prop-

---

[1] Of the Canadian Eskimo only those of Labrador and of Baffin island could perform this feat. It was commonly done by King Island Eskimo in Alaska, and is still performed by every self-respecting hunter in Greenland. Some of the Greenlanders can right the kayak without the paddle, using only an arm.

[2] *Cf.* p. 412.

erty than they could pack on their backs, carry in their canoes, and transport on their toboggans, sleds, or travois. Indeed, even the agricultural Iroquoians, who built new villages every ten or twelve years, and the tribes on the Pacific coast, who abandoned their houses for three or four months each summer and probably moved their village sites about once in a generation, had little desire to encumber themselves with personal property that was not readily removed.

It was only natural, therefore, that trade should be restricted mainly to small objects, either raw materials, food products, or articles of clothing and adornment. An Indian household was normally sufficient unto itself.[1] It provided its own shelter, clothing and food, weapons for fishing and hunting, and tools and utensils for domestic use. But the resources of all regions were not alike, and there were certain useful or desirable objects that many tribes could obtain through barter alone. Metallic copper, for example, which was valuable for tools and ornaments, occurred in a few localities only: around lakes Superior and Michigan, on the White river in Alaska, on the Coppermine river that flows into the Arctic ocean northeast of Great Bear lake, and in the centre of Victoria island in the Arctic archipelago. The Coronation Gulf Eskimo, who used the two last deposits, traded their copper east and west to other Eskimo tribes; and the Yellowknives bartered the Coppermine metal with Indian tribes to the south until the Chipewyans forcibly wrested the trade from their hands shortly before the establishment of European trading-posts on the shores of Hudson bay. The copper around the Great Lakes enriched not only the Iroquoian and other tribes of that area, but Indians far down the Mississippi and Atlantic Coast tribes from the bay of Fundy to Virginia; while from the Copper river, in Alaska, the metal passed in trade all along the Pacific coast as far as Vancouver island, and probably beyond.[2]

Concerning trade in other minerals we have less information. Nephrite from the Kobuk river, in northern Alaska, found its way to the Mackenzie delta; and the same mineral, present in the form of loose boulders on the Lower Thompson and Fraser rivers around Kamloops and Lytton, was traded over a wide area of British Columbia,

[1] Considering the household as the unit in a settlement of closely related families that rendered mutual assistance.
[2] There may have been another, less important source for copper in British Columbia itself.

even to the Queen Charlotte islands.[1] Most tribes had access to flint, chert, quartz, or quartzite within their own territories. There were several sources of obsidian, which was extensively used in British Columbia for knives, spear-points, and arrow-points; but the deposits of this mineral near mount Anahim furnished the southern Carriers with a valuable commodity to exchange with the northern branches of their tribe along the line of the present transcontinental railway. Obsidian derived from the Yellowstone Park region appears at scattered places on the plains, and may have been traded from tribe to tribe; but the Blackfoot, whose wanderings extended not only over the Canadian prairies, but far south of the International Boundary, may well have gathered the mineral themselves. It is probable, too, that they visited the "sacred quarry" in Minnesota to secure catlinite for the manufacture of pipes, since Catlin says that "all the tribes in these regions, and also of the Mississippi and the Lakes, have been in the habit of going to that place, and meeting their enemies there, whom they are obliged to treat as friends, under an injunction of the Great Spirit."[2] Nevertheless, in historical times at least, there was a brisk bartering of the finished pipes, probably also of the raw catlinite. The tribes of eastern Canada seem to have traded soapstone for the same purpose. This rock, however, was of greatest value to the Eskimo, who manufactured from it their cooking pots and lamps. Not only did they trade these articles from district to district along the Arctic and sub-Arctic coasts, but families often journeyed several hundred miles to fashion their own soapstone vessels and to carry home a surplus stock to barter with their kinsmen. Even wood was an important article of trade to the Eskimo between Coronation gulf and Baffin island, who lived so far beyond the limit of trees that their rivers deposited very little driftwood on their shores. Natives from the Coronation Gulf area visited the forests near Great Bear lake and Thelon river to obtain wood for their own use and for barter with neighbouring tribes to the westward, to whom a plank large enough to make a sled-runner

---

[1] Some Eskimo ruins in the Hudson Bay area and in Newfoundland contain small implements of nephrite whose source has not yet been discovered.
[2] Catlin, G.: Letters and Notes on the Manners, Customs, and Conditions of the North American Indians"; vol. i, p. 31 (London, 1842).

or a table was more valuable than ivory two or three times its weight.[1]

Trade naturally developed most in the regions of greatest prosperity, where the food supply was most certain and the population largest and most stable. The lowlands of eastern Canada vied with the Pacific coast in these respects. The Hurons and other agricultural tribes around the Great Lakes sold corn and tobacco to the Algonkians, receiving in exchange various furs.[2] These were the principal commodities that passed between the two peoples, but there were many other articles, such as canoes, nets, and ornaments of shell and copper. Indeed, the Algonkians probably derived less profit from their furs than from the sale of "medicines" (using that word to mean both herbal remedies, and magical amulets and rites), which were in great demand among all the tribes to the south and west.[3] Even to-day Cree "medicines" have a high reputation for efficacy among the plains' tribes, and are frequently bought and sold for what appear to us ridiculous prices.

Before Europeans penetrated far up the St. Lawrence, the Iroquoian natives had evolved a regular currency of beads, "wampum," which was manufactured by New England coastal tribes from clam and other shells. This wampum was carried in strings ("branches", as the old French writers called them) or woven into belts and sashes, a normal belt in the early eighteenth century containing eleven strands, each of about one hundred and eighty beads.[4] They were of two colours, white and purple, which had different symbolic meanings and different values. The Iroquoians estimated the entire wealth of their nations by the number of beads they possessed. In commercial transactions only loose beads or strings were used, the strings being measured by the fathom. The Jesuit Relations speak of a certain Huron who returned from a six months' trading journey with his gross receipts entirely in the form of wampum beads, of which he had fourteen thousand.[5] This shell currency, however, was not altogether aboriginal. In pre-European times the beads were so difficult to manufacture with nothing but

---

[1] The Haida are said to have bought planks for making boxes from the Tsimshian (Handbook of American Indians, article "Commerce"); but this must have occurred only rarely, because Queen Charlotte islands contain just as excellent stands of cedar and of spruce as the mainland.
[2] "Jesuit Relations," vol. xxxi, p. 209 *et passim;* Thompson: Op. cit., p. 261.
[3] "Jesuit Relations," vol. xvii, p. 211; Henry and Thompson: Op. cit., vol. i, p. 183.
[4] Lafitau: Op. cit., p. 505.
[5] "Jesuit Relations," vol. xxxiii, p. 185.

stone tools, that the output was limited, and only a very few reached the interior tribes and Canada. The introduction of iron increased the output a hundredfold, and as their markets expanded the coast natives flooded with their products all the interior country as far west as the Mississippi river, and northward beyond the lowlands of eastern Canada. Then, about the beginning of the nineteenth century, the fur-traders substituted a cheaper porcelain bead for the original bead of shell, and the currency became worthless.[1] The history of wampum thus offers a striking and in many ways unusual example of the economic revolutions brought about by the introduction of iron into primitive communities that had hitherto not known its use.

A similar phenomenon occurred on the Pacific coast of America, where beads made from dentalia and serpula shells, multiplied through the introduction of iron tools, became a definite currency in at least two areas, among the California Indians in the south and the Kutchin Indians of the Yukon district in the far north. The coast tribes of British Columbia, who either gathered the shells themselves or were in close contact with tribes who did, prized them mainly for trading purposes, preferring for their own use ornaments of the iridescent haliotis shell. The interior and northern natives preferred the beads: "Beads are the riches of the Kutchin and also the medium of exchange throughout the country lying between the Mackenzie and the west coast, other articles being valued by the number of strings of beads they can procure. . . . . . To be accounted a chief among the Kutchin, a man must possess beads to the amount of two hundred beavers."[2]

Even in pre-European times, when the production of shell beads and ornaments was more restricted, the Indians of the Pacific coast had developed commerce into a high art, and become the most enterprising traders on the continent. The stream of shell ornaments flowing northward met a stream of copper flowing south. Other streams of shell flowed inland, up the Fraser, Skeena, and Stikine rivers to the interior tribes, and across Bella Coola mountains into the territory of the Carriers. The oil of the oolakan or candle fish

[1] Cf. Beauchamp, W. M.: "Wampum and Shell Articles Used by the New York Indians"; Bull. New York State Mus., No. 41, vol. viii (Albany, 1901).

[2] Richardson, Sir J.: "Artic Searching Expedition, A Journal of a Boat Voyage through Rupert's Land and the Arctic Sea"; vol. i, p. 391 (London, 1851). Cf. Journal of Simon Fraser, Masson: Op. cit., ser. i, p. 221.

73454

A Kutchin chief with ornaments of dentalium shells. *(Reproduced from Richardson, Sir J.: "Arctic Searching Expedition, A Journal of a Boat Voyage through Rupert's Land and the Arctic Sea," vol. I, Pl. VII, London, 1851.)*

(*Thaleichthys pacificus*) passed from the Nass river outward to the Queen Charlotte islands, and inland by what is still called the Grease Trail to Kuldo on the upper Skeena river. "Chilcat" blankets travelled down from southeast Alaska to Vancouver island, elk hides travelled up from the south, and furs from the interior passed out to the coast and islands. Owing to visits from European vessels, the overland trade had already begun to swell in volume when Mackenzie approached the valley of the Bella Coola river, but the scenes he witnessed in that district faithfully reproduced the conditions of prehistoric times. "Every man, woman, and child," he says, "carried a proportionate burden, consisting of beaver coating and parchment, as well as skins of the otter, the marten, the bear, the lynx, and dressed moose skins. The last they procure from the Rocky Mountain Indians. . . Several of their relations and friends, they said, were already gone, as well provided as themselves, to barter with the people of the coast."[1]

During the winter months all the Pacific coast tribes held festivals, or potlatches, at which every visitor received a present more or less in accordance with his rank. They were not true presents, however, but loans payable with interest at some future potlatch under penalty of a loss in social prestige. Often the man who was holding the feast found himself short of gifts at the critical moment, and sought the assistance of kinsmen and neighbours, borrowing with one hand to lend with the other. These debts were strictly heritable; they descended from one generation to another until lost in the mists of antiquity. Every native of rank found himself inextricably enmeshed, and children were schooled to memorize their debts much as our own children learn the multiplication table. The most amazing feature of this "banking" system was its complete independence of any currency; for the loans, with few exceptions, were articles of everyday household use, principally the skins of various animals. The system was so deeply rooted in the social life that the natives have adapted it to modern conditions, substituting blankets, guns, and even dollar bills for the skins, horn spoons, and ornaments of earlier years. In a few cases at least, they have actually kept credit and debit accounts of their transactions in tiny notebooks.

---

[1] Mackenzie: Op. cit., p. 310.

Beneath the multiplicity of distinct languages along the coast of British Columbia there was a remarkable uniformity in the material culture of the various tribes and in the main features of their social life. On the plains, too, the Blackfoot, Sarcee, and Assiniboine closely resembled one another, although their languages contained scarcely a single word in common. Evidently trade, combined with wars, was a powerful levelling influence, spreading the different elements of culture over wide geographical areas. The "silent trade" so common in ancient times did not exist in Canada,[1] difficulties caused by language being overcome in other ways. Many natives were bilingual; the Kutchin, for example, learned the language of the Eskimo, their enemies from time immemorial.[2] Most tribes contained a few representatives of neighbouring tribes, fugitives, prisoners of war, or women purchased in marriage, who could serve as interpreters in case of need. The plains' Indians developed a complicated sign language that abolished the necessity of speech, and, after the beginning of the fur trade, the Indians of the Pacific coast, from California to Alaska, used a common trade jargon of two or three hundred words derived from the vocabulary of the Chinook tribe at the mouth of the Columbia river, with a few terms added from the Nootka and Salish. In northern Canada, and in eastern Canada outside the lowlands, language raised almost no barriers owing to the wide diffusion of the Athapaskan and Algonkian tongues. In those regions trade languished solely on account of the meagre resources, the isolation from centres of greater prosperity, and the scantiness of a population always in motion, and always fluctuating between abundance of food and starvation.

---

[1] Cf. Grierson, P. J. H.: The Silent Trade, Edinburgh, 1903. Early white explorers occasionally used the "silent trade" method in dealing with the Indians. Cf. Mackenzie: Op. cit., p. 217; Howley, J. P.: "The Beothuks or Red Indians, the Aboriginal Inhabitants of Newfoundland," p. 18 (Cambridge, 1915).
[2] Richardson: Op. cit., vol. i, p. 215.

CHAPTER IX

SOCIAL AND POLITICAL ORGANIZATION

PRIMITIVE MIGRATORY TRIBES

We have already seen how deeply the physiographic features of the country, its climate, fauna, and flora, stamped their impress on the lives of the aborigines. The geographical environment, however, influenced mainly the outward culture of the tribes or nations. Their inner culture, their social customs, political organizations, religious ideas and art, were all the products of a long evolution in which psychological and historical factors played the major rôle. Tribes shifted their homes during the centuries, came into contact with new neighbours from whom they borrowed new customs and new ideas, and at rare intervals produced great thinkers and great statesmen, like the half-mythical Dekanawida,[1] who directed their lives into new channels. Even the outward, material culture derived more from these historical causes than from the geographical environment. How else, for example, could we account for the great differences between the Iroquoians and the Beaver Indians, let us say, of the Peace River valley? The former were agricultural peoples with semi-fixed homes and well-made cooking vessels of pottery, the Beaver nomadic hunters who cooked their meat in vessels of birch bark or of woven spruce roots with the aid of hot stones; yet the Peace valley is no less fertile than southeastern Ontario, and contains as numberless deposits of clay suitable for making pots. If, then, the geographical environment fails to explain many of the apparently simple features in the economic life of the aborigines, still less can we make it our guiding star in discussing their social and religious life, which was so much more complex, and varied so greatly from one tribe to another. We seem, indeed, to be entering almost a new sphere, where causes and explanations lie concealed in a long chain of events and phenomena far beyond our vision.

The ultimate unit of social organization among the Canadian aborigines, whatever it may have been with the earliest races of man-

---

[1] For the history of this Iroquois statesman *See* Parker, A. C.: "The Constitution of the Five Nations"; New York State Mus. Bull. No. 184 (Albany, 1916).

kind, was the biological family, the man, his wife, and their children. Such units, often enlarged to include near kinsmen, could be found from one side of Canada to the other, dwelling in a bark wigwam in the eastern woodlands, in a skin tipi on the plains, in a snow hut along the frozen Arctic coast, and in a small partition within the huge communal wooden house on the shores of the Pacific ocean. Families of near kinsmen naturally kept together for mutual support, and among the migratory tribes in the east and north, where fish and game were seasonal and often scattered, they grouped themselves into small bands that roamed over separate territories and remained apart during the greater portion of the year, but usually amalgamated for a brief interval at certain seasons. Amalgamation

37026
Winter migration of an Eskimo community, Coronation gulf. *(Photo by D. Jenness.)*

was most frequent on the prairies, where the driving of the buffalo herds into pounds required the co-operation of many people; but there other groupings, similar in many ways to our fraternities, cut across the groupings by bands, at least in historical times. In Ontario, and on the Pacific coast, where the food supply was more stable and assured, families of near kindred still tended to hold together, but in those regions they were greatly overshadowed by larger social units, the village community, the clan, and the phratry, which will be considered later.

Let us trace first the organization of the simpler tribes, the Algonkians of the eastern woodlands, the Athapaskans of the Mackenzie basin, and the Eskimo along the Arctic and sub-Arctic coast. The vagaries of the food supply in these regions caused frequent dispersals and reunions of the aborigines. Now they wandered in individual families, now in small groups of three or four families together. At another time all the families in a district would combine into a definite band at some favourite fishing or hunting ground, and several bands generally united for a few short days each year to trade and to hold festivities. These fluctuations in the social groupings occurred among all the tribes, but were particularly marked among the Eskimo, who "reacted to the seasons, to their constantly changing environment, more than most of the inhabitants of our globe. . . . In winter, when the land lay bare and silent beneath the snow, when the caribou had migrated south, when the twilight hours were brief and the nights long, the natives (Copper Eskimos) had banded together into tribes, and tribe combined with tribe to wrest a precarious livelihood from the frozen sea by united effort. Food had been common to all, and their snow-houses had adjoined each other so closely that the families seemed absorbed in the group. With the returning sun and lengthening days nature had recalled its life; the seals had appeared on top of the ice, the caribou had come northward again, and the tribes of Eskimos had broken up into little bands. For a time they had lingered on the ice to hunt more seals; then, turning landward, they had pursued the caribou over the snow-covered hills and plains. Now the snow was vanishing, the caribou had scattered, and fish alone provided a sure livelihood until mid-summer. So my party, like many another throughout the country, was dividing up into its constituent households, each of which now toiled for itself alone. The tribe no longer existed; society had dissolved into its first element, the family."[1]

Each family group, and each band, had a nominal leader, some man who through courage, force of character, or skill in hunting, had won for himself temporary pre-eminence. The composition of the family groups, and consequently their leaders, varied from one season to another, but the band was a relatively stable unit with definite territorial boundaries. Theoretically, every individual in a band was equal to every other, so that its leader enjoyed few or no privileges, and held his position only so long as he could win popular support. Thus a Jesuit missionary states of a Montagnais band: "All the authority of their chief is in his tongue's end; for he is

---

[1] Jenness, D.: "The People of the Twilight," p. 136 f (New York. 1928). "Tribe" and "band" in this passage correspond to "band" and "family group" in the present chapter.

powerful in so far as he is eloquent; and, even if he kills himself talking and haranguing, he will not be obeyed unless he pleases the savages."[1] The same loose organization characterized the larger communities created when some of the bands amalgamated, as the Montagnais usually did during the season for catching eels, the Dogrib at the spring migration of the caribou, and the Eskimo during the season for sealing; for the leaders of the various bands were all of equal standing except in so far as one man might possess for the moment greater prestige.

An amalgamation of all the bands of a tribe, even for a few days only, was exceedingly rare, owing to the distances between their hunting-grounds and the difficulty of securing enough fish and game in one locality to support a large, if transient, population.[2] Outlying bands usually had contact only with their neighbours, who often belonged to a different tribe. Separation from their kindred then weakened the sense of unity; foreign influences brought in new customs and new ideas; and isolation facilitated the evolution of distinct dialects. Foreign marriages, disturbances of population caused by wars and famines, and many other factors aided the centrifugal movement. There was no chief for the entire tribe, no central organization, no sacred shrine or holy city recognized by all that could serve as a common rallying point. When the differences in language between two adjacent tribes were small, no greater, for example, than between Spanish and Italian, the border bands of each tended to merge into one another, so that it was impossible to decide where one tribe ended and the other began. By what means then can we distinguish them?

We may admit at the outset that the term tribe, strictly speaking, is hardly applicable to the eastern and northern peoples of Canada; for the word implies a body of people who occupy a continuous territory, who possess the same customs, speak the same language, and act as a unit in matters of offence and defence. It implies, further, a clear political separation from neighbouring peoples, usually associated in turn with differences in customs and in language. Doubtless there were real tribes of this character in the regions we are considering—the Beothuk of Newfoundland, the

---

[1] "Jesuit Relations," vi, p. 243.
[2] Cf. Ibid., n, p. 201.

Micmac of Nova Scotia, and perhaps the Yellowknives in the vicinity of Great Bear lake. But, in general, whether we examine the Algonkian-speaking peoples, the Athapaskan, or the Eskimo, the only clearly defined political unit was the band. It is true that neighbouring bands differed little except in the possession of different hunting-grounds, and that they frequently joined together for mutual support, but the compositions of these united groups varied continually as a band coalesced with its kindred, now in one direction,

43343

Summer migration of an Eskimo community, Coronation gulf.
(Photo by K. G. Chipman.)

now in another. Customs, too, like the colours in the spectrum, changed almost imperceptibly from one district to another as the bands encountered different influences; and the farther one receded from any given point, the greater, as a rule, became the variations in dialect. Hence the usual divisions into tribes, Naskapi, Montagnais, etc., for the eastern woodlands, Chipewyan, Yellowknife, and the rest for the Mackenzie basin, are to a considerable extent arbitrary; less so now than formerly, perhaps, because the bands are less numerous and more restricted in their wanderings, and the establishment of Indian reserves and trading-posts subjects them to local influences and conditions that were formerly lacking.

There is, of course, a justifiable basis for the tribal divisions; they provide a convenient method of classification that depends for its validity, like the differentiation of species in the biological world, on the relative amount of agreement or disagreement in certain more important characters—on geographical propinquity in this case and a feeling of kinship, on correspondences in dialect, and on the presence or absence of certain arts, beliefs, and practices. But it should be clearly understood that they were not tribes in the usual acceptation of that word; they were not coherent bodies of people united under a common rule, like the tribes of Africa or Polynesia; they were merely groups of scattered bands, very similar in speech and customs, that had no central governing authority, but through close neighbourhood and intermarriage possessed many interests in common. Among the Eskimo even loosely-defined tribes such as these were lacking, because the bands were dispersed over so wide an area that they lived in complete ignorance of all but their nearest neighbours; and yet they so closely resembled each other that one could travel hundreds of miles in certain regions without noticing any clearly marked differences. During the last fifty to seventy-five years, however, there has been not only a marked decline in the population, but a tendency for the remaining bands to concentrate at certain strategic points for the fur trade, so that we may now legitimately group the Eskimo also into tribes, if we wish, naming them from their geographical locations, or, in two rather exceptional cases,[1] from peculiar features in their culture.

The bands, as we have seen, were composed of families of near kindred, and kinship was reckoned in slightly varying ways, all different from our own Indo-European system. Few of the more primitive tribes in eastern or northern Canada, however, stressed the male line of descent to the exclusion of the female, or the female to the exclusion of the male[2]; they followed, that is to say, neither the patrilinear nor the matrilinear systems of organization, although there was a tendency, natural perhaps among migratory hunting peoples where the wives nearly always went to live with their husbands, to pay rather more attention to the male line. Marriage depended on blood relationship only,[3] and often occurred within the bands; but many were so small that they were practically exogamous units. The

[1] The Copper Eskimo of the Coronation Gulf area, who, until a few years ago, used native copper instead of stone for their tools and weapons, and the Caribou Eskimo between Hudson bay and Great Slave and Great Bear lakes, who, unlike other Eskimo, never hunted seals on the coast but depended almost entirely on caribou.

[2] The Micmac, possibly too the Malecite, and most of the Ojibwa had exogamous clans with descent in the male line. The Ojibwa north of lake Superior had similar clans with descent in the female line.

[3] This statement does not take into consideration special relationships brought about by adoption. or, among the Eskimo, by the practice of exchanging wives.

personal property of the native passed to a brother or sister, a son or a daughter, without question; it had so little value that it rarely occasioned any dispute. Often, indeed, his weapons and ornaments followed him to the grave, and his tent or bark cabin was abandoned and allowed to decay. "Real" property he had none, for the hunting territory and the fishing places belonged to the entire band, and were as much the right of every member as the surrounding atmosphere. Members of other bands might use them temporarily, with the consent of the owner band, or they might seize them by force; but land could not be sold or alienated in any way. It is true that in eastern Canada individual families, or groups of two and three families very closely related, have possessed their private hunting-grounds within the territory occupied by the band since the early days of European settlement; that they have handed them down from father to son, or in some cases to a son-in-law, in regular succession; and that the boundaries were so well defined by geographical features that in many districts we can map them to-day just as we map our counties.[1] Nevertheless, it does not appear at all certain that this system of land tenure pre-dates the coming of Europeans: for a similar partition of the territory of the band into family hunting grounds has occurred among the Sekani Indians at the headwaters of Peace river during the last hundred years, after the necessities of the fur trade compelled the families to disperse among different creeks and rivers.[2] That the Montagnais, and presumably also neighbouring tribes in eastern Canada, did not subdivide the band territory prior to the advent of the fur traders seems to be indicated by a passage in the "Jesuit Relations," written only thirty-two years after Champlain's first voyage up the St. Lawrence. Father Le Jeune there says: "Now it will be so arranged that, in the course of time each family of our Montagnais, if they become located, will take its own territory for hunting, without following in the tracks of its neighbours."[3]

---

[1] Cf. Speck, F. G.: "Family Hunting Territories and Social Life of Various Algonkian Bands of the Ottawa Valley"; Geol. Surv., Canada, Mem. 70, Anth. Ser. No. 8 (Ottawa, 1915).

[2] A man naturally returned to the same trapping ground year after year, because he knew all the haunts of the beaver in that district and could provide for their conservation. His winter trapping-ground was likewise his hunting-ground, so that the two terms became synonymous. This development from band to family ownership of territory was a logical response to the changed conditions, and might easily have occurred in eastern Canada within half a century. Cf. the growth of family ownership of maple groves among some of the Ojibwa. Thompson: Op. cit., p. 276.

[3] "Jesuit Relations," vol. viii, p. 57, 1634-6. Cf. Ibid., vol. xxxii, pp 269-271, which again imply that the ownership of the hunting territories was vested in the band, and not in individuals or groups of two or three families. The Ojibwa of Parry Sound, on lake Huron, assert that their hunting territories and maple groves still belong to the entire band, and have never been partitioned among the families; and Le Clercq states quite definitely that among the Micmac "it is the right of the head of the nation . . . . to distribute the places of hunting to each individual". Le Clercq: Op. cit. p. 237.

In the absence of chiefs and of any legislative or executive body within the tribes and bands, law and order depended solely on the strength of public opinion. There were no written laws, of course; merely rules and injunctions handed down by word of mouth from an immemorial antiquity, and more temporary taboos operative during the lifetime of an individual. Persuasion and physical force were the only methods of arbitrating disputes, social outlawry or physical violence the only means of punishing infractions of the moral code or offences against the welfare of the band or tribe. The band took cognizance of crimes that were believed to endanger the whole community, such as the infraction of important taboos or treasonable relations with an enemy; it left the individual families, with the help perhaps of near kinsfolk, to find their own redress for all other offences, from theft even to murder. A man who could gather a few followers around him might commit any number of excesses, but sooner or later he generally paid the penalty at the hands of some outraged victim, or was executed with the approval of the entire band. Fear of the blood-feud was a powerful restraint on murder, and social disapproval, more keenly felt in small communities than in large, checked the commission of many lesser crimes. Strangers, however, even people of a neighbouring tribe, might be robbed or killed with impunity; they had no rights, unless they married into a band or placed themselves under the protection of some powerful family.[1]

If there was no organization for the submission of disputes to arbitration or for maintaining law and order within the communities, neither was there any organization for prosecuting war with neighbouring peoples. Natives living outside the tribe were enemies, real or potential, to be carefully avoided unless they encroached on the hunting territories. Then it was the local band only that opposed the invasion, unless the menace became so serious that other bands voluntarily rallied to its aid. There was no mechanism for mustering an army, and often no means of appointing a leader for warriors who gathered of their own accord. In rare cases men of

---

[1] *Cf.* The oppression of the Yellowknives by the Chipewyans (Hearne: Op. cit., p. 201 ff). Also a few years later, when the Chipewyans declined, the outrages by the Yellowknives on the Dogribs and Hares (Simpson, T.: "Narrative of the Discoveries of the North Coast of America; Effected by the Officers of the Hudson's Bay Company during the years 1836-39," p. 318 (London, 1843); Back, Sir George: Narrative of the Arctic Land Expedition to the Mouth of the Great Fish River, and along the Shores of the Arctic Ocean, in the Years 1833, 1834, and 1835," pp. 457-8 (London, 1836)).

influence might be able to control their immediate followers, but they could not check desertion or separate action on the part of other volunteers. Furthermore, natives who lived from day to day on the game they secured by hunting, or the fish they captured in the lakes and rivers, could not undertake protracted campaigns, or band together in numbers where fish and game were scarce. Organized warfare was, therefore, impossible. Small parties might occasionally make sudden raids or incursions, individuals might treacherously massacre some families that slept peacefully in their tents, or attack them from ambush as they straggled along a trail; but there could be no massing of troops to wage a campaign, no pitched battles with a few thousand men on each side. So eastern and northern Canada lay an easy prey to any small but well-organized force of invaders that could overcome the resistance of the individual bands.[1]

5663

Cree camp at Oxford House. *(Photo by R. Bell.)*

The plains' Indians, although migratory themselves, had advanced one stage farther than the migratory tribes of eastern and northern Canada. They traced descent through the male line only, and the Blackfoot may have forbidden marriage within the band.

---

[1] The Montagnais campaign against the Iroquois in which Champlain participated (The Works of Samuel de Champlain, Champlain Society edition, vol. II, chapter IX) was far better organized than most raids by Algonkian tribes.

Families seldom wandered individually, in historic times at least, but scoured the country in small groups or in larger bands. The band was a stable body governed by an informal council of its leading men, one of whom acted as chief. All the bands of a tribe amalgamated for several weeks or months during the summer, and either selected a head chief, or tacitly acknowledged the authority of some band chief who possessed outstanding influence. At this season they adopted a military arrangement in their camps, pitching their conical tents in a circle, band by band, with the council tent or tent of the head-chief in the centre.[1] The tribe was thus a definite political unit sharply separated off from neighbouring peoples. There were three tribes in the Blackfoot nation, the Blackfoot proper, the Blood, and the Piegan, all very closely alike in language and in customs, and all united by common interests and a feeling of kinship; yet each of the three tribes retained its political independence unimpaired. The Sarcee differed from them in language only, being the fourth member of the Blackfoot confederacy that struggled for the control of the prairies against the confederacy of the Assiniboine and Cree. Clearly the plains' tribes had reached a higher level politically than the tribes of eastern and northern Canada. Nevertheless, they suffered from the same inherent weakness—the indefinite and uncertain authority of their chiefs. Father de Smet makes some pertinent comments on this subject:

" Each nation is divided into different bands or tribes, and each tribe counts several villages.[2] Every village has its chief, to whom they submit in proportion to the respect or terror which his personal qualities inspire. The power of a chief is sometimes merely nominal; sometimes, also, his authority is absolute, and his name, as well as his influence, extends beyond the limits of his own village, so that the whole tribe to which he belongs acknowledge him as their head. This was the case among the Assiniboines in the time of Tchatka. Courage, address, and an enterprising spirit may elevate every

---

[1] Except during the celebration of the sun-dance festival, when the head-chiefs of the Blackfoot and Sarcee tribes drew their tents back in favour of the woman whose vow initiated the festival. It is worth noting that Hendry's narrative of his journeys in 1754-1755 contains no reference to a camp circle, although he met large bodies of the Blackfoot. "Came to 200 tents of Archithinue Natives, pitched in two rows, and an opening in the middle; where we were conducted to the Leader's tent; which was at one end, large enough to contain fifty persons." " York Factory to the Blackfeet Country, the Journal of Anthony Hendry, 1754-55," edited by L. J. Burpee; Proc. and Trans. Roy. Soc. Canada, third series, vol. i, section ii, p. 337 (Toronto, 1907). This suggests that the camp circle may not have become fully established until some years after the introduction of horses.

[2] i.e. bands.

warrior to the highest honors, especially if his father or an uncle enjoyed the dignity of chief before him, and he has a numerous family ready to maintain his authority and avenge his quarrels. Yet when the seniors and warriors have installed him with all the requisite ceremonies, it must not be supposed that he, on this account, arrogates to himself the least exterior appearance of rank or dignity. He is too well aware that his rank hangs by a frail thread, which may quite easily be broken. He must gain the confidence of his uncertain subjects, or retain them by fear. A great many families in the village are better off than the chief; dress better, are richer in arms, horses, and other possessions. Like the ancient German chiefs, he gains the confidence and attachment of his soldiers, first by his bravery, more frequently by presents, which only serve to impoverish him the more. If a chief does not succeed in gaining the love of his subjects, they will despise his authority and quit him at the slightest opposition on his part; for the customs of the Indians admit no conditions by which they may enforce respect from their subjects." [1]

Cutting across the division of the plains' tribes into bands, however, was another division into societies or fraternities, whose members might belong to any band. Their number, organization, and functions varied somewhat from tribe to tribe. The Sarcee, who closely followed the Blackfoot, had five, all restricted to men; but one was a junior society in which young men had to enroll before they were eligible for the others. Each society held an annual dance that lasted four days, and during that period its leaders virtually controlled the entire camp. At other times three at least of the societies acted as police, under the general supervision of the head chief and tribal council; they regulated the life in camp and on the march, kept guard when enemies were near, and punished all infringements of the rules that governed the communal buffalo hunt. How serious might be this last duty can be seen from the functions of a similar police force among the Assiniboine.

" They first choose a band of warriors to hinder the hunters from leaving camp, either alone or in detached companies, lest the bisons be disturbed, and thus be driven away from the encampment. The law against this is extremely severe; not only all the Indians of the

---

[1] De Smet: Op. cit., vol. ii, p. 1124. *Cf.* Thompson: Op. cit., p. 364 ff.

camp must conform to it, but it reaches to all travellers, even when they are ignorant of the encampment or do not know that there is a hunt in contemplation. Should they frighten the animals, they are also punishable; however, those of the camp are more rigorously chastised in case they transgress the regulation. Their guns, their bows, and arrows are broken, their lodges cut in pieces, their dogs killed, all their provisions and their hides are taken from them. If they are bold enough to resist this penalty, they are beaten with bows, sticks, and clubs, and this torment frequently terminates in the death of the unhappy aggressor. Anyone who should set fire to the prairie by accident or imprudence, or in any way frighten off the herd, would be sure to be well beaten."[1]

Just how ancient these societies were we do not know. When the plains' tribes first came within the purview of history, about the middle of the eighteenth century,[2] their lives had been revolutionized by the horse, which spread quickly northward from one tribe to another after its introduction by the Spaniards into Mexico. It gave the Indians an unexpected mobility, vastly increasing the range of their migrations; and the ease with which they could now run down the herds of buffalo on horseback caused many woodland tribes to move out onto the prairies. So the great plains both of the United States and of Canada became a battling ground for a medley of tribes that jostled on each other's hunting territories until war became their natural sport. The discipline necessary for the old communal buffalo hunt on foot took on a military aspect, old institutions were modified to meet new conditions, and new customs, new institutions arose and spread from tribe to tribe with amazing rapidity. It seems not at all improbable that in pre-Columbian times, when the plains were sparsely inhabited by scattered bands of foot-wanderers, there were no societies, no organizations at all within the Canadian tribes, except the bands and families. Certainly several of the Blackfoot societies, which were more numerous than the Sarcee, did not arise until the nineteenth century.[3]

---

[1] De Smet: Op. cit., vol. iii, p. 1028.

[2] Hendry's narrative of his journeys in 1754 and 1755 shows that the Blackfoot were well provided with horses at that date, that the Assiniboine possessed them also, and that some were running wild on the Canadian prairies. In his introduction to the narrative Burpee suggests that "the earliest years of the eighteenth century would be nearer the mark, as the date when the Blackfeet first made use of the horse." "York Factory to the Blackfeet Country," p. 318.

[3] For detailed accounts of the societies of the plains' Indians, See Societies of the Plains Indians; edited by Wissler, Clark: Anth. Papers, Am. Mus. Nat. Hist., vol. xi (New York, 1916).

The advent of horses changed the Indians in other ways. Previously their most valued possession had been the buffalo-skin tent, which required from twelve to twenty-four hides, a number not easily procured by a hunter on foot. Now buffalo hides became so common as to be almost worthless; but horses gave the natives a new standard of value and a new medium of exchange. With them the warrior bought his wife, purchased high rank in the societies, or gained

73461

Blackfoot on the watch. *(Photo by Canadian National Railways.)*

possession of some sacred medicine-bundle that conferred on its owner great prestige. It was almost as honourable to steal an enemy's horses as to kill an adversary in battle, and raids for this purpose were a constant feature of camp life. In pre-Columbian days the bands of foot-hunters wandering over the plains with their pack-dogs were probably too scattered, and too slow of movement, to come into frequent contact with one another; but in the strenuous times, about the middle of the nineteenth century, when nearly all the Indians possessed firearms as well as horses, every tribe was permanently on a war footing and peace was a rare interlude in their lives. Each night they picketed their horses near the tents and set watchmen to guard against attack; and at frequent intervals small parties rode away to raid some enemy and return with scalps and horses. At this period the council of each tribe elected a special war chief to command the warriors in all major operations. So, with their compact organization and strong military proclivities they were a formidable barrier to European encroachment on the prairies.

In this connexion we may quote from De Smet again: " The Indian has the gift of being everywhere without being anywhere. These savages assemble at the moment of battle, and scatter whenever the fortune of war is contrary to them. The Indian puts his wife and children in shelter in some retired place, far from the scene of hostilities. He has neither towns, forts, nor magazines to defend, nor line of retreat to cover. He is embarrassed with neither baggage trains nor pack-horses. He goes into action when a favourable occasion is presented, and never risks himself without having the advantage of numbers and position on his side. The science of strategy is consequently of little use in operating against such a people. There is not on earth a nation more ambitious of military renown, nor that holds in higher estimation the conduct of a valiant warrior. No Indian could ever occupy a place in the councils of his tribe until he had met the enemy on the field of battle. He who reckons the most scalps is most highly considered among his people."[1]

The radical change that occurred in the plains' Indians through the introduction of the horse, even before there was direct contact with Europeans, is one of the most remarkable phenomena in history. It converted primitive parties of foot-hunters, isolated, timid, and circumscribed in their movements, into organized bands of daring warriors who extended their forays over thousands of miles. Not only did it ease their economic condition as long as the herds of buffalo lasted, but, by enlarging their contacts with each other and with neighbouring peoples, it caused a wide diffusion of social and religious ideas and a notable development in political life. It thus affords a striking example of the effect which the introduction of

---

[1] De Smet: Op. cit., vol. iii, p. 827.

a single new element of culture can produce upon a primitive people, an effect comparable, on a small scale, with the tremendous evolution of Japan after she threw open her doors to European commerce. It suggests, further, that in the early history of mankind some of the greatest and most rapid advances may often have resulted from solitary discoveries even less outstanding than the smelting of metal, the domestication of animals and cereals, or the invention of the wheel.

The Kootenay and some of the Salish Indians of southern British Columbia, who often crossed the Rocky mountains to hunt buffalo on the prairies, closely resembled the plains' tribes in their political organization, but lacked the semi-military societies.[1] The broken character of their country, too, and their dependence on fish for much of their food supply, kept the bands more separate, and, even after the introduction of horses (which the Kootenay obtained earlier than the Blackfoot), prevented their coalescence into the compact tribal units that were so characteristic of the plains' Indians from the beginning of the nineteenth century. So they were unable to offer serious resistance to European penetration, as did the Blackfoot across the mountains.

---

[1] *Cf.* the procedure before going to war, which resembled that of the plains' tribes before they were revolutionized by horses and firearms. Thompson: Op. cit., p. 462 f.

CHAPTER X

SOCIAL AND POLITICAL ORGANIZATION

IROQUOIANS AND PACIFIC COAST TRIBES

In the last chapter we considered only the most migratory tribes of Canada, those that wandered continually from place to place in search of a hazardous food supply. We saw that the primitive economic conditions under which they lived reflected themselves in a primitive social organization, and that the amelioration of these conditions among the plains' tribes through the introduction of the horse and firearms, combined with an increase of inter-tribal contacts, brought about a notable development in social and political life. We are prepared, therefore, to expect rather more complex types of society, and more intricate political organizations, among the less migratory tribes in southeastern Ontario and along the Pacific coast, who dwelt in semi-permanent villages and possessed food resources that were fairly stable and assured.

The history and organization of the Iroquoian tribes are obscure until the closing years of the sixteenth century, when they were grouped into three confederacies, the Huron around lake Simcoe, the Neutral around lake Erie,[1] and the League of the Iroquois south of the St. Lawrence. The two first were crushed by the third in the seventeenth century, and our information about them is very incomplete. However, all three confederacies appear to have been formed on the same pattern, so that it is necessary to describe only the League of the Iroquois.

This league contained several tribes[2] which were completely independent in domestic matters, but delegated their authority in external affairs to a council that represented them all. Every tribe was divided into four or more clans bearing animal names such as bear and turtle; and each clan was an exogamous unit, so that its

[1] The Erie tribe adjacent to the Neutrals remained outside of these confederacies, but shared the fate of the Neutrals and Hurons. The small Tobacco tribe, which in 1640 had nine villages in Grey and Simcoe counties, also stood aloof, although it perished with the Hurons.

[2] Five in earlier days, the Mohawk, Oneida, Onondaga, Cayuga, and Seneca. About 1722 the Tuscarora moved north from Carolina and entered the league, converting it into the "Six Nations.' The Huron confederacy contained four tribes; the number in the Neutral is not known.

members, men and women alike, had to marry outside it. Some writers believe that in earlier days each clan had its own village, and that the clans of one tribe were quite distinct from those of another, even when they bore the same names; a man of the Turtle clan in the Onondaga tribe, for example, could then marry a Turtle woman of the Mohawk tribe. In historic times, however, each clan was distributed through several villages, and clans bearing the same name, whatever the tribe, formed a single unit. There was also a grouping of all the clans of a tribe into two divisions known as phratries, which functioned mainly on ceremonial occasions.[1] Thus at feasts members of the two phratries occupied opposite ends of the ceremonial "Long House"; and when an Indian died the people of the phratry opposite to his own conducted the funeral. Politically, however, the division into phratries possessed little significance, the most important unit being the clan.

The clans themselves were subdivided. The Iroquoians had adopted a matrilinear organization that recognized descent through the female line alone. A boy belonged not to his father's clan, but to his mother's; it was from her that he inherited his name and family traditions. Every man had divided interests; for if parental affection attached him to his own children, who were members of his wife's clan, the clan to which he himself belonged attached him to his sisters' children who alone could be his heirs. The women were, therefore, the real guardians of all the names and traditions of a clan. Moreover, it was the women who controlled the long, bark cabins that sheltered up to twenty individual families. Every cabin recognized some elderly female as its ruler, or two females if it contained families derived from two lines of descent. Thus the clans were divided into what have been called maternal families, each of which comprised a "head woman or matron, her immediate male and female descendants, the male and female descendants of her female descendants, and so on."[2] An average maternal family numbered from fifty to two hundred persons, grouped in turn into individual families of husbands, wives, and children, similar to those of our own society.

---

[1] Whether there were phratries in the tribes of the Huron confederacy is doubtful.
[2] Goldenweiser, A. A.: "Early Civilization," p. 73, New York, 1922. My account of the League of the Iroquois is largely based on Chapter III in this book and on the paper by the same author in the Sum. Rept. 1912, Geol. Surv., Canada, pp. 464-475.

It will, perhaps, clarify this description of Iroquoian organization if we present its framework diagrammatically.[1]

League of the Iroquois

(Tribe)	Mohawk	Oneida	Onondaga	Cayuga	Seneca
(Phratry)	I				II
(Clan)	Turtle	Bear Wolf	Ball		Deer Hawk Great Snipe Little Snipe
(Maternal Family)		A		B C	
(Individual Family)		a	b	c d e	

The council that administered the affairs of the league was composed of nearly fifty chiefs or sachems, all of equal rank, and all selected from the maternal families. They assembled at irregular intervals, whenever necessity arose, to arbitrate on intertribal problems, to receive embassies, and to decide on peace or war with outside tribes. Being federal officials, they possessed no legal authority in matters that concerned only a single tribe or clan,[2] but in practice they wielded considerable power. The method of selecting a sachem was peculiar. His title was hereditary in some maternal family, so that the choice of a representative was limited. The matron of that family selected a candidate after consultation with other women of her family and clan; her selection was ratified, first by the sachems of the same phratry, then by the sachems of the opposite phratry, and finally by the entire council of the league, which called a great intertribal festival to install him in office. The same matron had power to depose him again if he failed to uphold the dignity of his position; after two warnings, she called upon him in company with a " warrior chief",[3] and formally divested him of office.

The authority possessed by the matrons of the maternal families would seem to constitute them the ultimate "powers behind the

---

[1] The table is, of course, much abbreviated. It subdivides only the Seneca tribe, and even in that tribe does not mark all the maternal families, but only those of one clan.

[2] There are differences of opinion on this point, however. *See* Morgan, L. H.: League of the Ho-de-no-sau-nee or Iroquois, Book i, p. 90 (New York, 1904).

[3] The status of these " warrior chiefs " is discussed later.

throne" in the political life of the Iroquois. It has even induced some writers to call their system of government a true matriarchate, i.e. a state that was ruled by women. There is no doubt that a few elderly women did exercise considerable power and gain high social

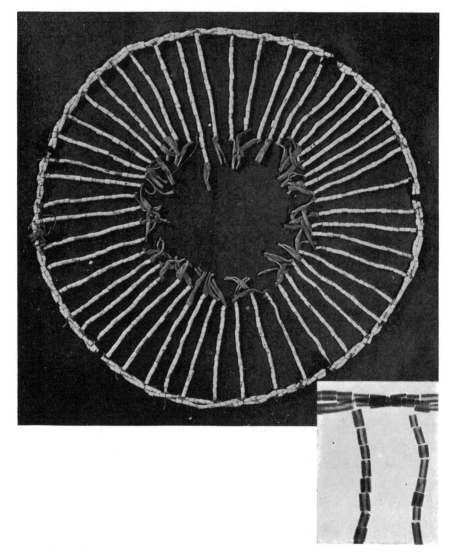

73465

The wampum circle with its fifty pendant strings, one for each sachem, that was entrusted to the Mohawk nation at the foundation of the Confederacy of the Five Nations. The X-ray photograph of some of the beads reveals how they were drilled from both ends. *(Photo by National Museum of Canada.)*

standing; but the majority seem to have possessed little influence, and the female sex as a whole was considered definitely inferior to the male. Such, indeed, was the opinion of every Indian tribe in the Dominion.[1] If women among the Iroquois enjoyed more privileges and possessed greater freedom than the women of other tribes, this was due, not so much to their matrilinear organization and the influence of the maternal families, as to the important place that agriculture held in their economic life, and the distribution of labour whereby the men confined their activities to hunting, fishing, trade, and war, leaving the entire cultivation of the fields and the acquisition of the greater part of the food supply to the women. The League of the Iroquois seems really to have been a male oligarchy in which each member of the governing council of fifty had to submit to more or less supervision by the women of his maternal family, principally to the supervision of one woman, its head.

Quite apart from this supervision by the women, however, the council suffered from another and more serious limitation. Its members obtained their position by birthright, not by military prowess or ability in other ways; and while they might declare peace or war in the name of the whole league, they could not control ambitious individuals who sought profit, revenge, or renown through sudden attacks on neighbouring peoples. Many of the so-called wars of the Iroquois seem to have been irresponsible affairs, organized and conducted without the consent and often without the knowledge of the council; for since the sachems were civil chieftains, not necessarily leaders in warfare or gifted with military talents, it was easy for a warrior who had gained a reputation for skill or valour to muster a band of hunters and start out on the warpath without notice. Iroquoian boys were trained to warfare almost from infancy, and the division of labour that left agriculture in the hands of the women gave the men ample leisure for raids and forays. There arose in consequence a group of warrior chiefs who attained considerable influence and sometimes rivalled the sachems themselves. It was these warrior chiefs indeed, not the sachems, who won most fame and honour during the Revolutionary War.

Even if the council had not been subject to these limitations, it was clearly impossible for so large a governing unit, that met for

---

[1] *Cf.* p. 52.

a few days only three or four times a year, to weld the various tribes and clans into a co-ordinated body politic. Only too often the tribes acted independently, so that one could be at peace with Algonkian neighbours who were being vigorously harassed by the others. As long as the league had only feeble Indian tribes to contend against it flourished and extended its boundaries, replacing losses in warfare by the wholesale adoption of captives; but when it encountered European forces accustomed to military discipline and unified under a single command, the looseness of its organization brought about disjointed action and hastened its disruption and downfall.

Law and order within the Iroquoian confederacies lay wholly within the jurisdiction of the tribes, resting in the final analysis with the individual villages. The penalty for treason or witchcraft was death, after summary trial and conviction before a council of the villagers; but compounding was permissible and usual in the case of all other offences. " They have only one method of justice for injuries, which is that the whole village must make amends by presents." [1] "For a Huron killed by a Huron, they are generally content with thirty presents; for a woman, forty are demanded, because, they say, women cannot so easily defend themselves. . . for a stranger, still more are exacted; because they say that otherwise murders would be too frequent, trade would be prevented, and wars would too easily arise between different nations."[2] The actual levy of presents took the form of voluntary contributions, but so great was the spirit of emulation among the Indians that it was seldom difficult to raise the necessary quantity of wampum and skins. Minor offences were punishable in the same way as murder, but for refractory individuals who continually disturbed the tranquillity of the community there loomed in the background outlawry, which deprived them of all legal protection and permitted any one to kill them at sight. On the whole, public opinion and the knowledge that the entire village would be held responsible for wrong-doing seem to have proved adequate safeguards, and the domestic life of the Iroquoians was probably no less peaceful than our own. Theft was comparatively rare, for land was the property of the community, surplus food was commonly shared with needier neighbours, the

---

1 "Jesuit Relations," vol. xv, p. 157 (1638-9).
2 Ibid., vol. xxxiii, p. 243 (1648-9).

long bark dwelling belonged to the maternal family, and personal property like the tools and weapons of the men, the household goods and utensils of the women, were so easily replaced that they possessed little value. Practically the only objects open to theft were the strings of wampum beads that served both as ornaments and currency; but such was the community spirit of the Iroquoians, so little did they esteem individual wealth, that a multitude of beads brought neither honour nor profit except so far as it gave the owner an opportunity to display his liberality by lavish contributions to the public coffers.[1]

The Iroquoians were a very democratic people. Their chiefs differed in no way from the rank and file, but depended solely on skill and valour in battle, dignity of bearing, and eloquence to maintain their prestige and influence. Captives, when not sacrificed, were adopted into the families, given Iroquoian wives, and regarded as citizens of full standing. There were no strata in society. Any man might become a warrior chief; he might become even a civil chief or sachem provided only that he belonged to one of the fifty maternal families in which that position was hereditary.

The various confederations of the Iroquoians, especially the League of the Iroquois, illustrate one method by which a group of primitive tribes may develop into nationhood and empire. The League had succeeded in breaking down the exclusiveness of each tribe by substituting the blood-price for the blood-feud, amalgamating clans with similar names, establishing a federal council and a federal treasury, and combining local autonomy with a certain measure of federal control. Doubtless, as time went on, it would have harmonized the conflicting positions of the civil and warrior chiefs, freed its leaders from the despotic interference of the heads of the maternal families, and by the subjugation of the neighbouring Algonkians, extended its sway from the Great Lakes to the Atlantic. The expansion of the European colonists checked its progress; but even though it never reached full blossom it will always remain a memorial to the political genius of the Iroquoian peoples.

Very different was the organization of the Indians on the Pacific coast of Canada, even although they too lived a comparatively

---

[1] *Cf.* Ibid., vol. xxxiii, p. 239. Weld, Isaac: "Travels Through the States of North America," p. 402, London, 1799.

settled life, and grouped themselves into clans and sometimes phratries. These British Columbia Indians, so far from being a democratic people, recognized three distinct grades of society, nobles, commoners, and slaves, of whom the commoners made up the bulk of the population.[1] Slaves were, generally, prisoners of war or their children, and, although well treated in most cases, possessed no rights of any kind. They could marry in their own class only, and could be put to death at the whim of their masters. Theoretically, too, commoners could marry only with commoners, and nobles with nobles;

Interior of a Coast Salish lodge at Esquimalt, B.C. *(Reproduced, through the courtesy of the Royal Ontario Museum of Archæology, from a painting by Paul Kane.)*

but the boundary line between these two grades was somewhat indefinite and intermarriage not unknown. Probably many of the commoners had the same origin as the nobles, but, being descended from younger sons and daughters outside the main line of inheritance, they had fallen lower and lower in the social scale until they lost all the recognized hallmarks of nobility.

Just as among the Iroquoians, the ultimate social unit in this area was the individual family, the ultimate political unit the village community. In the earliest days, according to Indian theory,

---

[1] MacLeod states that in the first half of the nineteenth century slaves composed about one-seventh of the population. MacLeod, W. C.: "Some Social Aspects of Aboriginal American Slavery"; Journal de la Société des Américanistes de Paris, vol. xix, p. 123 (Paris, 1927).

all the inhabitants of such a community (except, of course, the slaves) could trace their origin to a single family, but through wars and migrations other people came to settle in the same place, so that in course of time every village contained representatives of several genealogical families. Each genealogical family, that is to say, each group of families that claimed descent from a common ancestor, occupied with its retainers, commoners and slaves, one of the large plank houses so typical of this coast; sometimes, also, a second large house and a number of smaller dwellings when the original home became overcrowded. Every village of any size contained several such genealogical families, or "houses"[1] as we may conveniently call them; and, conversely, a single "house" often had representatives in several villages.

The union of two or more "houses" produced the clan, originally, it would seem, a geographical unit synonymous with village, but later, like the houses, distributed over several villages. Its distribution probably arose in various ways: by an increase of population that forced some of the individual families to seek new fishing-grounds; by wars and civil disturbances; and, most often perhaps, by intermarriage between the different villages. The community feeling that had sprung up while the clan was still a strictly geographical unit persisted after its dispersion, finding expression, for example, in the use of a common designation for all its members, and, in many districts, the employment of a special heraldic crest.[2] North of Vancouver island, among the Haida Indians of the Queen Charlotte islands, the Tsimshian of the Skeena and Nass rivers, the western Carrier adjacent to the Tsimshian, the Tlinkit along the Alaskan panhandle, and the Tahltan on the Stikine river behind them, the clans were grouped into still larger units or phratries, but this further systematization did not find favour among the Nootka, Kwakiutl, and Coast Salish peoples to the southward.

Among the three southern peoples just mentioned, marriage depended solely on the degree of kinship; neither the clan nor the village community entered into its regulation, although a small village might be practically exogamous because all its inhabitants belonged to the same kin. Property (using that term to include not

---

[1] In the same sense as the expressions "House of York," "House of Lancaster."

[2] Just as the Highland clans, the Macdonalds, the Argyles, etc., preserve their surnames and tartans in every part of the world, and retain a feeling of kinship with clansmen still living in the ancient glens.

only material things, but intangible possessions like the exclusive right to a certain song or dance) followed either the male or the female line among the Nootka, passing from a man to his own children, or to his sister's children, at will.[1] Among the Kwakiutl it passed from a man to his son-in-law, and from the son-in-law to his son, a curious inversion of the ordinary rules of inheritance that is not yet clearly understood.[2] North of Vancouver island the phratries (and consequently the clans) were exogamous, inheritance and descent rigidly followed the female line, and the whole structure of society was more systematized and sharply defined.[3]

It might appear at first sight that among these northern Indians of the Pacific coast we have merely a repetition of the exogamous clans and phratries, with matrilinear descent, which we remarked a little earlier among the Iroquoians. But there were several striking differences. Among the Iroquoians the clan was the exogamic unit, and the more important politically; the phratry had mainly a ceremonial significance, and is more likely to have arisen from the clans by a process of federation than the clans from the phratries by division. In northern British Columbia, on the other hand, the phratry was the exogamic and important unit, the clans probably subdivisions, originally local in origin, that later acquired a ceremonial character.[4] So in the general disintegration of native life that has resulted from the European occupation of Canada, the clans have outlived the phratries among the Iroquoians, whereas in British Columbia the phratries are showing themselves more tenacious of existence than the clans. This contrast between the two regions will remind us that two institutions superficially alike may on closer observation prove very different, and that even institutions that appear identical may conceivably have different histories, and owe their origins to entirely dissimilar causes.[5]

---

[1] Generally some of the property followed one line, some the other.

[2] Some writers have ascribed it to the influence of matrilinear peoples in the north; but this is doubtful.

[3] The Carriers of Fort Fraser, who, like other Carrier groups, imperfectly adopted the organizations of the coast tribes, seem to have reckoned clan and phratry through the female line, but rank through the male; whatever the rank of his mother, a man was not a nobleman unless his father was noble. At Stony Creek, near by, both parents had to be noble.

[4] The Iroquoian phratries were nameless; the British Columbia phratries all had names derived (for the most part) from birds and animals, and these phratric crests played a conspicuous rôle in the daily life.

[5] Thus there is not the slightest shred of evidence that the various phratric and clan systems of the American Indians, whatever may be their relation to each other, are connected in any way with the phratric and clan systems of the aborigines of Australia.

We have now followed our British Columbia Indians through an ascending series of groupings, from the individual family to the genealogical family or "house", then successively to the village community, the clan, and finally, among the northern tribes, the phratry.

73456

A Haida woman, with nose-ring and labret. *(Photo by R. Maynard.)*

Let us examine these phratries more closely among their three principal adherents, the Tlinkit, the Haida, and the Tsimshian. The two former recognized only two phratries, the Tsimshian four.

Phratries

Tlinkit:	*Raven; Wolf* (in some villages called *Eagle*)[1]
Haida:	*Raven; Eagle*
Tsimshian:	*Raven; Wolf; Eagle; Gispuwudwada* (a word of unknown meaning)[2]

There can be no doubt that these divisions did not arise independently. Whether the Tlinkit established the system first, and passed it on to their southern neighbours, as some writers believe, or whether its roots lie grounded in a time preceding the present arrangement of the population, does not matter for our present purpose. What is important is that the Indians themselves recognized its common origin, and that although the three peoples spoke different languages[3] and had different political interests, the phratric divisions overrode these boundaries. A Haida man of the Raven phratry, for example, could marry a Tlinkit or Tsimshian woman of the Wolf phratry, but not a Raven woman, even though he captured her in warfare. More than this, if a Haida Raven found himself by some accident in a Tlinkit village unknown to him, he naturally turned for hospitality and protection to its leading Raven inhabitant, and very rarely found his application refused.[4]

The clan and the phratry were social and ceremonial units, not political; they cut across geographical and even linguistic divisions. The smallest political unit was the village community. The largest was the same village community, or perhaps rather an indefinite number of neighbouring villages whose inhabitants possessed the same culture, spoke the same language, frequently intermarried, participated in joint festivals, and relied on each other for mutual protection. While every village had a definite leader, the head man or woman of its dominant clan (two leaders if there were two clans of equal strength), there was no leader for the amorphous group, which had no other bond than the ties of common interest. If enemies attacked a village its neighbours generally rallied to its support, and a village that

---

[1] A third division, called *Sanya*, in some of the southern Tlinkit villages, stood in certain ways outside the two main groups; its members could intermarry with either.
[2] The main emblem or crest of this last phratry varied. Some villages recognized the killer-whale, others the grizzly bear, still others the plant called fireweed. Barbeau, C. M.: " Growth and Federation in Tsimshian Phratries"; Proc. Nineteenth Inter. Cong. Americanists, p. 405 (Washington, 1917).
[3] Haida and Tlinkit, though perhaps genetically connected, differ from each other far more than French and English.
[4] There is some evidence that even in warfare enemies belonging to the same phratry often tried to avoid each other.

planned a raiding expedition invited neighbours to participate; but co-operation was always voluntary, unless the leader of the warring village had temporarily made himself so powerful that he could impose his will on others. There was no subordination of villages to a tribal organization, no tribes at all, strictly speaking, along this entire coast, although the convenience of the term has led to its frequent application to groups of neighbouring villages whose inhabitants spoke the same dialect. The broader divisions by language (Kwakiutl, Tsimshian, etc.) bore little relation to political organization, the only definite unit being the village.

Let us then examine the village more in detail. Its inhabitants were grouped into "houses", each belonging to a certain clan; and the "houses" contained people of three grades—nobles, commoners, and slaves. The nobles, of course, were the aristocracy, theoretically able to deduce their ancestry from the mythical founder of the "house". They, too, were graded according to rank, and their exact position in the scale made visible by the seats they occupied at feasts ("potlatches"), and the order in which they received invitations and presents. Each position carried not only a title, but many other privileges such as the ownership of a certain fish-weir or strip of hunting territory, the right to sing a certain song, execute a certain dance, carve or paint a particular design on the pillars and walls of the dwelling, or erect a special form of totem-pole. In every "house" there seem to have been more titles than people qualified by birth to fill them; and since no one could assume a title without giving a feast and making a lavish distribution of gifts, a man who wished to take out a new or higher "patent of nobility" could often choose between several. But the dignity of a title depended largely on the magnificence of the feasts given by its previous incumbents, so that by accumulating wealth and enlisting the support of relatives, a comparative parvenu could sometimes revive an ancient title that had temporarily lapsed, and raise himself above his fellow nobles. This happened most frequently after white colonization began, and the natives were able to acquire money and trade goods by working in canneries and other places; but even in pre-European times it was always a source of unrest, like the struggles for place and power in more civilized countries. Normally, the successor to a nobleman's

"A feast given at Nootka by Chief Macuina (Maquinna) to celebrate his daughter's coming-of-age." *(Reproduced, through the courtesy of the Public Archives of Canada, from atlas para el viage de las goletas sutil y Mexicana al reconocimiento del estrecho de Juan de Fuca en 1792, publicado en 1802.)*

rank and position was his son or nephew, depending on the precise method of reckoning descent;[1] and the man who held the highest title in a " house " received universal recognition as its chief.

Not only were the noblemen graded, but also their " houses ". The chief of the principal " house " in a clan was the local chief of that clan; if his clan predominated in a village, he was the head chief of the village, and if his village was more powerful than its neighbours, he was the most important man in the district. Obviously there was ample scope for rivalry whenever two " houses ", two clans, or two villages were approximately equal in strength. While a chief could perhaps count on the loyalty of the nobles, commoners, and slaves attached to his own " house ", he relied solely on his personal prestige to gain the support of the remaining chiefs.

We can now see more clearly the vast psychological chasm that separated the Iroquoian from the Pacific Coast system of organization. Each built its society upon the village community, the clan, and the phratry. But the Iroquoians, with a keen sense of democracy, permitted no social grading in their communities, no inequalities of rank, no inheritance of superior status. With an equally keen political sense, they subordinated their villages, clans, and phratries to the compact tribal units, and then federated the tribes into nations. They had the spirit of empire builders, although their empire, like the glow of sunrise in an Arctic winter, faded away before it reached full brightness. The West Coast Indians. on the other hand, evinced no political ability, and concerned themselves but little with the theory and practice of government. They lived in an atmosphere of the past, and turned mainly to social activities, to ceremonies and festivals suffused with the mystic light of religion and tradition, to pomp and display where nobles jostled each other for place and position, to art and song and masked dances that displayed the glories of their " houses " and names. Wealth opened the gates to rank and honour, and men laboured for years to obtain food and skins, dishes, and canoes, for grand festivals that would enable them to advance a few steps higher than their rivals. The culture was not a virile one, like the Iroquoian, but a rich hot-house plant, nurtured by isolation

---

[1] Among the matrilinear Iroquoians a man went to live at his wife's home, for the dwellings and all the furniture belonged to the women. In British Columbia the men owned the dwellings and the wife went to her husband's home and village. Later, if the tribe was matrilinear, her sons generally returned to their mother's village to take over the succession from their uncles.

in a peculiar environment, and incapable of withstanding a chill breeze from the outside world. Like Greece in the days of its decadence, it dazzled the more primitive tribes on its borders, and extended its influence farthest after decline had set in at the heart.[1] Despite its strange brilliance in ceremonialism and art, it had apparently reached full blossom at the coming of the white man, and was lacking in further potentialities for healthy and vigorous growth.[2]

---

[1] The phratric system, with the rudiments of gradation according to rank, reached the Rocky mountains within the last half century and began to establish itself among the Sekani at the headwaters of Peace river, and among the miscellaneous bands, largely Kaska, that now occupy the headwaters of the Liard and Pelly. It had penetrated to the Kutchin Indians on Peel and Porcupine rivers before the nineteenth century. We can hardly doubt (indeed, for the Sekani, there is definite proof) that these Athapaskan Indians had previously favoured the paternal line of descent, like their kinsmen to-day in the Mackenzie valley. But with the phratic system they adopted also the matrilinear organization of the coast tribes, a change which runs directly counter to the theory, more strongly advocated in Europe than in America, that in the development of human society a matrilinear stage invariably preceded the patrilinear.

[2] Such, at least, is the judgment of the writer. Not all students, perhaps, will concur in it.

CHAPTER XI

SOCIAL LIFE

Among primitive, as among civilized, peoples, the form in which society is organized profoundly affects every man, woman, and child in the community at every period of their lives. Yet the ordinary individual gives little attention to it, but accepts the society in which the accident of birth has placed him and directs his thoughts to more visible matters, to the daily task and the daily food supply, the joys and trials of human companionship, and the little events in the everyday life that seem to count most for human happiness and unhappiness. Man may be a social being, as Aristotle says, but when he reaches maturity he is also intensely conservative, and the institutions and forms of government that have moulded his life from childhood to manhood seldom excite his unqualified condemnation in after years. He has learned to adjust himself to them, like the fledgling sparrow that beats its way against the winds, and henceforward his desire is not to remodel them, not to create new social forms that will require his still further adjustment, but to enjoy all the good things that life in the now familiar society can offer him before old age and death come knocking at his door. The span from the cradle to the grave seems long to the youth, but at thirty years the end of the web is already coming within view.

Infancy the world over has the same needs and the same limitations. They make the babe completely dependent on its mother during the first few months of its entry into life. The Indian mother had no trained medical advisers to aid her in its upbringing, no stores where she could purchase warm clothing to protect it from the cold, no wheeled carriage in which she could convey it from one place to another. She suckled it for two years and even longer until it could masticate the meat and fish that predominated in the native diet,[1] clothed it, when clothes were necessary, in the furs that its father brought home from his hunting; and when the Indians moved camp, carried it on her back in a neat home-made cradle of skin,

---

[1] Iroquoian mothers could shorten the period a little through their possession of maize, squash, and beans.

wood, or birch bark.[1]   Little sisters and girl cousins played with it on the grass in the sunshine and guarded it inside the tent or cabin from the half-starved dogs that prowled around outside.   When sickness came, old women brought forth their bags of different simples, and medicine-men invoked their supernatural powers to retrieve

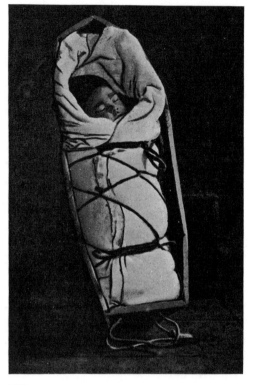

60610

Tsimshian baby in its wooden cradle.
(Photo by D. Jenness.)

and replace the infant's stolen soul, or to withdraw from its tiny body the magic bone or stone presumably implanted there by some evil sorcerer.   Mother-lore handed down from generation to generation taught the Indians many wise practices, but conditions of life were so hard, ignorance of certain elementary rules in child-welfare so general, that the infant mortality was terrific.

---

[1] The Coast Salish, Nootka, and Kwakiutl Indians of British Columbia attached to their cradles a pad, usually of cedar bark, that by slow pressure flattened the baby's forehead. They considered this deformation a mark of beauty. The Eskimo, and some of the Northern Indians, did not use a cradle, but strapped the baby against the back underneath the fur clothing.

In the southern parts of Canada children of both sexes up to the age of five or ten years usually went naked in mild weather. Their clothing was for protection only, not for modesty, although their mothers, like mothers everywhere, often sought to make it decorative.[1] They had more freedom than white children at this period,

27129

Interior Salish woman with baby in cradle.
(Photo by James Teit.)

playing in the open air the whole day, although every house and every tent kept an open door. There was no wall-paper they could damage, no books they might deface, no furniture and very few ornaments that they could mar or destroy. Most of the prohibitions

---

[1] Men could always appear naked without giving offence, and in some tribes even women. The presence or absence of clothing among primitive peoples had little relation to morals.

imposed on them, such as the widely-spread taboo against throwing fish bones to the dogs, applied equally to the adults of the community, so that they were exempt from the innumerable petty checks and restrictions that too often cramp the development of European children. They were exempt, too, from the discipline of corporal punishment that seems inseparable from civilized life, for an Indian parent, however provoked, rarely dreamed of inflicting more than a hasty push or blow. Yet their freedom did not mean licence. The smallness of their communities made every individual's life an open book to his neighbours and compelled every adult to take an active interest in each child, whether his own or another's. So, from their earliest years the children felt the full pressure of public opinion. Their elders always stood near to arbitrate their disputes and to apportion praise or blame, and no private chastisement in the home could have produced more effect than the outspoken reproof of the entire community.[1]

Freedom went hand in hand, too, with a primitive system of education, even although regular schools were lacking. The western bands of Carrier Indians who had absorbed much of the culture of the coastal tribes in British Columbia recognized two curricula: one secular, the other ethical and religious. The secular course was our manual training—instruction given at no set hours in the various tasks that the children would have to perform in later years. More peculiar was the ethical and religious course. On quiet winter evenings, when the people had gathered inside their big, plank houses, dimly lighted by one or two small fires, an old man seated in a corner would narrate some tradition or folk-tale of the distant past, and point the moral of the story with reference to the conduct of the children during the preceding hours. The education of children in other parts of Canada followed along the same general lines, but was not always organized into so definite a system.

At the age of about ten a boy's training became more rigorous. He then shot small game such as rabbits and squirrels, accompanied the hunters on their expeditions to become inured to the hardships of the chase, and performed many small duties around the camp. To harden the lads physically and mentally the Iroquois taught them to

---

[1] Cf. Hunter, John D.: " Memoirs of a Captivity among the Indians of North America," p. 12 (London, 1823)

endure torture.[1] The Pacific Coast tribes made them bathe in cold water daily, winter and summer alike, and whipped them with cedar boughs when they emerged. Among the Sarcee on the plains, the elderly man who supervised their training kept a bathing hole open for them all winter or made them roll naked in the snow; and when

27097

Tent, of fir-boughs and rushes, for the seclusion of an Interior Salish adolescent girl. *(Photo by James Teit.)*

the tribe moved camp he sometimes held them back for two or three hours and forced them to race the whole distance to the new settlement.[2] The Indians and Eskimo in northern Canada brought up their children less rigorously, but in that region the unavoidable hardships of life were so numerous that deliberate increase of them might have proved intolerable. Girls naturally escaped most of this physical training but received thorough instruction in all domestic duties.

[1] "Jesuit Relations," vol. xxxviii, p. 259.
[2] The best runners became scouts in later years.

Only a few minor ceremonies directly disturbed the current of the child's life during this early period, as when the parents of a Haida boy gave a special feast at the piercing of his ears and nose. The real crisis came with adolescence, which signified to the Indians, as to most primitive peoples, far more than the mere transition from childhood to maturity. They regarded it as a season fraught with mystery and danger, a time when the supernatural powers that controlled the phenomena of nature drew unusually near the individual and often marked out his destiny. In many parts of Canada both boys and girls spent part of the period in seclusion fasting and dreaming to establish communion with the unseen world; and those days and nights of solitude, of sleeping in lonely and often dangerous places awaiting a visitation from some unknown power, exerted a powerful influence on their undeveloped minds, especially on those who were innately imaginative. The intensified training that accompanied or followed it increased the effect. Except among the Eskimo the two sexes now kept aloof from each other, the girls often remaining in partial seclusion until marriage. The boys joined the ranks of the men, entering their semi-military organizations on the plains, or being initiated into the secret religious societies on the Pacific coast. The days of their childhood had ended, but, subdued by their recent experiences and a little awed, perhaps, by the responsibilities of their new status, they kept unobtrusively in the background for a year or two until familiarity with their position brought back confidence and self-reliance.

While adolescence seemed to the Indians a very critical period in the individual's life, marriage occupied a rather secondary place. The natives had strong family affections and scorned the celibate state so common at higher levels of civilization. Wedlock, however, brought little romance in its train, for the parents who in most cases arranged the matches gave more consideration to rank and influence, or to skill and courage in hunting, than to the inclinations of the young people themselves. Youths generally married about the age of eighteen or nineteen years, girls two or three years earlier. Often they were betrothed while still children, sometimes even before they were born; but these early betrothals were seldom binding.[1]   The

---

[1] Except on the Pacific coast, when the betrothal was ratified by an exchange of gifts. It could then be annulled only by a counterpayment that was likely to provoke ill-will.

youth of the plains, aided by his relatives, purchased his bride outright with horses, furs, and other gifts, but in eastern and northern
Canada he generally served her parents for a year (or until the birth
of the first child), presenting them with all the products of his hunt-

30969

Interior Salish girl wearing the fir-boughs and goat's
wool blanket that signify her adolescence. *(Photo by
James Teit.)*

ing during that period.[1] The Indians on the Pacific coast, with their
passionate fondness for ceremonies and trade, converted marriage
into a kind of commercial transaction. The husband bought his wife

---

[1] As Jacob served Laban for Leah and afterwards for Rachel.

and some of her prerogatives[1] in a series of feasts, and the wife's kinsmen repaid the bride-price in corresponding manner during the years that followed, adding interest for every child that issued from the marriage. Theoretically, the woman could dissolve the partnership after her redemption, but in practice the husband renewed the contract by a further distribution of presents to her kinsfolk.

Although few, if any, tribes entirely discountenanced polygamy, it was nowhere very common except in the Yukon basin and on the plains, where the leading men generally had two and three wives— sisters, as a rule, because they were more likely to live together in harmony. Marriage gave these prairie Indians such absolute control over their wives that divorce was rare, although the relatives of a woman who constantly suffered harsh treatment from her husband sometimes took her away for a period. For economic reasons divorce was practically unknown also in British Columbia, at least among the nobles, for we have little information concerning the domestic life of the commoners who made up the majority of the population. Elsewhere it was of frequent occurrence before the birth of children, in some of the more migratory tribes so frequent that the first few months of marriage seem to have been regarded as a period of trial union rather than of permanent partnership. The Athapaskans (and sometimes the Eskimo) even wrestled for each other's wives when these were young and good-looking, so that a strong man might arrogate to himself half a dozen young girls while a weakling secured only some cast-off woman or no wife at all.[2]

Marriage, as in all countries, brought increased responsibilities to the young couple. They divided their labours rather strictly, the more arduous and dangerous occupations naturally falling to the man, who devoted most of his time to hunting and fishing while his wife tended the home. He provided the meat and fish that formed the staple diet of the natives, while she collected the berries, nuts, and shell-fish that supplemented it at certain seasons. Among the Iroquoian tribes, which were in a transitional stage between migratory hunters and agriculturalists, the men cleared the forests for the maize crops, and the women planted, cultivated, and harvested them. The husband everywhere manufactured most of the house-

---

[1] e.g., the right to perform certain dances or paint certain figures on the front of his house.
[2] *Cf.* Hearne: Op. cit., p. 141 ff; Thompson: Op. cit., p. 163.

hold tools and carried on all the carpentry, a very important industry on the Pacific coast where the Indians made not only wooden houses and wooden canoes, but wooden dishes and ladles that supplied the place of crockery, and wooden chests for cooking and for storing everything from fish oil to dance-paraphernalia. The wife brought in the game from the hunting field and the firewood from the forest or beach. She gathered the berries and the shell-fish, dressed and cooked the meat, tanned the skins and made them into clothing, wove the

71403

Coast Salish woman weaving a blanket from the wool of the wild Mountain goat.
(Photo by Harlan I. Smith.)

blankets of mountain-goats' wool, the baskets of spruce root, the bags of cedar bark or basswood, and the mats of cedar bark or rushes; and in eastern Canada she fashioned the clay pots and birch-bark vessels that served as cooking utensils. Everything that needed sewing fell to her share, from the skin tipi to the birch-bark covering of the canoe. The plains' Indian never dreamed of helping his wife to set up the big skin tipi, any more than the ordinary native dreamed of cooking his own meals except in the hunting field.[1] Similarly, few women accompanied their husbands to the chase except as on-lookers or to participate in a drive. Each sex had its own duties which it performed without question. Close companionship developed a mutual affection between husband and wife that increased with the birth of children, of whom all Indians were extremely fond; and the inferior status of women seems to have been no obstacle to happy family life. The natives were probably just as industrious as Europeans, although their mode of life was different and periods of intense activity alternated more frequently with days of comparative idleness.

These days of idleness gave opportunity for many distractions and amusements. Some games were restricted to men, some to women, and in a few both sexes participated. Prominent among the amusements of men were athletic contests such as wrestling, running (horse-racing on the plains in more recent times), archery, hoop and stick, and a peculiar form of spear-throwing called snow-snake, practised in winter on the snow. Lacrosse, now so popular in America, had its home in the eastern section of the continent from Hudson bay to the gulf of Mexico, and the Micmac and Malecite Indians of the Maritime Provinces played an indigenous form of football. The Eskimo also enjoyed football, played in a slightly different way, and by women as strenuously as by men. Other ball games such as shinny were mainly women's pastimes, though played occasionally by men or by men and women together in certain tribes. For indoor amusement there were quieter pastimes like juggling, cat's cradle, and the ring-and-pin game.

More popular than any of these distractions were games of chance or guessing that appealed to the gambling instincts of the natives. Mackenzie thus describes the dice game that was prevalent all over eastern Canada: " The instruments of it consist of a platter or dish made of wood or bark and six round or square but flat pieces of metal, wood, or stone, whose sides or surfaces are of different colours. These are put into the dish, and after being for some time shaken together are thrown into the air and received again in the dish with consider-able dexterity, when by the number that are turned up of the same mark or colour the game is regulated. If there should be equal

---

[1] The Kutchin of the upper Yukon river were an exception; they allotted the cooking to the men.

numbers the throw is not reckoned; if two or four, the platter changes hands."[1] Guessing contests played with straws or sticks were more widely spread even than dice, being especially popular on the Pacific coast. Mackenzie saw one form of it among the Carriers: " We all sat down on a very pleasant green spot, and were no sooner seated than our guide and one of the party prepared to engage in play. They had each a bundle of about fifty small sticks neatly polished, of the size of a quill, and 5 inches long; a certain number of these sticks had red lines around them, and as many of these as one of the players might find convenient were curiously rolled up in dry grass, and according to the judgment of his antagonist respecting their number and marks he lost or won. Our friend was apparently the loser, as he parted with his bow and arrows and several articles which I had given him."[2]

Inordinate gambling connected with one game or another was almost universal in Canada, and the traditions of the Indians contain many stories of men who lost all their possessions. It was a fertile source of quarrels and bloodshed, particularly when the opponents in the games belonged to different tribes or bands. Some tribes played much more recklessly than others. In British Columbia the natives occasionally gambled away not only their clothing and other property, but even their wives and children. The Piegan Indians, on the other hand, " have some things which are never gambled, as all that belongs to their wives and children and in this the tent is frequently included; and always the kettle, as it cooks the meat of the children, and the axe as it cuts the wood to warm them. The dogs and horses of the women are also exempt."[3]

Devoted as they were to gambling, the Indians were even more passionately fond of dancing, which from its world-wide popularity would appear to be a natural response, conditioned by physiological rhythms, to certain emotional impulses. In Canada, as among primitive peoples elsewhere, dancing was generally the handmaid of religion, so much so indeed that Thompson asserted that all Indian dances had a religious tendency.[4] There was nevertheless much

---

[1] Mackenzie: Op. cit., p. 142.
[2] Ibid., p. 311.
[3] Thompson: Op. cit., p. 361. For gambling at the stick and dice games, and for Indian games generally, Cf. the voluminous monograph by Culin, Stuart: " Games of the North American Indians"; 24th Ann. Rept. Bur. Am. Ethn., 1902-3 (Washington, 1907).
[4] Thompson: Op. cit., p. 92. Cf. also Hewitt, J. N. B.: "Handbook of American Indians," art. "Dance."

dancing for mere pleasure, to celebrate success in hunting or in war, to welcome relatives and friends, or simply to while away a few leisure hours. The typical instruments were drums and rattles, the latter confined almost exclusively to religious ceremonies;[1] but their function was emotional only, the movements of the dancers rarely synchronizing with the drum beats or with the stress syllables of the songs. Men and women danced apart, usually singly, but often simultaneously, the men more violently than the women, whose movements seldom exceeded slight hops or a shuffling of the feet with gentle waving of the arms and swaying of knees and shoulders. On special occasions the usual gymnastic dances gave place to mimetic performances carried out with considerable skill. Forty Algonkins of lake Nipissing thus celebrated the attendance of some surrounding tribes at a " feast of the dead ": " The dance consisted of three parts. The first represented various encounters of enemies in single combat—one pursuing his foe, hatchet in hand, to give him the deathblow, while at the same time he seems to receive it himself, by losing his advantage; he regains it, and after a great many feints, all performed in time with the music, he finally overcomes his antagonist, and returns victorious. . . ."[2] Every region had its own types of dances, gymnastic and mimetic. Morgan lists no less than thirty-two for the Onondaga tribe alone. For in sorrow and gladness alike the Indian naturally turned to this diversion that he might express his emotions in song and rhythmic movements and enjoy the sympathy of his fellowmen.

Social amenities naturally reached their highest peak when a whole tribe assembled at some fishing or hunting ground, or the inhabitants of a village, scattered during parts of the year, had gathered at their homes. Every tent and every house then kept an open door that invited visitors to enter at any hour. Women gossiped at the cooking-places, men gathered in little groups to discuss the day's events. Most tribes held religious festivals at these seasons. The Ojibwa usually celebrated their *Midewiwin* or " medicine lodge " in the summer at the ripening of fruits and berries, and friends and relatives gathered from all the surrounding

---

[1] The Pacific Coast tribes had whistles with two or three notes, the Iroquoians and some eastern Algonkians a flute or flageolet; but they did not use these instruments for dance music.

[2] " Jesuit Relations," vol. xxiii, p. 213 (1642-43). *Cf.* " Menzies' Journal of Vancouver's Voyage"; edited by C. F. Newcombe, Archives of British Columbia, Mem. No. v, pp. 118-9 (Victoria, 1923).

districts to witness the initiation of candidates into the society of medicine-men.[1] The Iroquois had at least six major festivals throughout the year, beginning with the "maple festival" in the spring when the sap of the maple trees commenced to run, and ending with the great new year's festival (held not at our new year, but about February), when in addition to prayers and orations there were masked dances by the "false face society", and gambling with dice or peachstones.[2] The outstanding festival on the plains was the "sun-dance", celebrated about midsummer at irregular intervals of two or three years. The actual celebration, which was attended by every member of the tribe, lasted three or four days only, but its preparation and the ceremonies and games for which it gave occasion extended the period to almost a fortnight.[3] Even the primitive northern tribes like the Eskimo had their gatherings, although of brief duration owing to the uncertain food supply.

Naturally, it was on the Pacific coast, where the climate was mildest and food plentiful, that these half-social, half-religious entertainments most engrossed the attention of the aborigines. The Kwakiutl and Bella Coola Indians devoted almost the entire winter to feasts, masked dances, and ritual performances promoted by powerful secret societies that dominated the communities during this period and largely superseded the ordinary political arrangement into clans and houses. The northern tribes followed their example, but kept the societies more under control and extended the various festivals into other seasons of the year.

The daily life of the aborigines with its mingled work and play allowed ample scope for ambition. Except on the Pacific coast it was possible for any man to gain the leadership in his tribe through courage, sagacity, and eloquence. In the Iroquoian Confederacy only those who belonged to certain genealogical families might obtain election as sachems, but there were no restrictions on warrior chieftainships, and it was the warrior chieftains like Brant who exercised most influence during the Revolutionary wars. Even on the Pacific coast, if we may trust the folk-lore, men of lowly birth occasionally forced their way into the ranks of the nobles and won pre-eminence

[1] For a description of the *mide*, *See* Hoffman, W. J.: "The Midewiwin or Grand Medicine Society"; Seventh Ann. Rept., Bur. Ethn., 1885-86, pp. 143-300 (Washington, 1891).
[2] For details, *See* Morgan, L. H.: Op. cit., pp. 175 ff.
[3] For descriptions of the "sun-dance" in the different tribes, *See* Anthropological Papers, Am. Mus. Nat. Hist., vol. xvi (New York, 1921).

for themselves and their families. Many gained influence and wealth through medicine-power;[1] sometimes, indeed, the shaman had more authority than the chief. On the plains, men accumulated property for years in order to purchase a medicine-bundle, just as they hoarded skins and food on the Pacific coast to outdo their rivals in a potlatch. Women as well as men had their avenues of advancement. Many enjoyed high rank on the Pacific coast through the accident of descent; among the Iroquoians a few became matrons of maternal families. The great "sun-dance festival" of the plains' Indians brought together all the members of a tribe, from far and near; yet the Blackfoot and the Sarcee could not hold a sun-dance except in fulfilment of a woman's vow, and the woman whose purity and self-sacrifice permitted its celebration enjoyed fame and honour throughout her days. Both sexes alike could qualify as shamans, although in this sphere women rarely obtained the same prestige as men. Indian society was, therefore, far from stagnant. If the fields for ambition were narrow this was no more than inevitable among peoples of lowly culture whose horizons were limited to their own immediate vicinity.

The principal check on ambition, a salutary check in the main, was the socialistic character of Indian life. Rank and wealth gave no title to arrogance. Except at ceremonies chiefs dressed in the same way and ate the same food as the common people under them. Even the nobles on the Pacific coast lived little better than the slaves whom they could put to death for a mere whim. Not one of them would have dared to emulate many a petty chieftain in Africa and force his people to crawl before his feet or to starve while he had food in abundance. The fruits of the earth, the game on the land, and the fish in the water were for all men's use, and while every individual was entitled to the products of his labour no one might claim an unfair share to the detriment of his fellowmen. So we read of the Hurons: "No hospitals are needed among them, because there are neither mendicants nor paupers as long as there are any rich people among them. Their kindness, humanity, and courtesy not only make them liberal with what they have, but cause them to possess hardly anything except in common. A whole village must be without corn before any individual can be obliged

---

[1] *Cf.* the rise of Tchaka among the Assiniboine. De Smet: Op. cit., vol. iii, pp. 1108 et seq.

to endure privation. They divide the produce of their fisheries equally with all who come . . ."[1] The most ambitious native never dreamed of creating a tyranny or of subverting the established political constitution for his own advantage. So Indian tribes never knew those internal revolts that distracted the city states of ancient Greece and rendered our Saxon forefathers an easy prey to Danish and Norman invaders.

Neither did they suffer from those virulent diseases, smallpox and measles, that decimated their ranks in historical times. Some ailments they had before Europeans came, ailments due to malnutrition and other causes. For these they had specific remedies, principally herbal, a few of which are incorporated in our own materia medica. Skeletons from prehistoric graves seem to indicate a very healthy population, although the weaklings who died in infancy are probably very imperfectly represented in these remains. Hardships caused premature ageing in most tribes, and the aged and infirm were not always the objects of loving care. Among the Iroquoians and Pacific Coast tribes, where the conditions of life were easiest, they passed their closing years in comparative comfort, but among the more migratory peoples of eastern and northern Canada any who through illness or old age could no longer keep up with the march were abandoned on the trail or deliberately killed: " It is the custom of this tribe (Montagnais) to kill their fathers and mothers when they are so old that they can walk no longer, thinking that they are doing them a good service; for otherwise they would be compelled to die of hunger, as they have become unable to follow the others when they change their location."[2]

It is not easy to explain either historically or psychologically the great variety of methods employed by the Indians in disposing of their dead. The Iroquoians deposited them on platforms raised several feet above the ground, but collected them all at intervals of about twelve years, stripped them of their flesh, and piled the bones in a common pit. Other tribes in eastern Canada and on the plains sometimes practised platform (or tree) burial followed by inhumation, but most of them kept the two methods separate, adopting one

---

1 "Jesuit Relations," vol. xliii, pp. 271-273.
2 " Jesuit Relations," vol. iv, p. 199. *Cf.* vol. v, p. 103 et passim. Hearne: Op. cit., p. 218 f. Stefansson, V.: " The Stefansson-Anderson Arctic Expedition"; Anthropological Papers of the Am. Mus. Nat. Hist., vol. xiv, p. 283 (New York, 1919).

or the other according to individual circumstances. Tree or platform burial prevailed also in the timbered areas of northern Canada and in British Columbia, so that its range practically coincided with that of the forests. Almost equally widespread, however, was cairn-burial, common not only in the treeless Arctic and sub-Arctic together with certain sections of the plains, but in both British Columbia and Newfoundland. If we include with cairn-burial, deposition under

73457

Blackfoot (Blood) burial scaffold.

piles of logs and brush, its range actually covered the entire country outside perhaps the eastern woodlands. In eastern, central, and northern Canada the more migratory tribes frequently dispensed with every form of burial, simply abandoning the corpse inside the tent or wigwam and moving away to another camping-ground. The Chipewyan and Eskimo indeed often left it on the ground without protection of any kind, bestowing hardly more care on the bodies of their relatives than the west coast nobles accorded their slaves. Cave-

burial and its equivalent, burial under overhanging cliffs, were practised in Newfoundland and in British Columbia. In the latter
region the dry air of certain caves brought about natural mummification, which the Tsimshian sometimes effected artificially for persons of rank.[1] Cremation occurred among the Assiniboine, and their
Cree neighbours around Nelson river,[2] and was the usual custom
west of the Rockies from the Yukon to the northern end of Vancouver island, where it gave place to inhumation or burial in cairns
or trees. The interior Salish, who lived in the arid portion of the
Fraser valley, adopted a novel method of interment. They laid their
dead at the bases of steep slopes and covered them effectively with
rock-slides.

Familiar with the sight of death from their earliest years, the
Indians viewed its approach with stoical equanimity. It was not
that they expected rare joys in a life to come, a Valhalla of feasting
and revelry or a Paradise where beautiful houris administered to
every want. Some tribes located the land of spirits in the sky, others
in a world beneath this earth, still others somewhere in the west along
the path of the setting sun. Wherever it lay, the soul that reached
it enjoyed happiness indeed, but only a shadowy happiness compared with the joys of earth. And since the journey to it was long
and dangerous, so that many perished along the path, the Indians
placed food and other objects in the graves of their loved ones to
help them on their way, and some of the Ojibwa kindled a fire on
every fresh tomb four nights in succession to illumine the " solitary
and obscure passage to the country of souls."[3] Many tribes held
that there were two separate spirit-lands, one for shamans and great
warriors, the other for common people; or one for those who had
lived uprightly according to tribal law, the other for sorcerers and
the evil-minded. The doctrine of reincarnation found general
acceptance, but in too vague a form to produce much influence. For
although the beliefs concerning the afterlife, which were almost as
numerous as the tribes, sufficed to rob death of its terrors, few of them
held out such promise of happiness, or carried such faith, as to offer
much cheer to the dying or comfort to those who were left behind.

---

[1] Perhaps, also, the Micmac of Nova Scotia. Le Clercq: Op. cit., p. 302.
[2] Cf. The Kelsey Papers, p. 12. Documents relating to the Early History of Hudson Bay; edited
by J. B. Tyrrell, Toronto, The Champlain Society, 1931, p. 231.
[3] De Smet: Op. cit., vol. iii, p. 1047. The Ojibwa on the north shore of lake Huron placed tobacco
in the hand of the corpse to pay for its passage across the river of death.

" He has gone to the sand-hills," the Blackfoot would say of some-one recently deceased, and the thought brought little solace to them.[1] Yet there were a few happy exceptions, as in the pathetic incident recorded by Thompson: " With regard to the immortality of the soul; and the nature of the other world, the best evidence of their belief I learned from a [Chipewyan] woman; her husband had traded with me two winters. They had a fine boy of six years of age, their only child; he became ill and died; and according to their custom she had to mourn for him twelve moons, crying in a low voice ' She azza, She azza ' (my little son) never ceasing while awake, and often bursting into tears. About three months after, I saw her again, (making) the same cry, the same sorrowful woman, her husband was kind to her; about six months after this I saw her again, she no longer cried, ' She azza,' and was no longer a sorrowing woman; I enquired of her the cause of the change. She replied, when my little son went to the other world, there was none to receive him, even his Grandfather is yet alive; he was friendless, he wandered alone in the pitching track of the tents (here she shed tears), there was none to take care of him, no one to give him a bit of meat. More than two moons ago, his father died, I sorrowed for him, and still sadly regret him, but he is gone to my son, his father will take great care of him. He will no longer wander alone, his father will be always with him, and when I die I shall go to them."[2]

---

[1] Ibid., Op. cit., vol. ii, p. 526. McClintock, W.: " The Old North Trail," p. 148 f, London, 1910.
[2] Thompson: Op. cit., p. 164 f.

CHAPTER XII

RELIGION

Europeans, realizing the brevity of man's earthly career, regard it as a training-school for another life to come, and seek in religion a guide to the thought and conduct that offer apparently the best preparation for the hereafter. Christianity teaches them to weigh all earthly gains and losses, all seeming good and ill, in the balance of eternity, and to forego many things that appear desirable here and now for a greater good beyond the grave. The Indians pinned little hope to the uncertain hereafter. They sought from religion help and guidance in this present life alone, and with full consciousness of the limitations in their own knowledge and power, they summoned to their aid the mysterious forces surrounding them in order to obtain during their mortal span all the blessings that their hearts desired. Long life and health, success in hunting and in war, medicine power, prosperity, fame, happiness, and the gift of happy children— these were the things for which the Indians prayed, these the blessings that they demanded from their religion. They realized, nevertheless, that this life also is uncertain, that no religion could release them from all its trials and perils, and, like mortals everywhere, they submitted in blind resignation to the misfortunes that inevitably cross man's path.

Of the many phenomena that affected their welfare the majority lay beyond both their understanding and their control. The sun that rose daily in the east, gladdening all the earth with its rays, set again in the west without their volition. Its movements, so vital for human existence, stood apart from all human activities. The seasons came and went, and land and water changed to their rhythm, bringing now abundance, now want, to the various tribes of men. The wind blew as it listed, often imperilling their canoes, and the clouds that gathered on the mountains without apparent cause hurled bolts of lightning upon their tents. The animal, the bird, and the fish, each had a power and an intelligence resembling and yet unlike those of the hunter who sought them for his daily food. If superior cunning enabled him to circumvent the swift-footed deer, he in turn was circumvented by the still more cunning wolverine. Year after year, again, the salmon came to the Indian's rivers from some unknown ocean home, as though they appeared for his special benefit alone. There were seasons when game abounded, and his camp was filled with meat; and other seasons when animals were so scarce that they seemed to avoid his neighbourhood deliberately. Then there were diseases that came suddenly and unseen, striking down as with invisible arrows the strong and the weak alike. Finally, many of the barriers that separated man from nature vanished in dreams and visions, when the sleeper seemed to travel in far distant places and to have contacts with the world of animals that were impossible in normal waking hours.

All these things the Indian perceived and pondered. The earth to him was a flat expanse of land and water that ended somewhere beyond the horizon. The sky was similar to this earth, although man could see only its under side. Some tribes, observing perhaps the clouds that pass beneath each other and hide the faces of the sun and moon, believed there were several worlds above this one, and correspondingly several underneath. No Indian could conceive of the earth as an immense ball rotating on its axis and revolving around the sun, governed by the same mysterious forces that direct the course of an arrow from its bow. Astronomy, meteorology, physics, these and other sciences were as yet unborn, and the Indian interpreted the phenomena of nature in spiritual terms, projecting his own mentality into the processes he saw at work around him. Spiritual forces akin to those in his own being caused the sun to rise and set, the storms to gather in the sky, the cataract to leap among the rocks, and the trees to bud in the springtime. A mentality similar in kind to his animated the bird, the animal, and the fish. The same reason, the same emotions that actuated all his movements, actuated also all that moved on earth, in water, and in sky. Reason and emotions were present, it is true, in varying degrees, and accompanied by different powers, some greater and some less. But ultimately (although few if any Indians consciously reached this generalization) all life was one in kind, and all things, potentially at least, possessed life.[1]

Life was inseparable from force or power, and power could express itself in many ways and under many disguises. There was

---

[1] Thus the Ojibwa of lake Huron predicate a "soul" and a "shadow" even in rocks and stones.

power in water, in the tree that spread out its leafy branches, in the rock that man trampled beneath his feet. Even if the power lay dormant, yet every now and then it manifested itself in unmistakable guise. The placid water arose in tempestuous waves, and the rock split with a noise like thunder before it tumbled down the mountain-side. Birds had the power of flight, and of beholding from their aerial vantage-point things that were hidden from human eyes. The fish explored the secret waters. Of the animals some were strong, some weak, some ferocious, and some timid, some slow of foot, and some speedy; but each species had its own peculiar powers, and each in its wanderings acquired a special knowledge. Man's powers were great, but none knew better than he their limitations. Air and water were closed domains to him. He could run, but many an animal could outstrip him. He could fashion tools and weapons, but he could not ensure the accuracy of his marksmanship nor the safety of his canoe. He could plan a course of life, but forces unforeseen might change the issue. In a battling-ground of manifold forces or powers he stood alone, striving with the limited powers at his command to win a happy livelihood for himself and his kindred.

The Indian, however, had neither the inclination nor the training for metaphysical speculations. Although this theory of the universe supported the whole fabric of his religious life, it is doubtful whether he ever formulated it clearly in his mind, or expressed it in words, any more than the ordinary European comprehends or expresses all the philosophical ideas implied in Christian rites and ceremonies. For the Indian, like mankind elsewhere, concerned himself less with the nature of things around him than with their effect on human welfare; and recognizing that some things exerted a greater influence than others, he tended to magnify the former at the expense of the latter. It was not the quietly running stream that arrested his attention, but the foaming cataract; not the gentle zephyr, but the thunder; not the insignificant porcupine, but the mighty buffalo. For power, though universal perhaps, was graded, and whatever had little power could safely be neglected. Thus he peopled his world with numerous " powers ", some great, mysterious, and awe-inspiring, some small and of little or no account. Furthermore, following man's tendency everywhere, he gave them such anthropomorphic traits as speech and knowledge, even ascribed to them human or partly human forms. So the "power" of the cataract became its "spirit", the "power" of the buffalo a kind of supernatural man-buffalo.

Here a confusion of thought arose which seems to pervade all Indian religion. The "power" of the cataract was only an attribute, but the "spirit" was a distinct entity, immanent in the cataract, of course, yet conceivably capable of a separate existence. It carried the same name as the cataract, and the name heightened its individuality, giving it the status of a definite supernatural being. Similarly the "power" of the buffalo became a supernatural king-buffalo that lived in a mysterious buffalo-land, and yet was immanent in every single buffalo; and the power or vitality of the corn, a corn goddess who was present in every blade and ear. Some spirits were vague and nameless, others as definite as the deities of ancient Greece and Rome. But ultimately they were no more than personifications of the mysterious forces which the Indians saw working in nature around them, and which they were unable to account for except as they accounted for themselves.

Just as these mysterious forces varied in their powers, so the spirits varied also. Above a multitude of *genii locorum*, obscure and usually nameless, rose higher beings like the plains' thunder-god who perpetually warred against the water-spirit, the Eskimo sea-goddess Sedna who presided over the supply of seals, and the sun or sky-god, recognized under different names by many different tribes, who looked down upon all that happened here on earth. Every tribe had several such deities, generally more or less co-ordinate; only the Bella Coola Indians of British Columbia arranged them into a regular hierarchy culminating in a great sky-god, the All-Father Alkuntam. The sky-god always occupied the highest position, but many tribes regarded him as too remote, too detached from human affairs, to require much attention or worship. So the Haida Indians, while acknowledging the supremacy and occasionally offering a few prayers to the "Power of the Shining Heavens", reserved nearly all their sacrifices for the ocean spirits, especially the Killer Whales; and the Montagnais, who believed Atachocam created the world, "spoke of him as one speaks of a thing so far distant that nothing sure can be known about it."[1] Yet in two regions at least the sky-god reigned supreme. The Huron and other Iroquoian tribes offered vows and sacrifices not only " to

---

[1] "Jesuit Relations," vol. vi, p. 157; *cf.* iv, p. 203.

the Earth, to Rivers, to Lakes, to dangerous Rocks, but above all, to the Sky . . . They have recourse to the sky in almost all their necessities, and respect the great bodies in it above all creatures, and remark in it in particular, something divine."[1] Similarly, Father de Smet writes of the plains' tribes: "All these Indians believe in the existence of a Great Spirit, the Creator of all things . . . They think this great medicine pervades all air, earth and sky; that it is omnipresent, omnipotent, but subject to be changed and enlisted on their side in any undertaking if the proper ceremonies and sacrifices are made. It is the author of both good and evil according to its pleasure, or in accordance with their attention to their mode of worship . . . Power is its attribute, and its residence is supposed by some to be in the sun."[2]

Although the great body of the Indians lingered in a polytheistic stage, yet in several parts of Canada, particularly on the plains, the more speculative had arrived at a true monotheism. Their All-Father was not the omniscient and benevolent Being of the Christian religion who created and governs this universe to fulfil some unknown purpose. Neither was it an intellectual principle, like the λόγος or νοῦς of Greek philosophers. Rather it was the personification of the mysterious powers or forces operating in man's environment, forces that were conceived as emanations from some higher force. The Algonkians called both this higher force and its individual manifestations *manito*, the Iroquoians *orenda*, and some Siouan tribes *wakanda*. Comparative religion, however, already recognizes the conception under the term *mana*, the name that was applied to it by the natives of Melanesia and Polynesia, who likewise made it the foundation of their religion.

The supernatural spirits of the Indians, like the mysterious forces which they personified, might be either helpful or harmful, but they were not ethical forces in any sense. Indian thinkers hardly attacked the problem of evil in the world. The tribes on the plains considered that their All-Father was the ultimate source of both good and evil, and attempted by rituals and prayer to gain only the blessings. The western Carriers of British Columbia now make *Sa* a sky-god of righteousness who punishes violations of the moral code, but this is

1 Ibid., vol. x, p. 159.
2 De Smet: Op. cit., vol. iii, p. 1064 f; *cf.* p. 939.

perhaps the result of Christian teaching. The Iroquoians alone[1] vaguely perceived the great depth of the problem. They predicated a dualism in nature, like the ancient Persians, and in various elaborate myths described how two rival spirits, one good and one evil, fought for the mastery of the universe, and how the good spirit finally overcame his adversary without being able to undo all his mischievous creations. After all, the main problem for every tribe of Indians, as it is for all mankind, was not the explanation of evil, but its avoidance. Since many of the forces or supernatural beings in nature were hostile or at least productive of evil, it behooved the native either to render these powers innocuous, or to ward off their influences by other means.

29145

Effigies of two men in a canoe, made of twigs by a Nootka Indian and secluded in the forest to give success in sealing. *(Photo by G. A. Cox.)*

The easiest method of rendering them innocuous was by propitiation. The Indian, therefore, offered them gifts, as he did to his fellow-countrymen. " I have remarked two kinds of sacrifices," says a Jesuit missionary among the Hurons. " Some are to render them (the supernatural powers) propitious and favourable; others

---

[1] The Ojibwa and some of the Cree recognized a Good Spirit (*Kitchi Manido*) and a Bad Spirit (*Madji Manido*), but they seem to have paid little regard to the latter prior to the teachings of the Jesuit missionaries.

to appease them, when they have received in their opinion some disgrace from them, or believe they have incurred their anger or indignation. Here are the ceremonies they employ in these sacrifices. They throw some Tobacco into the fire; and if it is, for example, to the Sky that they address themselves, they say, Aronhiate onne aonstaniwas taitenr, ' O Sky, here is what I offer thee in sacrifice; have pity on me, assist me.' If it is to implore health, taenguiaens, ' Heal me.' "[1] A Cree told Thompson that during the great smallpox epidemic of 1781-82 " what little we could spare we offered to the Bad Spirit to let us alone and go to our enemies. To the Good Spirit we offered feathers, branches of trees, and sweet smelling grass."[2] Minor powers received the same attention. In every part of the Dominion the Indians made offerings at waterfalls and rapids, at passes in the mountains, at trees or rocks that stood solitary, at every place that seemed in any way dangerous or uncanny. The offering might be only a whiff of tobacco, or a stick added to a pile that had already accumulated; but always its purpose was the same, to propitiate the supernatural force or being that lurked in the vicinity. Special regard was paid to the spirits that controlled the food supply. The Indians of the Pacific coast held a solemn ritual at the arrival of the salmon-run to propitiate the spirit of the salmon, the Eskimo deposited gifts beside every bear carcass, and the Montagnais when moose were scarce threw grease on the fire saying, " Make us find something to eat."[3] During the great Sun-Dance festival on the plains many Indians tortured themselves to win the favour of the Sun or Sky-god, and the Iroquoians and neighbouring Algonkians sacrificed white dogs as thank-offerings and to ward off impending evil. It is noteworthy, however, that the human sacrifices so common in the higher civilization of the Aztecs of Mexico were rare in Canada, and confined to the two regions where the social organization was most advanced, the Iroquoian area and the Pacific coast.

Even more important than gifts or sacrifices were the taboos observed by the natives that they might give no offence to the supernatural powers. The number of taboos was almost limitless, and they affected every phase of social life. There were prohibitions that

---

1 "Jesuit Relations," vol. x, p. 159.
2 Thompson: Op. cit., p. 337; cf. p. 324.
3 "Jesuit Relations," vol. vi, p. 173. Other tribes, e.g. the Carrier, followed the same practice as the Montagnais.

applied only at certain seasons, as in summer, or at certain epochs in life, as at puberty or on the death of relatives. Thus among some British Columbia tribes no mourner might approach a river where the salmon were running. Other prohibitions were incumbent at all times and on every individual in the tribe. Often their exact significance was lost in antiquity, and their only sanction a vague feeling that violation was anti-social and would bring ill-luck to the individual or the community. Yet there were many taboos, particularly those relating to animals and fish, for which the sanction was clear and the purpose definite. The eastern Indians prohibited the throwing of beaver bones to the dogs lest the beaver spirit should resent the indignity shown to its incarnated forms and withdraw them altogether from the hunters' reach. For a similar reason no refuse might be cast into the salmon rivers of the Pacific coast, and, in certain parts of the Arctic, no caribou meat could be cooked on the sea ice when the Eskimo were hunting the seals. Violation of all such taboos was sin, and sin brought punishment, from which the British Columbia and plains' Indians saw no way of escape unless the supernatural powers mercifully yielded to entreaty and consented to overlook the transgression. But in eastern and northern Canada many natives believed that public confession would blot out the offence,[1] and the Iroquoians sometimes made a white dog their scapegoat, casting their sins upon this victim after strangling it in sacrifice to the unseen powers.

It was not sufficient merely to avoid giving offence to the supernatural powers. The Indians needed their active aid. Sometimes they could obtain this by prayer alone, and in trouble or in danger the natives from one end of Canada to the other had recourse to prayer, calling on the supernatural powers for aid and protection.[2] An old plains' Indian would often ascend a hill at daybreak and beseech the sun-father to bless the people in the tents below. In time a few prayers became stereotyped into formulæ and so degenerated into incantations; but usually the supernatural world appeared too close and too real for mere formal incantations to provide the necessary emotional satisfaction.

---

[1] Cf. Boas, F.: "The Eskimo of Baffin Land and Hudson Bay"; Anth. Papers, Am. Mus. Nat. Hist., vol. xv, p. 120 (1901); Keith in Masson: Op. cit., ii, p. 127.

[2] Cf. "Jesuit Relations," vol. vi, p. 205.

All tribes firmly believed that prayer combined with fasting and ceremonial purity exercised a powerful influence on the unseen world, particularly if the suppliant was at the age of adolescence. Almost inevitably he would be granted a vision that would bestow on him supernormal powers, or give him one or more supernatural protectors. The type of vision varied tribally according to traditional patterns. On the plains an Indian would hear a voice, or behold a strange being, human or animal, that would promise its help in the crises of life. Among the Carriers and other tribes of British Columbia the spirit of a dreamer might journey to some distant cavern in the mountains, where it would hear the beating of a drum and the noise of singing. Whatever variations the visions might display, their purpose was the same everywhere; they provided a means whereby man could divert to his own use some of the mysterious forces around him, and prevail against the difficulties of his environment. So, throughout nearly the whole of Canada, boys, and sometimes girls, passed days and even months in partial solitude, striving under the direction of parents and relatives to obtain a guardian spirit. Such experiences always aroused feelings of the deepest awe, and few Indians dared to reveal their visions afterwards from fear of offending the spiritual world and forfeiting its blessings. Very typical, however, is the following description given by an early missionary among the Hurons.

"A certain man who urged us to baptize him, had, when but fifteen or sixteen years of age, retired into the desert to prepare himself by fasting for the apparition of some demon. After having fasted sixteen days without eating anything, and drinking water only, he suddenly heard this utterance, that came from the sky: 'Take care of this man and let him end his fast.' At the same time, he saw an aged man of rare beauty who came down from the sky, approached him, and, looking kindly at him, said: 'Have courage, I will take care of thy life. It is a fortunate thing for thee, to have taken me for thy master. None of the demons, who haunt these countries, shall have any power to harm thee. One day thou wilt see thy hair as white as mine. Thou wilt have four children; the first two and the last will be males, and the third will be a girl; after that, thy wife will hold the relation of a sister to thee.' As he concluded these words, he held out to him a piece of human flesh, quite raw. The youth in horror turned away his head. 'Eat this,' said the old man, presenting him with a piece of bear's fat. When he had eaten this the demon withdrew, ascending toward the sky, whence he had come. After that, he often appeared to him and promised to assist him. Nearly all that he predicted then has happened."[1]

As visible symbols of these increments of supernatural power, or of the protection of guardian spirits, the Indians wore tokens or amulets attached to their clothing, or suspended by cords around the neck. These were objects they had seen in their visions, or that their guardian spirits had prescribed for them; and although in many tribes they were merely the shrivelled skins of birds or animals,[2] they possessed the same value and received the same reverence as the crucifixes which many Indians have substituted for them to-day. An Algonkin Indian lovingly preserved a hair, which he worshipped as a little divinity. "It is a hair," he said, "that I have pulled from the moustache of the Manitou. That hair has saved my life a thousand times, when I have been in danger of losing it. I would have been drowned a hundred times had it not been for this hair. It is this which has enabled me to kill moose, has preserved me from sickness and has made me live so long. I have cured the sick with this hair; there is nothing that I cannot do with it. To ask me for it is to ask for my life . . . . He therefore took his tobacco pouch, from which he drew a smaller one, and from the latter a third, neatly embroidered in their fashion with rows of porcupine quills, which he placed in my hands. I opened it, and found it filled with down, in which the hair was wrapped."[3]

Unlike the negroes of Africa, the Indians seldom worshipped or made fetishes of these amulets, because they were not the actual repositories of power but only symbols, and, therefore, useless without the special visions and contacts with the supernatural world that gave them validity. So an Indian whose guardian spirit seemed to fail him in a crisis often threw away its symbol, and the victorious warrior who stripped an enemy of his charms derived no benefit from them. Still less did the Indians worship the other amulets with which they bedecked their persons, amulets not connected with the doctrine of a guardian spirit, but founded on sympathetic or associative magic. Thus Eskimo women living near the magnetic pole sewed the skins

[1] "Jesuit Relations," vol. xxiii, p. 155.
[2] Cf. Catlin, G.: Op. cit., p. 36 ff.
[3] "Jesuit Relations," vol. xxv, pp. 123-125.

of terns to their garments that they might endow their unborn sons with the skill of the tern in fishing, and some Indians on the plains carried curious natural stones[1] shaped like miniature buffaloes to give them good luck and success in hunting. Their attitude here was not different from that of the European who carried a lucky coin in his pocket, or who stuck pins into an image of wax in order to create shooting pains in his enemy.

52789

Sarcee medicine-pipe bundle resting on a horse travois outside the owner's tipi; the head-dress associated with the bundle is covered beneath the blanket. *(Photo by D. Jenness.)*

In the opinion of most Indians guardian spirits could neither be inherited nor transferred; they protected only the individuals who had acquired them by prayer and fasting, and each generation had to repeat the quest anew. But the dwellers on the plains modified the doctrine. Without abolishing the usual quest they held that a man might purchase a vision and with it the blessing originally imparted by the supernatural world. In practice this led to the ritual buying and selling of visions and their symbols when they seemed to possess peculiar efficacy, and ultimately some of the plains' tribes came to

---

[1] Frequently fossils.

own several " medicine-bundles " that were sanctified by antiquity, accorded the highest social value, and impressively transferred from one individual to another, generation after generation.

In a sphere like religion, which was largely dominated by emotion, the Indians naturally displayed great individual differences. Those who were intensely emotional, or endowed with keen imaginations, easily persuaded themselves that they could commune with the supernatural world and draw upon its resources at will. Visions came to them in the day as well as by night. Sometimes they fell into trances, or induced a condition of hysteria which both they and their fellow-countrymen interpreted as possession by a spiritual force. Their apparent intimacy with the unseen powers marked them off from the rank and file of the natives, who sought their mediation in times of trouble. So they became the medicine men or shamans of their communities, prophets and seers and healers of diseases, or else sorcerers and witch-mongers whenever they used their talents for antisocial purposes. Sometimes the medicine-men and the sorcerers formed two separate classes, the former working openly for the welfare of their tribesmen, the latter secretly, and under penalty of sudden death if their machinations became known. Often the same man (or woman) stood ready to fulfil either rôle for a suitable reward, although caution generally prevented him from directing his sorcery against the members of his own band or village. Youthful aspirants commonly apprenticed themselves to older practitioners, and frequently developed a professional technique after the fashion of doctors in civilized communities. Some even tried to heighten their prestige by conscious jugglery, performing several sensational tricks that are well known from other countries, such as sword-swallowing and walking over red-hot embers.

Here and there in Canada the medicine-men banded themselves into guilds or fraternities, the most notable, perhaps, being the *midewiwin* or medicine-lodge of the Ojibwa. The higher grade members in this lodge exercised great influence in the various bands, and the summer initiation ceremonies attracted spectators from far and near. Organized priesthoods, especially among primitive peoples, tend to develop esoteric doctrines different from those of the laity, and there is some evidence that the religious beliefs of the ordinary Ojibwa were cruder and more animistic than those officially

Tlinkit medicine-man and his incantations. (Reproduced from an illustration by Edward de Groffs, Sitka, Alaska).

expounded by their medicine-lodge. But any chasm that existed was comparatively small, for the aborigines of Canada, even their medicine-men, seem to have been incapable of the flights of philosophical fancy that were so characteristic of the priesthoods in Polynesia.

The secret societies of the Pacific coast were primarily religious organizations, fraternities of initiates who, like the worshippers of Dionysos and Orpheus, had placed themselves under the patronage of certain supernatural powers. They retained this simple character when they spread to the natives in the interior of British Columbia, never attaining (at least among the Carriers) the tremendous social and political influence which they exerted on the coast. During the winter festivals of the Kwakiutl and other southern tribes the members impersonated their patrons and deliberately deceived the uninitiated, who firmly believed the grotesque masked figures parading in their midst to be supernatural beings from above. But these western secret societies often restricted their membership to the upper classes; and they used their power for social purposes only, not for the moral or spiritual uplift of the people. So, although they stimulated the arts of sculpture and painting, they did not progress, like the mysteries of the Mediterranean world, beyond the crude beliefs of the laity, or attain to any higher plane in either ethics or religion.

In the weakly organized tribes of eastern and northern Canada the medicine-men always played a very important rôle, their influence depending solely on their individual personalities. A man of strong character could become both the spiritual and the political leader of his band, its bulwark against foes of the visible and of the invisible realm alike. But in the south and west, where the communities were more firmly knit together, the medicine-men as a class held a definitely subordinate place. The official heads of the tribal religions were not necessarily medicine-men at all, but leaders in the civil life. The Iroquois appointed special sacerdotal officers, " Keepers of the Faith ", to supervise all matters pertaining to religion and to officiate at festivals. On the plains any Indian of wealth and standing could acquire one of the coveted medicine-bundles, and the chief, not the medicine-men, regulated the time and place of the sun-dance. Among the Kwakiutl, Bella Coola, and other tribes of the Pacific coast the heads of the various "houses" and clans maintained a careful control over the secret societies and invariably occupied the most important seats at all public ceremonies. There is no indication that any Canadian tribe, except perhaps the Ojibwa, would ever have evolved a powerful priesthood exercising supreme authority in the religious sphere, comparable with the priesthoods that have arisen at many different levels of civilization, and in many different parts of the world, including the North American continent itself.

Dance of Haida (?) Indians at Esquimalt, B.C. *(Reproduced, through the courtesy of the Royal Ontario Museum of Archæology, from a painting by Paul Kane.)*

The crude beliefs of the aborigines could not withstand the impact of European civilization without considerable reinterpretation. The early missionaries and settlers derided or condemned their dreams and visions as foolish illusions, or as traffic with the hosts of Satan. Amulets and charms that might seem to have guarded against sickness in earlier days failed absolutely to mitigate the terrible ravages of the newly introduced plagues, smallpox and measles. The medicine-men who summoned their supernatural helpers, beat their drums, and shook their rattles, themselves fell victims to the diseases that carried off their kinsmen. European trappers and traders disregarded with impunity regulations and taboos that had been scrupulously observed for untold centuries, and branded as idle superstition things that had been held most sacred from the remotest antiquity. It was useless to pretend (as the more conservative natives still do in certain places) that the Indian and the white man

706

A Kwakiutl house with legendary figures painted on its front. *(Photo by G. M. Dawson.)*

were radically different, that the religion that was good for the one might not be good for the other, and that each race ought to follow in the footsteps of its forefathers. Both the economic and the social conditions had changed. It was the white man, not the supernatural beings of the old-time Indian's world, who now controlled many of the necessary and desirable things of life, firearms and ammunition, steel knives and hatchets, glass beads, woollen cloth, and all the gew-gaws of civilization. The Indian who followed in his forefather's footsteps, who clung to the old religion and observed all the old ceremonies and taboos, seriously handicapped himself in the competition with his fellow-tribesman who imitated the dress and customs of the new rulers of the land and from conviction or self-interest embraced Christianity. The old religion had to change under the changed conditions if it was to survive at all. In most places, of course, it has not survived, even although it has so determined the interpretation of the newer faith that some of its elements still hold their ground wherever the Indians preserve a semblance of their former life. Yet here and there before it yielded it did make a resolute attempt to set its house in order and to adjust itself to the altered environment.

The principal adjustment was in the direction of pure monotheism. Every tribe had possessed a sky-god who ranked among the higher supernatural beings, even if he did not always occupy the foremost place. In reaction to Christian teaching the Indians exalted him into a " Great Spirit " of righteousness, the master of the universe and the direct author of all that happens here below. It is true that the Hurons and the plains' tribes had almost reached this conception in pre-European days,[1] but they had failed to emphasize the moral nature of their sky-god and had allowed the doctrine to remain entangled in a mass of polytheistic beliefs and a still cruder nature-worship. The clash with Christianity purified their notions, and the impulse toward monotheism extended to other tribes.[2] Yet the " Great Spirit " still remained a peculiarly Indian god who favoured his redskin children, although he had allowed them to pass under the rule of the white man; and many natives dreamed of a day when he would banish the usurpers to their homes across the sea, and restore the country to its rightful possessors.[3]

Out of these dreams and garbled versions of Christian teaching arose some curious religious revivals instigated by Indians who claimed to have received direct revelations from the sky. Best known of these is the " New Religion " propagated by a Seneca sachem named Handsome Lake in the closing years of the eighteenth century. His followers, numerous even to-day among the Iroquois, assert that three spiritual beings sent by the Great Spirit restored him to life as he lay insensible on his couch, showed him the torments that the evil-minded endure in the future life, and sent him

[1] It is not impossible that the imperfect monotheism of these Indians was itself a very early reaction to vague Christian ideas carried from tribe to tribe across the continent before any white explorers reached the far interior.

[2] For a recent example among the Eskimo, See Rasmussen, Knud: " Across Arctic America," ch. xxviii (New York, 1927).

[3] The Indians of northern British Columbia, particularly the Tsimshian, still talk occasionally of " driving the white man back to Boston," i.e., to the United States.

forth to preach the gospel of temperance and morality.[1] Similar but cruder revivals spread northward during the nineteenth century from the state of Oregon through the Salish and Carrier tribes to the Sekani, at the headwaters of the Peace river; and symptoms of the same phenomenon appeared in the Mackenzie basin. But the movement in these regions was of short duration, and after this dying protest from their old religion the natives immediately transferred their allegiance to the Christian church.

---

[1] For details *See* Morgan, L. H.: Op. cit., pp. 217-248. Parker, A. C.: " The Code of Handsome Lake"; New York State Mus., Bull. 163 (Albany, 1912).

CHAPTER XIII

FOLK-LORE AND TRADITIONS

Very few men in civilized or uncivilized communities have the gift of genuine creation. They can modify and improve on what is known already, but they cannot evolve an entirely new style of architecture, or a type of literature unlike any that has gone before. Similarly, when a people borrows folk-tales from surrounding peoples —and tales, or at least incidents in them, are transmitted more easily perhaps than anything else—it cannot assimilate them if they differ radically from its own folk-tales, but modifies them to conform to ideas and patterns that are already familiar and imposes on them the individuality inherent in its own legends and traditions. A few tales, of course, often remain imperfectly assimilated and preserve their alien flavour. Nevertheless, taken in the aggregate, the folk-lore of each people has its own peculiar character, and mirrors, often with great clearness, the lives and thoughts of its exponents.

The absence of writing among the Indians gave their folk-lore (using that word in its broadest significance) a higher and more important rôle than it possesses in civilized countries. It supplied the place of text-books in the education of the children, teaching them the traditional history, morality, and religion of their tribes both directly and through the ceremonies that in many cases dramatized the tales. In British Columbia men used the folk-tales as public records, citing them to prove their claims to various rights and privileges, such as that of painting certain emblems on their houses. On the plains men validated their sacred medicine bundles by the legends attached to them, and in the east they established the claims of their bands to certain hunting and fishing territories by the recital of ancient traditions. There were many tales so closely interwoven with the social and religious life of the British Columbia and plains' Indians that they were considered personal property, and although known to other individuals might be recited only by their owners or at certain definite times and places. It was as though the stories attached to the name of Aeneas might be told only by the kings of Rome and their descendants, or the legend of Isis and Serapis only by the high priests of the temples when they officiated at the unveiling of the statues of the great mother.

It is not possible to distinguish in Indian folk-lore between myths in which supernatural beings play a leading rôle, historical or

62152

Bella Coola Indian dramatizing the supernatural being Echo.
(Photo by Harlan I. Smith.)

quasi-historical traditions, and simple folk-tales where the only, or at least the principal, characters are human beings. We might attempt, with more success, to discriminate these elements in Homer, for when the tales concerning the fall of Troy and the wanderings of Odysseus obtained their present form, the world of Olympus and heroes of semi-divine birth had receded into a distant past, and the ordinary mortal pursued his course through life without thought of visible interference from the unseen supernatural powers. But the world of the supernatural has always seemed very close to the Indians from the most ancient times down to to-day. It figures even in personal narratives of the nineteenth century, vitiating many accounts of their early contacts with Europeans that in all other respects appear historical.

Abandoning, then, the usual classification into myths, traditions, and folk-tales proper, we may profitably adopt a division that the Indians themselves employed. Every tribe, except those in the extreme north of Canada, separated its tales into two cycles, those that referred to the world of to-day with its familiar mountains, lakes, and rivers, and those that related to a supposedly earlier epoch before the earth and its inhabitants had assumed their present form.[1] In that mythical "golden age," the Indians believed, man could freely communicate with the animals, which had the same thoughts, the same emotions as human beings and could even lay aside their animal dress at will. But mighty tricksters or heroes transformed the world, and a chasm began to separate man and the animals, which could no longer discard their animal forms except in their homes, far removed from human view,[2] or on special occasions when they visited the fasting Indian to confer on him their blessing.[3]

The folk-lore of the first cycle, then, inevitably abounds in nature tales, especially tales in which animals are the principal actors. There are anecdotes about beaver and mice, about a contest between owl and squirrel (resembling our "Fox and Crow"), and endless other stories of a similar character. No one has yet explained satisfactorily why such tales should have appealed to nearly every people both in the new world and the old.[4] Not that they are exactly alike in all

---

[1] There are, of course, many border-line tales which might fall into either category.

[2] Many, perhaps most, Indians believed that each species had its individual home, where the animals could assume human form and live like human beings.

[3] Radin's interpretation of the Indian's guardian-spirit would make his visitor not the individual animal, but the prototype of the species. "Anthropology in North America," by Franz Boas, Roland B. Dixon, Pliny E. Goddard, A. A. Goldenweiser, A. Hrdlicka, William H. Holmes, Robert H. Lowie, Paul Radin, John R. Swanton, and Clark Wissler, pp. 283-291 (New York, 1915). This seems to represent the view of some philosophical medicine-man rather than of the lay Indian.

[4] Boas suggests as one reason that the individual animal in these tales is confused with the species, which is permanent and known to every generation, whereas human actors must be distinguished by individual names which in time lose their significance (ibid., p. 343).

regions. The negroes of west Africa portray the animal actors in considerable detail, ascribing to them all the characteristics and emotions proper to man himself. The Indians of Canada, on the other hand, generally make of each animal a type, as in the fables of Æsop. The coyote is a treacherous creature, the wolverine both treacherous and gluttonous, the deer timid, the raven greedy, the buffalo brave and honourable but rather stupid. Many of their tales, however, lack even this amount of characterization, and a bird or animal has no other identity than that afforded by its name and outward description.

More interesting than these nature tales are the ætiological and genealogical myths and the trickster and hero stories that are also attached to the first cycle. The Iroquoians and Eastern Algonkians have given us long cosmogonic myths in which the various episodes follow each other in more or less logical sequence. Another systematic account comes from Bella Coola, on the Pacific coast, where the Indians had a fantastic but unusually well-ordered conception of the universe and its origin, built around the belief in the sky-god Alkuntam. Elsewhere these tales are short and utterly disjointed, even when the same characters figure as the principal actors. Nearly every tribe has in fact numerous tales that flatly contradict one another, for there was no organized priesthood to collate all the versions, reducing them to harmony, and individual families handed down their own traditions regardless of whether they conflicted or not with the traditions of their neighbours.

Although the Indians had innumerable ætiological myths explaining, for example, how daylight began, why winter and summer alternate, why the raven is black and the sea-gull white, and why the chipmunk has stripes along its back, yet there were no true creation stories, no myths attributing to the will of a creator the genesis of stars and planets, earth and water, day and night, the seasons, animals, and plants.[1] The great Manitous or high deities of the Indians were not " fathers of gods and men," like Zeus and Brahma, and they could not be invoked as the ultimate causes of all things. Apparently the Indians felt no necessity for an ultimate cause, but assumed that the phenomena of nature had always existed some-

---

[1] Boas: Op. cit., p. 325 f. Boas there states that the only Indians in America north of Mexico who possessed true creation myths were some tribes in northern California.

where, and in their ætiological myths merely described how they had been brought into their present relationship with man.

The principal character in many of these myths is a powerful "trickster" known to the different tribes under various names. The Algonkians of eastern Canada call him Glooscap, Nanibush, or Wisakedjak; the plains' Indians name him "the Old Man"; the Salish Indians of British Columbia identify him with the coyote; and the Pacific Coast tribes with the raven. Whatever his name, animal or otherwise, he is always what the Carriers call him, "the trickster", who delights in playing pranks on every one and everything. He invites the ducks to a new kind of feast so that he may twist their necks while they are dancing, and he frightens away his daughters with a rumour of enemies that he may surreptitiously eat all their food. The tales of his adventures and misadventures (for as often as not he over-reaches himself) would fill an entire book. They provided the folk-lore with a comic element that never failed to amuse the Indians, old and young alike.

Another group of tales widely spread over the Dominion relates how the "trickster", or else a separate culture hero, roams over the earth rearranging phenomena and destroying all the devouring monsters that prey upon mankind. There was no place for altruism in the character of the "trickster" himself, so that whenever he appears as the hero of these tales he performs his services unintentionally, merely to gratify his personal whims. But whenever there is a separate character, as among the Carriers, we have a hero analogous to Perseus or St. Andrew, a genuine crusader who fights and sometimes dies for the cause of humanity. Many tales in this group afford interesting glimpses of tribal life during pre-European days, and a few reveal touches of true romanticism. Thus in one Carrier story the hero begins life as a despised orphan, marries the daughter of a powerful chief through the help of his supernatural guardian, wins fame and honour by his skill and courage and becomes the champion of the countryside. After destroying various monsters that ravage the villages he receives a mortal wound in the death agonies of a supernatural lynx. His countrymen then carry home his body for honourable burial, but his widow, overwhelmed with grief because a faulty stitch in his moccasin had caused his death, commits suicide.

In the tales of the second cycle, those that refer to the world of to-day, human actors definitely gain the foreground and animals drop back to a secondary place. The Indians believed—and in many regions still believe—that a stump could momentarily change to a man, that the caribou could push back the hood from its face and gaze out of a human countenance, that the snake or the owl could

73462

"Legend of the burning buffalo grass," a ceremony held by the Blackfoot at the first full moon in June. *(Photo by Canadian National Railways.)*

address the sleeping Indian in his own tongue. These things, however, happened rarely and not to all individuals, whereas there were many other tales of equal interest that they could narrate around their fires; adventures of the chase and of war, experiences of travellers among distant tribes, rivalries of chiefs and of medicine-men, medicine paraphernalia and their histories, and the ever-changing incidents of village and camp life. Each tribe, of course, set its own stamp on these anecdotes, making them conform to certain patterns and reflect its own social life. The Eskimo had few tales of animals transforming themselves into men, but many stories of encounters with strange half-human beings, of shamans and their conflicts, of blood-feuds and quarrels over women, of orphans who grew up to avenge the murders of their parents, of famines, and long journeys by land and sea in search of food. The Indians on the coast of British Columbia told of the rivalry of chiefs, of potlatches and the struggles for wealth and position, and of journeys up and down the coast for trade and warfare.[1] From the plains there are anecdotes of the march and of the buffalo hunt, accounts of the search for medicine-power and of the origins of amulets and medicine-bundles, and endless stories of raids for scalps and horses. Tales of war and of medicine-power were popular, also, among the Iroquoians and eastern Algonkians, but these tribes have absorbed so many European tales during the last three centuries that it is not easy to disentangle their original folk-lore, except the myths that belong to the first cycle.

It is noticeable that in every area, but particularly on the plains, many tales are frankly modelled on exactly the same plot. A story that describes the origin of a certain medicine-bundle will be repeated with the change of a few names for several other bundles, as though this particular plot has carried a special appeal. Another stylistic feature, common in European folk-lore also,[2] is the repetition of the same incident over and over again for the purpose of holding the listener in suspense and retaining his interest. Thus in a Tsimshian tale a woman cries out for aid, and the animals come one after another to offer their services. Each asks the same question and receives the same answer, until the words become a refrain that lingers in the mind and serves as a text for the entire story. Many plains' and west coast tales specialize in repeating the incident four times. Four brothers in succession will start out on a journey and only the youngest be successful, or a man will undergo four tests and succeed only at the last. In this respect the folk-lore parallels some of the religious rituals, which were commonly repeated four times; and it reminds us of the use of the number seven in the ancient rituals and folk-lore of western Asia.

---

[1] Boas has successfully reconstructed many phases in the social life of the Tsimshian solely from their mythology (Boas, F.: "Tsimshian Mythology," p. 393 et seq. 31st Ann. Rept., Bur. Am. Ethn., 1909-1910 (Washington, 1916)). Such a procedure however, requires extraordinary caution. The Sekani Indians at the headwaters of Peace river, for example, absorbed many myths from the Carriers and Tsimshian which pre-suppose potlatches and distinctions of rank, although neither ever became established among the Sekani.

[2] Cf. the story of the "Three Billy-Goats that go to the Mountain."

The most noteworthy feature about Indian folk-lore, however, is its purely anecdotal character. The emotions it portrays are few and simple—fear and anger, pity and love, jealousy and hatred—and even these are implied rather than expressed. Nowhere is there any attempt to analyse the characters, to depict their motives, or to introduce any psychological reflections. The stories relate nothing but events, and either end as soon as an incident is complete or pass on immediately to the next episode without comment. The moral tales familiar to us from other parts of the world found little favour in Indian literature, which seldom condemns wrongdoing or represents the coward and villain as more unfortunate than the brave and upright. It is true that one or two tribes in British Columbia, notably the Tahltan and the Carrier, had a kind of moral tale, and that they even emphasized the moral by a short sentence at the conclusion. Such are the stories of abused orphans who receive the aid of supernatural powers in avenging their wrongs, stories that end with expressions like " do not mock the poor." But even among these tribes the moral sentence often seems little more than a stylistic feature, a convenient literary device for bringing a tale to its conclusion. It is seldom the true *raison d'être* of the story or an integral part of it, for other tribes that relate exactly the same tales omit the appended moral.

Although they were not moral in form, a large proportion of the tales undoubtedly had a considerable ethical influence, especially when narrated at night in the fitful firelight by some old man or woman who could add the comments suggested by a long experience of life. Public recitals of war-exploits, too, such as occurred among the Iroquoians before they set out on the war-path, stimulated the youths to military valour. The great " sun-dance festival " of the Blackfoot, at which the whole tribe extolled the purity of the sun-dance woman and her predecessor, the warriors recited their earlier deeds, and the elder men related the tribal traditions, had something of the character of a prolonged spiritual revival;[1] while in British Columbia the personal ownership of many tales, and their elaborate dramatization at public festivals under the mantle of religion, gave them the inherent value and force that we associate only with the stories of the Old Testament.

---

[1] The sun-dance, of course, had other aspects besides the religious and moral. It provided an opportunity for social reunions and for much gaiety and festivity.

The historical value of Indian traditions is comparatively slight, their value, that is to say, to the ethnologist who seeks to reconstruct the origins, migrations, and developments of the various tribes. For this there are several reasons. In the first place the traditions are not fixed even in a single tribe, but the versions given by one family contradict those of another so frequently as to cast doubt upon the credibility of them all. We should not expect complete agreement, of course. That was lacking even in Polynesia, where the traditions of the natives were the special concern of a priesthood that strove to hand them on unchanged from one generation to another.[1] But in Indian tribal traditions there is scarcely a semblance of agreement concerning movements and events in pre-European times. Even on the Pacific coast, where the nobles were so deeply engrossed in matters of rank and inheritance that they kept count of potlatches and debts for three or four generations, traditions of events that happened more than a century and a half ago show little congruity, so that we cannot rely upon them unless they are supported by considerations of another character. It would almost seem that the Indians lacked interest in plain, historical facts, or at least found them difficult to understand without invoking such a wealth of supernatural causes and interferences that to-day we cannot separate the fanciful from the real. Many other peoples would have preserved fairly reliable records of a great constitutional change such as the formation of the League of the Iroquois, which commenced only about the time of Columbus and was not perfected until a century later. Yet, although we know the names of its principal founders, Dekanawida and Hiawatha, we have very little authentic information concerning their lives, which have become swallowed up in impossible legends.

Another reason for the unreliability of Indian traditions is the manner in which they were re-interpreted as they spread from tribe to tribe. There are stories that are known almost from one end of the Dominion to the other, as well as to many tribes in the United States. Waterman cites a good example.[2] It is a tale about a girl and a dog, which is quoted by certain Eskimo tribes to explain the origin of sea mammals, by others to explain the origin and diffusion

---

[1] Percy Smith collected in New Zealand and Rarotonga long genealogies that traced back the history of certain families for nine or ten centuries. The earlier portions of the two lists, which covered the period preceding the separation of the Maoris of New Zealand from the Rarotongans, virtually coincide, so accurately had each island group preserved its traditions.

[2] Waterman, T. T.: " The Explanatory Element in the Folk-Tales of the North American Indians"; Jour. of American Folk-Lore, vol. xxvii, pp. 24, 28 et seq. (1914).

of the different races of mankind. The Tlinkit Indians repeat the same story to account for the Milky Way, and the Blackfoot Indians to explain the origin of their " dog society," an organization of comparatively recent growth. There are tribes that make it explanatory of nothing, but narrate it as a mere anecdote. The story is highly fantastic, and obviously nothing but an ancient folk-tale variously re-interpreted by the different tribes to suit their needs. Even if it were not a tissue of impossibilities, we should certainly err if we regarded it as the true explanation of the Blackfoot " dog society." Similarly we often find two tribes with the same migration tradition, although it can hardly be true of both. New myths and new traditions arose so easily, indeed,[1] that even when a tradition seems purely local and contains no improbable episodes we dare not accept its authenticity unless we can adduce other evidence to its support.

Practically the only value the folk-tales possess for reconstructing the earlier history of the Indians comes from an analytical study of their diffusion. If two tribes now widely separated both relate the same complex story, we know that they have been in contact with each other at some period in their history, or else that one or both of them has derived it from an intermediate tribe. Tales like the girl and dog story, mentioned above, are so ancient that we can hardly hope to discover their original sources or to trace the historical contacts suggested by their present diffusion. There are certain themes, such as stories about giants and dwarfs, that may even belong to the infancy of the human race, and have reached America with the first immigrants. Others, again, are so simple and natural that they could spring up in any country, and their distribution has no historical significance. Thus both our Indians and the aborigines of Australia have a tradition concerning a great flood, which we cannot reasonably connect with the biblical account or with each other. Still, when we find among the Chukchee and Koryak tribes of northeastern Asia, and again on the Pacific coast of Canada, a whole series of similar anecdotes in which the raven plays a leading part, and when we are confident that these anecdotes were current in both regions before the arrival of Europeans, we can safely assume that the two groups of natives, although now separated by hundreds of miles, were

---

[1] The Hopi Indians of Arizona have a myth to explain the origin of horses, although horses reached America only with the Spaniards. Waterman: Op. cit., p. 33.

at one time in direct or indirect contact or sprang perhaps from the same stock.

In spite of the example just quoted, the comparative study of folk-tales has hitherto yielded little result. This is partly due no doubt to the disruption of the tribes by European colonization and the fur trade, which brought the Iroquois across the Rocky mountains and the Cree to the delta of the Mackenzie river. The extensive dissemination of folk-tales produced by these historic movements now conceals their true diffusion in pre-European times. It is safer to rely on culture elements less easily transmitted, such as resemblances in social organization or material possessions, and to use the folk-lore as subordinate evidence.

As commonly recorded by ethnologists, Indian folk-lore seems dull and dreary to the average European. It is derived in most cases through a native not thoroughly conversant with English and unable with his limited vocabulary to translate or explain the full implications of the words or episodes. An ethnologist rarely speaks any Indian language fluently, and the more literary he makes his texts the more likely he is to misinterpret the originals. Yet the fault lies less with the ethnologist than with the stories themselves. Our psychological background does not permit us to adopt the attitude of the Indian and to look for supernatural interferences in the most pedestrian events. It offends our reason and destroys our interest to find this obtruding on every page, especially when it takes a form not familiar in European mythology. Moreover, most of us have outgrown the stage of enjoying mere anecdotes and prefer literature of a less superficial character. Doubtless certain animal tales are suitable for children, and some of the traditions provide excellent material for a writer of romances who can select what he pleases and build up the remainder according to his fancy. But the vast bulk of the folk-lore carries no popular appeal and is of interest to the professional ethnologist alone.

Nevertheless, a few tales, a very few, stand out like flowers from a tangle of bushes and deserve the brush of a great artist. Such is the Tsimshian story given below, which in spite of its exoticism and impossibilities appeals to our hearts on account of its warm humanity: [1]

---

[1] Unpublished MS. belonging to the author.

56880

Bella Coola Indian wearing the "Thunder" mask. *(Photo by Harlan I. Smith.)*

"The son of a chief married a girl of his own village. They lived happily together for many months, and the woman was about to bear a child. One morning she awoke very ill; by evening she was worse, and at midnight she died, the child being still unborn. The people mourned over her body for two days, and buried her on the morning of the third day.

The husband, stricken with grief, slept each night on his wife's grave. The people carried presents of food to him, but he declined to eat. At last his mother went and begged him to eat; and he entered her house and ate whatever she offered him. But at night he returned to his wife's grave and slept there.

The weather grew colder, and snow began to cover the ground. At first he cleared it away from the grave and slept on the bare ground; but when the snow grew deeper and the cold more rigorous he slept in his hut.

Spring came, and he went to visit his wife's grave again. As he drew near it he saw a little boy gathering fireweed;[1] very quietly it entered the grave with a bunch of flowers, then came out again and began to pick more. The man concealed himself and watched. Sometimes the boy gathered flowers and took them inside the grave, sometimes he gathered other things. And all the time the man watched from his hiding place.

Now, as he pondered over this, he determined to try and catch the child. He returned to his house, speaking to no one, took down his tools, and made four tiny bows, which he covered with red paint. Next he cut some branches of the saskatoon tree and made four tiny arrows, which he feathered with great care. The villagers were glad to see him working again, although they did not know what he was doing, for they grieved that he should weep each day at his wife's grave.

Three days after he had first seen the boy the man returned to the grave, carrying his bows and arrows in a bag upon his back. Again he saw the boy, who was now a little bigger. When he entered the grave the man ran forward and planted a bow and arrow in the ground near by. He planted the second bow and arrow a little farther down the trail toward the village, and the third and fourth a little farther still. Then he hid and waited.

---

[1] Like the leaves on the trees, the child is born in the spring.

Soon the boy came out of the grave again. He laughed softly when he saw the first bow and arrow, and ran to examine them. At first he seemed afraid to touch them with his hands; but presently he pulled out the arrow and looked at it. It was very beautiful, and a low laugh escaped him as he strung it on the bow and began to play with it. Looking around, he saw the second bow and arrow, and ran to get them likewise. Now he noticed the third, and, dropping the first two sets, which were rather heavy for him, he ran to gather them also. Both the third and fourth he gathered up and carried inside the grave, then returned a few moments later for the first and second. The man waited for some time longer, but when the boy did not reappear, he returned home pondering.

Now he made six more bows and arrows and set them out in the same way as before; and the boy came out of the grave and gathered them. Many more he made and also told his parents what he had seen. Twelve of the most noted medicine-men gathered in his father's house while he went out and planted them about six feet apart in a long line that led from the grave to the village. Then he rejoined the people in the house and they waited.

The boy was growing bigger now. He came out of the grave. gathered the bows and arrows three at a time, and returned for more All day he worked, carrying his burdens into the grave; and nearer and nearer he approached the village, while the medicine-men watched him in silence through the part-open door. The last bow and arrow had been planted in the ground just behind the house. Thither the boy came, timidly, to draw it out; but just as he turned to go back the chief medicine-man ran swiftly and silently behind him, in a kind of trance, and caught him in his hands. The boy gave one frightened cry and shrivelled almost to nothing. The other medicine-men inside the house shook their rattles and sang their songs. They approached the child, one by one, and breathed on him, trying to restore him to life. Then they carried him inside the house, and sang over him for three days and three nights. On the fourth day the boy became truly alive. He was the man's own son, who had been buried in the grave with his mother but had been granted the semblance of life because of the father's constant weeping.

The boy was now alive, but he was not happy. He would not eat, but cried night and day. The villagers, unable to rest, called in a wise woman from another village and promised to pay her bountifully if she would cure the child. She came and listened to his weeping and to his constant cry 'Dihl he Dihl he'; and she laughed as she heard the words. 'I thought it was something big and great that the child wanted,' she said. 'What he wants is only a little thing. He craves for the full free life of man, not the half life he enjoyed in the grave. He wants his cousin to accompany him half-way up yonder mountain where the giant spruce trees grow, and the people to set fire to the spruce trees so that the hot gum may fall on the bodies of them both as they stand underneath. Then the people must wash him and his cousin beneath a waterfall.'

As the old woman instructed they did. The hot gum that fell on the children's bodies they washed off beneath a tumbling waterfall. Thus the boy gained the full free life for which he craved, and cried no more.[1] The people named him " The Dead Woman's Son ". And the heart of his father was glad as he watched him hunting and playing with his cousin, both growing up to manhood together."

---

[1] All life is one. The gum that supplies life to the tree revived also the boy.

CHAPTER XIV

ORATORY AND DRAMA, MUSIC AND ART

Among the tribes of the plains and eastern woodlands the reciting of folk-tales at family gatherings and the recounting of war deeds or tribal legends at public festivals provided the Indians with a "school of rhetoric" for the development of those oratorical talents that in democratic communities seem indispensable for public leadership. Eloquence ranked second only to skill and courage in hunting and in war. So essential was it to every leader for the maintenance of his prestige and power that it provoked the exclamation from an early Jesuit missionary, "There is no place in the world where Rhetoric is more powerful than in Canada . . . It controls all these tribes, as the Captain is elected for his eloquence alone, and obeyed in proportion to his use of it, for they have no other law than his word."[1] In eastern Canada and on the plains the tribes were so loosely organized, and so frequently involved in war or engaged in communal hunts, that concerted action was impossible without unanimity in the tribal councils, and unanimity was impossible without the employment of every art of persuasion and rhetoric. The Pacific Coast natives with their sharp divisions into nobles, commoners, and slaves naturally laid greatest emphasis on lineage, but they also held eloquence in high esteem, and their public orators who functioned on ceremonial occasions were men of rank in the communities. Among the primitive northern tribes alone eloquence counted for little, because there the struggle for existence was so constant and the political organization so tenuous that prestige and authority came only from outstanding personality combined with physical prowess, success in hunting, or accredited influence over the spiritual world.

The Indians spoke slowly and deliberately, as a rule, but not haltingly, being rarely embarrassed for words in which to clothe their thoughts. They could develop an argument logically, and employed repetition, rhetorical questions, and sarcasm with telling effect. Wit and humour were conspicuously absent from their

---

[1] "Jesuit Relations," vol. v, p. 195.

speeches, for, unlike the Eskimo, they seldom relished jokes, either practical or verbal, and anything savouring of humour would have appeared highly undignified in a public oration.[1] Their sentences were short and straightforward, frequently adorned with similes and metaphors. Metaphors, indeed, had an unusual fascination for the eastern Indians, particularly the Iroquoians,[2] who frequently cast entire orations in this figure, so that when translated literally they sound florid and artificial to European ears. " Onontio," said the chief of an Iroquois embassy to the French governor at Quebec, " thou hast dispersed the clouds; the air is serene, the sky shows clearly; the sun is bright. I see no more trouble; peace has made everything calm; my heart is at rest; I go away very happy."[3] Like most orations, however, Indian utterances derived their force largely from the manner of their delivery and lost much of their effect when reduced to print. The invariable dignity of the orator, the easy flow of his words, and the magnificence of his gestures, preserved his speeches from the taint of bombast and justly earned him a very high reputation for eloquence.

Festivals, like council meetings, gave frequent opportunities for oratory, but even more for dancing. Some of the mimetic dances were primitive dramas—when a war party, for example, mimicked its attack on an enemy camp, or an Eskimo hunter his capture of a seal. Real drama with impersonation of characters and a slight attempt at stage setting occurred only on the Pacific coast, and among the interior tribes of British Columbia, who adopted part of the culture of the coast people. Some dramas were for entertainment purposes and for enhancing the prestige of particular individuals, as when a man impersonated the mythological being or animal that birthright made his distinguishing crest. Thus, only a few years ago a Carrier Indian, supported by relatives and friends, gave a special feast that would enable him to impersonate a caribou, a privilege he inherited from his uncle much as a feudal nobleman in Europe might have inherited the right to wear a certain robe. As the guests gathered near the feast-house two rifle shots resounded in

---

[1] There was much jesting, often very coarse, in the dramatic festivals of the west coast natives, but not in formal speeches.
[2] " Metaphor is largely in use among these peoples; unless you accustom yourself to it, you will understand nothing in their councils, where they speak almost entirely in metaphors." " Jesuit Relations," vol. x, p. 219.
[3] " Jesuit Relations," vol. xxvii, p. 303.

the vicinity and a fictitious caribou, bounding from the woods, headed toward the rear entrance, followed by two hunters wearing the full accoutrements of the chase. When the people flocked inside the building, the mock caribou leaped from behind a curtain into their midst and as quickly leaped from sight again. Dancing and feasting followed this simple drama, which was enacted in broad daylight and served only to enhance the actor's prestige.

58522

Actors in the "Cannibal" dance, Bella Coola. *(Photo by Harlan I. Smith.)*

More solemn, and often more elaborate, were the religious dramas performed at night by secret societies and visible only by the flickering firelight that left the recesses of the feast-houses in deep gloom. Men dressed as wolves howled eerily, masked figures representing supernatural beings stalked about the hall, and monstrous birds and animals, carved of wood and operated by hidden ropes, descended mysteriously from the roof or rose through concealed doors from beneath the floor. The uninitiated audiences gazed awestruck on these ceremonies, not knowing how the marvels were produced and fully convinced that the supernatural world had taken visible form in their midst.

One of the most remarkable of these performances was the " mystery " play in which the Bella Coola Indians and their neighbours at Kimsquit depicted the regeneration of nature in the spring. Actors of small stature, wearing different masks, represented the various shrubs and trees of the district; two " old women " played the part of midwives; the " south wind," arrayed as a handsome young man, was the doctor who repelled attacks from a life-destroying " north wind "; and Mother Nature herself was a large wooden figure seated in the middle of the room just behind the fire. She gave birth first to the willow, a lively sprite who danced around the fire before disappearing behind a curtain. The gooseberry followed him, then the nettle, grass, the black cottonwood, the aspen, and all the other plants, to the number of two or three hundred, in the order of their sprouting.[1] No doubt both the acting and the stage settings were crude and even coarse, yet it was true drama that strove to represent a really beautiful idea.

The Indians spent weeks and months in rehearsing for these performances and in practising the songs that accompanied them. Virtuosos were engaged to compose the songs, and special craftsmen to manufacture the necessary paraphernalia, which was secretly destroyed at the conclusion of the ceremonies. Drama stimulated the arts of carving and painting by placing a premium on ingenuity, since individuals and villages often rivalled one another in the magnificence of their displays. Yet much of the elaborate stage-setting in vogue during the nineteenth century was probably due to the introduction of iron tools and the use of appliances like hinges and pulleys that were unknown in pre-European days. Very few early explorers saw the secret dances, and the exoteric performances of at least one tribe, the sophisticated Nootka, were changing even in Vancouver's day, as Menzies' Journal bears witness: " During this time a number of the Natives were equipping themselves in the

---

[1] McIlwraith, T. F.: Op. cit.

adjacent houses, and now assembled at the Chief's door in a group of the most grotesque figures that can possibly be imagined, dressed, armed, and masked in imitation of various characters of different Countries, some represented Europeans armed with Muskets and Bayonets, others were dressed as Chinese and others as Sandwich Islanders armed with Club and Spears; the rest were equipped either as Warriors or Hunters of their own nation. After a party of them armed with long spears entered and were drawn up at the further end of the House, the Actors came in one at a time and traversed the Area before us, with the most antic gestures. If a Warrior he showed the different evolutions of attacking an enemy, sometimes crouching down, sometimes retreating, at other times advancing with firm steps and eyes steadily fixed on the Commanders who were seated in the middle of our group, and to whom all their feigned aims and motions were directed, sometimes with much pointed archness as to occasion some alarm of their intentions being real. The Hunters equipped with various marks and implements, shewd all the wiles and stratagems usual in taking or chasing different Animals as Deer, Bears, etc. While those armed with Muskets represented Sentinels or went through various motions of the manual exercise. And those representing the Sandwich Islanders traversed the Area in the different attitudes of wielding their Clubs or darting their Spears, and as each finished his part he retreated back and took his station among the masked group at the further end of the house."[1]

In the secret society dramas of the Pacific coast and the religious ceremonies of many other tribes any mistake in the performance of a ritual song was regarded so seriously that it frequently invalidated the entire ceremony and occasionally led to the death of the unfortunate culprit.[2] For just as the old Greek bard attributed his minstrelsy to Apollo, and the mediæval churchman derived his hymns from some divine inspiration. so the Indians ascribed many of their songs to dreams and visions in which they were brought into close communion with the supernatural powers and received the songs as blessings. Singing furnished both their poetry and their music, for they recognized no rhythm in language apart from song, and there

---

1 Menzies: Op. cit., pp. 118-119.
2 To avoid such a catastrophe some British Columbia tribes appointed men with unusually retentive memories to lead the singing and give the cue for the proper changes, since there were often as many as fifteen or twenty songs in a single ceremony.

were no true musical instruments except the primitive flageolet of eastern Canada.

They had many varieties of songs—dance songs, game songs, ritual songs, songs of war, of love, and of medicine—not every variety,

50918

A Coronation Gulf Eskimo with his drum. *(Photo by Sir G. Hubert Wilkins.)*

of course, invariably present in every tribe. Most of them contained only a few significant words, many none at all, but merely vocables, for the words were generally of minor importance except in mocking songs like the nith songs of the Hudson Bay and Greenland Eskimo.

There were several reasons for this. In ritual songs handed down from one generation to another expressions became archaic and finally meaningless. Then there was a frequent transmission of songs from group to group and from tribe to tribe even when the latter spoke unrelated languages, and in such transfers both the words and the music underwent modification; so some of the ritual songs of the western Carrier contained what were undoubtedly Tsimshian words, although so greatly transformed that they were no longer intelligible. Often again the original compositions bore only catchwords whose explanations soon became lost. But perhaps the principal reason was that the emotions found their outlet not in the words[1] but in the music, the metre, the more or less variable rhythm, and the motor activities that accompanied the singing, just as we ourselves give little heed to the words of a dance song provided the music is pleasing and both rhythm and metre appropriate.

There was no part-singing in the music of the aborigines; men merely sang the melodies an octave lower because of the lower range of their voices. The songs were much more irregular than ours, for not only did the music modify the words (e.g., by changing their accents), but the words affected the melodies far more than we permit in our sophisticated art where the music is so often divorced from any text and developed for its own sake entirely. There were rhythmic patterns corresponding sometimes to our verses and refrains, but they were seldom uniform throughout a composition. The measures were generally in two, three, or four-part time, but sometimes also in five and even seven part; five-part time was fairly common on the Pacific coast.[2] Yet the natives seldom adhered to any strict measures, but altered the time continually, sometimes from exigencies of breath, sometimes to suit the words and their dominating accents. It is quite common, in fact, to find long, rhythmic units without any recognizable measures at all.

The octave naturally provided the basis for the musical scale, though most Indian songs ranged less than that interval and a play of melodies on octaves (apart from the differences in men's and women's voices) was rare. Its divisions, however, did not coincide exactly with the tones and semitones familiar to Europeans. The

[1] No doubt the words of new songs aroused some emotion, especially in their composers.
[2] Boas, F.: " Primitive Art," p. 340, Oslo, 1927.

natives constantly used intervals of less than a semitone, although it is not certain that they were a fixed part of the melodic systems.[1] There were both major and minor tonality, the major predominating as it does in most parts of the world, and the minor often expressing melancholy and doubt; but the full tone systems of our keys were lacking. Eskimo songs occasionally modulate from major to minor, an exceedingly rare feature in primitive music and hardly known in Indian songs. On the other hand, many Indian songs have a tendency to begin on a high note and gradually descend, ending on the lowest,

An Eskimo song.

whereas the songs of the Arctic Coast Eskimo have generally an upward curve and return at the close to about the level of the beginning.[2] Undoubtedly the different tribes of the Dominion had their own musical styles which scholars will probably decipher through a closer study of their songs.

Native songs have considerable value in the history of the development of music, but they seldom give genuine pleasure to Europeans who are acquainted only with the somewhat rigid and circumscribed musical styles of our modern civilization. The melo-

---

[1] Densmore, F.: Chippewa Music—ii, Bull. 53, Bur. Am. Ethn., p. 14 (Washington, 1913).
[2] Roberts, H. H., and Jenness, D.: "Eskimo Songs," pp. 404-5; Report of the Canadian Arctic Expedition, 1913-1918, vol. xiv (Ottawa, 1925).

dies are nearly always exceedingly brief, and the constant repetition of only a few syllables on the same or approximately the same melodic theme becomes very monotonous. The irregular time is confusing, and the unfamiliar intervals often raise a suspicion that the singer is flattening or sharpening his notes unintentionally. We should remember, however, that it is hardly fair to compare our collections of Indian songs with European songs, for not only did all Indians sing, but nearly all, whether musically gifted or not, composed songs, and our collections have been gathered at haphazard without regard to their musical value, and often from very indifferent singers. There are certainly some very beautiful melodies, especially in Eskimo songs, if one has only time and patience to separate the gold from the dross.

The impact of civilization had little effect on Indian music, but it exerted so profound an influence on aboriginal art that to-day we can hardly unravel the old art forms from those that have grown up during the last two or three centuries. This is particularly the case in eastern Canada, where the natives have been subjected to intensive acculturation since the seventeenth century, have intermarried largely with Europeans, and in many districts have lost practically all their Indian characteristics. In the prehistoric graves and village-sites of this eastern area we find realistic figures of animals, birds, and human beings carved on stone pipe-bowls, or modelled on pipe-bowls of clay, but artistically the work is rather crude, certainly much inferior to the stone sculpture and clay modelling of central America or of many parts of the Old World. Sculpture in wood was hardly more advanced, if we may judge from the remark of Charlevoix, " Their (Huron) cabins . . . . were adorned with figures in relievo, but of very coarse workmanship,"[1] and from the grotesque wooden masks still used by the Iroquoian False-Face societies. It is true that the grotesqueness of these masks is intentional and that they display a certain anatomical exactness; nevertheless, the carving seems coarse and unrestrained, as though sculpture was held in little esteem. The backs of modern Iroquoian cradle-boards are sometimes ornamented with elaborate floral carvings and bird figures, but these are the work

---

[1] Charlevoix, P. E. X. de: " Journal of a Voyage to North America"; translated from the French, vol. 2, p. 128 (London, 1761). Lescarbot speaks more favourably of the carving in the Maritime Provinces: " Our Souriquois and Armouchiquois have the art both of painting and carving, and make beasts, birds, and men in stone and also in wood, as prettily as good workmen in these parts." Lescarbot: Op. cit., p. 98.

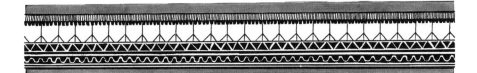

Typical designs in the art of the Canadian aborigines. From top to bottom: painting on a Naskapi robe; engraving on an Alaskan Eskimo snuff-box; beadwork on a Sioux "garter"; porcupine-quill work on a Slave gun-case; painting on a Haida bow. (*Copied and arranged by Douglas Leechman.*)

of European craftsmen or of Indians thoroughly trained in the traditional arts of French Canada.[1]

The old painting of the eastern Indians is as little known as their sculpture, although some early writers refer to it casually. "They often curry both sides of elk skin, like our buff skin, then variegate it very prettily with paint put on in a lace-like pattern."[2] Another author speaks of "a mixture of different colours which they use for daubing the face, or for representing upon their garments certain figures of wild beasts, birds, and other animals such as are supplied by their imaginations."[3] Geometric designs were apparently no less common than realistic, and both were often deeply tinged with religious symbolism. The Indians of the Maritime Provinces, perhaps also of eastern Quebec and Labrador, seem to have preferred curved lines in their paintings, like their Algonkian neighbours to the south, whereas the Ojibwa and Cree employed the angular patterns so characteristic of the tribes on the plains. All these Indians have now practically abandoned the ancient styles, employing European designs in what little painting still survives.

On the plains there was no sculpture worthy of mention, and the realistic paintings on robes and tents were pictorial records rather than expressions of an artistic impulse. Geometric figures on rawhide bags (parfleches) showed considerable skill in line-drawing and often produced pleasing effects, but their unceasing repetition of straight lines, zigzags, triangles, and rectangles had the taint of monotony. The only Indians, indeed, who excelled in either sculpture or painting were the natives on the Pacific coast, where both these arts attained an unexpected brilliance.

The newly awakened interest in the handicrafts of primitive peoples has directed considerable attention to this coast, partly because of the high quality of the carving and painting, still more, perhaps, because of its bizarreness and originality. While it is quite common to find a high conventionalization of realistic art in different parts of the world, these conventionalizations have nowhere taken exactly the same form, or developed the same peculiar style, as among the Indians of British Columbia. It was a style that origin-

---

[1] Some of these cradle-boards were manufactured for the Indians at St. Regis. Beauchamp, W. M.: "Aboriginal Use of Wood in New York"; Bull. 89, N.Y. St. Mus., p. 168 (Albany, 1905).
[2] "Jesuit Relations," vol. iii, p. 75.
[3] Le Clercq: Op. cit., p. 95.

ated long before any Europeans touched these shores, for we can discern it on the stone mortars and whale-bone[1] clubs that have been recovered from prehistoric shell-heaps. The modern artists of the Pacific coast have but carried on the ancient tradition and applied it a little more widely. They look upon their figures with the eyes of an anatomist, dissect them as it were, and rearrange the parts to suit the shape of the object that they are decorating. In the simplest representations they appear to be working with the skins of birds and animals. Thus a frog carved on the walls of a circular dish will reveal one lateral profile on one side and one on the other, as though the sculptor had draped the skin over and around the vessel, cut out the centre and treated the dish as the batrachian's body. Similarly, a human figure carved on the rounded front of a house-post or totem-pole creates the illusion that the artist has divided his model down the back, spread it, and attached it to the pole in two halves. The same process of " dissection " or halving is applied to plane surfaces also, as in the paintings on the flat boards of houses and the paintings and carvings on wooden boxes. Evidently the artistic tradition requires that certain significant parts of each figure shall be represented whether they would normally be visible or not. It is exactly the same reasoning as that of the European child who endows a human profile with two eyes or two ears, although only one of each should be shown in this perspective.

The Indian artist, however, goes much farther than the child. Limitations of space in the field that he is decorating, and a strong desire for symmetry and balance, will make him distort the different elements in a figure, disjoint, and rearrange them without regard to their proper anatomical positions. He may place the tail of an animal above its head, the wings of a bird beside its legs. Then he conventionalizes many elements—represents joints, for example, by circles, eyes by circles, rounded rectangles and other more complicated designs; and he utilizes these conventionalized, half-geometric patterns as purely decorative features wherever he wishes to avoid blank spaces. Furthermore, his psychological attitude towards the animal world, his belief that animals are fundamentally like men, though clothed in different forms, leads him frequently to depict them as human beings, but with the addition of fixed symbols to

---

[1] I.e., bone of whale, not baleen.

differentiate one animal from another. Ears placed in line with the eyes denote a human being, ears situated above the head an animal. A long tongue protruding from the mouth connotes a grizzly bear, even though the rest of the figure is human, and by the same convention two large incisor teeth and a squamous tail denote a beaver.

62244

A painted wall-board that was used as a sliding partition in a Tsimshian initiation ceremony. The design is supposed to represent a woodpecker. *(Photo by National Museum of Canada.)*

This extraordinary style of art varies slightly from tribe to tribe along the coast so that we can usually distinguish without difficulty the productions of the southern peoples, the Coast Salish and the Kwakiutl, from those of the Haida and Tsimshian in the north.[1] The differences, however, are of a somewhat minor character and need not detain us here. In every district the art was both highly conventionalized and highly symbolic, the figures representing definite characters drawn from the local traditions and myths. We may admire the artists' control of their technique, the excellence of many of their carvings, and the splendidly decorative effect of some of the paintings. The huge totem-poles and house-posts will impress us by their savage dignity; silver bracelets and slate dishes delight us by the delicacy of their engravings. But the grotesqueness of the figures, unredeemed, as in the art of the New Zealand Maoris, by exquisite scrollwork or other softening features, soon wearies us; and the conventionalization is

[1] *Cf.* Boas, F.: "Primitive Art," p. 287 *et seq.* (Oslo, 1927).

too involved, the symbolism too obscure and too far removed from our trends of thought for us to assimilate this exotic style of art, which, however attractive in certain respects, fails to blend with our traditional styles. We can understand and appreciate better, perhaps, the fine portrait masks that are also found along the British Columbia coast, especially in the southern part where the artists more frequently abandoned the usual conventionalized style and strove after absolute realism.

The small ivory carvings of the Eskimo deserve a few words of commendation, particularly the animal figurines and sculpturings in high relief. The earlier engravings were practically limited to geometrical patterns, but since the introduction of iron the Eskimo have developed a vivid picture-writing remarkable for its delicacy and the life of the individual figures. The finest carvings and engravings in ivory come from Alaska, where the art is now thoroughly commercialized, but the natives of Baffin island and Labrador also produce some excellent figurines.

The peculiar paintings and carvings of the Pacific Coast natives had their counterpart in the "Chilcat" blankets, which the Tsimshian Indians of the Skeena and Nass rivers, and their Tlinkit neighbours in southeastern Alaska, wove from goat's wool and shredded cedar bark on a primitive, shuttleless loom. The ground or field of this blanket was divided into three panels, of which the middle and largest usually contained a representation of an animal figure, so conventionalized that it resembled discrete blocks of geometrical designs with one or more human-like faces standing out in bold relief. The side panels, which were practically identical with each other, contained similar geometric patterns arranged without definite relation other than a regard to symmetry. The gracefully curved lines, the symmetry of the block patterns and the soft colours, black, pale blue, pale yellow, and white, combined to make these blankets very decorative. The oldest specimens, however, have only very simple geometric designs like those on the blankets made by the Coast Salish Indians farther south, so that probably the more ornamental forms that copy the style of painting did not originate until comparatively recent times, after the early fur trade had brought unexpected wealth to the Tsimshian and stimulated a rich growth of ceremonial life with coincident developments in sculpture and weaving.[1]

Basketry was another art, widely spread throughout the Dominion, which yet attained its highest development in British Columbia, not along the northern part of the coast, however, but in the southern part among the Nootka Indians, the Salish, and the Chilcotin. All these tribes employed a variety of techniques, the Nootka, who often used only the finest materials no thicker than

36458

Coiled baskets of the Thompson River Indians. *(Photo by National Museum of Canada.)*

ordinary string, preferring as a rule the " bird-cage " weave, whereas the Salish and Chilcotin Indians specialized in coiled basketry. Both groups made different types of baskets, some round and some rectangular, and they wove into them figures of birds and animals as well as more conventional geometric designs. The handsome coiled baskets of the Thompson River Indians with imbricated patterns in black, pale yellow, and red have found a ready market in European

---

[1] This would explain why the men had to draw the patterns for the women to copy in their weaving. If the style had been old the women would have required no assistance.

stores, especially since the natives have adapted their shapes to European requirements and equipped them with lids and handles. No baskets were made on the plains, and those of the northern and eastern tribes were much inferior to the western baskets, although the Labrador Eskimo now produce some graceful forms through instruction they have received at the Moravian missions. The Ojibwa, however, wove soft bags of elm bark that rivalled in workmanship and beauty the splendid bags made by several tribes in British Columbia, or the bags, manufactured by the Nez Percé Indians in the United States, that circulated among the Blackfoot.

An art very similar to basketry, but confined to the Canadian aborigines and to adjacent tribes in the United States and Alaska, was "embroidery" with porcupine quills, goose quills, or moose hair.[1] Here the Indians obtained their finest results by using a small bow as a loom and locking the quills within a simple checker weave. The strands of the warp hardly showed in the finished article, and the weft was totally invisible, being concealed by slight corrugations in the quills where it cut across them.[2] The natives coloured the quills with their usual vegetable dyes, and although these colours were limited in number they were softer than the aniline dyes that have now replaced them in everything except some basketry. The designs were exclusively geometrical and of necessity angular forms such as crosses and diamonds, but their rhythmical repetition and the harmony of the soft colours gave a very pleasing effect. Unfortunately, the art has now disappeared entirely except in one or two remote districts in the basin of the Mackenzie.[3] Silk work replaced it for a time in certain regions, and Indian women, some of whom were trained in Quebec convents, decorated coats, gloves, and moccasins with floral designs skilfully embroidered in silk on the soft moose skin. This art in turn is vanishing, leaving only the beadwork that still persists among most Indian tribes and even among the Eskimo of the Arctic. The beadwork patterns are mainly floral, owing probably to the strong influence of early French-Cana-

---

[1] Many of the "moose-hair" specimens are really of horse-hair, sold for this purpose to the Indians by the Hudson's Bay Company.

[2] Cf. Orchard, W. C.: "The Technique of Porcupine-quill Decoration Among the North American Indians"; Cont., Mus. of the American Indian, Heye Foundation, vol. iv, No. 1 (New York, 1916).

[3] Some of the eastern Algonkians, e.g. the Ojibwa, decorate birch-bark baskets with porcupine quills, which, however, are not woven, but merely laid side by side with the ends pushed through holes in the bark.

dian art;[1] but the plains' Indians generally retain their old geometric designs. Some of these plains' costumes are very striking, particularly the moccasins and vests on which parti-coloured triangles, squares, and zigzags, all arranged with perfect symmetry, stand out in brilliant relief on a solid field of blue or white. Almost equally gorgeous are the Eskimo coats from Hudson bay that reproduce the earlier insertions and fringes of caribou fur in beadwork. One cannot but feel, however, that the newer style in this Eskimo region is less appropriate and attractive than the old, for the hard brilliance of the beads seems scarcely to harmonize with the subdued colours and silken texture of the fur.

The potter's art did not flourish in Canada, apparently because its inhabitants were marginal peoples who acquired the technique from elsewhere and scarcely realized its potentialities as a medium of artistic expression. Tribes to the southward understood the use of slips, and both central America and Peru produced exquisitely designed vessels richly coloured with geometric and naturalistic figures. Canadian pottery was never painted, and with the exception of the pipes already mentioned, comprised only the wide-mouthed jar forms that are requisite for cooking vessels. Some of these were not ungraceful, especially certain Iroquoian types with well-made, cornice-like rims; but the majority were coarse in texture, poorly shaped, and without any decoration except crudely drawn chevrons, parallel lines, and cross-hatchings. If pottery-making had ever taken root among the skilled artists of British Columbia, it might have blossomed into beautiful shapes and colours like the wares of the tropical and sub-tropical peoples of America; but the seeds that sprouted in eastern Canada, on the southern prairies, and along the shores of the Arctic, found the soil too barren to nurture their growth and bring them to full maturity.

---

[1] For a contrary view *See* Davidson, D. S.: " Decorative Art of the Têtes de Boule of Quebec"; Indian Notes and Monographs, vol. x, No. 9, pp. 149 *et seq.* (New York, 1928).

CHAPTER XV

ARCHÆOLOGICAL REMAINS[1]

Although the many diverse languages and customs of the aborigines suggest that the country was occupied for countless centuries before its discovery by Europeans, the remains of its prehistoric inhabitants are seldom conspicuous, and in many districts hardly discoverable even with careful research. There are no architectural ruins similar to the cliff dwellings in the southwest of the United States, the stone temples, walls, and highways of Central America and Peru, or the brick and stone monuments of the Old World. Stone entered into the construction of dwellings only on the Arctic and sub-Arctic coast-lines, where alone we find habitations, still partly intact, that lead us back to the centuries preceding Columbus. The bark wigwams of the eastern Indians were impermanent structures frequently dismantled and removed to another site, and the skin tents of the plains' and Mackenzie River tribes left no marks except circles of stones or faint depressions in the soil. West of the Rocky mountains, and in southeastern Ontario, the Indians occupied the same village sites for several years in succession; but even in those regions few traces of their dwellings remain, because the wood of which they were built rapidly disintegrated with the moisture and changing temperature.

Yet if Canada is not wealthy in prehistoric remains it is by no means barren. Even though the ancient dwellings have disappeared with hardly a trace, though most of the implements and utensils used by the earlier Indians have fallen into dust, many objects have been preserved that help us to reconstruct their history. Wood, horn, and skin may often have disintegrated, but bone, antler, stone, pottery, ivory, and shell remain, and although the story they tell is partial and one-sided, we can often fill in the gaps from our knowledge of the historic Indians. The kitchen-middens on both the Atlantic and the Pacific coasts contain not only the empty shells of the molluscs on which the aborigines feasted, but objects of stone, bone, and native

[1] I have received much assistance in this chapter from my colleagues, Mr. Harlan I. Smith and Mr. W. J. Wintemberg, Archæologist and Assistant Archæologist, respectively, of the National Museum of Canada.

copper that were either discarded or lost when they moved away. The old village sites in southeastern Ontario and along the St. Lawrence contain, in addition, amazing quantities of broken pottery, and pottery (which, though fragile, is almost indestructible) appears near the International Boundary in all three Prairie Provinces. The dry soil along the Fraser river in the interior of British Columbia has preserved fragments of cord-woven basketry that generally crumbled to pieces in more humid regions. Thus the southern parts of Canada possess many valuable relics of the distant past; and though the northern interior is almost barren, the Arctic and sub-Arctic coast-lines, where the floors of the old dwellings remain perpetually frozen beneath the surface soil, rival, in the abundance of their treasures, the richest sites anywhere in America.

Graves, though generally less fertile than village or camping sites, have in many places yielded valuable remains. Much of our knowledge of the Beothuk Indians of Newfoundland comes from the implements they deposited in caves and rock shelters beside their dead. Burial customs, as we have seen, varied greatly in different parts of Canada. Wherever cremation was common, as on the Pacific coast, or the dead were laid on scaffolds or on the surface of the ground, comparatively little has survived. But stone cairns and shell-heaps often contain both human and other remains, and in southeastern Ontario the plough of the farmer has exposed many pits or ossuaries where the Iroquoians had deposited the bones of their dead with the tools and utensils that they had used in life.

The Indians have left other records of their ancient occupation in addition to dwelling-places and graves. In British Columbia, and more rarely on the prairies, there are petroglyphs or boulders sculptured with strange designs about which the present natives know nothing. Commoner still are pictographs or rock paintings, many also prehistoric, although some on the upper Fraser river, and perhaps elsewhere, were made as late as the nineteenth century. Then there are traces of old quarries where the Indians mined their soapstone, chert, and other minerals, old trails over which they wandered, stone cairns, food-caches, and fish-weirs that were constructed before the white man came. Finally, explorers travelling in the Arctic archipelago far beyond the historic range of any Eskimo tribe now extant have found stone dwellings and tent-rings, graves, and caches on Melville, Bathurst, and other islands, even on the extreme north of Ellesmere island within 8 degrees of the north pole.

Archæological investigations, however, face at the outset a very serious difficulty; for the aborigines, familiar with no writing except picture-writing, have left behind no literature that might help to fix

52001

Petroglyph near the Bella Coola river, four miles from the village of Bella Coola.
(Photo by Harlan I. Smith.)

the dates of these various remains. We may know from the ignorance of the present day natives concerning their origin, and from the absence of any iron tools, that they antedate the arrival of Europeans two or more centuries ago; but this hardly begins the inquiry. In other parts of the world we can sometimes determine the approximate period of a ruin through the presence of objects imported from a country whose history is already known, as when we find in Cretan house-sites ornaments that were peculiar to well-established dynasties of Egypt. But Canada, like the rest of the American continent, seems to have been entirely cut off from the civilization centres of the Old World until the end of the fifteenth century,[1] and any foreign objects its soil contains are either intrusions from the United States, where their origin and date are hardly less obscure, or else of recent introduction, like the Chinese coins that are occasionally unearthed near Vancouver and other places, and the bronze figurine from northern India that was dug up at Kincolith, on Nass river, some twenty-five years ago.[2] The only possible starting point, then, for the elucidation of the earlier history of our aborigines is the appearance of Europeans on the scene, of Jacques Cartier on the east coast in 1534, and of Russian, Spanish, and English navigators and fur-traders on the west coast in the eighteenth century. For Europeans brought iron tools and weapons that instantly replaced most of the stone implements previously in use, and archæological sites from this and subsequent periods invariably reflect the change.

In the absence of historically fixed dates for pre-European times the Canadian archæologist must fall back on the slender evidence afforded by changes in the geological or biological conditions. Thus in some parts of Canada, notably in the Arctic, the coast-line has risen thirty or forty feet since certain dwelling-sites were deserted, and several inches of soil have accumulated over their ruins. Such conditions indicate the lapse of many centuries, but unfortunately we cannot determine the rates at which the coast-line rose or the soil accumulated, and, therefore, cannot measure the interval in years. To find one ruin resting directly on top of another (as in so many Mediterranean sites) is extremely rare; but provided that soil, vegetation, and other conditions are similar, we may logically assume that a site buried eighteen inches beneath the ground is older than one buried only twelve inches, and by this criterion we can occasionally determine the sequence of remains within a restricted area.

---

[1] The transitory visits of the Norsemen to the east coast of Canada about the year 1000 A.D. appear to have left no impression on the aborigines.

[2] Boas, F.: " A Bronze Figurine from British Columbia"; Bull., Am. Mus. Nat. Hist., vol. xiv. pp. 51-52 (1901).

Certain archæologists have attempted to calculate the antiquity of the shell-heaps on the coast of California by estimating the probable population of the sites and the number of empty shells an Indian would throw out each day; but such a method seems impracticable, in Canada at least, where we can neither estimate the probable population nor the proportion of shell-fish in the native diet. We can, however, obtain the minimum ages of a few heaps by examining the forests that have covered them since their formation. "In 1897 there stood on one heap that was eight feet high the stump of a Douglas fir that showed over four hundred annual rings. This heap must have been abandoned before 1497; before an earlier date still, in fact, because there was a second stump on it larger and presumably older, although its rings could not be counted because the centre was hollow. A Douglas fir cut down on another and higher shell-heap many years ago showed four hundred and twenty annual rings, so that this heap was abandoned before 1500. We know neither how many years had elapsed between the abandonment of these shell-heaps and the growth of the trees, nor the rate at which the shell-heaps themselves had accumulated; but if the upper layers are at least 400 years old, the lower ones must be considerably more ancient. There seems no reason to believe that the two shell-heaps just described are the oldest along this coast. Others may be centuries older, preceding perhaps the Christian era. We may derive from tree-growths minimum dates for a few, but unless we can obtain some geological indications, there seems little hope of discovering the true age of any heaps except the most modern."[1]

Let us now examine each region in turn and see what light archæology has been able to throw on its inhabitants during the long, dark period that preceded the coming of Europeans. We will begin our survey with eastern Canada. In Nova Scotia, New Brunswick and Prince Edward Island, prehistoric shell-heaps, camping sites, and graves reflect almost the same culture as that of the Algonkian tribes, Micmac and Malecite, who occupied this region in the seventeenth century. The coastal shell-heaps, however, rarely if ever contain gouges or grooved axes of stone, both of which are fairly common in the interior; and since these objects do not occur in post-European

[1] Smith, Harlan I.: "Kitchen-middens of the Pacific Coast of Canada"; National Museum of Canada, Bull. 56, p. 46 (Ottawa, 1929).

sites it seems possible that they indicate the habitation of the province by some earlier tribe than the Micmac and Malecite who linger there to-day. The abundance of pottery in the prehistoric shell-heaps supports this hypothesis, for none of the early writers appears to mention its presence, except Lescarbot, who says, without stating his authority, that it had formerly been used by the Micmac, but discontinued before his time.[1] We should remember, on the other hand,

56861

Shell-heap or kitchen-midden near the mouth of the Fraser river, B.C., showing the stumps of the trees that grew above it after its formation. Much of the heap has been removed. *(Photo by Harlan I. Smith.)*

that there are no detailed accounts of the Micmac or Malecite Indians before the seventeenth century, when they had already been in contact with Europeans for a hundred years, so that Lescarbot may be quite correct in believing that pottery had disappeared in the interval, even though it lingered for a much longer period among the Iroquoians. We may conjecture, too, that the natives had little use for gouges and grooved axes at the seashore, and, therefore, left them inland at the winter hunting-grounds; although in that case we might reasonably expect to find one or two stray specimens in the shell-

[1] Lescarbot: Op. cit., vol. iii, p. 195.

heaps. But then the rarity of stone or pottery pipes, both inland and on the coast, again arouses our suspicion that there may have been an earlier population, for it suggests that smoking was a new trait but lately introduced into the Maritime Provinces from the Iroquoians to the west. Such pipes as have been found closely resemble Iroquoian types,[1] indicating that either the Iroquoians or the Maritime Algonkians, perhaps both, were newcomers into southeastern Canada. There the problem rests to-day, and we must leave it unsolved pending further excavations.

None of the Maritime remains hitherto excavated bears any indications of great antiquity,[2] nor can we prove with certainty that Algonkian or any other tribes had occupied this region more than a century or two before the coming of Europeans. A grave at Red Bank, in Northumberland county, New Brunswick, contained burnt human bones and a number of stone implements deeply stained with red ochre like the remains of the mysterious " Red Paint " people in the neighbouring state of Maine,[3] although the implements themselves in no way resembled " Red Paint " types. On the other hand, knobbed gouges, plummets, adze blades, and long slate spear-points of typical " Red Paint " forms have been unearthed in various parts of New Brunswick and Nova Scotia, but neither associated with deposits of red ochre nor in circumstances that would indicate great antiquity. It seems safer, therefore, to regard these specimens not as the work of a distinct people, but as local variants from the more usual Algonkian forms. Altogether, archæological investigations in the Maritime Provinces have been singularly disappointing. They have elucidated some obscure features in the culture of the inhabitants that were not recorded by the early missionaries and explorers, but they have failed to prove conclusively that there was any occupation of this area before the eleventh or twelfth century A.D.[4]

Archæology has been a little more successful in the lowlands of the St. Lawrence River valley, where we find two kinds of prehistoric village remains. In the one, besides the usual stone axes, bone awls, and other implements, there are fragments of clay pots that had

---

[1] The special pipe developed by the Micmacs appears to be post-European.
[2] The shell-heaps are much smaller and shallower than those on the coast of Maine.
[3] For these " Red Paint " people, See Moorehead, W. K.: " Archæology of Maine"; Andover, Massachusetts, 1922. Moorehead claims for them great antiquity.
[4] It is hardly credible, nevertheless, that it was entirely uninhabited before and for several centuries after the beginning of the Christian era.

rounded bases, overhanging or cornice-like rims, and, occasionally, handles; curved pipes made of stone or earthenware and frequently carved or modelled into human, bird, or animal forms; and now and again an ornament made of shell. Many of the arrow-heads are of bone or antler; those of chipped stone are sometimes equipped with barbs or stems, but more often, perhaps, present the outline of a simple isosceles triangle.[1] The pottery, too, has been modelled into shape, not built up by the alternative method of coiling.[2] Sites with these remains persist into European times, when shell beads become more numerous and iron knives and axes appear. We recognize them as the village sites of an agricultural people, because the refuse deposits always contain charred corn and beans; and we can be certain, too, that they mark the locations of Iroquoian settlements, for some of them are actually mentioned by the early Jesuit missionaries, although the majority were abandoned before their time.

The second group of sites yields very different remains, which we can likewise identify as typical of the Algonkian tribes in northeastern America. Arrow-heads of bone are here very scarce, and those made of stone are more frequently barbed or stemmed than triangular. The pots, of inferior texture, are manufactured by the coiling process as often as by modelling, and are without collars, overhanging cornices, or handles. Pipes and shell ornaments seem rare, but in their place are occasional objects of copper and many stone implements not present in Iroquoian remains, such as gouges, grooved axes, pestles shaped like bells or cylinders, and polished ornaments that, according to their form, are classified into gorgets, banner-stones, and amulets.[3] All these Algonkian sites are prehistoric, revealing no traces of European contact, and since many of them lie in what was Iroquoian territory in the sixteenth century we know that they must precede the Iroquoian occupation of the St. Lawrence lowlands, even although as yet we have found no actual super-imposition of remains. There are no storage pits for grain on these Algonkian sites, nor any indication that their inhabitants were acquainted with the cultivation

---

[1] In New York the triangular forms predominate almost to the exclusion of the other types. Parker, A. C.: "Origin of the Iroquois"; Am. Anth., n.s., vol. xviii, p. 484 (1916). On the other hand stone drills are rare or lacking in Iroquoian sites south of the border, but not uncommon in Ontario. They are very plentiful in Algonkian sites.

[2] For a description of Huron pot-making See Sagard, T. G.: "Histoire du Canada," vol. 1, p. 260 (Paris, 1866).

[3] The few two-holed gorgets discovered on Iroquoian sites were probably derived from the Algonkians.

of maize. Both agriculture and smoking, therefore, seem to have come into southeastern Canada through the Iroquoians.

At what period, then, did the Iroquoians reach the St. Lawrence valley? Parallel discoveries south of the International Boundary, and a close study of the culture, traditions, and dialects of their various tribes, tend to fix the date at around 1300 A.D. Parker would bring them from the Ohio valley to Detroit or the Niagara river, where he believes they split into two branches, one, the ancestors of the Hurons, Mohawks, and Onondagas, moving along the northern shores of lakes Erie and Ontario; the second, which later separated out into the Seneca, Erie, and other tribes, traversing the southern shores.[1] Other authorities prefer to suspend judgment on the movements and cultural groupings of the various tribes pending the results of further investigations.[2] Meanwhile, Wintemberg has dispelled one illusion by finding an Iroquoian camping site as far east as Kegashka, beyond the Natashkwan river; for his discovery proves that the prehistoric Iroquoians controlled not only the valley of the St. Lawrence but a considerable portion of the gulf, and that the party met by Cartier off the Gaspe coast was not, as is commonly supposed, a mere scouting expedition cruising in unknown waters.

The Algonkians who preceded the Iroquoians, like those of the Maritime Provinces, were pottery-makers, although their kindred north of the St. Lawrence watershed used vessels of birch bark for cooking their food. Parker has discovered at Lamoka, in the state of New York, a stratified refuse heap left by two distinct peoples, the lower deposits by a long-headed tribe that knew no pottery, the upper by a round-headed tribe with pottery.[3] He estimates the antiquity of the heap at from two thousand to four thousand years. which is very much greater than a reasonable estimate for any site yet discovered in eastern Canada. We have not found, indeed, any site in the lowlands of the St. Lawrence where pottery is absent, except a small and rather insignificant camping place at Red Mill, near Three Rivers. Yet we are confident that pottery was not an independent invention of the Algonkians, but came to them from more civilized tribes to the south. Possibly it was introduced from

---

[1] Parker, A. C.: Op. cit., p. 483.
[2] Cf. Skinner, A.: "Notes on Iroquois Archæology"; Indian Notes and Monographs, Mus. of the American Indian, Heye Foundation, pp. 21 ff (New York, 1921).
[3] Parker, A. C.: American Anthropologist, n.s., vol. 30, pp. 515-6 (1928).

the mound-building tribes in the Ohio valley, for there are graves and mounds in Ontario that contain gorgets of shell and stone, copper axes, awls, and beads similar to specimens that have been unearthed in Ohio, Indiana, and other parts of the United States. Only a few of these remains have been excavated by trained investigators, so that while we are certain that they belong to the prehistoric period, we cannot actually prove that they precede the Iroquoian occupation of the province.[1] Several of the graves, we may note in passing, contained considerable quantities of red hematite, like the grave at Red Bank in New Brunswick. But red was a favourite colour with the Indians in many parts of North America, so that we should not attach too great significance to this feature.

The Prairie Provinces and the Mackenzie basin have proved barren fields for the archæologist, apparently because their inhabitants have always been migratory peoples who never stayed long enough in one place to leave extensive remains. In the southern parts of the Prairie Provinces are burial mounds similar to those of Dakota and other states to the southward. They contain, besides a few human bones, fragments of crude pottery, shell beads, and other stray objects already recorded by early explorers of the plains, so that they add very little to our knowledge. Stone cairns and circles of stones that held down the edges of tents are numerous from the International Boundary to the Arctic ocean, but many of them are quite recent, often no older than the present century. Occasionally we find tent-stones so covered with lichens or buried in the turf that we feel sure they date from pre-European times, but digging reveals nothing except perhaps a few flakes of chert or quartzite. The plough of the farmer often turns up a grooved stone hammer or a tubular stone pipe which we recognize as characteristic of the plains' region, and here and there one stumbles on long rows of boulders that, mosaic-like, trace out some geometrical design or a human or animal figure. But nowhere have archæologists found evidence of other inhabitants than those of the present day, or traces of even their occupation earlier than a century or two before the arrival of the white man.

The village sites, graves, and camping places in the valleys of the Thompson and Fraser rivers, and the innumerable shell-heaps or

---

[1] Wintemberg, W. J.: "Artifacts from Ancient Graves and Mounds in Ontario"; Trans. Roy. Soc., Canada, Third series, vol. xxii, sec. 11, pp. 175-202 (Ottawa, 1928).

kitchen-middens that fringe the coast-line of British Columbia, have been investigated sporadically for half a century. The shell-heaps vary in length from a few yards to one or two miles, and in depth from a few inches to nine feet. The smaller ones are often entirely modern, and a few of the larger ones have grown within the last hundred years, for the Indians of this region still consume large quantities of clams and cockles; but the giant heaps now buried in dense forest certainly date from many hundreds of years ago, in some cases perhaps even thousands.

One would naturally suppose that in such a region archæologists could find a sequence of remains that would permit a reconstruction of the cultural history back to and beyond the beginning of the Christian era. Yet the researches of fifty years have added very little to our knowledge. No doubt difficulties of excavation have militated against any great success. No archæologist has ever possessed funds enough to remove a heavy stand of timber, and then excavate carefully, layer by layer, a solid mass of refuse and earth measuring perhaps three hundred yards long, seventy feet wide, and five feet deep, to take only a moderately large shell-heap. They have run trenches in different places and in various directions; occasionally they have tried to follow the operations of workmen who were razing part of a shell-heap to make a new railway track[1] or a site for a lumber-mill; but hit-or-miss operations of this character can never produce the same results as systematic and complete excavations. We must remember, too, that in the moist, warm climate of the British Columbia coast everything made of wood, horn, skin, or vegetable fibre, the materials most commonly used by the historic natives, decays completely within a century, that the Indians of this region were ignorant of pottery, and that the only specimens we may expect to find in the shell-heaps are stray objects of bone or antler, shell, or stone. Two men may dig for a week without uncovering more than a dozen specimens that are worth carrying away.

A few words, then, will sum up all that we have learned from the prehistoric shell-heaps of the British Columbia coast and from the stone cairns that seem to be more or less contemporary with them.

---

[1] At Eburne, for example, now called Marpole, within the city limits of Vancouver.

Two types of Indians occupied the coast-line in those early days, the one with very narrow faces and heads, the other with very broad. The former type has either disappeared, or else it has now so merged with the prevailing broad-headed type that it escapes detection. The builders of the shell-heaps practised trephining, a custom now unknown, but their graves, unlike those of the historic Indians, seldom contain anything except human bones. Their rectangular

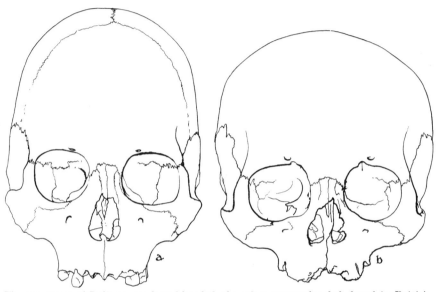

The two types of Indians, one broad-headed, the other narrow-headed, found in British Columbia shell-heaps. The latter type seems absent from the present Indian population of the coast.

houses were similar in ground plan at least to the large plank dwellings that survived until the latter half of the nineteenth century; their tools, weapons, and household equipment, so far as we have recovered them, closely parallel those in use during historic times; and their carvings in stone and bone (for all carvings in wood and horn have disappeared) seem to belong to the same general school of art as the totem-poles, masks, ladles of goat's horn, and other carved objects so prominent among the present-day tribes of the Pacific coast. Altogether there appears to have been no radical change in the material culture of this region, no great disturbances of population, for many centuries.

If we examine the region a little more closely, however, we notice a few differences between the shell-heap remains in the northern part of the province and those in the south. The heaps on the Queen Charlotte islands contain grooved adzes and hammer heads that have not been found on southern Vancouver island or on the mainland opposite. Conversely, the shell-heaps around the mouth of the Fraser river yield several objects that are not known from farther north, such as tubular pipes, clubs made from the bones of whales, plain celts with the hafts in which they were mounted, and stone figures of seated human beings holding bowls in their laps. Undoubtedly these differences have a certain significance. If we correlate them with the present-day differences in language, and with the slight variations in material culture and social organization that are apparent along the shores of British Columbia, we seem to discern in the far-distant past a movement of Salishan-speaking peoples from the interior to the coast, some down the Fraser valley to its mouth, others into the basin of the Bella Coola and the fiord into which the river empties. It is true that inland, in the valleys of the Fraser and Thompson rivers, the prehistoric culture revealed by ancient house-sites and graves differs markedly from any coastal culture with which we are familiar, and merges imperceptibly into the historic culture of the Interior Salish tribes that still inhabit those valleys. But one can readily believe that a primitive people moving from an arid plateau of limited economic resources down to a moist littoral, heavily forested and abounding in fish, game, and fruits, might abandon its earlier mode of life within a few years and adopt the culture of the new tribes with which it came in contact.

The Eskimo of the Arctic coast and their kinsmen along the shores of the Labrador peninsula now claim our attention. Historically they were the first aborigines in the New World to come into contact with Europeans, for we cannot doubt that they were the Skraelings encountered about 1003 A.D. by the adventurous Norsemen who sailed across from Greenland to the coast of North America. Although practically no archæological work was undertaken in their territory until the twentieth century, it has already yielded some rather unexpected results. The climate of the Arctic has exerted an important influence on the character, number, and condition of the ancient remains, for the absence of trees made the Eskimo more dependent than Indian tribes on stone, bone, antler, and ivory, which the permanently frozen soil has maintained in perfect preservation. Moreover, there was a period in Eskimo history when from Coronation gulf to Labrador many of the natives dwelt in houses built of stones and bones of whales roofed over with turf, and the ruins of these dwellings still stand out prominently in the barren landscape. The archæologist faces special problems in the shortness of the summer season and the difficulty of transporting his supplies. He has trouble in excavating, too, because even in midsummer the ground is invariably frozen below the first few inches. On the other hand, he has the immense advantage of finding on every side innumerable old village-sites that will undoubtedly repay investigation.

Without entering into minute details, then, we may summarize briefly the earlier history of our Canadian Eskimo so far as we have deciphered it from their remains.[1] They seem to have been divided many centuries ago into two, possibly three, distinct groups, all closely alike in some ways, in others very different. The interior region that stretches between Hudson bay and those two vast expanses of water, Great Bear and Great Slave lakes, harboured a number of tribes that seldom or never visited the sea, but subsisted entirely on fish and land animals, principally the caribou and the musk-oxen. Dependence on migratory animals caused ceaseless movements within a fixed radius, so that these Eskimo possessed no permanent habitations, but built temporary huts of snow during the winter months and moved into tents of skin at the approach of spring. Their primitive culture —for they were the most primitive of all Eskimo tribes—and their migratory life without fixed habitations did not permit the accumulation of any definite remains. We know of the existence of the group by inference only, from the handful of its descendants still occupying this region and from the tribes that, breaking away in prehistoric times, moved out to the Arctic coast and the shores of Hudson bay.

The second group of Eskimo occupied the littoral from the delta of the Mackenzie to Hudson strait and probably Labrador; offshoots even spread over the now uninhabited islands of the Arctic archipelago and entered Greenland. During the winter months they dwelt in permanent houses built of stones and turf; and like their kindred

[1] The chief authority is Mathiassen, T.: "Archæology of the Central Eskimos"; Report of the Fifth Thule expedition, 1921-24, vol. iv (Copenhagen, 1927). Cf. also Jenness, D.: "Origin of the Copper Eskimos and Their Copper Culture"; Geog. Rev., vol. xiii, pp. 540-55 (New York, 1923); and "A New Eskimo Culture from Hudson Bay"; Id., vol. xv, pp. 428-437 (New York, 1925).

in north Alaska down to the twentieth century, they depended for their livelihood mainly on the great sea mammals, seals and, wherever they existed, whales and walruses. Many of their tools, weapons, and household objects differed from those used in the Arctic to-day, and their stone houses are now unoccupied and falling into ruins. Yet their civilization (named Thule from the site in North Greenland where it was first discovered) must have lasted many centuries, for in Hudson bay the land has risen twelve or thirteen metres since they erected their earliest houses, and four or five metres since they built their latest a few generations before their discovery by Europeans. They were then swamped, apparently, by an invasion from the inland group of tribes, who spread over the whole coast-line as far as Coronation gulf. What set the inland tribes in motion, and the date when they first pushed outward, we do not know, but it seems not improbable that these disturbances in the Hudson Bay area and in Baffin island extended as far as Greenland, and caused that southward movement of Eskimo along the west coast of the island in the fourteenth century, which brought about the destruction of the more northern colonies established by the Icelanders. In the isolation of Southampton island a modified form of the old Thule culture persisted right down to 1902, when all the inhabitants, except four children who had been adopted by a mainland tribe, perished through an infectious disease contracted from a whaling vessel.

The third ancient division of the Canadian Eskimo is more doubtful. Various old ruins that stretch all the way from the northwest coast of Newfoundland to Ellesmere island, but which centre, apparently, around Hudson strait, have disclosed harpoon heads and other objects so unlike those normally associated with Thule remains that they surely denote either a very peculiar phase of that culture, or else a culture that is entirely distinct.[1] It resembles in a few points the culture of the extinct Beothuk Indians of Newfoundland, suggesting that the latter formerly inhabited the southern part of Labrador peninsula in such close proximity to the Eskimo that the two peoples borrowed certain traits from each other. These, however, are hypotheses that cannot be proved without further excavations in Labrador and the eastern Arctic.

---

[1] It is known, tentatively, as the Dorset culture, from cape Dorset, in the southwest corner of Baffin island where it was first discovered. Jenness, D.: " A New Eskimo Culture in Hudson Bay"; Geog. Rev., vol. xv, No. 3, pp. 428-437 (July, 1925).

Although archæological discoveries have opened up for us a vista into the history of the Eskimo during the past thousand, or it may be two thousand, years, they are very far from disclosing the origin of this peculiar people or deciphering the beginnings of its strange civilization. The culture revealed by the oldest remains yet

69170

Soapstone cliff at Fleur-de-Lys, Newfoundland, where Eskimo (?) quarried out their pots in pre-European times. *(Photo by D. Jenness.)*

examined is so well integrated, so perfectly adapted to the peculiar conditions of an Arctic coast-line, that it could hardly have evolved within a few years, but was rather the slow growth of many centuries. We have discovered no trace of such a growth within Canada itself, and several indications point to the development of a still earlier culture on both sides of Bering strait.[1] Even this earlier culture, however, is far from primitive, so that ultimately we may have to seek along the Arctic shores of Siberia for the birthplace of Eskimo

[1] Jenness, D. "Archæological Investigations in Bering Strait"; National Museum of Canada, Bull. 50, pp. 77 f (Ottawa, 1928). Collins, H. B.; "Prehistoric Art of the Alaskan Eskimo"; Smith. Misc. Coll., Pub. 3023 (Washington, 1929).

civilization, and for the origin of this remarkable people. Nevertheless some writers believe that the barren land west of Hudson bay, where a primitive Eskimo group still lingers, was the original home of the entire people, and that somewhere along the Arctic shores of Canada we may yet find traces of that transitional stage when it first adapted itself to life on the seacoast.[1]

1 Steensby, H. P.: "An Anthropogeographical Study of the Origin of the Eskimo Culture"; Meddelelser om Grønland, vol. 53, pp. 39-228 (København. 1917).

CHAPTER XVI

WHO ARE THE INDIANS?

The archæological remains we have just considered carry us back only a short distance into the history of the occupation of Canada. They tell us neither who the Indians are, where they came from, nor how long they have been in possession of the country. The solutions of these problems cannot, in fact, be found in Canada alone, nor even in North America, because they are inseparably bound up with the history of man throughout the whole of the western hemisphere. In the ebb and flow of tribal movements during the long centuries before Columbus, few if any of our aborigines occupied exactly the same territories as they occupy to-day, and some of them, like the Iroquoians, undoubtedly reached Canada from the south.

Our present problem leads us into a realm of pure theories, which, however well founded on established facts and on the inferences that flow logically from them, are liable, nevertheless, to complete or partial overthrow from some fresh discovery in either the Old World or the New. There are really three problems that we should unravel. First, are the Indians autochthonous, and, if not, where did they come from? Second, how long have they occupied this hemisphere? And, third, if they were not autochthonous, what route or routes did they take in travelling hither?

Let us consider the first problem. If the Indians were autochthonous, we should expect to find in this hemisphere traces of earlier types, both in the human and in the simian world, from which they have developed or branched off. But nowhere have we discovered a more primitive type of man than the Indians who inhabit it to-day, no remains that would correspond to Piltdown or Neanderthal man in Europe, Rhodesian man in South Africa, *Sinanthropus* in China, or the ape-man of Java, *Pithecanthropus erectus*. America, again, has known none of the higher anthropoid apes,[1] our nearest of kin

---

[1] One must view with suspicion, until it is verified beyond doubt, the peculiar ape reported to exist in the Rio de Oro region of Venezuela by Montandon, George: " Découverte d'un singe d'apparance anthropoide en Amérique du sud"; Journal de la Société des Americanistes de Paris, nouvelle série, tome xxi, pp. 183 ff (Paris, 1929).

in the animal world, derived, perhaps, from the same remote ancestors in the early Tertiary. On the other hand, many mammals, such as the *Elephas primigenius,* the red deer and the reindeer, migrated

A Chukchee woman and her children, northeast Siberia. Except for their clothes they are hardly distinguishable from Canadian Indians. *(Photo by Captain J. Bernard.)*

from the Old World to America in Pleistocene times, and it is reasonable to suppose that man could have followed in their footsteps.

Other facts also suggest an origin for our Indians outside America. Pleistocene man has left numberless indications of his presence in nearly every part of the Old World, from England to China and from Siberia to South Africa, but in the New World few if any. We may reasonably infer, therefore, that if America was inhabited at all during the Ice Age, its population was exceedingly scanty. Again, no one can doubt that at least the majority of our Indian tribes so closely resemble the peoples of northeastern Asia that they must derive their ancestry from the same source, and the physiography of the two continents favours a migration eastward into America, corresponding to the movement of so many Pleistocene mammals, rather than a migration westward out of America into Asia.[1] We may feel certain, then, that our aborigines are not autochthonous, but sprang from an older race or races that originated somewhere in the eastern hemisphere.

Having now answered our first question we may pass on to the second; how long have the Indians occupied America? We stated in the last paragraph that we have found few, if any, indications of their occupation during the Ice Age. Scientists have indeed set up many claims for their presence during this period. They have reported the remains of Pleistocene man in the Argentine pampas. At Vero, Florida, workmen unearthed human skeletons that seemed to lie beside the bones of *Elephas columbi,* an animal that may have become extinct before or about the close of the Ice Age. In Colorado, Oklahoma, New Jersey, and elsewhere stone arrowheads and other implements have been found in association with extinct animals in strata that appear to have been laid down during the Glacial period.[2] The number of such " discoveries " probably reaches more than half a hundred. Many, however, have been definitely disproved by later researches, and others rendered doubtful. If a few have never been refuted, their very fewness, compared with Old World discoveries, makes us hesitate to accept their authenticity, knowing that it is often very difficult to detect disturbances in the soil, that some of

---

[1] Turkestan and Siberia, broadly speaking, are immense grasslands unbroken by high mountains, but with low ranges running east and west that might canalize to some extent, but hardly check, a drift of animals and their primitive hunters towards the Chukchi peninsula. North America, on the other hand, has the formidable Rocky mountains that almost cut off the north Pacific coast and Alaska from the rest of the continent. A northward drift from the centre of the United States through grassland, sub-Arctic forests, mountains, and tundra would require many radical and successive changes in the mode of life to meet conditions that grew more difficult at every advance. This assumes, of course, that conditions at the end of the Ice Age were not very dissimilar to those of to-day.

[2] *Cf.* Hrdlicka, A.: " Early Man in South America"; Bur. Am. Ethn., Bull. 52 (Washington, 1912). " Skeletal Remains Suggesting or Attributed to Early Man in North America"; Bur. Am. Ethn., Bull. 33 (Washington, 1907); and the excellent discussion in Boule, M.: " Les Hommes Fossiles," pp. 395-434 (Paris, 1921).

the now-extinct Pleistocene mammals may have survived into comparatively modern times, and that errors may creep in from other sources. In the light of our present knowledge it is safest to conclude that the western hemisphere was uninhabited during the Glacial period, although we must be willing to revise this opinion should new discoveries produce overwhelming evidence to the contrary.

Nevertheless, the Indians are by no means recent immigrants into America. Early civilizations grow rather slowly, as we know from the histories of Egypt and Mesopotamia, and a long preliminary period of agricultural development and experimentation in the dressing of stone, a gradual progress through hundreds of years, must have been necessary to produce the Mayan civilization that flourished in Central America at the beginning of the Christian era. Then the amazing number of languages[1] and the diversity of customs and physical types throughout the two continents are further evidence of long occupation, as long perhaps as twenty thousand years, or roughly from the final retreat of the ice-sheets to the present day. Even this length of time might seem too short, considering the slowness of such changes in other parts of the globe, were it not probable that many of these differences developed in the Old World and characterized some of the tribes before they reached America. For we can hardly believe that they all entered in one body and at no time received any further accessions from the outside; but rather that they came in many scattered bands separated by wide intervals of time, although they followed the same established route or routes. If the first bands arrived just at the close of the Pleistocene, they may have left those implements in the gravels at Trenton, New Jersey, whose position Wissler and Spier seem inclined to attribute to heavy floods produced by the melting ice-sheet.[2] Apart from this one instance, however, there seem to be no solid grounds for assigning quite as great an antiquity to any known aboriginal remains. Doubtless many of them date back several millenia, although we have no means of arriving at their true age because nowhere is there any

---

1 We do not know how many different linguistic families there are in North and South America combined. Powell, in 1891, estimated fifty-eight in the region north of Mexico alone (Powell, J. W.: "Indian Linguistic Families"; 7th Ann. Rept. Bur. Am. Ethn., pp. 1-142 (Washington, 1891)), but later investigations have brought that number down to about thirty, with the probability of still further reduction in the future.

2 Spier, Leslie: "The Trenton Argillite Culture"; Anth. Papers, Am. Mus. Nat. Hist., vol. xxii, pp. 167-226 (New York, 1924). Wissler, Clark: "The Present Status of the Antiquity of Man in North America"; Scientific Monthly, March, 1916, pp. 234-238.

chronology for the period preceding the First Mayan Empire, which opens its time count in 613 B.C. The case is different in northern Europe, for there clay varves have given us a definite time scale into which we can fit certain physiographic, climatic, botanical, and cultural changes; in America geologists have not yet succeeded in tieing together the various varve counts into a consecutive series. Some scientists have tried to obtain a time count by other methods. Thus

Sun temple at Chitzen Itza, showing the high development of architecture among the Maya Indians of Central America. *(Photo by courtesy of Peabody Museum, Harvard University.)*

Allison counted the number of light and dark bands on a stalagmite overlying charcoal and an engraved mastodon bone in a limestone cavern near Pineville, Missouri, and calculated that the cavern had been inhabited from about 16,080 B.C. to 11,730 B.C.[1] His assumption, however, that these light and dark bands represent annual layers is generally discredited, and his deductions meet with no sup-

[1] Allison, Vernon C.: "The Antiquity of the Deposits in Jacob's Cavern"; Anth. Papers, Am. Mus. Nat. Hist., vol. xix, pp. 297-335 (New York, 1926).

port. Not until we succeed in establishing an absolutely reliable time scale for the period between the Ice Age and the beginnings of written history, will our estimates of the antiquity of many pre-European sites, and of the length of time the Indians have occupied America, be any more than guesses.

Leaving our second problem only partly answered let us take up the third, what route or routes did man use in coming to America. During a part or parts of Pleistocene time northeastern Asia seems to have been joined to Alaska, providing an easy passage for the migration of the bison, reindeer, and other animals into America. If man did actually inhabit this continent during that period, he must surely have taken the same route, because it offered him the only land connexion then in existence, and with the primitive tools at his command he could hardly have built an ocean-going vessel. The bridge was severed some time during the latter part of the Pleistocene, leaving the present narrow strait that unites the Arctic ocean with the Bering sea. But whether it persisted until most of the ice-sheet retreated, and so was available for the passage of early man from northeastern Asia into America, remains as yet uncertain.

Of the other land connexions between America and the Old World none endured later, apparently, than the Miocene.[1] Man was still unborn when Antarctica broke away from South America, so that it is idle to speculate on human migrations between the two hemispheres along that route. North America, Greenland, Iceland, and Europe may have been joined together in the early Teritary, but we may be sure that no dim tradition of their union inspired Plato's fanciful story of Atlantis, that mythical continent buried beneath the ocean, which Lewis Spence has recently resurrected to explain the rise of the Mayan civilization.[2] The submerged archipelagos, or perhaps continents, in the Pacific, postulated by Macmillan Brown in order to link the scattered South Sea islands with one another, and with Asia and South America, find little or no support among competent geologists.[3] Such theories of submerged continents over which man could wander back and forth throughout the globe naturally

---

[1] Matthew, W. D.: "Hypothetical Outlines of the Continents in Tertiary Times"; Bull., Am. Mus. Nat. Hist., vol. 22, pp. 353-383 (New York, 1906). Scott, W. B.: "The Origin of the Mammalian Faunas of North and South America"; Dollo-Festschrift der Palaeobiologica, pp. 254-262 (Wien und Leipzig, 1928).

[2] Spence, Lewis: "The Problem of Atlantis," London, 1924.

[3] Brown, J. Macmillan: "Peoples and Problems of the Pacific," vol. i, ch. xx (London, 1927).

fire the imagination of the layman, but they all lack solid geological foundation, and are really not needed to explain the many problems created by human migrations.[1]

It is clear, then, that apart from the possible land-bridge at Bering strait, man can have reached America only by water across the Pacific or the Atlantic ocean. Have we any reason to suppose that there was a migration across the Atlantic before the voyages of the Scandinavian Vikings about the year 1000 A.D. and their successors from southern Europe in the fifteenth century? Professor Wiener claims that the negroes of West Africa made numerous voyages to America in the centuries before Columbus, introducing not only tobacco, maize, and other plants, but the foundations of the Mayan calendar and religion.[2] Certainly the Atlantic is much narrower between West Africa and Brazil than at any other place, and both the equatorial currents and the winds favour a passage there from the Old World to the New. Nevertheless, the pre-Columbian aborigines showed not the slightest trace of negro or European admixture, and no well-informed ethnologist will accept the African origin of maize or tobacco, still less of the Mayan calendar. It seems quite certain, indeed, that America was entirely unin-fluenced by either Europe or Africa until the fifteenth century, for even the three-year sojourn of the Vikings somewhere on the north-east coast produced no permanent effect on the Indian tribes inhabit-ing that area. Only in one region did pre-Columbian Europeans leave some slight trace—in southwestern Greenland, the home of an Icelandic colony from 990 A.D. until the sixteenth century. There Mathiassen has unearthed a few Icelandic relics in the old Eskimo settlement of Inugsuk,[3] and certain authorities derive two or three words in the local Eskimo dialect from old Norse. Yet this very exception is peculiarly instructive, because it shows that unless the conditions are favourable to receptivity, the influence of one culture on another, even after generations of contact, may be almost negli-gible. The Icelanders were more advanced in many ways than their neighbours, yet they produced little effect on the material culture of the Eskimo, or on their social and religious life.

[1] I am indebted to Mr. W. A. Johnston, of the Geological Survey, Ottawa, for assistance in these geological matters.
[2] Wiener, Leo: " Africa and the Discovery of America"; 3 vols. (Philadelphia, 1919).
[3] Mathiassen, T.: " Inugsuk, A Mediaeval Eskimo Settlement in Upernivik District, West Green-land"; Meddelelser om Grønland, vol. lxxvii (Copenhagen, 1930).

If man failed to conquer the Atlantic before the tenth century or, if he conquered it, failed to survive after he reached the New World, we could hardly expect him to have crossed in pre-European times the broader and equally stormy Pacific. Yet there are strong arguments to support the theory that he journeyed from southern Asia and the Malay archipelago through the islands of the south Pacific and settled on the coast of either North or South America, introducing into this hemisphere certain customs and implements that were previously unknown. Sullivan states that a skull discovered at Punin, in Ecuador, is of definitely Australoid type and akin to Melanesian skulls;[1] and several European anthropologists claim that some skulls unearthed at Lagoa Santa, in Brazil, and others discovered later in southern California, differ radically from ordinary Indian skulls, but closely resemble the skulls of the natives in the New Hebrides, New Caledonia, and other parts of the Melanesian archipelago.[2] Rivet, again, finds so many parallels in grammatical structure and vocabulary between the Malayo-Polynesian group of languages, particularly its Melanesian dialects, and the Hokan group in California, that he postulates their derivation from the same linguistic stock.[3] Then there are several customs that are common to the South Sea islands and America, such as the chewing of betel-nut and lime in Melanesia, and of the coca-leaf and lime in South America; the cutting off of a finger in sign of mourning; trepanation; masked dances; feather head-dresses and cloaks; the use of shell-money, shell-trumpets, pan-pipes, and musical bows. The early navigators of the north Pacific coast compared the forts, carved house-posts, whale-bone clubs, and cedar-bark beaters of British Columbia with the forts, house-posts, and clubs of far-off New Zealand and the tapa-cloth beaters of central Polynesia. Mauss, again, finds all the essential features of the British Columbia feast or potlatch reproduced in Melanesia.[4] Turning to the field of mythology, we have among the Luiseño and perhaps Gabrielino Indians of southern California elaborate cosmogonies without parallel else-

---

[1] Sullivan, L. R., and Hellman, Milo: "The Punin Calvarium"; Anth. Papers, Am. Mus. Nat. Hist., vol. xxiii, pt. VII (New York, 1925).

[2] *Cf.* Verneau, R.: Crânes d'Indiens de la Colombie, L'Elément Papoua en Amérique, L'Anthropologie, vol. xxxiv, pp. 353-386 (Paris, 1924).

[3] Rivet, P.: "Les Malayo-Polynésiens en Amérique"; Journal de la Société des Américanistes de Paris, vol. xvii, pp. 141-278 (Paris, 1926).

[4] Mauss, M.: "L'extension du potlatch en Mélanésie"; L'Anthropologie, vol. xxx, pp. 396-7 (Paris, 1920).

where in America, but so strongly reminiscent of Polynesian myths that Kroeber declares " either an Oceanic influence or an extraordinary coincidence has occurred."[1] If we go further, and, following the guidance of some enthusiasts, allow our imaginations to run amok, we may see the trunks of Indian elephants carved on Mayan monuments, and derive the calendrical system of the Mayas and the beginnings of agriculture in America through Malaysia and southeastern Asia from a hypothetical source in ancient Egypt. But we need hardly resort to such far-fetched flights of fancy to sustain the theory of a trans-Pacific migration when so many more obvious parallels lie ready to our hand.

Such a migration, nevertheless, is far from proved. There is no evidence that the Polynesians reached the open Pacific before the middle of the first millenium A.D., and archæologists have found no traces of earlier inhabitants in the South Sea islands. The Polynesians doubtless drove or carried some Melanesians into the eastern Pacific, but that these Melanesians could have introduced into America, between the fifth and the fifteenth centuries, all the widespread innovations attributed to them (for most of the parallels are with Melanesia rather than with Polynesia) seems highly improbable. We can hardly believe that the isolated Beaver Indians, for example, who had little or no contact with tribes south or west of Peace river, severed a finger in imitation of immigrants who landed less than a thousand years before somewhere on the coast of California or farther south, and then lost their identity amid a host of alien tribes. It is far more probable that the custom arose independently in America, where it has a very wide distribution, or else that the ancestors of our Indian tribes brought it from the Old World ages before the Polynesians began their wanderings over the Pacific ocean. Some of the other oft-cited parallels, such as the use of shell-money, of the blowgun, and of feather head-dresses and cloaks, may be cases of convergent evolution, since they are not so complex that the human mind could not have evolved them independently in several different places. Certain correspondences, too, may be more apparent than real. Thus, the chief resemblance between the house-posts and totem-poles of British Columbia and the house-posts of the New Zealand Maoris lies

---

1 Kroeber, A. L.: " Native Cultures of the Southwest"; University of California Publications in Am. Archæology and Ethnology, vol. 23, No. 19, p. 397 (Berkeley, California, 1928).

in their common superimposing of figures one on top of another; the elaborate scroll-work so characteristic of all Maori carving is quite foreign to our west-coast natives. We can hardly conceive of a direct migration from Polynesia to British Columbia, and if the house-posts in the latter region were inspired from abroad, why do they not appear farther south along the coast of North America?[1] It would be easier to accept the theory of a migration across the Pacific if all the culture parallels between the Indians and the Malayo-Polynesians were concentrated in one part of America, whether British Columbia, California, or Peru. But when writers attribute to these immigrants customs as widely diffused as masked ritual dances, which were practised from South America to Ontario and British Columbia, and terrace-cultivation, employed from Peru to Arizona—when they ascribe to the same source the tree-dwellings of tropical South America, the blow-gun known from Brazil to Ontario, and the bark-beaters used from Brazil to British Columbia, we begin to wonder why immigrants numerous enough to affect so profoundly the cultures of the tribes in two continents should yet have disappeared so completely within a thousand years that their very existence is open to serious question.

We must frankly admit, however, that certain analogies between the two regions are too striking to dismiss without grave consideration, and too numerous, in the aggregate, to seem the result of pure chance. If we agree that the " Lagoa Santa " people were racially akin to the Melanesians,[2] we must either subscribe to a migration across the southern Pacific, or regard the Melanesians and the "Lagoa Santa " people as descendants of a race that divided in Asia and sent one branch to the southeast, through the Malay archipelago, and the other into America, by the same route, presumably, as the forefathers of our other Indians. The wide distribution of " Lagoa Santa " remains, and the apparent age of some of them,[3] seem to favour the latter hypothesis. Again, if the Hokan group of languages really belongs to the Malayo-Polynesian stock, we must acquiesce in its introduction by way of the southern Pacific; but the arguments in support of this relationship have not yet been subjected to a rigor-

---

[1] The early Spanish explorers mention what seem to be the totem-poles in Chile. Lacham, R. E.: " The Totemism of the Ancient Andean Peoples"; Jour. Royal Anthropological Institute, vol. 57, p. 72 (London, 1927).
[2] For a contrary opinion See Hrdlicka, A.: " The Origin and Antiquity of the American Indian"; Ann. Rept., Board of Regents of the Smith. Inst., 1923, p. 493 (Washington, 1925).
[3] e.g. the Punin calvarium. See Sullivan and Hellman: Op. cit.

ous examination. After all, whatever conclusion we may reach will not seriously affect the problem of the origin of our aborigines, or the route by which they entered America; for the vast majority of the Indians are certainly not of Melanesian extraction, but of Mongoloid, and indubitably occupied America thousands of years before the Christian era.

The north Pacific, up to 51 degrees north latitude, was a more formidable barrier to migration than the south, because there were no chains of islands to serve as stepping stones from one hemisphere to the other. Within the last two centuries some fishing junks carried by the Japanese current have occasionally drifted across to this side, and a few of their occupants, always men only, have survived the exposure and privation.[1] But these occurrences have been rare, and there is no proof that survivors would have escaped massacre in pre-historic times. The cultures of the British Columbian and Alaskan natives reveal no traces of Japanese or Chinese influences, although they have many links with the native cultures of northeast Siberia. We can, therefore, safely reject the possibility of a direct migration by sea from eastern Asia to America, for which it would be difficult to discover any supporting evidence.

There remain, then, only two routes, one by sea from Kamschatka to the Aleutian islands and thence to the mainland of America, the other across Bering strait. Both have numerous advocates, the former in Europe rather than in America, whose scholars appreciate more fully, perhaps, the dangers of navigation in the stormy and fog-ridden Bering sea. No one can assert that it is impossible for small, open boats to make the three hundred mile traverse from the Komandorski islands off Kamschatka to Attu, the westernmost island of the Aleutian chain, but the feasibility of a migration, or series of migrations, along this route seems exceedingly doubtful. Jochelson's failure to find any early Indian remains in the Aleutian shell-heaps and village-sites, any culture different from that of the present islanders before their contact with the Russians,[2] is another strong argument against this route; for no one doubts that the islanders themselves reached their present home from the mainland of America, not from Kamschatka.

---

[1] *Cf.* Brooks, C. W.: " Report of Japanese Vessels Wrecked in the North Pacific Ocean, from the Earliest Records to the Present Time"; Proc., Cal. Acad. Sci., vol. vi, 1875, pp. 50-66 (San Francisco, 1876).

[2] Jochelson, W.: Archæological Investigations in the Aleutian Islands"; The Carnegie Institute of Washington, Pub. No. 367 (Washington, 1925).

We come now to our final route—across Bering strait. Concerning its feasibility there is happily no doubt, since it is followed even to-day by the natives of both continents. The writer saw two open skin boats (*umiaks*) cross over to America in the summer of 1926, one manned by Eskimo from East cape, the nearest point of Siberia to Alaska, the other by Chukchees from a village some fifty miles to the northwest.[1] A hundred years ago there was a well-

67784

Chukchee from the Siberian coast approaching Little Diomede island, Bering strait, on their way to Alaska. *(Photo by D. Jenness.)*

defined trading route that commenced at Anadyr, the Russian mart near Bering sea, crossed Bering strait to Kotzebue sound, then continued overland to the mouth of the Colville river and eastward to the delta of the Mackenzie. Identical remains in ancient house ruins on both sides of the strait attest to a similar movement backwards and forwards several centuries before any Europeans had penetrated to northeastern Siberia, and what was possible for primitive man seven or eight centuries ago was surely possible thousands of years earlier, seeing that the coast-line has changed but little since Pleistocene times. Indeed, we have evidence that at least one migration did occur several thousand years ago, either by this route, or, less probably, by way of Kamschatka and the Aleutian islands; for

---

[1] The distance across the strait is only fifty miles, and the land on both sides is high enough for each continent to be visible from the other on a clear day. Natives crossing today generally spend a night at one or other of the two islands, Big and Little Diomede, that are situated exactly in the middle of the strait.

the mythology of the Koryak and other tribes in northeastern Asia so closely resembles that of our Pacific coast Indians (Tlinkit, Haida, etc.) that the two groups of aborigines must once have been close neighbours.[1] It does not affect the main issue, the peopling of America by way of Bering strait, whether our Pacific Coast Indian tribes developed part of their culture in Asia and subsequently crossed over into America, or whether the group of tribes now living in northeastern Asia separated off on this continent and returned from America to Siberia. In either case their separation provides the same evidence that man was migrating across this strait thousands of years ago, and renders still more probable our theory that most, if not all, the migrations into America followed the same route.

In the absence of any more plausible hypothesis, then, let us imagine the ancestors of our Indians drifting in small bands, generation after generation, into the northeast corner of Siberia, whence the distant view of new hunting grounds lured them across Bering strait. Ascending the valley of the Yukon river they crossed the divide to the upper waters of the Mackenzie, and so passed down through Alberta and Saskatchewan into the United States. Perhaps some of the earliest immigrants worked through the Rocky mountains into British Columbia; for the glaciers were in full retreat fifteen thousand years ago, and the Pacific coast with its abundance of fish and game would have seemed an earthly paradise to hunting tribes that had wandered down from the far north. As the movement from Asia continued and the population on this continent increased, certain tribes were pushed farther and farther south until the vanguard finally entered South America and proceeded to spread over that continent from Colombia to Patagonia. Families of close kindred became divided in the course of centuries, bands that had once been neighbours moved to widely separate homes, and new environments, new contacts, developed differences of speech and customs in peoples who had formerly spoken and lived alike. Thus was evolved the extraordinary multiplicity of tribes and languages, although part of this multiplicity doubtless existed in the migrating bands before they reached America. What caused the original drift from Asia, and the exact date of its commencement, we may never discover.

---

[1] Cf. Jochelson, W.: "The Koryak"; Mem., Am. Mus. Nat. Hist., vol. 10; Jesup North Pacific Expedition, vol. vi, pp. 354 et seq. (Leiden, 1908). Boas, F.: "Migrations of Asiatic Races and Cultures to North America"; Scientific Monthly, Feb., 1929, pp. 112-117.

Probably, in the beginning, it was only one phase in the general expansion of mankind that followed the retreat of the ice-sheets.

Hrdlicka conjectured, partly on anatomical grounds, that the Algonkians, the Siouans, the Iroquoians, and some other tribes (including the " Lagoa Santa " people of South America) were among the first to enter America.[1] There would seem to be more hope of discovering who were the latest. Geographical considerations appear to limit the choice to two peoples, the Athapaskans, whose territory resembles a mighty wedge driven into the heart of North America, and the Eskimo, who once fringed the whole Arctic and sub-Arctic coast-line from the gulf of Alaska to the north shore of the gulf of St. Lawrence, including both sides of the bridge-head at Bering strait. If these peoples were actually the latest immigrants we would expect them to retain more traces of their Asiatic affiliations than Indian tribes farther south. Both do, in fact, share numerous customs and beliefs with Asiatic tribes, but this may be plausibly ascribed to the diffusion of culture traits across Bering strait. Moreover, the Algonkians and the Indians on the Pacific coast also share some of these customs and beliefs; they too, for example, propitiate slain bears, like many Athapaskan, Eskimo, and Siberian tribes. Of greater significance would be the linguistic kinships between the Athapaskan and the Sinitic (Tibeto-Chinese-Siamese) languages of eastern Asia, and between Eskimo and Uralian, should any of these relationships be verified by future research. For we have been unable to discover any connexion whatever between other Indian languages, and any languages in the Old World, except possibly between Hokan and Malayo-Polynesian.

The origin and affiliations of the Eskimo have given rise to considerable controversy. Some scholars, following Boas and Steensby, consider them but an offshoot of the Indians. According to this theory their original home was the inland country around Great Bear and Great Slave lakes, whence for some reason they moved out to the coast, developed a peculiar littoral culture, and spread east and west over the shores of the Arctic and sub-Arctic.[2] Bogoras, on the other hand, places their earlier home on the Siberian side of Bering strait, and believes that they did not enter America until

---

[1] Hrdlicka, A.: " The Origin and Antiquity of the American Indian"; Ann. Rept., Board of Regents of the Smith. Inst., 1923, p. 493 (Washington, 1925).
[2] Cf. Steensby: Op. cit., pp. 41-228.

about a thousand years ago.[1] Archæology appears rather to support the latter theory, but with the date of entry into America pushed back another two or three thousand years. It is worth noticing that Professor Ruggles Gates, when testing the blood-groupings of the Mackenzie Delta Eskimo, obtained in 50 per cent of his cases a reaction for agglutinogen B, the agglutinogen that is more dominant in eastern Asia than in Europe. Such a percentage among Eskimo seems too high to attribute to any white admixture, even though the number of cases examined was small.[2] Since pure-blood Indians appear to possess neither this agglutinogen, nor agglutinogen A,[3] its presence in nearly pure-blood Eskimo, if substantiated, would suggest a separate origin for the two peoples, and lend additional strength to Bogoras' theory that the Eskimo have migrated from Asia into America within comparatively recent times.

Scientists are divided, also, concerning the possible kinship of the Eskimo with some of the upper palæolithic peoples of Europe. Sollas claims as typically Eskimo a skull that was found at Chancelade, in the Dordogne district of central France, and Sullivan sees an equally great resemblance to the Eskimo type in a skull found at Obercassel, near Bonn in Germany. Keith and others deny any similarity.[4] Theoretically, it would seem not impossible that the generalized Eskimo type established itself somewhere in the Old World towards the close of the Glacial period, and that some of its representatives penetrated to western Europe. But this will not solve the problem of the relationship of the Eskimo to our Indians or to the peoples of northern Asia. Nor does it throw any light on their history and wanderings from the closing centuries of the Ice Age to the end of the first millenium A.D.

Of the questions with which we commenced this chapter only one can we claim to have answered with reasonable certainty. The Indians are not indigenous to America, but have migrated hither from the Old World, probably by way of Bering strait. How long

---

[1] Bogoras, W.: " Early Migrations of the Eskimo between Asia and America"; Compte-Rendu, Congrès International des Américanistes, 21st session, 2nd pt., at Goteborg, 1924, pp. 216-235 (Goteborg Museum, 1925).

[2] Personal communication from Professor Ruggles Gates.

[3] Snyder, L. H.: " Human Blood Groups: Their Inheritance and Racial Significance"; Jour. Physical Anthropology, vol. ix, No. 2, pp. 233-264 (Geneva, New York, 1926).

[4] Sollas, W. J.: " The Chancelade Skull"; Jour., Royal Anthropological Inst., vol. lvii, pp. 89-122 (London, 1927). Sullivan, L. R.: " Relationships of the Upper Palæolithic Races of Europe"; Nat. Hist., vol. xxiv, No. 6, pp. 682-696 (New York, 1924).

they have been here no one can say. The continent seems to have been uninhabited during the Glacial period, but the first immigrants may have arrived as far back as fifteen or twenty thousand years ago. The latest immigrants were perhaps the Eskimo, who may have entered America not many centuries before the Christian era. At the end of the first millenium A.D. a few small parties of Malayo-Poly-nesians may possibly have landed somewhere on the Pacific coast between California and Peru, but it seems highly improbable that they could have influenced in any way the aboriginal tribes of the Dominion.

CHAPTER XVII

INTERACTION OF INDIANS AND WHITES

Over and over again in the course of the world's history great changes and occasionally advances in civilization have resulted from the clashes of peoples who previously had marched along separate roads. Such an advance occurred in Japan during the nineteenth century after she threw open her doors to European commerce, and a similar change is taking place in China to-day. In these countries the clash has perhaps benefited materially and mentally both the white race and the yellow, for no one can question their equality in mental endowment, or their ability to assimilate whatever most appeals to them in each other's culture. Very different, however, has been the result of the impact of civilization on many primitive peoples throughout the globe, peoples who, though perhaps not inferior mentally, had lagged so far behind in material progress that they seemed unable to make any far-reaching contributions to European social or economic life. The civilized world is intolerant of these peoples, whom it has neither the time nor the patience to protect and train for three or four generations until they can bridge the gap between the old conditions and the new. So the world is strewn with their wreckage, in Australia, in Melanesia, and in parts of Africa and the two Americas. Yet here and there some alleviating factor has intervened for their protection. Geographical isolation, an extreme climate, some special trait of character or culture, or immunity from certain diseases has guarded them from too sudden an onslaught, permitted their gradual adjustment to the altered environment, and enabled them to participate in the march with the rest of mankind either as independent units for a time, or assimilated in blood, language, and culture with the invaders. The Canadian aborigines have experienced both these effects. Some tribes have been wrecked beyond the possibility of salvage; others, after the first disasters, have courageously stopped the leaks and are beginning the voyage afresh; and many are still struggling, with the breakers looming not far ahead.

Whatever their fate has been, whether they have weathered the storms or foundered, they have not failed to leave a permanent impression on the immigrants who invaded and occupied their territories. The early French-Canadian settlers came from a land intersected with splendid highways which the mild climate rendered serviceable for wheeled vehicles at every season of the year; and quiet rivers linked together by a network of canals permitted the safe and easy transport of freight in cumbersome barges. The new land of which they took possession had no roads at all, and the rivers were so swift, and so full of cataracts and rapids necessitating portages, that barges were totally impracticable and even a light row-boat a very unsatisfactory craft. In winter the rivers and lakes were frozen over, and the land buried under a mantle of soft snow that impeded the movements of men and animals alike. For his own preservation the settler had to adopt the methods of travel and transportation evolved long before by the Indian, to use in winter the snow-shoe and the toboggan, in summer the birch-bark canoe. With these he borrowed also the moccasin so convenient for travelling in deep snow, fur mittens, fur caps (or capotes), and sometimes the moose-skin legging. In Greenland about the same period, Danish colonists were accustoming themselves to the Eskimo dog-sled, which later became the orthodox means of transport along the shores of the Canadian Arctic.

The Indians contributed also to the food supply of the early settlers. Wheat, especially the older varieties, did not thrive in the Maritime Provinces or on the lower St. Lawrence, but the farmer soon found a satisfactory substitute in the Indian's maize. To this he added other aboriginal farm products, the bean, the pumpkin, and the squash. He borrowed, also, tobacco, which, though not a food, spread with amazing rapidity into every corner of the globe, and to-day is grown for commercial purposes in several districts of eastern Canada. For tobacco was indigenous to America, and unknown to the world before the discoveries of Columbus and his successors. The Spaniards in Mexico, the English in the United States, and the French in Canada, all learned its use almost simultaneously from the Indians.

These may seem no small contributions from primitive savages,[1] but they tell only half the story. The Indians taught the settlers woodcraft and the habits of the strange game with which the forests

---

[1] The contributions from the entire American hemisphere were, of course, far more extensive. Cf. Nordenskiöld, E.: "The American Indian as an Inventor"; Jour., Royal Anthropological Inst., vol. lix, pp. 273-307 (London, 1929).

abounded. They manned the canoes of explorers and fur traders, served them as guides and hunters through the wilderness, and showed them the trails and the canoe routes. Many of our highways in Ontario follow the routes of ancient trails, and our railroads cross the mountains over passes first used and pointed out by the Indians. They and their half-breed descendants have always been the mainstay of the fur trade, which, expanding rapidly into the remotest corners of the Dominion, led to the discovery of fertile lands and mineral wealth, with subsequent colonization and development. We may safely say that large tracts of the Dominion would either be little known to-day, or entirely unknown, if the country had not been inhabited at the time of its discovery.

Many tribes acquiesced quietly in the invasion of their territories, others, particularly the Iroquois and the natives of the plains, offered strong opposition. Whether they resisted or submitted, all alike paid the same heavy price for their contact with civilization, some even before they had actually encountered Europeans. The first plague that afflicted them was smallpox, which decimated them periodically from the early seventeenth century until the second half of the nine-teenth. Nearly all the early writers describe its ravages. " None of us," says Thompson in 1781, " had the least idea of the desolation this dreadful disease had done, until we went up the bank to the camp and looked into the tents, in many of which they were all dead, and the stench was horrid; those that remained had pitched their tents about 200 yards from them and were too weak to move away entirely, which they soon intended to do; they were in such a state of despair and despondence that they could hardly converse with us, a few of them had gained strength to hunt which kept them alive. From what we could learn three-fifths had died of the disease. They informed us that as far as they knew all the Indians were in the same dreadful state as themselves."[1]

A medical historian states that " the path of smallpox, from the time it was introduced among the Montagnais in eastern Canada, until it reached the most westerly tribes both in Canada and the United States, may be followed only too easily. It left behind it a broad and a well-blazed trail. Appearing in 1635 among the Montag-nais, who dwelt near Tadoussac on the lower St. Lawrence, it spread

---

[1] Thompson: Op. cit., p. 321 f.

with great rapidity north and south, east and west, invading in turn the numerous tribes which occupied territory extending from the Atlantic in the east to the Great Lakes in the west, and from James bay in the north to the Atlantic seaboard in the south. By the year 1700 smallpox had spread over half the continent, leaving a trail of death and devastation. As we have seen, smallpox was present among the Indians of the Canadian west in 1738. Then, the Sioux, Monsoni,[1] Crees, Piegans, and Assiniboines were infected, so that

46655

"The old graveyards are small, but the new ones large and overflowing." A Haida graveyard in 1919. Marble slabs sculptured by white men have replaced the old memorial columns of wood. *(Photo by Harlan I. Smith.)*

one hundred years after the introduction of smallpox into Canada all the tribes that roamed the Canadian plains from the eastern to the western limits of the country were infected. The disease kept pace with, and at times outstripped, the progress of the white man. As to the number of deaths one can only hazard a guess. Suffice it to say that it played no mean part in the reduction to a mere handful of the once numerous tribes that roamed the plains."[2]

[1] A subdivision of the Cree.
[2] Heagerty, J. J.: "Four Centuries of Medical History in Canada," vol. 1, p. 56 f (Toronto, 1928).

Smallpox was the deadliest, but by no means the only, plague that afflicted the aborigines. Typhus carried off one-third of the Micmac in Acadia in 1746, and in the winter of 1902-3 destroyed the entire Eskimo population of Southampton island in Hudson bay. About 1830 the British Columbia Indians suffered heavy losses from influenza, a malady that spared none of the tribes during the great epidemic of 1918.[1] Pulmonary afflictions, especially tuberculosis, attacked the natives at an early date and ever since have caused a high mortality. Between 1891 and 1901, a malady that official records designated as "consumption" carried off 65 Indians of the Sarcee tribe alone, reducing its already diminished population from 240 to 203. These diseases, if known at all in America before its discovery by Europeans, were certainly very rare, and they exacted a heavier toll because the natives had never developed the slightest immunity.

Of shorter duration than diseases, because Europeans finally awoke to its menace, but, while it lasted, almost equally destructive of aboriginal society, was alcohol. The Indians, unlike many other primitive peoples, had no alcoholic beverage in prehistoric times, and from the earliest days of settlement they abandoned every restraint in their frenzy for the white man's firewater. "They do not call it drinking unless they become drunk, and do not think they have been drinking unless they fight and are hurt. However, when they set about drinking, their wives remove from their wigwams the guns, axes, the mounted swords (spears), the bows, the arrows, and (every weapon) even their knives, which the Indians carry hung from the neck. . . . Immediately after taking everything with which they can injure themselves, the women carry it into the woods, afar off, where they go to hide with all their children. After that they have a fine time, beating, injuring, and killing one another. Their wives do not return until the next day, when they are sober. At that time the fighting can be done only with the poles of their wigwams, which they pull to pieces to allow this use."[2]

These excesses that Denys witnessed in the Maritime Provinces during the seventeenth century, every trader and explorer observed throughout the length and breadth of Canada down to the middle of the nineteenth. Whisky and brandy destroyed the self-respect of

---

[1] About three hundred Indians in the Mackenzie valley, almost 10 per cent of the population, died of influenza in 1928.
[2] Denys: Op. cit., p. 444.

the Indians, weakened every family and tribal tie, and made them, willing or unwilling, the slaves of the trading-posts where liquor was dispensed to them by the keg. Even the fur traders recognized its evils and gladly supported the government when it finally prohibited all sale to the Indians under penalty of a heavy fine.

Disease and alcohol demoralized and destroyed the Indians just when they needed all their energy and courage to cope with the new conditions that suddenly came into existence around them. The old order changed completely with the coming of Europeans. Stone tools and weapons gave place to tools and weapons of iron; cooking vessels of clay, skin, bark, and wood to metal pots; the fire-stick to the flint and steel, and bows and arrows to firearms. Once a tribe had made these changes it could not revert to its former condition because it had lost most of its earlier skill in chipping knives and arrowheads of flint, in grinding out stone axes, and fashioning serviceable bows. Any withdrawal of the trading-posts upon which the Indians were now dependent would have caused endless hardships and widespread starvation. Firearms in particular could not fail to cause a complete revolution in a country so rich in game as Canada, for even the old muzzle-loading gun greatly simplified the food-quest. " With an arrow they killed only one Wild Goose; but with the shot of a gun they kill five or six of them. With the arrow it was necessary to approach an animal closely; with the gun they kill the animal from a distance with a bullet or two."[1]

This was only one result of the introduction of firearms, and perhaps not the greatest. The gun was superior for warfare also, and the tribes that first acquired the new weapon immediately employed it against their less fortunate neighbours. So the seventeenth, eighteenth, and, on the plains, the first half of the nineteenth, century were periods of constant strife and unrest. In eastern Canada the Algonkians and Hurons, assisted by the French, assaulted their old enemies the Iroquois until the latter obtained firearms from the Dutch, vigorously assumed the offensive, and more than evened up the score. Micmac Indians crossing from Nova Scotia to Newfoundland completed the annihilation of the unfortunate Beothuk, and the Cree raided south and west over the Prairies, down the Mackenzie to its delta, and up the Peace river into the

[1] Denys: Op. cit., p. 443.

Rocky mountains. In the north the Chipewyans, obtaining guns at Churchill, oppressed the more distant Athapaskan tribes and kept them from visiting the trading post until smallpox decimated all the bands and the traders opened new posts on the Mackenzie.

Furs, always more furs, the traders demanded in return for the steel tools, the guns, ammunition, liquor, and other perquisites of civilization that they held out as bait to the various tribes. Previously the Indians had paid little regard to the smaller fur-bearing animals, which held an insignificant place in their food supply. To meet this new and unceasing demand they trapped intensively, and when they had depleted their own hunting-grounds expanded into new areas, often invading the territories of their neighbours. The Cree drove the Eskimo out of James bay, and the Slave and Beaver from the districts around Athabaska lake and Slave river. The Ojibwa spread westward into the Red River country and the state of North Dakota; the Iroquois pushed out to the rich beaver area near lake Winnipegosis, then a little later into the foothills of the Rockies and beyond them to the headwaters of the Fraser. Thompson gives a vivid picture of what happened west and northwest of lake Winnipegosis.

" The Nepissings, the Algonquins and Iroquois Indians having exhausted their own countries, now spread themselves over these countries, and as they destroyed the Beaver, moved forwards to the northward and westward: the natives the Nahathaways (Cree), did not in the least molest them; the Chippaways and other tribes made use of traps of steel; and of the castorum. For several years all these Indians were rich, the women and children, as well as the men were covered with silver broaches, ear-rings, wampum, beads, and other trinkets. Their mantles were of fine scarlet cloth, and all was finery and dress. The canoes of the fur-traders were loaded with packs of beaver, the abundance of the article lowered the London prices. Every intelligent man saw the poverty that would follow the destruction of the beaver, but there were no chiefs to control it; all was perfect liberty and equality. Four years afterwards (1797) almost the whole of these extensive countries were denuded of beaver, the natives became poor, and with difficulty procured the first necessities of life, and in this state they remain, and probably forever. A worn out field may be manured, and again made fertile; but the beaver, once destroyed cannot be replaced: they were the gold coin of the country, with which the necessaries of life were purchased."[1]

On the plains the advent of the fur trade and the introduction of horses produced a similar result. Firearms and horses converted the buffalo hunt into a royal sport that attracted tribes from far and near. "Last year," wrote De Smet in 1848, "110,000 buffalo robes with skins of elk, gazelle, deer, bighorn, otter, beaver, etc., and 25,000 salted tongues, were received in the warehouses of St. Louis."[2] The tribes that jostled together on this amazing hunting-ground combined the buffalo chase with ceaseless wars, and raided each other for firearms, horses, and scalps until the whole area from the Rockies to the Great Lakes became a perpetual battlefield. The Blackfoot confederacy (Blackfoot proper, Blood, Piegan, and Sarcee), with its back to the Rockies, contested the field with the Assiniboine and Cree to the east and north, pushing its raids even to the gates of Fort Garry. The same confederacy fought with the Shoshone and other tribes of the United States, and repelled in its rear attacks from the Kootenay and Salish Indians who crossed the mountains to share the buffalo hunt. War and confusion reigned everywhere while the buffalo diminished apace. About 1879 the herds at last failed to appear, and the Indians, dying of starvation, had to accept unreservedly the conditions laid down by the white man.

Contact with Europeans thus revolutionized the economic conditions in every part of the Dominion, although the changes did not always take place as suddenly and completely as on the prairies. In British Columbia the canneries that sprang up at the mouths of the Columbia, Fraser, and Skeena rivers depleted the salmon on which the Indians had depended for their daily food. The musk-ox disappeared from the barren lands, and both there and in the Labrador peninsula the herds of caribou dwindled in numbers or changed their migration routes. Throughout the whole country, indeed, there was a serious diminution in the food resources of the tribes that depended on fishing and hunting, all the tribes, that is, except the Iroquois and some of their Algonkian neighbours who cultivated maize. No longer was each tribe a self-contained and self-supporting unit, but from the Arctic to the prairies and from the Atlantic to the Pacific all alike found themselves inextricably enmeshed in the economic

[1] Thompson: Op. cit., p. 295 f.
[2] De Smet: Op. cit., vol. ii, p. 635.

system forced upon them from without. One by one they ceded their territories to the invaders, and wherever European colonization was proceeding, submitted to confinement on narrow reserves. The needs of the colonists then became their needs also, and in place of their former self-sufficiency, they were reduced to purchasing most of the necessities of life at European trading stores.

60670

A typical fur-trading post, with its Indian cabins and church. Macleod Lake, B.C., in the territory of the Sekani. *(Photo by D. Jenness.)*

Parallel to this revolution in the economic conditions was a complete breaking down of the old social order, of the systems of law, government, and religion on which their societies rested. Trapping, which compelled the dispersal of the individual families during three-fourths of the year, weakened the strong community spirit engendered by common settlements and co-operative action in warfare, fishing, and hunting. The fur traders, with one or two notable exceptions, thought only of multiplying skins, and regarded with more or less veiled contempt the institutions and customs of the natives who furnished their annual turnover. They appraised the Indian not by his character or tribal standing, but by the number of skins he could bring in each spring, and they bestowed their favour only where it seemed most likely to enhance their profits. "Post" natives disregarded or undermined the prestige of the chiefs and elders, who could not enforce their authority without incurring the displeasure of the traders or running foul of the white man's law-courts. Often, indeed, the traders appointed new chiefs whom they bolstered up with presents and with all the authority at their command. In British Columbia the abolition of slavery destroyed one of the main pillars in the social and political life, and the new standard of wealth enabled commoners and even ex-slaves to hold lavish potlatches and to usurp titles and privileges that traditionally could belong only to nobles. Every one then became a chief, as an old nobleman mourned; there were no longer commoners or slaves. The old order received its final death-blow when potlatches also fell under the ban of the law, and the Indians were forbidden to perform the religious ceremonies or hold the social functions that tradition linked inseparably with feasting and the giving of numerous gifts. On the plains the military organization of the Indians became useless when there were no more buffaloes to hunt, and the strong arm of the white man forbade raids on neighbouring tribes. The chiefs became chiefs only in name, for the real authority had passed for-ever from their hands; and the Europeans who usurped their lands recognized no distinctions of rank, but brushed to one side every Indian alike with feelings of mingled pity and contempt.

Ancestor-worship in China, and Zoroastrianism in Persia and India, have held together their adherents even in the face of extreme social and economic upheavals. But the nature-worship of the Indians was too vague, too eclectic to withstand the assault of a highly organized proselytizing religion like Christianity, or to serve as a rallying ground for the bands and tribes that struggled without guidance to adjust their lives afresh. Taboos and superstitions of various kinds had formed its buttresses, and when the taboos were disregarded with impunity by the white man, and the super-stitions aroused only incredulity and ridicule, the entire edifice toppled down in ruins. The epidemic of smallpox hastened its downfall, for in those days of trial and suffering that would have tested the strength of any religion the Indians called on their dei-ties, their guardian spirits, and their medicine-men in vain. In certain places they tried to build up their religion anew on foun-dations borrowed from Christianity, but except among the Iroquois, with whom the doctrines of Handsome Lake still count a few adherents, the building could not last. When the missionaries of a dominant race can invoke the aid of economic interests, they meet with little resistance from ill-organized religions. Although most of the tribes still cling to some of their old superstitions and beliefs, all of them very quickly transferred their allegiance to one or other of the Christian churches.

Economically and socially, then, the Indians were cut adrift from their old moorings at the very time when their ranks were being decimated by previously unknown diseases. Such results from contact with Europeans were perhaps inevitable, although human foresight exercised without regard to selfish interests could have eased the transition to the new conditions and prevented much hardship and suffering. The picture, of course, had its brighter side. Europeans put an end to war, the blood-feud, infanticide, and the abandonment of the aged and sick. They equipped the Indians with better tools and weapons, taught them to build more comfortable homes, and introduced agriculture and stock raising to replace the vanished game. But when survival or extinction depends on the measure of a people's adaptability, even an amelioration in the conditions of life may bring disaster; for success and failure in adaptation depend only partly on the external conditions, partly, also, on psychological factors that are not easily recognized or controlled.

Actually, most tribes have survived, though in some the decline has been rapid and extinction seems not far remote. At the risk of repeating what was stated in earlier chapters and what may appear in Part II of this book, we may briefly outline their histories and present status.

The most fortunate Indians, perhaps, were the tribes of the Maritime Provinces and of the St. Lawrence valley who bore the brunt of the first invasion. The settlers were then coming in small numbers to a country still entirely unknown, and they depended on the goodwill of the natives for the security of their families and homes. Life was very simple in the sixteenth and seventeenth centuries. Few people could read or write, and steam engines, telegraphs, and newspapers had not yet stirred men's thoughts. Many of the differences between the pioneer and the Indian were superficial only, and the chasm that separated the two peoples could be bridged without great difficulty. Moreover, in those early days there was a shortage of women in the new colony, and Indian girls trained in the convents made excellent wives for isolated farmers and fur traders. Intermarriage was, therefore, very frequent in French Canada, the more frequent because the French, like the Spanish and south Europeans generally, have never developed the extreme prejudice against racial admixture that characterizes the north Europeans. These conditions endured with little change for over a hundred and fifty years, allowing racial blending and acculturation to increase with each succeeding generation until most of the descendants of these eastern Indians became entirely absorbed into the white race, or so completely lost their original characteristics that they were no longer distinguishable. If considerable numbers still cling to the reserves that were allotted to them long ago, it is not because they are in most cases incapable of holding their own under modern conditions, but because as wards of the government they enjoy certain economic advantages which they would lose by accepting citizenship.

The tribes north of the St. Lawrence, and the Ojibwa bands north of the Great Lakes, have readjusted their lives less perfectly. Their territories were heavily forested, permitting of agriculture only in certain localities, and then only after extensive clearing. The fur trade kept them moderately prosperous in earlier days, but the game has greatly diminished since white trappers have encroached on their domains, prospectors, mining and lumber companies have invaded the region, and finally the railways have driven thin lines of settlements through some of the best hunting-grounds. So trapping brings in ever dwindling returns, while the needs of the Indians have increased rather than decreased. The enterprising white man despises them for their unprogressiveness, and mining and lumber camps undermine both their morale and their morals. Miscegenation occurs slowly, but only with the lowest class of whites who bring about no improvement. So civilization, as it flows past their doors, seems to be entrapping them in a backwash that leaves only one issue, the absorption of a few families into the aggressive white race and the decline and extinction of the remainder.

The plains' tribes did not incur the full pressure of the European invasion until the second half of the nineteenth century, when small farming communities were springing up along the old trading routes, the antelope and buffalo were disappearing, and a railway threatened to bisect the territory. To clear the prairies for closer settlement the government then set aside certain tracts for occupation by the Indians alone, and undertook the difficult task of transforming them from purely hunting peoples into agriculturalists on the wheat lands and raisers of cattle and horses on the plateaux. For a period the Indians stagnated, unable to stifle their longing for the old free days of buffalo hunting and the excitement of the chase. Some of the bands then responded vigorously, especially the Blackfoot, who to-day contribute their full quota to the car-loads of grain that find their way to the flour mills. Others never recovered from the transplanting. The Sarcee, for example, after their removal to a rather infertile tract of land on the outskirts of Calgary, submitted only half-heartedly to a forced agriculture and stock raising that yielded little profit and few thrills. Ill success in these occupations increased their apathy, and proximity to a city that scorned them as tourist attractions only, and to white farmers who deemed them unworthy of a white man's wage, still further lowered their morale. They lost all desire to recuperate, all ambition to stand on their feet in the economic world. So they are fast declining, and probably within another century this tribe will be no more.

The inland tribes of British Columbia experienced much the same difficulties in readjustment as the plains' Indians, and faced the situation with equally varying results. The Kootenay, who occupied a splendid ranching country, energetically seized hold of the new career that opened out to them, a career that fostered their love of horses and involved no tremendous upheaval in the social sphere; but many of the Salish and Carrier bands, condemned from a nomadic hunting life to a quiet tilling of the soil, became spiritless and started down the road to decline. The tribes of the coast, absorbed in ceremonies and rituals that emphasized the ever-present rivalries and class distinctions while feignedly commemorating the glories of a visionary past, received only a very short warning before the European invasion broke on them in full force. They could not change the entire economic and social framework of their lives before the flood of settlement rolled over their villages and submerged the inhabitants beyond all hope of rescue. Helplessly they were tossed at the mercy of the tide, unable to gain a secure foothold. The survivors to-day, with few exceptions, feel that their race is run and calmly, rather mournfully, await the end.

62164

The transformation of the Indian. A Chilcotin cowboy.
(Photo by Harlan I. Smith.)

Nearing their end also, it would seem, are the Athapaskan tribes of the Mackenzie valley. Yet civilization did not come to them suddenly, nor did it require from them revolutionary changes. Apparently these Athapaskans were less virile than other tribes, lacked stamina and self-confidence in the presence of unforeseen difficulties and of situations for which there were no parallels. They had scattered like sheep before the advance of the Crees in the eighteenth century, and evaded in terror the Eskimo who occasionally ascended the river a hundred or more miles from its mouth. Nevertheless they could not endure bondage or the loss of their former freedom. The trading-posts that destroyed their economic independence destroyed also their weak moral and mental fibre, dissipating any resistance they might have offered to the tuberculosis that now seems endemic and the epidemics of influenza and other diseases that periodically sweep through their ranks. Sturdier peoples would have thriven under the new economic régime, which offered security and reasonable prosperity in place of perpetual hardship and strife; but the Athapaskans lacked vigour to react to the stimulus and are slowly fading away in despair.[1]

The Eskimo of the Arctic and sub-Arctic coasts differed from the Indians not only in their mode of life, but in temperament. They were a hardy, resourceful people, fond of laughter and cheerful even in extreme adversities. Their resourcefulness permitted their rapid and easy adaptation to the new conditions, and their exceptional mechanical ability enabled them to grasp and use effectively even modern inventions like the marine gas-engine. The diseases that ravaged all the aborigines of Canada impaired their numbers but neither lessened their courage nor lowered their vitality. Ever since these natives came into close contact with Europeans they have served the white man loyally, as hunters and drivers of dog-teams, and more recently as seamen and engineers on small power-boats. If medical attention and instruction in hygiene reduces the present high death rate, and a wise regulation of the fur trade or the successful establishment of reindeer introduces an era of continuous prosperity, thereby preventing the recurrence of the famines that were so destructive of the race in past ages, the Eskimo will undoubtedly rebuild their lives on a secure foundation and play an important rôle in the development of Canada's far north.

---

[1] It may be that the same psychological weakness has contributed to the decline of the Athapaskan-speaking Sarcee, who did not descend to the prairies until a few centuries ago.

It is not possible now to determine what will be the final influence of the aborigines on the generations of Canadian people still to come. Doubtless all the tribes will disappear. Some will endure only a few years longer, others, like the Eskimo, may last several centuries. Some will merge steadily with the white race, others will bequeath to future generations only an infinitesimal fraction of their blood. Culturally they have already contributed everything that was valuable for our own civilization beyond what knowledge we may still glean from their histories concerning man's ceaseless struggle to control his environment.

THE INDIANS OF CANADA

PART II

CHAPTER XVIII

MIGRATORY TRIBES OF THE EASTERN WOODLANDS

In the first part of this work we outlined in bold relief the main features in the lives of our Indians and Eskimo, considered *en masse,* and discussed what little we know concerning their origins and earlier histories. In this second part we will briefly pass in review each physiographic region, sketch the chief characteristics of its principal tribes and summarize their histories since their contact with Europeans. We may logically open our account with the eastern woodlands, with the migratory tribes of Algonkian speech that did not till the soil; and commence with the extinct Beothuk Indians of Newfoundland.

BEOTHUK

The word Beothuk meant probably " man " or " human being," but early European visitors to Newfoundland considered it the tribal name of the aborigines who were inhabiting the island. They gave them also another name, " Red Indians," because they smeared their bodies and clothing with red ochre, partly for religious reasons, apparently, partly as a protection against insects.[1] They may have been lighter in colour than the Indians of the Maritime Provinces,[2] from whom they differed in several ways. Thus, they had no dogs, and did not make pottery, but cooked their food in vessels of birch bark.[3] For sleeping places within their bark wigwams they dug trenches which they lined with branches of fir or pine. Their canoes, though made of birch bark like those of other eastern tribes, were very peculiar in shape, each gunwale presenting the outline of a pair of

---

[1] Just as the Montagnais of the Labrador peninsula smeared themselves with seal-oil. Hind, H. Y.: " Explorations in the Interior of the Labrador Peninsula"; vol. i, p. 177 (London, 1863).

[2] This assertion of some eighteenth century writers, however, seems rather improbable.

[3] There seems to be no evidence that they used soapstone cooking vessels like the Eskimo. Probably it was the latter, not the beothuk, who worked the soapstone quarry at Fleur-de-Lys, on the northeast coast of Newfoundland (*See* illustration, p. 231).

crescent moons; and they speared seals with harpoons modelled on an archaic Eskimo type. Many of their graves contain bone ornaments of curious shapes and etched with strange designs. We know nothing concerning their political organization except that they were divided into small bands of closely related families, each with its nominal leader. Some meagre vocabularies of their language suggest that they spoke two or three dialects of a common tongue, although the entire tribe could hardly have numbered much more than five hundred individuals when Cabot discovered Newfoundland in 1497.

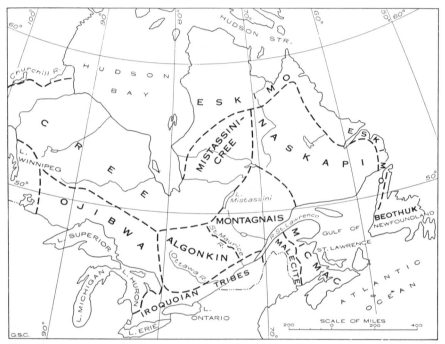

Approximate distribution of the eastern Algonkian tribes in 1525 A.D.

The European fishermen who settled around the shores of the island in the sixteenth, seventeenth, and eighteenth centuries resented their petty pilfering, and shot them down at every opportunity, the French even placing a bounty on their heads; and the Micmac who crossed over from Nova Scotia in the eighteenth century hunted them relentlessly far into the interior. The Beothuk attempted to retaliate, but, armed only with bows and arrows, they could not withstand the combined attacks of white and Micmac, and the last known survivor died in captivity at St. Johns in 1829. One or two families may have escaped from the island and found asylum among the Montagnais of Labrador, for an old woman, discovered by Dr. Frank Speck in 1910 among the Micmac of Nova Scotia, claimed to be the half-breed daughter of a Beothuk refugee. But Nancy Shawanah-dit, the captive who died in 1829, was the last " Red Indian " ever seen by white men, and the year of her death marks the date of their extinction.[1]

MICMAC

The Micmac ("Allies"), who united with the French and Eng-

72218

A Micmac woman. *(Photo by Frank Speck.)*

lish settlers to exterminate the unhappy Beothuk Indians of New-foundland, occupied at the time of their discovery not only the whole province of Nova Scotia, including Cape Breton island, but the north-ern portion of New Brunswick and the neighbouring Prince Edward island. They were a typical migratory people who lived in the woods

[1] Most of what we know about the Beothuk will be found in Howley, J. P.: " The Beothucks or Red Indians, the Aboriginal Inhabitants of Newfoundland"; Cambridge University Press, 1915.

during the winter months hunting moose, caribou, and porcupine, then moved down to the seashore in spring to gather shell-fish, to fish at the mouths of the rivers, and to hunt the seals near the coast. Like most Algonkian tribes they lived in conical wigwams covered with birch bark, and they made canoes and household utensils from the same material; but they manufactured also large wooden troughs for boiling their food, and even cooking pots from clay—unless indeed the numerous fragments of pottery found in Nova Scotia shell-heaps were the work of some earlier tribe. Their canoes resembled the peculiar Beothuk type more than the usual Algonkian, and their dialect was so different from those of the tribes around them, and from the Algonkian dialects spoken about the Great Lakes, that it suggests they may have been late intruders into the Maritimes, coming perhaps from the northwest.

The tribe was divided into several exogamous clans, each having its own symbols which its members tattooed on their persons, painted or worked in porcupine quills on their clothing, carved into ornaments to wear on their chests, and painted on their canoes, snowshoes, and other possessions. One clan used a cross as its symbol, to the great astonishment of the early missionaries, who immediately reinterpreted it for the promotion of Christianity. The chiefs of the various bands had comparatively little authority; one of their main duties, apparently, was to assign hunting territories to the different families. The war leaders were often not the actual chiefs, but men who had distinguished themselves in intertribal fighting; for in spite of their rather isolated position the Micmac fought with Algonkian tribes in the south, Iroquoian tribes in the west, and Eskimo and Montagnais on the north shore of the gulf of St. Lawrence. Their weapons were stone tomahawks,[1] bows and arrows, spears with two-edged blades of moose-bone, and bone or stone knives for scalping their foes. From mimic fights beforehand they augured the issue of their war-parties, and they celebrated their victories with savage feasts and dances at which they generally tortured to death their male prisoners, but spared the women and children for absorption into the tribe.

Micmac mothers strapped their babies to wooden cradles ornamented with painted designs, wampum and porcupine-quill embroid-

---

[1] But *See* footnote, p. 298.

ery. Marriage was a solemn ceremony preceded by a year or more of betrothal, when the youth resided with the parents of his future bride and gave them the products of his hunting. Equally solemn were the funeral rites, when the Indians wrapped their dead in birch-bark rolls, deposited them, seated as in life, within round, shallow graves, and burnt, or buried with them, all their implements and utensils to serve their needs in the after life. Elaborate ceremonies, too, attended the installation of chiefs, at least in historical times. It is, therefore, very surprising that the writers of the seventeenth century, to whom we owe most of our information concerning the Maritime Indians,[1] record no ceremony or ritual for the period of adolescence, which Indian tribes elsewhere regarded as the greatest crisis in a man's or woman's lifetime. Yet it is highly probable that every youth fasted to obtain a guardian spirit, since the medicine-men who pretended to cure diseases by incantations, by breathing and blowing on their patients, and by various juggling tricks, made the usual claim that it was through fasting and prayer they had gained the favour of the supernatural world. No youth, in any event, could participate in the councils of the tribe until he had proved his manhood by killing either a moose or a bear.

These old customs of the Micmac have long since disappeared and are now practically forgotten; for the tribe quickly took up agriculture, submitted to the teachings of the Jesuit missionaries, and intermarried freely with the French colonists who settled in their midst. Like their neighbours, the Malecite, they were faithful allies of the French throughout the wars of the seventeenth and eighteenth centuries. It is doubtful whether any pure-blood representatives of the tribe still exist, but their mixed descendants, to the number of nearly 4,000, which about equals the original population, occupy several small reserves in the Maritime Provinces and in Quebec, and a few families survive in Newfoundland. Of their old handicrafts only basketry persists to any great extent, and even this has been modified to meet the requirements of the market. In their mode of living to-day the majority of the Micmac are hardly distinguishable from poor whites.

---

[1] Especially Denys, Le Clercq, Lescarbot, and Biard in the " Jesuit Relations." *See* Bibliography, Appendix B.

MALECITE

The Malecite (the meaning of the name is uncertain) so closely resembled the Micmac in their customs that the early writers seldom distinguished the two tribes clearly. Their dialect, however, was quite different, and they raised considerable crops of maize, so that they were rather less dependent on fishing and the chase than their neighbours, who seem not to have practised agriculture before the seventeenth century. Politically, the Malecite were completely independent, and indeed on one occasion actively hostile to the Micmac. The boundary between the two tribes was roughly the height of land separating the waters that flow into the St. John river from those that enter the gulf of St. Lawrence. The territory of the Malecite, however, stretched beyond the drainage basin of St. John river to the shore of the St. Lawrence opposite Tadoussac, and included also part of the state of Maine. They joined with several Algonkian tribes to the southward to form a loose confederacy generally known as the Abenaki ("Eastern") Confederacy, which supported the French against the English colonists of New England and the league of the Iroquois. Driven across the border into Canada, they shared the same fate as the Micmac, being confined to a few reserves in New Brunswick and Quebec. To-day they number about 800, approximately the same as in pre-European times, but all the present population bear a strong infusion of white blood.

MONTAGNAIS AND NASKAPI

These two tribes (*Montagnais*, "Mountaineers"; *Naskapi*, "rude, uncivilized people") were the first to come into close contact with Europeans, yet they have remained, in some districts, almost more primitive than any other Indians in Canada. This is partly due, no doubt, to the character of the country they inhabit, for it covers so vast an area, and much of it is so rugged and inhospitable, that even to-day it has not been fully explored. The territory of the Montagnais comprised the huge square bounded on one side by the north shore of the gulf of St. Lawrence between the St. Maurice river and Seven Islands, on the other by the height of land that separates the waters flowing into the St. Lawrence from those flowing into James bay. The Naskapi occupied a still larger area; they roamed the entire Labrador peninsula east of a line from Seven Islands to lake Nichikun, and a second from lake Nichikun to Ungava bay, with the exception of the narrow belt of coast-line from Ungava bay to the strait of Belle Isle, which was controlled by Eskimo.

Both the Montagnais and the Naskapi, like the Micmac, were nomadic peoples ignorant of agriculture and living exclusively by hunting and fishing. Their dialects were almost identical, and their customs so closely alike that the two tribes were hardly distinguishable. Such differences as did exist arose in the main from differences in their environments, for the Montagnais country was a well-wooded area abounding in moose, whereas much of the Naskapi territory was

54584

Camp of a Naskapi family. *(Photo by F. W. Waugh.)*

open plateau covered with grasses and lichens, the natural feeding-ground for herds of barren-ground caribou. The Montagnais, therefore, covered their conical wigwams with birch bark and hunted principally the moose during the winter months, moving down the rivers in the spring to spear salmon and eels, and to harpoon the seals that were then plentiful along the shores of the St. Lawrence. The Naskapi, on the other hand, covered their wigwams with caribou skin, and hunted the caribou from midsummer until early spring, when some of them moved down to the coast, like the Montagnais, while others remained inland to fish in various lakes and rivers, and to hunt hares, porcupines, and other small game.

The southern Montagnais wore practically the same costume—robe, breech-cloth, leggings, and moccasins—as the tribes in the Maritime Provinces, like whom, also, they generally went bareheaded in winter, while protecting their arms with detachable sleeves pinned in front and behind. But the harsher climate in the interior of the Labrador peninsula compelled the Naskapi, and some of the more northern Montagnais, to adopt the tailored shirt of the coastal Eskimo, and to fit it occasionally with a hood for winter use. The Naskapi nearly always adorned these shirts with geometrical patterns, which they printed in red (now in paints of various colours) by means of curious stamps carved from bone or antler.

Neither the Montagnais nor the Naskapi possessed any true tribal organization. Each was divided into a number of small bands that were interrelated by marriage, but politically quite distinct and in possession of separate hunting areas. Even these bands had no organized government, for though certain individuals might be designated chiefs, they wielded little or no authority. In the wars waged by the Montagnais against the Micmac and Iroquois it was a general council of the warriors that decided the plan of campaign, and in the actual fighting each man was practically a law unto himself, although the leaders generally arrayed their forces in definite order before an attack. The weapons of the Montagnais were clubs, spears, bows and arrows, and knives to cut off the heads or remove the scalps of fallen foes. A few warriors may have adopted the shields covered with moosehide, and the coats of mail fashioned from wooden slats, which the Iroquois often used to protect their bodies against arrows; for it was from the Iroquois that the Montagnais learned to fortify their camps with barricades of trees. The Naskapi, who fought only with the Eskimo, used the same weapons as the Montagnais (which, indeed, served both tribes for hunting even more than for war), but dispensed with the club, the armour, and the shield. They seem to have made no prisoners except perhaps women, whom the hunters probably took for wives, whereas the Montagnais imbibed all the ferocity of their Iroquois foes, and savagely inflicted on male captives the most cruel tortures in their power.

Montagnais and Naskapi women carried their babies in bags ("moss-bags"), not in the wooden cradles preferred by the Algonkian peoples around them. Girls in the more northern tribe enjoyed making and dressing dolls, an amusement rare among Indian children, and probably stimulated by the neighbouring Eskimo. Adolescent girls of both the Montagnais and Naskapi tribes passed a period in seclusion, and boys fasted to obtain the blessings of the unseen world. Parents gave away their daughters in marriage without any ceremony, and without much consideration for their wishes; but a son-in-law had to serve his wife's parents for a year before he could take back his wife to his family. The Montagnais wrapped their dead in birch bark, buried them in the ground, and held a memorial feast; but the Naskapi deposited them on scaffolds or suspended them from trees, adopting burial in the ground only after their contact with Europeans.[1]

The Naskapi and the Montagnais believed vaguely in a great sky god to whom they occasionally offered smoke from their pipes. Of more concern to them, however, were the numberless supernatural beings whom they postulated in the world around them, and the souls of the animals on which they depended for their food supply. They strove to avoid giving offence to these animals by the observance of various taboos, and they trusted to the guardian spirits acquired in dreams, and the fancied powers of their medicine-men, to ward off attacks from malicious spirits and to shield them from the sorcery of their fellowmen. An early Jesuit missionary regarded these two peoples as the most superstitious of all Indians on account of the abnormal credence they placed in dreams and visions, although in reality they were no more credulous than other tribes. Medicine-men conjured up their familiars inside cylindrical lodges (just as the witch of Endor conjured up Samuel for Saul), and inquired from them the cause of some tribesman's sickness, or the broken taboo that was responsible for the scarcity of game. To prove the genuineness of their calling they sometimes allowed themselves to be lashed —hands, body, and feet—with stout caribou thongs, released themselves by jugglery, and cast out the thongs to the awe-struck spectators. Lay Indians frequently divined their success or failure in the chase by scrying, or by the marks on the scorched shoulder-blade of

---

[1] See Turner, L.: "Ethnology of the Ungava District, Hudson Bay Territory"; Eleventh Ann. Rept., Bureau of Am. Ethn., p. 272 (Washington, 1894). James McKenzie, writing of the Naskapi who frequented the southern coast of the Labrador peninsula in 1808, said that they buried their dead in the ground, with the utensils and wearing apparel they might need in the after life (McKenzie, James: "The King's Posts"; in Masson, ii, p. 418). The Montagnais often raised their dead on scaffolds, but only in winter, apparently, and as a preliminary to burial in the ground ("Jesuit Relations," vol. v, pp. 129-131).

an animal; and to give them good fortune in their hunting they carried ceremonial pack-straps ornamented with representations of their visions.

Contact with Europeans was disastrous to both tribes, although the Montagnais welcomed Champlain with enthusiasm when his musket gained them a signal victory over the Iroquois. For the latter, armed by the Dutch of Pennsylvania, raided far into the Montagnais territory, exterminating several bands and scattering others. Later, the game supply diminished owing to intensive slaughter with firearms; the moose disappeared entirely from certain districts, and on the barren grounds the depleted herds of caribou ceased to visit many of their ancient haunts. The struggle for existence then became harder and starvation more frequent. The fur trade helped the Indians until white men encroached on their best trapping and hunting grounds; then it called for greater effort and yielded diminishing returns. Measles and other diseases decimated their ranks, and many of the interior natives, urged by missionaries to settle on the coast, fell victims to lung afflictions aggravated by the damp sea air.[1]

So both the Montagnais and the Naskapi declined rapidly. To-day the two tribes combined number less than four thousand, although the Montagnais (with some Algonkin and Malecite allies) once mustered 1,000 warriors at the mouth of the Saguenay river. Mooney gives them a pre-European population of 5,500, which seems a very conservative estimate.[2] Most of the survivors are still hunters and trappers, more or less enchained to the trading-posts where they dispose of their furs for rifles, ammunition, woollen clothing, cloth tents, sewing-machines, gramaphones, and other products of our modern civilization. The Naskapi in the centre and north of the Labrador peninsula have been too isolated to mingle much with Europeans, but the majority of the Montagnais carry an infusion of white blood in their veins.

ALGONKIN

Adjoining the Montagnais in the east, and merging in the west with the Ojibwa of the Great Lakes region, were a number of scattered bands commonly classed together as Algonkin, from the

---

[1] Cf. McKenzie, James: " The King's Posts"; in Masson, op. cit. ii, p. 426.
[2] Mooney: Op. cit., p. 24.

name[1] applied by Champlain and his contemporaries to the bands below Ottawa, who made common cause with the Montagnais against the inroads of the Iroquois. As in their geographical position, so

74876

Algonkins in aboriginal dress. *(Reproduced from "Works of Samuel de Champlain, edited by H. P. Biggar," vol. 3, p. 44, The Champlain Society, Toronto, 1929.)*

[1] The meaning of the name is not quite certain. One authority suggests its derivation from a Micmac word signifying " at the place of spearing fish and eels (from the bow of a canoe)."

also in their customs and beliefs, they held an intermediate place between the peoples that flanked them on either side: they had the wooden cradle-board, the double-headed drum, and, in the western bands at least, the annual festival to the dead and the totemic clan system of the Ojibwa, but they lacked, like the Montagnais, the rice and maple-syrup industries and the secret medicine-society of the western tribe. A few bands along the Ottawa, through their proximity to the Hurons, learned to grow a little maize, and a few squashes and beans; but their methods were so primitive, and their dread of Iroquois raids so constant, that agriculture added but little to their food supply. In the seventeenth century the Iroquois drove them to the north and east away from the lower Ottawa and St. Lawrence rivers, but when the power of the Iroquois declined they gradually drifted back to their old territories. Few in numbers, and scattered in small bands over a large, densely wooded area where the best hunting and trapping districts lay in the hills away from the main routes of travel and settlement, they exercised hardly any influence and received very little attention throughout historical times. Many of their women married white trappers, lumbermen, and pioneer farmers, and their descendants have merged imperceptibly into the civilized communities that now occupy their territory. The remainder, numbering a little over 2,000 (the majority, perhaps, of mixed blood), are restricted to a few reserves in eastern Ontario and western Quebec. There, some raise a little garden produce, and serve as licensed guides to the sportsmen who visit their districts to fish and hunt. Others, notably the Tête-de-Boule band on the upper waters of the St. Maurice river, still support themselves in their old nomadic fashion by hunting and trapping, but purchase with their furs, at the trading-posts, most of the necessities of life except food.

It is difficult to estimate the numbers of the Algonkin in the early sixteenth century when Cartier sailed up the St. Lawrence, for before the French missionaries and fur traders had visited all their bands, more than a century later, the tribe had suffered heavy losses from introduced diseases, and some of its bands had been scattered by the Iroquois. A reasonable estimate of the pre-European population would place it between 3,000 and 4,000.

OJIBWA

Numerically the Ojibwa or Chippewa (both are forms of the same word, which signifies " people whose moccasins have puckered seams ") were the strongest nation in Canada, totalling even to-day around 20,000.[1] They controlled all the northern shores of lakes Huron and Superior from Georgian bay to the edge of the prairies, and at the height of land north of lake Superior where the rivers begin to flow towards Hudson bay they united with their near kinsmen, the Cree. So numerous were they, and so large a territory did they cover, that we may separate them into four distinct groups or tribes, viz., the Ojibwa of the Lake Superior region,[2] the Mississauga (" people of the large river-mouth ") of Manitoulin island and of the mainland around the Mississagi river, the Ottawa (" Traders ") of the Georgian Bay region,[3] and the Potawatomi (" people of the place of fire ") on the west side of lake Huron within the state of Michigan, some of whom moved across into Ontario in the eighteenth and nineteenth centuries. Three of these four tribes, the Lake Superior Ojibwa, the Ottawa, and the Potawatomi, formed a loose confederacy that became known in the eighteenth century as the Council of the Three Fires.

Each tribe, as among other Algonkians, was subdivided into numerous bands that possessed their own hunting territories and were politically independent of one another, though closely connected by intermarriage. The majority of the bands were small, numbering probably not more than 300 to 400 individuals; and each contained an indefinite number of exogamous totemic clans in which the children inherited the totems of their fathers.[4] These clans had no political functions and very little religious significance, but being distributed among all the bands they gave the nation a certain unity, since fellow clansmen regarded one another as close kinsmen even when they belonged to different tribes. The real political unit was the band. Each had its own leader, who normally handed on his

---

[1] It is possible that they were exceeded by the Cree.

[2] These are often called Saulteaux, from their meeting place at the falls (Sault) of Sault St. Marie.

[3] In the early seventeenth century, when they first became known to Europeans, the Ottawa seem to have occupied part of Manitoulin island also.

[4] Skinner states that some of the Saulteaux clans north of lake Superior were matrilinear, i.e. children inherited the totems of their mothers (Skinner, A.: " Notes on the Eastern Cree and Northern Saulteaux"; Anth. Papers, Am. Mus, of Nat. Hist., vol. ix, pt. i, p. 149 f (New York, 1911)). But around lake Nipigon at least they were patrilinear (Cameron, D.: " The Nipigon Country, 1804"; in Masson, op. cit., ii, p. 246).

rank to his son; but the power and prestige attached to the position varied with the individual. There was no chief for a whole tribe, still less a leader who could unify the entire nation.

595

Ojibwa Indians in front of their birch-bark lodge. *(Photo by T. C. Weston.)*

The chief of a band was generally, but not always, its war captain. If he planned a raid against the Sioux or the Iroquois, the principal enemies of the Ojibwa, he first consulted his own followers, then sent either his personal lieutenant or a selected envoy with a pipe and tobacco to invite the participation of neighbouring bands. The envoy delivered his message to the assembled hunters, lit the pipe and handed it around the company. Those who were unwilling to join the war party passed it on without smoking; for no man who put it to his lips could refuse, without deep disgrace, to take part in the enterprise. The Ojibwa were braver warriors than most of the eastern Algonkians, and preserved much stricter discipline on the march. They used the same types of arms as their enemies—the bow and arrow, knobbed wooden club, knife, and a round shield covered with moosehide; and while the fighting lasted they spared neither man, woman, nor child. Whoever slew an enemy carried home the scalp for the victory dance, and thereafter enjoyed the privilege of wearing an eagle feather in his hair. Unlike the Montagnais and the Micmac, however, the Ojibwa never tortured their prisoners, and regarded the Iroquois with special loathing because of their inhuman conduct toward enemies who fell into their hands.

All the Ojibwa tribes subsisted to a considerable extent on vegetable foods. They gathered and stored away, in the late summer, vast quantities of the wild rice that grew in the shallow water around the edges of the lakes. In spring they collected the syrup from the maple trees, and in summer large stores of berries, which they preserved for the lean months of early winter. So, although they did not practise agriculture (except some of the Ottawa bands adjacent to the Hurons), they were not so completely dependent on fish and game as other Canadian tribes that did not cultivate maize. Nevertheless, they were as keen hunters, and as keen fishermen, as other Indians. Every winter the families scattered into the woods to pursue the moose; in spring and summer they killed beaver and smaller game, and caught suckers, pickerel, and pike; and in autumn, at the close of the rice harvest, they speared the larger fish—trout, whitefish, and sturgeon—that spawned at that season close to shore. These varied resources caused their lives to be no less migratory than those of their kindred to the east, whom they closely resembled in their extensive use of birch bark for canoes and wigwams.[1] The more southern Ojibwa, in early historical times at least, made clay pots, but too few to supersede the birch-bark utensils which, after all, were more satisfactory for a people constantly in motion.

Partly because the living conditions were a little easier, perhaps,[2] and partly because they were in contact with more advanced tribes in southeastern Ontario, in Michigan, Wisconsin, and Minnesota, the Ojibwa enjoyed a richer social life than the other Algonkian tribes of eastern Canada. The clans held annual feasts, and in the autumn of each year the people celebrated an All Souls' Day or Festival of the Dead, when they burnt a little food for the shades[3] of the departed

---

[1] The Ojibwa wigwam was dome shaped, however, and often covered with rushes instead of bark. For a good description of one See Grant, Peter: "The Saulteaux Indians"; in Masson, ii, p. 329.

[2] Yet the Ojibwa, like the Cree, often suffered from famine during the winter, and had the same dread of *windigos* or supernatural cannibals.

[3] They distinguished the shade or image of a man from his soul, believing that the former remained near his grave, or haunted the habitations of his kindred, whereas the latter went to the land of souls in the south.

and feasted and danced until morning. A pleasing ceremony accompanied the naming of each child; when the relatives and friends had gathered for the feast, the grandfather (or another elderly kinsman) took the child in his arms and called on all the great powers in the spiritual world to impart their blessing to its name. Neighbours joined in a feast over every bear laid low by a hunter's club, and they partook of the first game a boy killed, even if it were no larger than a rabbit. There was much jollity, too, in the sugar-making camps of early spring, and at the rice harvesting later in the summer. Food was generally plentiful at those seasons, giving leisure for dances and other pastimes. The men played lacrosse or gambled with bone dice, while the women either watched them or played a special ball game of their own.

The most notable event of the year, however, was the holding of the Midewiwin, or celebration of the Grand Medicine Society, a secret religious organization, open to both sexes, that exercised great influence among the Ojibwa, but existed nowhere else in Canada except among some of the neighbouring Cree. The full organization recognized four grades of membership;[1] even the lowest required a long period of preliminary instruction and the payment of heavy fees, and as the fees increased with each grade, only a few individuals ever attained the highest. The members, *mede,* were the principal doctors or medicine-men of the communities, and, like our own doctors, generally derived much profit and prestige from the practice of their profession. In treating the sick they employed mainly herbal remedies, some of them undoubtedly beneficial, such as the application of balsam gum to wounds, the majority utterly useless. Yet they effected many cures, most often, it would seem, from psychological causes, because the Ojibwa ascribed a soul and power to every tree and stone, and believed that their medicine-men, through the favour of the supernatural world, could attach this power to human beings. But they also believed that many supernatural spirits were unfriendly, and that by enlisting the aid of these hostile powers, or sometimes by purely sympathetic magic, the medicine-men could harm and even slay their fellowmen. So, a dread of witchcraft constantly infected their minds, converting into the grossest superstition what might have been a really beautiful religion.

---

[1] Some Potawatomi members of the society, now living in Parry Sound, recognize only one grade, and give an account of its ceremonies slightly different from the descriptions recorded from other bands.

In early historical times the Ojibwa recognized both a supreme good spirit, a sky-god who ruled the universe through a host of subordinate spirits, and a supreme evil spirit, sometimes regarded as a monstrous supernatural serpent. This dualism arose, probably, through Christian teaching, although the belief in a great sky-god may belong to aboriginal times. Men often prayed to the good spirit and offered him smoke from their pipes, or on special occasions a burnt offering of white dogs. But, regarding him as too remote to concern himself often with human affairs, they generally trusted to the subordinate spirits, and made each adolescent boy fast and dream in solitude to obtain one as his guardian.[1] Every hunter of note carried a " medicine-bag " containing herbs, roots, feathers, wooden images, and other objects revealed to him in his visions or taught him (for a price) by some medicine-man; usually, too, a drum to accompany his medicine-songs. In addition to the *mede*, or members of the Grand Medicine Society, there was an unorganized class of seers or conjurors who delivered their oracles from within cylindrical shrines exactly after the manner of the Montagnais.

The Ojibwa buried their dead in the ground and deposited with them food and tobacco for the four days' journey to the land of souls, whose ruler, according to the esoteric doctrines of the *mede*, was Nanibush, the great trickster and culture hero of the tribe[2] and the secret patron of the Grand Medicine Lodge. There, the souls dwelt in happiness, hunting and feasting and dancing as on earth. Hence relatives, while throwing away their own property to display their grief, dressed a dead man in his best apparel and deposited in the grave all his tools and equipment so that he might use their souls in his new abode.[3] If a chief had won great renown in war his kinsmen sometimes placed his body on a high scaffold, and suspended beside it the scalps he had taken, and other tokens of his valour. Thus they ensured that the prestige and honour he had gained during his earthly career would attend him without fail in the hereafter.

Despite their numbers and the large extent of territory they occupied, the Ojibwa did not play a very prominent part in the

---

[1] Many parents made their daughters, also, seek guardian spirits during their periods of seclusion. A man who wished his son to become a great medicine-man often made him sleep on a scaffold or in a "nest" in a tree.

[2] *See* Part I, p. 189.

[3] *Cf.* Champlain (Champlain Society edition), vol. i, p. 120, for the same practice among the Montagnais. It was indeed almost universal in Canada.

history of the Dominion. They fought with the Sioux southwest of lake Superior, participated in the wars against the Iroquois, and supported the French in their struggle against the English. The Ottawa were close friends of the Hurons, from whom they learned to cultivate maize; and their proximity to the Ottawa river gave them control of the main route to the lower St. Lawrence and the trading-posts of the early colonists, for the upper St. Lawrence was blocked by the hostile Iroquois. After destroying the Hurons, therefore, the Iroquois turned their arms against the Ottawa and drove them from Georgian bay. Some fled west towards lake Superior; others took refuge with their Potawatomi kinsmen in the United States. Half a century later many of these refugees returned to Manitoulin island and the north shore of lake Huron, where their descendants still survive.

36741

Ojibwa Indian women in a birch-bark canoe. *(Photo by F. W. Waugh.)*

About the beginning of the eighteenth century, when the strength of the Iroquois commenced to wane and a portion of the Ottawa were moving back into Canada, the main body of the Ojibwa suddenly entered on a career of expansion provoked by the diminution of the beaver within their domains. Many Missisauga moved into the old territory of the Hurons between lakes Huron and Erie, pushing out the Iroquois who had taken possession of the land; some of the Lake Superior Ojibwa occupied parts of Manitoba, Wisconsin, and Minnesota; and some spread eastward along the north shore of lake Huron into Georgian bay.

In these regions they have remained throughout the settlement of the country, becoming more and more closely confined to the numerous reserves that the government has set aside for their use. In southeastern Ontario they earn a rather meagre livelihood by farming; farther north, around the Great Lakes, they still hunt the moose and trap the fur-bearing animals, although game is decreasing, and white farmers and lumbermen have invaded many of their old hunting-grounds. Some find employment as guides and canoe-men, others eke out the diminishing supply of fish and meat with a little garden produce. New lumber and mining camps, new settlements and towns are springing up around them, and the old migratory life of hunting is fast becoming impossible. Nothing will then remain for them except the rather tedious occupations of the white man, in which the Indians are handicapped by lack of experience and training. Whether they can patiently endure continuous and monotonous toil, so unlike the strenuous but intermittent exertions of the chase, is uncertain; and modern industry has little sympathy for the unsteady labourer, especially if he differ in appearance and speech from the ordinary workman. So the future of the Ojibwa is not alluring. Doubtless a few will break altogether with their old traditions, merge their interests with the white man's, and prosper. The majority will be less fortunate. Some will join the ranks of our casual labourers; others will struggle against penury on miserable farms; and many families will succumb altogether, helplessly cast adrift in a strange and complex world that they are unable to comprehend.

CREE

The Cree (Cree: contraction of Kristineaux, the French form of a name, of unknown meaning, that a portion of the tribe applied to itself) were closely related and almost equal in number to the Ojibwa, whom they flanked on the north and west. Like the Ojibwa, too, they occupied an immense area of country. On the north they were bounded by the coast-line from Eastmain river nearly to Churchill; on the east by lakes Mistassini and Nichikun. Their western limits are uncertain, but in the early sixteenth century they appear to have wandered over part of the country west of lake Winnipeg, perhaps between the Red river and the Saskatchewan. As soon as they obtained firearms from Hudson bay, however, they expanded westward and northward, so that by the middle of the eighteenth century they controlled northern Manitoba and Saskatchewan as far as Churchill river, all northern Alberta, the valley of Slave river, and the southeastern part of Great Slave lake. Some of them had even raided up the Peace river into the Rocky mountains, and others down the Mackenzie to its delta almost within view of the Arctic sea, preceding in both directions the explorations of Sir Alexander Mackenzie. The acquisition of firearms by surrounding tribes, and a terrible epidemic of smallpox that devastated them in 1784, checked their further expansion. The Cree then became demoralized through spirituous liquors, underwent constant attack from the Blackfoot confederacy, and were decimated by a second epidemic of smallpox about 1838. From these disasters they never recovered, but remained scattered in whatever districts they found themselves, earning a meagre livelihood by hunting and trapping. Like some of the Athapaskan peoples, they took on the colour of the tribes with whom they had most contact, so that to-day we can divide them into two large groups:

(1) Plains' Cree, living on the prairies. These we shall consider in a later chapter.

(2) Woodland Cree, usually called Swampy Cree or Muskegon. They include not only the bands around the southern part of Hudson bay, but those living on Peace, Athabaska, and Slave rivers and on Athabaska and Great Slave lakes.

Like the Naskapi—but to an even greater extent—the Cree embellished themselves with tattoo marks, a practice not common among Algonkian tribes. Their women had a widespread reputation for beauty; in fact, so experienced a traveller as Mackenzie considered that they were better proportioned, and possessed more regular features, than any other Indians within the boundaries of Canada. In the more southern parts of their area the Woodland Cree dwelt in birch-bark wigwams, either dome-shaped like the Ojibwa wigwam. or conical like the dwellings elsewhere in the east;

A Cree Indian. (*Painting by Paul Coze.*
Reproduction rights reserved by the artist.)

farther north, where the birch trees were small and stunted, they substituted coverings of pine bark or the hide of the caribou.[1] The bands living around James bay often used soapstone pots for cooking their food instead of the usual birch-bark vessels, a practice they learned probably from the Eskimo. For scraping their skins, too, they employed a curved knife that resembled the everyday knife of Eskimo women, although bands west of Moose Factory used a chisel-shaped tool after the manner of the plains' tribes. Since the winter was rather more severe in the territory of the Woodland Cree than farther south, many of them eschewed the tanned hides of the Ojibwa and Algonkians, and wore in their stead coats and blankets made of woven hare skin, or of soft, warm caribou fur, similar to the coats of the Naskapi and some of the Montagnais. Other features differentiating them from their southern neighbours were the absence of mats, and of baskets made from roots or split twigs, together with the relative unimportance of fishing, which the Cree scorned in early days as unworthy of a hunter, and resorted to only from necessity.

The game in most repute were the woodland caribou, moose, beaver, and bear, but owing to the relative scarcity of these animals many bands subsisted in winter principally on hares, which they caught in snares made from the bark of the willow. Hares, like several other northern mammals, undergo periodic increase and decrease; they disappear almost completely every ninth winter and remain scarce for a year or two afterwards. During these seasons shortage of food caused many natives to die of starvation and sometimes led to cannibalism, which inspired no less horror among the Indians than among us. It must have occurred fairly frequently, however, for the early fur traders and explorers mention several instances[2] and it occupies a prominent place in the legends of the tribe, which abound in stories of *windigos*—human beings transformed into supernatural man-eating giants through the eating of human flesh. In spring and autumn the Cree secured many ducks and geese, and in the winter many grouse and ptarmigan; but naturally these minor foods could only supplement, not replace, the meat of the larger mammals.

---

[1] For a description of the tent of the northern Cree *See* Hearne: Op. cit., p. 74 f.
[2] *Cf.* " Twenty Years of York Factory, 1694-1714, Jérémie's Account of Hudson Strait and Bay"; translated by Douglas, R., and Wallace, J. N., p. 40 (Ottawa, 1926).

As among most Algonkian tribes, the only real social units were the bands and the families. Some bands from the Albany river westward developed totemic clans on the analogy of the Ojibwa, but these never gained a firm foothold and are now practically forgotten. Adolescents passed a period in seclusion fasting for visions, and men served their wives' parents for a term, although there was no formal marriage ceremony. Widows and orphans received the kindly treatment usually afforded them by Algonkian Indians, who differed in this respect from the Eskimo and from most of the Athapaskan-speaking tribes. Old people who could no longer keep up on the march were abandoned to starve, or killed at their own request. The dead were buried in the ground amid much lamentation and self-torture, and every year the Cree held a feast in their honour.

All these customs the Cree shared with the Ojibwa, like whom they had a ceaseless fear of witchcraft. Conjurors, indeed, wielded more influence than the so-called chiefs. In many districts there was a secret religious organization copied from the Grand Medicine Society of the Ojibwa, but its celebrations were concealed from the sight of the laity and its power was comparatively slight.[1] More deeply embedded in the lives of these Indians were the innumerable taboos and hunting customs intended to propitiate the spirits of the game. Every hunter carried a medicine-bag to help him in the chase, and in many bands every hide was ceremonially decorated with stripes and dots of red paint.

Even in Sir John Franklin's day the Cree had degenerated and were no longer the adventurous hunters and warriors who had traversed half the Dominion. The white man's liquor and the white man's diseases had left their mark, and recurring epidemics of diseases only intensified the effect. Tuberculosis became almost endemic in many districts, as it has among the tribes of the Mackenzie valley; and the Cree suffered heavily from epidemics of influenza in 1908 and 1909, and again in 1917. Their number (including the Plains' Cree) seems to have fallen away but little, for they registered about 20,000 in 1924; but many of the present day Cree carry a perceptible strain of European blood. Being a

---

[1] At the beginning of the eighteenth century the Lake Superior Ojibwa joined the Cree in their visits to the trading posts on Hudson bay, and the two tribes became closely intermingled. So the Cree whom Mackenzie describes (op. cit., p. xci ff) have all the characteristics of the Ojibwa. In early times they were probably much more distinct.

marginal people requiring large tracts of territory to ensure a livelihood by hunting and trapping, they have witnessed a ceaseless
encroachment on their hunting grounds and a steady diminution in
the supply of game and of fur-bearing animals. Semi-starvation
and diseases have lowered their physique, and the pitying scorn of
the white man destroys their morale and robs them of self respect
and pride of race. Their regeneration and preservation is thus both
an economic and a psychological problem. It requires their diversion
into new fields of activity as the old mode of life becomes more and
more impracticable, and their rehabilitation mentally so that they
can enter into competition with the white man on an equal footing.
A few families in the Peace River area have successfully taken to
horse raising, but in most parts of their territory the Cree seem now
to have neither the inclination nor the courage to strike out along a
new path, even when they are presented with the opportunity.

CHAPTER XIX

AGRICULTURAL TRIBES OF THE EASTERN WOODLANDS

When Jacques Cartier sailed up the St. Lawrence river in 1535 he found Iroquoians cultivating the land and controlling the country around the present site of Montreal; but when Champlain followed him sixty-eight years later this region was occupied by Algonkins, and the only part of Canada controlled by Iroquoians was the peninsula of southern Ontario south and west of lake Simcoe.[1] In the early seventeenth century, " the Hurons (or Wyandots), allied in origin and language to the Iroquois, numbered about 16,000 souls, and dwelt in several large villages in a narrow district on the high ground between lake Simcoe and Georgian bay of lake Huron. Their dwellings were bark cabins, clustered within stoutly palisaded walls, and near each fortified town were fields of corn, beans, pumpkins, and tobacco. Agricultural in habit, keen traders, and in the main sedentary, these semi-naked savages made short hunting and fishing excursions, and laid up stores for the winter. They were better fighters than the Algonkins[2] around them, yet were obliged gradually to withdraw northward and westward from Iroquois persecution, and during the period of the Jesuit missions were almost annihilated by the latter. To the southwest, across a wide stretch of unpopulated forest, were the allies and kindred of the Hurons, the Tionontates, called also Petuns, or Tobacco Nation, a term having its origin in their custom of cultivating large fields of tobacco, which commodity they used in a widespread barter with other tribes. To the southeast of the Petuns, west of lake Ontario and on both sides of the gorge of Niagara, were the peaceful Atiwandaronks, who, being friends alike of Iroquois, Algonkins, and Hurons, were known as the Neutral Nation. To the eastward of the Neutrals, strongly entrenched in the interlocking basins of the Genesee and the Mohawk, lay the dread confederacy of the Iroquois, who in time were to spread like a pestilence over the lands of all their neighbours."[3]

---

[1] Hewitt (J. N. B., article " Hurons," Handbook of American Indians North of Mexico) asserts that the vocabulary collected by Cartier on Montreal island indicates that the inhabitants were Hurons, who must subsequently have retreated to the westward. Yet the pottery and other objects dug up at Montreal resemble most closely remains from Mohawk and Onondaga sites in New York and Vermont, and the traditions of these two tribes bring them from the St. Lawrence. The affiliations of Cartier's Hochelagans are, therefore, still unsettled.

[2] i.e. Algonkians, including both the Algonkin proper and the Ojibwa.

[3] " Jesuit Relations," vol. 1, p. 22.

HURONS

The confederacy of the Hurons (Old French *Huron*: a bristly, unkempt knave) consisted of four separate tribes, the Bear, the Cord, the Rock, and the Deer, together with a few smaller communities[1]

74877

Hurons in aboriginal dress. *(Reproduced from "Works of Samuel de Champlain, edited by H. P. Biggar," vol. 3, p. 135, The Champlain Society, Toronto, 1929.).*

[1] These smaller communities were mostly Iroquoian, but one at least was Algonkian, showing how slight was the barrier imposed by their different languages.

that united with them at different periods for protection against the
League of the Iroquois. The real name of the confederacy was
Wendat ("Islanders" or "Dwellers on a Peninsula"), whence the term
Wyandot subsequently applied to the mixed remnants of both the
Hurons and the Tobacco people; and the strongest tribe was the
Bear, which contained about half the population. When Champlain
visited the country in 1615 the Hurons occupied eighteen villages,
all situated within a few miles of one another; but the number varied
at different dates, for no settlement lasted longer than from twelve

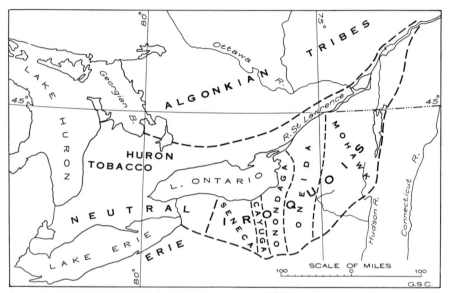

Approximate distribution of the Iroquoian tribes in 1525 A.D. Based partly on map
in Beauchamp, W. M.: "A History of the New York Iroquois"; N.Y. State Museum,
Bull. 78. The boundaries between the Huron, Tobacco, and Neutral nations, and
what tribe or tribes controlled the north shore of the St. Lawrence river, are not
known.

to twenty years on account of the depletion of the fuel supply and
the exhaustion of the unfertilized soil. Only eight of the eighteen
villages were fortified with palisades and ramparts; to these the
inhabitants of the remainder fled for refuge in times of danger, if
indeed they did not scatter to the woods like sheep. Owing to the
size of the dwellings, each of which housed from eight to twenty-four
families, with an average of five or six persons to a family, a village
seldom contained more than twenty or thirty dwellings, irregularly
arranged at short intervals from each other to avoid complete destruc-

tion by fire; for the carelessness of the Indians and the inflammable nature of their bark huts made fires of very frequent occurrence. Naturally there was no privacy when all the actions of a family were open to the view of other families within the hut. Yet the homes of the Hurons were quiet and peaceful, and dissensions

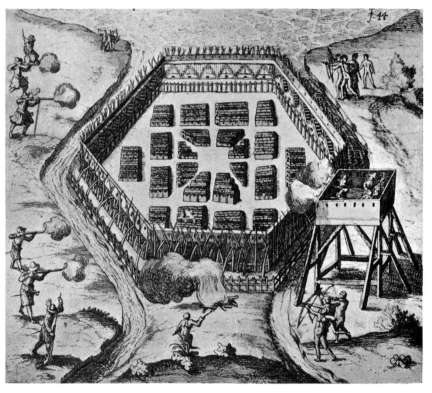

74878

Hurons and French attacking a palisaded Onondaga village. *(Reproduced from "Works of Samuel de Champlain, edited by H. P. Biggar," vol. 3, p. 135, The Champlain Society, Toronto, 1929.)*

within a village infrequent, though common enough between the different tribes that made up the confederacy.

The cornfields lay close to the villages, and all around were dense woods that sheltered large numbers of deer and bears. Well-defined paths radiated toward neighbouring villages, but there were no bridges spanning the numerous rivers and streams. These could be crossed occasionally on fallen tree trunks, but most often only by swimming or wading.

For their food supply the Hurons depended principally on maize, with beans and pumpkins as subsidiary crops. Fish was fairly plentiful, but meat rather scarce, although in the autumn of the year the hunters drove the white-tailed deer into pens and killed considerable numbers. Under normal conditions every family was self-sustaining; it owned (in usufruct) a plot in the cornfields, obtained its own fish, and was allotted a share of the venison secured in the communal hunt. The planting, weeding, and harvesting of the crops devolved on the women, but the men assisted them occasionally, agriculture being no disgrace to an able-bodied Huron hunter as it was to an Iroquois. As soon as the planting ended, however, the men scattered in all directions to trade with neighbouring peoples, or to raid the camps of the Iroquois south of the St. Lawrence, so that only a minimum force of warriors remained in the settlements to protect them against attack. June to September, in fact, were favourite months for the Iroquois themselves to raid the Hurons, partly because travel was easiest at that season, and partly because the country was then so largely denuded of its men. Both warriors and traders returned about September, when the women were harvesting and storing away the corn; and they devoted the rest of the year to hunting and fishing. During November, several parties established camps on the islands at the bottom of Georgian bay to capture with seines the sturgeon, whitefish, and trout that spawned close to shore during that month. Some made brief hunting and fishing excursions between December and March, but the majority loitered around the settlements; for those months were taken up with festivals and council meetings, which kept the people in such constant motion travelling from one village to another as to leave little time for other pursuits.

On the whole, the men had more leisure than the women, for while the former hunted and fished, traded with neighbours and raided the Iroquois, built houses and canoes and fashioned their various tools and weapons, the women performed all the household work as well as the work in the fields. It was they who gathered the winter's supply of fuel,[1] who made the clay cooking pots and the bark vessels that served for dishes,[2] the wicker baskets for carry-

---

[1] In March and April, because in the late spring and summer berry picking and the cornfields engaged all their attention.

[2] The men sometimes carved wooden bowls from tree knots, and they constructed their bark canoes without the aid of the women. Among the Algonkians the men made the frames of the canoes, but the women sewed together the strips of bark.

ing in the grain, the bark chests for storing it safely during the winter, and the rush mats that closed the doorways of the cabins and overlaid the dirt floor where the inmates slept. It was the women, too, who gathered all the berries, converted the raw hides into clothing, and collected and twisted the fibre of the basswood and nettle from which the men made their fish nets. They had occupations, indeed, that could keep them busy at every season, but, like the men, they looked forward with zest to the winter, when they could paint their faces, bedeck themselves with ornaments, and participate in the festivals and dances.

These festivals, which in all cases had a religious significance, have been classified by an early missionary under four heads: singing feasts, farewell feasts, feasts of thanksgiving, and feasts for deliverance from sickness,[1] the last being apparently the public ceremonies that accompanied admission into one of the numerous medicine societies. They were held in the village council-house, an exceptionally large cabin erected at the same time as the ordinary dwellings; and they lasted from one to fifteen days, according to their importance, the number of the guests, and the supply of food. The sachems and old men, who had charge of the arrangements, issued invitations in the form of sticks to the sachems of neighbouring villages, who then regulated the size of their delegations in accordance with the number of sticks they received. Singing and dancing signalized every feast, but the so-called "singing" feasts, held for various reasons, but especially as a preparation for the war-path, ranked first in public estimation, with the exception of the Feast of the Dead, which was celebrated only once in every ten or twelve years. On that occasion each family of Hurons solemnly resurrected the bodies of relatives who had died since the preceding feast, removed and burned the decayed flesh (or wrapped the body, if still intact, in a new robe), and transported the bones to a common sepulchre for reinterment with the rest of the tribal dead. Since all the tribes reinterred their dead at the same time, the entire country was drowned in tears for nearly a fortnight, although feasting, archery contests, and liberal distributions of presents throughout the proceedings mitigated the strain of the prolonged mourning and even introduced a measure of entertainment.[2]

---

[1] " Jesuit Relations," vol. 10, p. 177 f. *Cf*. Sagard, vol. ii, p. 286.
[2] For details *See* " Jesuit Relations," vol. 10. p. 279 ff; Sagard, chapter xvi.

During the period from autumn to spring, and especially during the various festivals, the Hurons spent much of their time in gambling. The favourite outdoor game was lacrosse, in which the villages often contended against each other, not without frequent

Hurons gambling with cherry-stones. *(Reproduced from Lafitau, Mœurs des Sauvages Amériquains, vol. 2, p. 341, Paris, 1724.)*

dissensions and quarrels. Indoors they gambled with straws and plum-stones, women against women and men against men. The losers generally bore their discomfiture with equanimity even when they parted with all their possessions; but when some hot-headed individual assaulted and murdered his antagonist, as happened not infrequently, his entire village was held responsible for the crime and mulcted in a heavy indemnity.

It was during the winter festivals that the medicine-men appeared most prominent, although they exerted great influence at every season of the year. There were at least three orders among them: conjurers who claimed to cause rain and sunshine; seers who claimed to discover lost objects and to divine the future; and practitioners who pretended to diagnose the causes of disease, to replace a sick man's missing soul, and to extract from his body some object mysteriously implanted there by the evil arts of some other practitioner.[1] Candidates prepared themselves for these professions by a prolonged period of fasting. There were in addition several medicine societies to which admission was gained through sickness and dreams. Dreams, indeed, were the gods of the Hurons, to use the expression of an early missionary. A man would abandon a journey, turn back from the war-trail, or give up some other weighty enterprise, if a dream that came to him in the night seemed to predict misfortune; for he believed that his soul, wandering abroad while the body slept, had brought him a warning which he dared not neglect. So medicine-men often ascribed sickness to a disharmony between the soul and the body, an unfulfilled longing in the soul causing disease in the physical frame. Whatever that longing might be the clansmen did their utmost to satisfy it, and the medicine-man who diagnosed its supernatural source supervised the patient's admission into the appropriate medicine society. Many of the strange dances and feasts described by the early missionaries seem to have been performances of these medicine societies, which were as little understood by their European eye-witnesses as they are by us to-day. Possibly they played the same rôle among the Hurons as fasting and dreaming at puberty among the Algonkians, their object being to place the youth of the nation under the protection of supernatural guardians whose aid they could summon in later years.

---

[1] Cf. " Jesuit Relations," vol. 10, p. 193 f.

Unlike the Algonkians, the Hurons demanded no period of servitude from a youth who sought a girl in marriage. He wooed her with presents, and, having gained her consent, obtained the consent of her parents,[1] who invited the relatives and friends of both parties to the wedding feast. Every woman in the village presented the bride with a load of firewood, for unless the wedding took place in the early spring, she would have been hard pressed to gather fuel enough to supply the needs of her new household throughout the autumn and winter. Divorce was easy for both sexes. Either might leave the other on any pretext whatever, the husband carrying away his tools and weapons, the wife her cooking pot and household utensils. Girls generally followed the mother in such cases, while the boys accompanied the father.

If marriage seemed an affair of little moment, that could be passed over with a simple feast, death, on the contrary, called for elaborate rites to smooth the course of the soul in its after life. Unlike their near kinsmen, the Neutrals, who kept the corpse in the cabin until it no longer retained any semblance of humanity, the Hurons buried their dead almost immediately, but buried with them also food, weapons, ornaments, and other articles whose outward forms had been valued in this life, and whose souls (since to the Hurons every object, not man alone, possessed a soul) would be equally indispensable in the next. Fellow tribesmen supplied food to the relatives and mourners, and during the interment (or deposition on a scaffold),[2] distributed presents to "wipe away their tears." For ten days thereafter the husband (or the wife) lay prone in the cabin eating sparingly of the meanest food; and for a year he remained in mourning, unable to remarry till the close of that period. Later, at the great Feast of the Dead already mentioned, the entire nation renewed its mourning and buried a large portion of its wealth in the public ossuaries, thereby enriching, as it believed, the souls of its dead by supplying their needs in the unseen home.

With the Algonkians to the north and east the Hurons maintained a firm friendship; in fact they often gathered berries along the northeastern shores of Georgian bay in territory that strictly belonged to the Ojibwa. At one period they fought with their

---

[1] Perhaps of her mother only, who would consult other women of her clan.

[2] Babies, and persons killed in war, frozen to death, or drowned, were buried in the ground, the babies along some pathway in order that they might be reincarnated in women passing by. All others were wrapped in bark and deposited on a platform. "Jesuit Relations," vol. 10, p. 163, 269 f.

neighbours the Tobacco people, but cemented a close alliance with that nation before Champlain penetrated into southeastern Ontario.[1] The only enemies of the Hurons at that time were the Iroquois south of the St. Lawrence river, whose hands were lifted against every

Huron feast of the dead. *(Reproduced from Lafitau, Mœurs des Sauvages Amériquains, vol. 2, p. 457, Paris, 1724.)*

neighbour that refused to enter their League. The warfare between the two confederacies took the form of raids and counter-raids, in which little mercy was shown to age or sex and many of the male

1 " Jesuit Relations," vol. 20, p. 43.

prisoners underwent barbarous tortures before death brought their sufferings to an end. The offensive weapons on both sides were clubs and bows and arrows; for tomahawks were not used, apparently, prior to contact with Europeans.[1]   Many warriors used slat armour and wicker shields, covered with rawhide to make them impenetrable to bone- or stone-pointed arrows; but they quickly abandoned this armour when it proved defenceless against the bullets of muzzle-loading guns.   Neither confederacy had a really efficient military organization, although, unlike the Algonkians who had to fish and hunt at every stage of a campaign, they could employ their total man-power and escape many commissariat difficulties through the possession of corn, which gave them a portable food supply and could be cultivated and harvested by the women alone. Both Hurons and Iroquois, however, made the raising of levies not a national issue, but a matter for individual " captains," who bought the services of volunteers with presents, outlined the objective and plan of attack, and, as far as they possessed the authority, disposed of any prisoners that were taken.   Under such conditions it was impossible to carry out a co-ordinated campaign with separate bodies of troops, or even to establish discipline in a single war-party, where the individual warriors could drop out whenever they wished and incur no other penalty than a loss of public esteem.   If lack of proper organization weakened their powers of attack, it lessened also their powers of defence, so that an early missionary could exclaim of the Hurons (and the same was true of the Iroquois at that time) " They take no precautions against surprise, they are not careful to prepare arms or to enclose their villages with palisades; their usual recourse, especially when the enemy is powerful, is flight."[2]

The struggle between the two confederacies might have continued indefinitely if the Iroquois had not acquired from the Dutch a far larger supply of firearms and ammunition than the Hurons could

[1] Jacques Cartier gives a word for hatchet in his Hochelagan vocabulary, but does not state that it was ever used in warfare. De Vries, speaking of the Mohawk a century later, says " The weapons in war were bows and arrows, stone axes and clap hammers " (De Vries, David Pietersz: Voyages from Holland to America, A.D. 1632 to 1644, translated by Henry C. Murphy; Collections of the New York Hist. Soc., ser. 2, vol. iii, pt. 1, p. 95 (1852)). De Vries may well be mistaken, however, for the archæological remains of the Iroquoians yield no stone tomahawks, unless indeed the Indians sometimes used in war the stone adzes commonly employed for felling trees. Abbé Maillard, an eighteenth century writer, describes the manufacture of stone tomahawks by the Micmac, but his description is not convincing (Maillard, A. S.: " Account of the Customs and Manners of the Micmackis and Maricheets, Savage Nations Now Dependent on the Government of Cape Breton," p. 26 (London, 1758)). On the other hand, the Huron warrior in the old illustration on p. 289 certainly carries a tomahawk, apparently of stone.   The iron or steel-bladed tomahawks constantly mentioned in accounts of Indian wars originated, of course, with the whites.
[2] " Jesuit Relations," vol. 10, p. 95.

obtain from the French fur traders on the lower St. Lawrence. This gave the Iroquois a signal advantage which they grasped without delay. In 1648, when the Hurons had been already weakened by smallpox and other diseases introduced by Europeans, the League of the Five Nations launched a determined attack on their settlements and destroyed three or four villages. Then, instead of returning to their homes as usual, they secretly passed the winter in southeastern Ontario, and renewed their attacks in the following spring before the snow had left the ground. Many of the Hurons were killed or carried away into captivity. The remainder fled in all directions, to the Tobacco nation, the Neutrals, the Eries, and even to the French settlements on the lower St. Lawrence. Against each of these people in turn the victorious Iroquois turned their arms. First they drove out the Tobacco nation, together with the Hurons who had found shelter among them. Then they destroyed the Neutrals, although the latter, in violation of their neutrality, were holding large numbers of Huron refugees as prisoners.[1] Finally, they attacked and destroyed the Erie nation. Through these campaigns the survivors of the Hurons became scattered far and wide. One portion took refuge with the Potawatomi tribe in the United States, and after many vicissitudes, including a temporary stay on Manitoulin island, in lake Huron, settled in Oklahoma, where their descendants in 1905 numbered 378 individuals. Those who fled to the French near Quebec had the choice between further warfare and voluntary absorption by the Iroquois. The majority chose the latter alternative, and are now indistinguishable from other members of the Mohawk and Onondaga tribes. A small number clung to their alliance with the French, and ultimately obtained a reservation at Lorette, a few miles outside the city of Quebec. There they still live, their village returning a population of 399 in the census of 1924. Few if any of these Lorette Indians, however, are of pure blood, and many show not the slightest trace of their part-Indian lineage. With hardly an exception, too, they have adapted themselves to the civilization around them, and settled down to the same life of peaceful industry and toil as their neighbours in French Canada.

---

[1] The remnants of this confederacy, and a few of the Hurons, were absorbed by the Seneca tribe of Iroquois.

TOBACCO NATION AND NEUTRALS

The Tobacco people, or Tionontati ("There the mountain stands"), and the Neutrals,[1] were in all their customs hardly distinguishable from the Hurons whose disasters they shared. The Tobacco nation was far less numerous than the Neutral, having only nine villages (in 1640) to the latter's twenty-eight (in 1626). They had very little direct contact with Europeans, for the Hurons, fearful of losing their trade as middlemen, would not allow any passage through their territories to the Ottawa river and the French settlements in Quebec, and the upper St. Lawrence was blocked by the Iroquois.[2] The Neutrals, but not the Tobacco people, waged fierce wars against some Algonkian tribes in Illinois, and treated their prisoners with unexampled cruelty, torturing even the women, whom other Iroquoian tribes nearly always spared and adopted into their families. The Neutrals, too, had the strange custom, unknown elsewhere in Canada, of killing every animal they encountered, whether or not they needed it for food, lest it should carry a warning to other animals of its kind and keep them out of reach when food was needed.

IROQUOIS

The constitution of the League of the Iroquois ("Real adders", a name given to them by some neighbouring Algonkians) has been outlined in an earlier chapter; and the map on page 290 shows the approximate locations and boundaries, about 1600 A.D., of the five tribes or nations that made up the confederacy. In order from east to west they were as follows:

(1) Mohawk: "Man-eaters."
(2) Oneida: "A rock set up and standing."
(3) Onondaga: "On the hill or mountain."
(4) Cayuga: "Where locusts were taken out."
(5) Seneca: A distorted variant of Oneida, the two names having a common origin.

All these tribes closely resembled in their customs and beliefs the Huron and other Iroquoian tribes that they destroyed in south-

[1] The name that the Neutrals applied to their confederacy is not known, although we know the names of some of the constituent tribes. The Hurons called them Attiwandaronk, "People who speak a slightly different tongue"; and the Neutrals applied the same name to the Hurons. "Jesuit Relations," vol. 21, p. 193. The Tobacco nation consisted apparently of one tribe only, subdivided into two clans, the deer and the wolf.

[2] According to Sagard (p. 807) the Neutrals would have found it difficult to use the St. Lawrence route because they were not skilful in the use of canoes.

eastern Ontario; but the survival of the Iroquois proper down to the present day has enabled us to obtain some additional information concerning their aboriginal condition that the early explorers and missionaries failed to record from their Canadian kinsmen, although it probably held good for them also. We know, for example, that the Iroquois held annually six or eight festivals that were associated with the cultivation of the soil and the ripening of wild fruits and berries. There was a festival, lasting seven days, when the corn was planted; another, of about the same duration, when it was green; a third, that

Model of an Iroquois "long-house" of bark, in the Rochester Municipal Museum.
(Photo by courtesy of A. C. Parker.)

lasted for four days, when it was harvested; and, in addition, minor festivals at the ripening of strawberries, raspberries, and beans. But the outstanding event in the Iroquois ceremonial year was the great mid-winter festival that extended over seven or eight days, the morning of the fifth day being reserved for the sacrifice of a white dog and the two or three final days for games. Certain elected officials had charge of all these festivals; they levied contributions of food from each household, fixed the dates for the ceremonies, and appointed orators to open them with an appeal to the Great Spirit[1] and a prayer

---

[1] In prehistoric times perhaps to Jouskeha, the benevolent sun-god, or according to another interpretation, the personification of the quickening forces in nature.

of gratitude to the three sister goddesses, Corn, Bean, and Squash. Songs and dances followed the opening ceremonies and continued throughout the duration of each festival, with intervals for feasting and games. The Iroquois had also a Feast of the Dead, which must have been closely analogous to the Huron feast of the same name. None of the early writers, however, has actually described the Iroquois rites, and we have definite proof of their existence among the Mohawk, Onondaga, and Oneida alone.[1]

Every individual in the tribe participated in the harvest festivals, and presumably also in the Feast of the Dead; but only members could take part in the elaborate ceremonies of the various medicine societies. The best known of these, and the only one that persisted, with slight changes, down to modern times, was the False-Face Society, whose members every spring and autumn covered their faces with grotesque masks, raided the houses to drive away the demons that caused disease, then adjourned to the " long " or council-house of the village to hold their dances. More influential than the False-Face Society, however, were the Medicine, the Dark Dance, and the Death Feast, even though women controlled the last two societies and comprised more than half the membership. Undoubtedly these organizations had a very prominent place in the lives of the Iroquois before and for some time after the coming of Europeans, although the obscurity that still envelops them tends to mask their real importance.

The Iroquois seem to have regulated marriage much more strictly than the Hurons, who permitted their youth to select their own wives, subject to the approval of the girls' mothers. Among the Iroquois, on the contrary, it was the young man's mother who chose his bride, and arranged the match with the girl's mother without regard to the young couple's inclinations or wishes. The two families then exchanged food and presents, and the youth was informed that henceforth he and the girl were man and wife, that they must live together in the hut of her family and provide for each other, he by hunting and fishing and she in the cornfields. Fathers had no jurisdiction whatever in the match and were usually not consulted, but

---

[1] " Jesuit Relations," vol. 53, p. 213 (1669-70). W. J. Wintemberg unearthed nearly a hundred graves in a prehistoric village site at Roebuck, Ontario, left by an eastern group of Iroquois, probably the Onondaga; yet he found no trace of scaffold burial or of ossuaries. Possibly these customs were adopted later from the Hurons, or they may have been sporadic only among the Five Nations.

the mothers might seek the advice of elderly people in their own clans. In some cases a woman would marry her young son to a widow twice his age, or her daughter to an elderly warrior. In these

73990

Masks worn by members of the False-Face Society.

circumstances divorce was naturally easy, yet not as frequent as one might imagine, because it brought discredit on both parties, and particularly on the man. The name given to a child at birth received public confirmation at the green corn and mid-winter festivals; but at adolescence, or a little later, the child discarded this name at the same two festivals and assumed another name which it generally retained through life.

The largest tribe among the Iroquois was the Seneca, the most aggressive the Mohawk. Being the two flank members, they often encountered different enemies, and owing to the loose organization of the confederacy were forced to act independently. So it was the Seneca who were chiefly responsible for the destruction of the Huron, Tobacco, and Neutral nations, and the Mohawk who principally harassed the Algonkins and Montagnais north of the St. Lawrence, and the Abenaki and other Algonkian tribes in the Maritime Provinces, New Hampshire, and Maine. The Oneida, Onondaga, and Cayuga generally provided contingents for all major operations, but complications frequently arose through one tribe in the confederacy concluding a peace, which the others ignored or refused to accept. This lack of cohesion was a constant source of weakness to the league, even though it sometimes caused almost as much embarrassment to its enemies. Thus in the seventeenth century, when the French were congratulating themselves on the establishment of a hard-won truce with the Mohawks, and, breathing a new sense of security, were moving freely up and down the St. Lawrence, they found themselves unexpectedly assailed by parties of Onondaga or Seneca who recognized no cessation of the warfare, but slaughtered or carried away captive every unfortunate Frenchman they encountered.

The aid that Champlain rendered the Montagnais in 1609 when he defeated the Mohawk on lake Champlain began that bitter feud between the Iroquois confederacy and the French that blocked the latter's expansion southward and made the Iroquois staunch allies of the English down to the capture of Quebec by Wolfe. For in Champlain's day the Iroquois were still unacquainted with firearms, and, lacking any superiority in weapons, fought with their neighbours on nearly equal terms. The Mohawk, who occupied the most vulnerable position on the eastern flank, suffered more heavily than the other tribes in these conflicts, being almost annihilated by the Algonkians in the latter half of the sixteenth century, and again by the Conestoga, an Iroquoian tribe on their southern border, at the beginning of the seventeenth. The wholesale adoption of captives, and the acquisition of firearms from the Dutch, who began to settle in Pennsylvania about 1615, turned the tide in favour of the Mohawk and other members of the Iroquois League, who gradually overwhelmed their enemies one after another and extended their sway over all the territory from Tennessee to the Ottawa river and from the Kennebec river in Maine to the southern shore of lake Michigan. During the seventeenth century the French, through their missionaries, made numerous attempts to win the goodwill of the confederacy, and succeeded in inducing a large number of the Indians, mainly Onondaga and Mohawk, to move into French Canada, accept Christianity, and join their fortunes with the French and Algonkians. The league then outlawed these proselytes, but some of their descendants survive to-day at Caughnawaga, St. Regis, and Oka in the province of Quebec, while others, whose forefathers manned the canoes of the fur-trading companies during the eighteenth and early nineteenth centuries, occupy a small reserve not far from Edmonton in Alberta.

It may have been the numerous ups and downs of fortune they endured, and the high proportion of foreign elements in the tribe, that made the Mohawk of the seventeenth century the most aggressive nation in the confederacy and, at the same time, perhaps the most savage.[1] Its war parties raided Ontario and Quebec almost to the shores of James bay, so that even to-day the mere mention of its name causes a shudder of fear. and hatred in the hearts of many Ojibwa, Cree, and Montagnais.[2] Although the rules of the confederacy strictly prohibited cannibalism, we find records of several cases in which the Mohawk cruelly sacrificed a prisoner to their war-god Aireskoi and divided up the body to be devoured in the different villages. We should add perhaps, in common justice, that among themselves the Mohawk were as hospitable and charitable as the other Iroquois, or indeed as any tribe in Canada; and that they never abandoned the aged and infirm, as was the custom among the Algonkians. Moreover, these outbursts of superstitious savagery occurred only when they were depressed by a great calamity; in the later wars of the eighteenth century they and all other Iroquois con-

---

[1] Although the Jesuit missionary Burgess considered that the Oneida were the most cruel. "Jesuit Relations," vol. 57, p. 193.

[2] The nearness of the Mohawk to European settlements magnified their importance in the eyes of the early writers. Probably there were few or no real Mohawks in many of the Iroquois war parties that raided north of the St. Lawrence.

ducted themselves in fairly close accord with the rules that were prevalent among European nations at that time. In any case extreme torture of prisoners was an exceptional event, by far the larger number being adopted into the various families and incorporated into one or other of the tribes as members of full standing.

The League of the Iroquois did not function as a unit during the American revolutionary war, but permitted its tribes to act independently according to the wishes of the members. The Oneida and a portion of the Tuscarora (an Iroquoian tribe that was driven out of North Carolina and accepted into the confederacy about 1722, transforming it henceforth into the " League of the Six Nations") espoused the cause of the Americans, while the remainder joined the British side. When peace was concluded, the majority of the pro-British Iroquois settled in Ontario on lands assigned to them by the Crown. Others joined them in later years, so that to-day more than two-thirds of the Indians officially classed as Iroquois reside in Canada.

At no period in their history were the Iroquois a numerous people: Lloyd estimates that at the coming of Europeans their total population (excluding the Tuscarora) was only 16,000, distributed among the tribes as follows: Mohawk, 3,000; Oneida, 1,000; Onondaga, 3,000; Cayuga, 2,000; and Seneca, 7,000.[1] From 1642 until the close of the seventeenth century the league suffered tremendous losses through wars, diseases, and defection to French Canada. losses that were only partly repaired by the continuous adoption of captives. In 1668, indeed, Huron and Algonkian ex-captives made up two-thirds of the Oneida tribe;[2] and about the same time the Seneca became a medley of Neutral, Erie, and Conestoga remnants with only a small inlying stratum of the original Iroquois. In the eighteenth century all five tribes absorbed an appreciable number of Europeans, and ever since, the two races have slowly intermingled. Consequently, though the number of " Iroquois " living on reserves in Canada and the United States to-day approximates 16,000, very few of them, if any, can lay claim to pure Indian descent, and in all probability many have no real Iroquois blood at all in their veins. No small percentage has broken away from the reserves and merged

---

1 Morgan, L. H.: League of the Iroquois, p. 227. Estimates of the population during the seventeenth and eighteenth centuries vary greatly, and we have no real means of checking their accuracy.
2 " Jesuit Relations," vol. 51, p. 123.

successfully with the surrounding population, a few even attaining national fame. Those who still cling to the reserves are in the main fairly prosperous, and within another century will undoubtedly disappear as separate communities. Yet their old confederacy, through its opposition to the French, largely affected the composition of the present population through the whole of the North American continent, and for this reason alone, if for no other, has earned a prominent place in every Canadian history, and in every history of the United States.

CHAPTER XX

PLAINS' TRIBES

ASSINIBOINE

The plains' tribe that lived nearest to the Iroquoians during the early seventeenth century was the Assiniboine ("the people that cook with hot stones"), who had probably separated off from the Dakota Sioux only a few generations before. They were then hunting in the country around the Lake of the Woods and lake Nipigon, and, though depending mainly on the chase, gathered large quantities of wild rice,[1] which they cooked, like their neighbours the Ojibwa, in clay pots and vessels of birch bark. By the eighteenth century, however, most of them had moved away to the northwest,[2] and divided into two branches, one of which lived on the edge of the forest northwest of lake Winnipeg, in close contact with the Cree, while the other centred about the valley of the Assiniboine river a little to the southward.

The acquisition of horses and firearms about the middle of the eighteenth century increased the range of their movements, and shifted their centres a little farther west. With their Cree allies they fought bitterly against the Blackfoot confederacy for the control of the Canadian prairies; and they waged war on the Sioux, Mandan, and other tribes of the United States, and the Kootenay and Salish tribes across the Rocky mountains. Their hunting grounds now embraced all the prairies of Canada, and the buffalo provided them with tents and daily food. They slaughtered entire herds by driving them into pounds, and roasted the meat on spits, or boiled it in hide bags by means of hot stones;[3] for they had now abandoned the clay pots and birch-bark vessels that had served their needs when their home lay farther to the eastward. But constant wars and

---

[1] "Jesuit Relations," vol. 54, p. 193.

[2] Some remained in the Red River district until the end of the century. McDonnell, John: " Some Account of the Red River"; in Masson, op. cit., ser. i, p. 278.

[3] According to Lowie the women always roasted the meat, and only the men, when travelling alone, sometimes boiled it (Lowie, R. H.: "The Assiniboine"; Anth. Papers, Am. Mus. Nat. Hist., vol. iv, pt. 1, p. 12 (New York, 1909)). Yet Denig, in the early nineteenth century, found boiling the commoner method, and noticed no distinction based on sex (Denig, Edwin Thompson: "Indian Tribes of the Upper Missouri"; edited with notes and biographical sketch by J. N. B. Hewitt, Forty-sixth Ann. Rept., Bur. Am. Ethn., 1928-1929. p. 581 f (Washington, 1930)).

foreign diseases, particularly smallpox,[1] thinned their ranks; and when Europeans pushed forward their settlements into the prairies, and the herds of buffalo disappeared, the Assiniboine, unable to continue their old free life, submitted to confinement on various reserves. The southern branch found a retreat at Fort Belknap, in Montana; the northern, commonly known to-day as Stonies, settled on several small reserves in Saskatchewan and Alberta, the larger number going to Morley, between Calgary and Banff. Several generations of separation have developed slight differences in dialect and customs between the two branches, owing mainly to the closer contact between the Stonies and the Cree; but they still remember their common origin, and, though enrolled under different flags, consider themselves a single people.

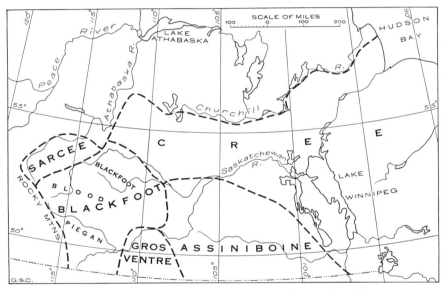

Approximate distribution of the plains' tribes in 1725 A.D.

In historical times, then, the Assiniboine were a typical plains' tribe living in large conical tents or tipis made of buffalo hide. They moved their camps from place to place even more frequently than

[1] Cf. "The Prairie all around is a vast field of death, covered with unburied corpses, and spreading, for miles, pestilence and infection. . . . The Assiniboines, 9,000 in number, roaming over a hunting territory to the north of the Missouri, as far as the trading posts of the Hudson's Bay Company, are, in the literal sense of the expression, nearly exterminated. They, as well as the Crows and the Blackfeet, endeavoured to flee in all directions, but the disease (smallpox) everywhere pursued them." Maximilian, Prince of Wied's, Travels in the Interior of North America, 1832-1834, in Thwaites, R. G.: "Early Western Travels"; vol. 22, p. 35 (Cleveland, 1906).

the Algonkian tribes of the eastern woodlands, for though the more northern bands, through their proximity to the forests, secured many moose, beaver, bear, and porcupine, the existence of the tribe as a whole depended on the migratory buffalo. Each family owned several dogs, which, hitched to the poles of the travois, dragged the household possessions in summer and winter alike.[1] Rivers that the Indians encountered in their wanderings they generally forded or swam; but not infrequently they ferried themselves across in bull-boats, which were tub-like vessels covered with buffalo or moose[2] hide and paddled from the front. Thus they followed the wanderings of the buffalo herds, dispersing into small bands during the winter months when the buffalo were more scattered and hunting difficult,[3] and reuniting in spring for the great sun-dance festival and the driving of the herds into pounds.

Foot-wanderers whose only transport animals are dogs must necessarily be slow of movement and circumscribed in their range. Hence, the contacts of the Assiniboine with the hostile Blackfoot confederacy were comparatively slight in early times. The weapons of all the plains' tribes in Canada were practically identical. Besides the ubiquitous bow and arrow, there were a long-handled spear for close fighting, and three or four types of stone-headed clubs, as well as a wooden knobkerrie. Some men wore "Jackets of Moose leather six fold, quilted and without sleeves" as a protection against arrows;[4] and a notable warrier generally carried a shield of painted buffalo hide, decorated on its outer surface with painted scenes or figures derived from the vision in which he had received his supernatural blessing. Whatever protection this blessing afforded him then attached itself in part to the shield, which guarded its owner in battle and rested beside him in his grave.[5] Whether he carried a

---

[1] The webbed frame attached to the Assiniboine travois for holding the baggage was circular, the Blackfoot made both a circular and a rectangular (ladder-like) frame; and Assiniboine women, when erecting their tipis, fastened three poles together to form a base, whereas the Blackfoot women fastened four. Numerous other differences of a similar character distinguished one plains' tribe from another, apart from differences in social customs, religious rituals, and language.

[2] "York Factory to the Blackfoot Country", p. 329. A few Assiniboine who travelled down to the trading post at York Factory on Hudson bay learned to make birch-bark canoes from the Cree, but the majority of the tribe, and the Blackfoot, were ignorant of their use. "An Adventurer from Hudson Bay; Journal of Matthew Cocking, from York Factory to the Blackfoot Country, 1772-73"; edited by L. J. Burpee, Proc. and Trans., Roy. Soc., Canada, 3rd ser., vol. ii, sec. ii, pp. 104, 114, 116 (Toronto, 1908).

[3] On Red river, according to John McDonnell (1793-1797), "they generally winter together in large camps, and make what the French call parcs, an enclosure of wood in the form of a fence and circular, into which they drive whole herds of Buffalo." Masson: Op. cit., i, p. 297.

[4] "An Adventurer from Hudson Bay," pp. 110-111.

[5] Among the Assiniboine. Among the Blackfoot and Sarcee the shield, the special shirts, and the war-bonnets were regarded as "medicine-bundles," and transferred at intervals, with the appropriate rituals and songs, from one warrior to another.

shield or not, however, every warrior had a war charm specially made for him by some old medicine-man.[1] A few individuals had special skin shirts and elaborate war-bonnets that were thought to aid their wearers in battle; but the right of wearing them came only from a vision, or by purchase from a man who himself had received permission in a vision.

Two Assiniboine Indians running a buffalo, from a painting by Paul Kane. *(Photo by courtesy of the Royal Ontario Museum of Archæology.)*

The introduction of horses and firearms gave the same stimulus to warfare that it gave to buffalo hunting. The horse materially widened the field of conflict, for enemies 200 or 300 miles away, who previously could be reached on foot only after many days of hard travelling, were now within measurable distance for a raid; and firearms were more accurate and deadly than arrows that could not penetrate a shield.[2] The Assiniboine, like the other plains' tribes, became infected with the war fever, and divided their energies between the exciting buffalo hunt and raids and counter-raids against their enemies. Flashes of sunlight from a mirror, the precursor of the

---

[1] The charm might be only the head of a loon, but its cost was fairly standardized, being in later years a horse.
[2] *Cf.* David Thompson's Narrative, p. 411.

modern heliograph, and columns of smoke dampened at intervals with a blanket, passed the warning from camp to camp whenever foes were lurking in the neighbourhood. A warrior who dreamed of killing an enemy regarded the dream as a prophecy, enlisted a band of volunteers, and (with the consent of the military society or soldiers' council) sallied out to capture scalps and horses. Paintings on the outside of his tent portrayed his exploits, and the eagle feathers in his war-bonnet recorded the number of enemies he had slain. Women danced around the scalps that his party brought back to camp, and older warriors recited their own exploits to encourage the younger generation. In communities infected by such war passion, and devoid of an hereditary class of chiefs and nobles, valour and success in battle offered the surest road to honour and high rank.

No people, however, can devote itself exclusively to war and hunting; there are many activities and events in the daily life of a camp that call for public recognition and public ceremonies. The Assiniboine gave names to their children in a pleasing ceremony that closely resembled the Ojibwa ceremony on such occasions; an old man, or a prominent warrior, took the infant in his arms and conferred on it a name ostensibly derived from a propitious dream, or from a successful feat in battle; all the assembled relatives and friends then embraced the child in turn and added their benediction. In the latter half of the nineteenth century parents distributed gifts when their daughters reached maturity, and, at the marriage of their children, arranged formal processions of their relatives to bear presents of food and clothing, and to lead strings of horses, between the tipis of the groom's parents and the bride's.[1] In earlier days there seems to have been no marriage ceremony; the suitor made his offer through the medium of an old man, and the girl moved over to his lodge at night,[2] if her parents accepted the bride price.

Funeral rites were more elaborate than marriage rites as in nearly all Indian tribes. Occasionally the Assiniboine cremated their dead,[3] or deposited notable warriors on the surface of the ground

---

[1] Lowie: Op. cit., p. 40.
[2] Denig: Op. cit., p. 511.
[3] *Cf.* " This morning his body was burned according to their way, they making a great feast for him y[t] did now after y[t] y[e] flesh was burned his Bones were taken and buried with Loggs set up round of about ten feet Long." The Kelsey Papers, p. 12.

beneath cairns of logs and stones;[1] but usually they followed the procedure described by De Smet:

" They bind the bodies with thongs of rawhide between the branches of large trees, and, more frequently, place them on scaffolds, to protect them from the wolves and other wild animals. They are higher than a man can reach. The feet are always turned to the west. There they are left to decay. When the scaffolds or the trees to which the dead are attached fall, through old age, the relatives bury all the other bones, and place the skulls in a circle in the plain, with the faces turned toward the centre. They preserve these with care, and consider them objects of religious veneration. You will generally find there several bison skulls. In the centre stands the medicine pole, about twenty feet high, to which Wah-kons are hung, to guard and protect the sacred deposit. The Indians call the cemetery the *village of the dead*. They visit it at certain seasons of the year, to converse affectionately with their deceased relatives and friends, and always leave some present."[2]

The principal deities of the Assiniboine were the sun and the thunder, which were regarded, at least in historic times, as direct manifestations of the Great Spirit, the ruler of all things. Both deities received public worship at the sun-dance and horse-dance festivals held during the summer months, and on solemn occasions individual Indians frequently made them offerings of tobacco smoke and prayed for long life, health, or success in some special venture. But the Assiniboine, like the eastern Indians, placed less reliance on these " higher " powers than on the supernatural blessing supposedly bestowed in a vision, generally in answer to fasting and supplication. To the average Indian this vision brought only an indefinite assurance or conviction of some supernatural power who watched over his every action, and stood ready to help in times of crisis; but to some it brought special powers or privileges, e.g., power to heal diseases with herbal remedies or else by supernatural means, authority to establish a dancing society, or the privilege of painting on the outside of the tent an episode in the dream itself.

---

[1] Maximilian, in Thwaites, vol. 22, p. 393, Denig says "the grave is excavated to the depth of about 5 feet, and made large enough to contain the implements before referred to, which are all buried with the body, the grave filled up and large rocks rolled upon it. . . . Very brave and formerly renowned warriors sometimes requested not to be interred in any way, in which case they are placed inside their lodge propped up . . . . and the whole is thus left on the plains." Denig: Op. cit., p. 572 f.

[2] De Smet: vol. iii, p. 1141.

So Assiniboine society recognized, besides a military society of noted warriors, four classes of men more or less distinguished from the rank and file, viz., two orders of medicine-men, the owners of painted tents, and the founders or leaders of various dancing societies.

The medicine-men, however, and the owners of painted tents, enjoyed little prestige unless they distinguished themselves also in warfare. It was the military society, comprising all the bravest and most active men between the ages of twenty-five and thirty-five, that controlled every large camp. Nominally the leader of the society received his orders from the dominant chief, but since it was only through the military society that the chief could enforce his wishes, he dared not oppose its expressed opinion. The society policed the camp and regulated the buffalo hunt,[1] received delegations from other tribes, and authorized raids for scalps and horses. On special occasions its members dressed in full battle array, danced to the accompaniment of drums and singing, and recounted their individual exploits, with the avowed purpose of impressing the laity with their strength and of stimulating the popular zeal for warfare.

The number of dancing societies varied at different periods as old ones ceased to exist and new ones arose to take their place. Their purpose was mainly social, although fellow members aided one another in daily life. In one alone was the religious aspect prominent, in the "horse-dance,"[2] whose members annually set up an altar inside an enlarged tipi and offered incense and tobacco smoke to the sun, the thunder, and the earth. Nearly all dancing societies restricted their membership to men, but even in 1820 women had a special order of their own. Candidates paid an initiation fee of varying amounts, and (in the second half of the nineteenth century at least) the societies held annual dances when the bands united in early summer for the buffalo-hunt and the sun-dance.

Some recent events on the Stoney reserve at Morley illustrate rather clearly how such dancing societies might arise. An Indian named Cough Child, or Crow Child, had a vision in which the Great Spirit appeared to him and said "You must sleep on a mountain four successive nights. The thunder will clap over your head, and at each clap you will daub white paint on your cheek. Afterwards you

---

[1] For these duties *See* part I, p. 128.
[2] This society may not be older than the middle of the nineteenth century.

will return to your people, heal their diseases, and restore the old religion of prayer and the offering of smoke from the medicine-pipe, now so fallen into decay through Christian teaching that the Indians have lost their earlier power." Acting on these instructions, as he claimed, Cough Child hired drummers and singers, daubed white paint on his person and his clothes, painted a thunder-bird on his blanket as a visible token of his mandate, and held a public dance. With his breath alone he seemed to heal patients who were brought to him from all around. His fame spread far and wide. Cree Indians in the north sent messengers asking him to come and cure them, Sarcee went from Calgary to beseech his aid. An Indian from distant Utah brought a child that Cough Child might restore its eyesight, but sadly returned home with his child still blind. Every patient the prophet cured bought from him a feather to wear whenever it thundered, and, like the prophet, daubed his cheeks with white paint that the thunder might pass him by. Many wore their feathers at all times,[1] thereby acknowledging the leadership of Cough Child and their enlistment among his followers. They had the feeling of membership in a regular society, although (so far as we know) their leader had given it no name and did not organize an annual dance. It remained an embryonic society until its disappearance, because the conditions of life had changed and the old organizations and beliefs were rapidly passing away.[2]

The greatest religious event in the Assiniboine year was the sun-dance. "They often speak of it in the course of the year, and look forward to its immediate arrival with joy, respect, and veneration."[3] The leader was a man who had inherited the privilege and received the necessary instruction from his father. After a ceremonial buffalo-hunt to provide the necessary food, the united tribe moved to some previously chosen site and erected a sacred pole which had been cut down after the manner of an enemy and dragged to the camp amid great rejoicing. To this pole, and to the rafters of a gigantic lodge, the people lashed their offerings to the Great Spirit or his manifestation, the sun-god, and the leader addressed

---

[1] In 1921 a Sarcee woman living on a reserve near Calgary had one of Cough Child's feathers attached to her necklace, and a visitor from the Assiniboine reserve at Morley wore another in her hair.

[2] Cough Child's vision of the Great Spirit, his revolt against Christianity, and attempted restoration of older beliefs and customs bear some analogy to the Messianistic phenomena that occurred among other tribes, notably the Iroquois and the interior tribes of British Columbia, at the end of the eighteenth and early part of the nineteenth centuries. See part I, p. 183 f.

[3] De Smet: vol. III, p. 937.

a prayer on behalf of the entire tribe. The ceremonies proper lasted three days. On the first the people danced; on the second the medicine-men displayed their conjuring tricks; and on the last the whole camp banqueted, giving dog's flesh a prominent place among the meats.

When the Blackfoot and some other plains' tribes celebrated the sun-dance the most sensational incident, though actually an unessential one, was the voluntary torture endured by a few young warriors to excite the compassion and favour of the Great Spirit. These misguided devotees allowed their breasts or shoulders to be pierced with sharp skewers and attached by stout thongs to the sacred pole or to a heavy buffalo skull; and they strained at the pole, or dragged the skull, until they either broke loose or friends and relatives took pity on their sufferings and in some way or other secured their release.[1] The Assiniboine, however, seem not to have associated self-torture with the sun-dance, but only with preparations for war. Men who aspired to lead a war party lay out in the rain or snow for three or four nights fasting and praying to the Great Spirit for favourable visions; and some of them gashed their arms and breasts with knives the more to excite his pity.

We have no reliable estimate of the numbers of the Assiniboine before the first quarter of the nineteenth century. At that period the population seems to have fluctuated between 8,000 and 10,000, distributed among sixteen or seventeen bands. Four thousand or more perished in the terrible smallpox epidemic of 1836, and the tribe declined steadily thenceforward until it was confined to reserves. To-day it numbers roughly 2,500, half of whom live in Alberta and Saskatchewan, the remainder in the United States.

PLAINS' CREE

In pre-European times the Plains' Cree probably comprised only those few small bands in northern Saskatchewan and Manitoba that periodically moved out from their home on the edge of the forest to hunt the buffalo herds on the prairies. There they jostled against older plains' tribes, and allied themselves with the Assiniboine against

---

[1] A full description of the festival among any one of the plains' tribes would require a whole chapter, which is more space than can be allotted in this book. For an eye-witness' account of a Blackfoot sun-dance half a century ago the reader may consult McLean, J.: " The Blackfoot Sun-Dance": Proc. Can. Inst., 3rd ser., vol. vi, 1887-1888, pp. 231-237 (Toronto, 1889).

the Blackfoot and Sarcee. The introduction of horses and firearms induced other bands of Cree to join them, and their numbers swelled until they became a serious menace to all the tribes along what is now the International Boundary. They spread over northern Alberta to the Peace river, raided through the country of the Blackfoot to the Rocky mountains, and southward to the posts of the fur-traders on the Missouri river. Smallpox decimated them in the eighteenth century, as it did many other tribes in the United States and Canada, and between 1835 and 1858 diseases and wars reduced their number from about 4,000 to barely 1,000.[1] When the disappearance of the buffalo, about 1878, deprived the remnants of the tribe of their means of livelihood the government distributed them among various reserves in the three Prairie Provinces, combining them in one or two places with Assiniboine.

The Plains' Cree claim that they were formerly divided into twelve bands, each of which had its own chief. Possessing only a weak culture of their own, they quickly assimilated many of the customs of their neighbours, particularly of the Assiniboine, their allies, and of the Ojibwa who mingled with them on the east. They had one military society only, to which entrance was gained by some valorous deed. From the Assiniboine they probably derived the ceremony of the sun-dance;[2] perhaps also some of their dancing societies, although most of the Cree societies were more definitely religious than the Assiniboine, three at least aiming to increase the success of the hunters. There were two ceremonies that they probably borrowed from the Ojibwa, an annual smoke-offering and prayer to the Great Spirit, and an annual feast to the dead. On the whole, their customs were similar to those of the Assiniboine, although every plains' tribe, of course, differed in many ways from every other.

BLACKFOOT

The strongest and most aggressive nation on the Canadian prairies in the middle of the eighteenth century was the Blackfoot, whose territory stretched from the Rocky mountains well into Saskatchewan, and from the North Saskatchewan river almost to the upper Missouri in the United States. On their southeastern flank

---

[1] Hind, H. Y.: North West Territory, Reports of Progress; together with a preliminary and general report on the Assiniboine and Saskatchewan exploring expedition, p. 46 (Toronto, 1859).
[2] The Cree sun-dance, strictly speaking, was a dance to the thunder, not to the sun-god.

were the Gros Ventre, usually friends but sometimes enemies, who retreated south before the end of the century and played no further part in Canadian history; to the north and northeast were the Assiniboine and Plains' Cree, often friendly in the middle of the eighteenth century,[1] inveterate foes towards its close; northwest, the little tribe of the Sarcee, who affiliated themselves wholeheartedly with the Blackfoot, although their Athapaskan tongue bore not

58569

Tipi of a Blood Indian medicine-man, with his medicine-bundle suspended outdoors.
(Photo by G. Anderton.)

the slightest resemblance to the Algonkian speech of their allies; on the west were the Kootenay and Salish tribes of British Columbia, who often crossed the passes of the Rockies to harass the Blackfoot and share the spoils of the buffalo-hunt; and in the southwest, south, and southeast were Shoshonean, Siouan, and other tribes as hostile as the Assiniboine and Cree. So the Blackfoot became the Ishmaels of the prairies, their hands being raised against every neighbour

---

[1] Cf. "York Factory to the Blackfoot Country," pp. 340, 344, 350; "An Adventurer from Hudson Bay," p. 110.

except the insignificant Sarcee, and occasionally the Gros Ventre, who sought the shelter of their confederacy.

There were three tribes in the Blackfoot nation, the Blackfoot proper, the Blood, and the Piegan,[1] the southernmost or Piegan being numerically almost as strong as the other two combined. Each tribe was an independent unit under its own chief, so that whenever they came together they pitched their tents in separate camp circles and regulated their affairs by separate councils. A common language, common customs, a tradition of common origin, and frequent inter-marriage prevented open warfare between them, despite frequent feuds; against their enemies they presented a united front. Yet even in their own eyes the union was too imperfect to require a common name, and the use of the term Blackfoot to cover all three tribes was really an unwarrantable extension by the early whites.

In their outward life the Blackfoot tribes hardly differed from the Assiniboine. Both were buffalo-hunting peoples living in skin tents and roving the prairies in search of the buffalo herds.[2] Both wore the typical costume and ornaments of the plains' tribes,[3] and both used dogs and travois to transport their household possessions. In both nations the social units were the families and the bands, and cutting across the divisions into bands was a society, or societies, whose members held annual dances, and performed police and other duties whenever the bands came together in summer and pitched their tents in the characteristic circle.[4] Both nations, again, wor-shipped the sun and the thunder, the manifestations of the Great Spirit, and held the annual ceremony of the sun-dance. Underlying all these outward conformities, however, there were considerable differences in the social and religious life.

The Blackfoot treated their women more harshly than the Assini-boine, whose code demanded almost the same conduct from men and

[1] The word Blackfoot (a translation of the Indians' own name for themselves, *Siksikauwa*) refers to the moccasins, either because they were painted black, or besmirched by prairie fires. Piegan comes from a word meaning "poorly dressed robe," but its real significance, as of the name Blood, is unknown, the Indians giving several contradictory legends.

[2] In Cocking's Journal we read "I found in an old tent-place belonging to the Archithinue (Black-foot) Natives, part of an earthen vessel, in which they dress their victuals; it appeared to have been in the form of an earthen pan." (" An Adventurer from Hudson Bay," p. 109); and again " Their Victuals are dressed in earthen pots, of their own manufacturing; much in the same form as Newcastle pots, but without feet: their fire tackling a black stone used as flint, and a kind of ore as a steel, using tuss balls as tinder, (i.e.) a kind of moss" (Do., p. 111). From these passages it would appear that some at least of the Blackfoot, like the Assiniboine of a slightly earlier period, used cooking vessels of pottery, which they abandoned before the end of the century in favour of hide vessels, probably because it was too difficult to transport pottery on the horse-travois.

[3] There were minor differences in ornamentation; the Assiniboine, for example, commonly worked a large rosette on the front and on the back of the robe, the Blackfoot seldom.

[4] The Assiniboine had only one military society, the Blackfoot several. *See infra.*

women alike. The Blackfoot, on the contrary, seem to have encouraged their young men to practise seduction, and then scorned the women who yielded to their advances, and, if they were married, mutilated and even killed them. The name given to a boy at birth lasted only until his first war-party, when his comrades conferred on him a new name, often in mockery. This name, too, he discarded later in favour of one more befitting his manhood years; but even his manhood name was not always permanent, being subject to change at will. While still very young every boy adopted another of about his own age to be his inseparable companion, and this Damon and Pythias relationship lasted all through their lives. Several other plains' tribes were familiar with the same custom, but seem to have observed it less systematically.

Like the Assiniboine, the Blackfoot often deposited their dead in trees, but they did not perform any subsequent ceremony over the fallen bones. Men and women who had been prominent in their communities, they laid out on hill-tops inside their tents, after weighting down the edges of the skin with stones. Many of the " tent-rings " still visible on the prairies are, therefore, burial-rings, not the sites of ancient camps.[1] Women, and sometimes men, lacerated themselves at funerals, and widowers commonly assuaged their grief by going immediately on the war-path.[2]

Each of the military societies of the Blackfoot, which were known collectively as All-Comrades, had either one or two leaders who sat in the tribal council when the bands united during the early summer. As in the military society of the Assiniboine, these leaders arranged for the policing of the camp,[3] the organization of the buffalo hunts, and the guarding of the tribe on the march. There were ten or twelve military societies in each tribe, some of which opened their ranks to a limited number of women. Membership was by purchase only, but a man generally passed automatically from one society to the next, at intervals of four years, by selling the regalia

---

[1] In the nineteenth century, and probably also in the eighteenth, the Blackfoot sometimes wrapped their dead in robes, deposited them among rocks, or on solitary cliffs, and covered them with logs. Maximilian in Thwaites, vol. 22, p. 121.

[2] Wissler states that in more recent times a Blackfoot suffering from an incurable disease would frequently run amok, though without mania, and attempt to kill as many people as he could, even his own family, before taking his own life. He regards this as a variant, and in some respects, a survival, of taking to the war-path (Wissler, C.: " The Social Life of the Blackfoot Indians"; Anth. Papers, Am. Mus. Nat. Hist., vol. vii, p. 32 (New York, 1912)). Cocking remarks that " The Asinepoet (Assiniboine) Natives are oftentimes guilty of suicide, on very childish grounds "; " An Adventurer from Hudson Bay," p. 112.

[3] " They appear to be under proper discipline, and obedient to their Leader, who orders a party of Horsemen Evening and Morning to reconitre"; " York Factory to the Blackfeet Country," p. 339.

he possessed in the old society and purchasing the corresponding regalia of the new. Thus the societies were roughly graded, young men entering the lowest and proceeding at intervals to the higher grades. But if the Blackfoot had carried out the system to its logical conclusion the higher societies would have contained old men only, the lowest only youths. Partly to prevent this, apparently, every

74879

A Blood Indian girl. *(Photo by courtesy of Canadian National Railways.)*

grade had to include at least four old men among its members; and many individuals purchased membership in the higher societies without relinquishing their affiliations with the lower. Since there were no special qualifications for members, and no means of expelling them, we may presume that every man in the tribe joined at least one society for a time, and the majority passed through several.

Of dancing societies, both the purely social and those with religious functions, the Blackfoot possessed even more than the Assiniboine. An outstanding feature in all these societies, whether dancing or military, was the formal acquisition by purchase of the ceremonial objects and the songs that went along with membership. The same formal transference of ceremonial objects pervaded the entire religious life of the Blackfoot, giving it a character quite distinct from that of other plains' tribes.[1] It affected even the significance of the annual sun-dance; for whatever may have been the earlier history of this festival (and doubtless it was a composite of many different rites), among the historical Blackfoot it was primarily the fulfilment of a vow, made by a virtuous married woman at a time of crisis, to purchase a sacred sun-dance bundle from some other woman in the tribe. The formal erection of a central pole loaded with offerings to the Great Spirit, the self-torture of warriors, and the ceremonial cutting of buffalo tongues by women who had dedicated themselves to this form of thanksgiving, these and other episodes in the festival, such as the annual dances of the various societies, all seemed to the Blackfoot subsidiary to that one indispensable event, the transfer, with due ceremony, of a sacred medicine-bundle.[2]

These sun-dance bundles, however, formed but one group in a numerous series of medicine-bundles, the other most outstanding groups being the beaver and pipe bundles. The pipe bundles were associated with the worship of the thunder, the beaver with tobacco cultivation; for the planting of tobacco was a sacred ceremony among the plains' tribes, and its smoking on formal occasions just as necessary a ritual as it was among the Iroquoians.[3] A medicine-bundle might be anything from a few feathers wrapped in skin or cloth to a multitude of miscellaneous objects—skins of animals and birds, roots, rocks, stone pipes, etc.—kept inside a large rawhide bag, in which every article had a definite significance and called for a special song whenever its owner exposed it to the light. Owners and their wives incurred many obligations and taboos, but they enjoyed considerable prestige in the tribe and believed that possession of a sacred

[1] Except the Sarcee.
[2] The buffalo-hunt that generally preceded the Blackfoot and Sarcee sun-dance lacked the ceremonial character of the corresponding hunt among the Assiniboine, with whom it was really a part of the festival.
[3] *Cf.* David Thompson's Narrative, p. 365.

bundle brought them prosperity and good fortune. Hence there was much rivalry for their ownership, and the man who expended most of his property in purchasing one could always recuperate his loss by selling it again. The formal transfer was a solemn ceremony that

74882

Blackfoot crossing the Elbow river, Alberta. *(Photo by courtesy of Canadian National Railways.)*

generally extended over many days and even weeks; for the new purchaser had to learn not only the significance of all the objects in the bundle, but the full details of the visions to which they traditionally owed their origin, and the songs, in a large bundle numbering perhaps half a hundred, that established their validity.

Painted tents, special war-shirts, amulets, everything in fact that originated from a vision, the Blackfoot regarded in the same light as the medicine-bundles. Each was a symbol of some blessing bestowed on its original owner by the powers of the supernatural world, and that blessing could be retained for mankind by handing down the symbol with the original vision-story and songs. The symbol alone, the medicine-bundle or the painted tent, was worthless without the vision-story and the songs, for only through a perfect knowledge of these " formulae " could each successive owner resurrect, in his imagination, the spiritual experience of the first. It was this necessity of obtaining, as far as possible, the same spiritual experience that differentiated the Blackfoot cult of " medicine-bundles " from the almost world-wide belief in an amulet, a religious statue, or a grave relic conveying good or ill luck from one generation to another.

An epidemic of smallpox in the eighteenth century, and epidemics of smallpox and measles about the middle of the nineteenth, greatly diminished the numbers and strength of the Blackfoot along with the other plains' tribes. Mackenzie estimated that there were from 2,250 to 2,500 warriors in the three tribes of the confederacy in 1801, which would give a population of about 9,000.[1] Hind in 1858 estimated 300 tents in the Blackfoot tribe, 400 in the Piegan, and 250 in the Blood; reckoning eight persons to a tent, this gives a total population of 7,600.[2] Six hundred died of starvation just after the disappearance of the buffalo twenty-five years later. The remainder then settled on reserves in Montana and in Alberta. To-day there are about 2,200 living in the former state, and slightly more than this number in Alberta.

SARCEE

The Athapaskan dialect spoken by the Sarcee (" Not Good ") Indians of Alberta seems most closely related to the dialect of the Beaver Indians dwelling on the Peace river, and the traditions of the

---

[1] Mackenzie: Op. cit., p. lxx.

[2] Hind: Op. cit., p. 115. An estimate in 1835, just before the worst epidemics, gave the Blackfoot 300 tents, the Piegan 500, the Blood 400, the Gros Ventre 250, and the Sarcee 100; Private Papers of Sir James Douglas, 1st ser., ser. C, No. 12, Bancroft Collection of Pacific Coast MSS., University of California.

two tribes assign them a common origin. Present-day Sarcee claim
that their territory ranged from the Peace to the Red Deer rivers,
and that they allied themselves more closely with the Blackfoot tribe
than with either the Blood or the Piegan. Mackenzie estimated that
they consisted only "of about thirty-five tents, or one hundred and
twenty men," which would give a population of about 280;[1] but their
real number was two or three times this amount, judging from other
estimates made in the early years of the nineteenth century.[2] In

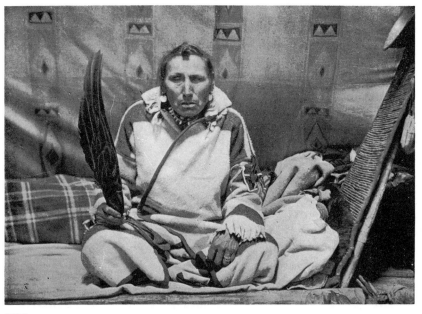

53312

A Sarcee chief inside his tipi. *(Photo by D. Jenness.)*

any case they constituted a small and rather unimportant tribe, which
would almost certainly have disappeared from the prairies had it
not sought the protection of the Blackfoot. In organization, customs, and religious beliefs it was a weak reflection of its more powerful ally, only its language, and perhaps a slight inferiority in the
average stature, betraying its separate origin. For the Sarcee had
similar divisions into bands and military societies, similar marriage

[1] Mackenzie: Op. cit., p. lxx.
[2] " The Sussees are about ninety tents and may number about 650 souls " (David Thompson's
Narrative, p. 327). Franklin allows them 100 tents (Franklin, J.: " Journey to the Shores of the Polar
Sea," vol. 1, p. 170 (London, 1824)). The same estimate appears in the private papers of Sir James
Douglas quoted in a preceding footnote.

and funeral rites, purchased the Blackfoot medicine-bundles with their rituals, and copied their institution of an annual sun-dance initiated by a woman's vow to purchase a sun-dance medicine-bundle. They shared, too, all the misfortunes of the Blackfoot, and when the latter were confined to reserves, received a small and rather infertile tract of land a few miles south of Calgary. There they have steadily declined, partly through apathy, partly through the ravages of tuberculosis, which has carried off a large proportion of the children during the last half century. In 1924 their reserve returned a population of only 160, a total that included a number of Cree and Blackfoot who had married into the tribe or joined their fortunes with it.

GROS VENTRE AND SIOUX

The Gros Ventre or Big Belly[1] Indians who roamed over the southern part of Saskatchewan about 1750 were an offshoot of the Arapaho, one of the many tribes that hunted the buffalo on the prairies of the United States. They were organized on much the same lines as the Blackfoot, having graded military societies and other institutions that differed only in secondary details from the corresponding institutions of their neighbours. After harassing some of the fur-trading posts on the Saskatchewan towards the close of the eighteenth century, they retreated to the south under pressure from the Assiniboine and Cree,[2] and ceased to exert any further influence on the development of the Canadian prairies.

On some small reserves in Manitoba and Saskatchewan to-day there live a few Dakota Sioux,[3] survivors and descendants of the bands that, under their leader, Sitting Bull, rebelled against the United States government in 1876, annihilated the force of General Custer that was sent against them, and found asylum in Canada. Previous to that date they crossed the International Boundary line comparatively seldom, although they bitterly opposed the inroads of the Ojibwa, Assiniboine, and Blackfoot into the prairies farther south. Strictly speaking, therefore, they are not a Canadian tribe, and we may pass them by without further mention.

---

[1] A mistaken rendering of their tribal sign, which expressed the name given to them by their Arapaho kinsmen, Hituena, "Beggars." Their language was Algonkian, not Siouan, as erroneously shown on the folded map at the end of this volume.

[2] David Thompson's Narrative, p. 235.

[3] Sioux is an abbreviation of an Ojibwa word meaning " rattle-snake " or, metaphorically, " enemy."

A Sioux Indian. (*Painting by Paul Coze.*
Reproduction rights reserved by the artist.)

CHAPTER XXI

TRIBES OF THE PACIFIC COAST

From the plains we pass to the Pacific coast of Canada, neglecting for a time the inland tribes of British Columbia because most of them patterned their lives after their neighbours on the coast. The material culture of the coastal tribes[1] hinged on the shoals of salmon that annually ascended the creeks and rivers, and on the abundant stands of free-grained cedar trees; for the salmon provided them with an assured supply of food throughout the year, and the cedar furnished timber for dwellings, canoes, and household utensils, and bark for clothing and mats. While there were local differences in the shapes of the houses and canoes, and in the character and proportion of other foods than salmon, these variations were on the whole less noticeable than differences in social organization, in religious beliefs, and in tribal ceremonies and rituals. The three northern tribes, the Tlinkit of southeastern Alaska, the Haida of Queen Charlotte islands, and the Tsimshian of the Nass and Skeena rivers, possessed well-integrated social systems based on exogamous phratries and clans that recognized descent only in the female line; and they eschewed or kept in strict subordination all other groupings that tended to override their systems. The Kwakiutl, Bella Coola, and Nootka tribes farther south recognized no phratric divisions, hesitated between matrilineal and patrilineal descent, between clan exogamy and clan endogamy, and permitted a rank outcrop of secret religious societies to dominate the clan groupings during the mid-winter months. Clans and secret societies, together with the unique style of painting and carving that accompanied them, tended to fade away among the Coast Salish, and disappeared altogether on the shores of the state of Washington. Considering this progression, it would seem logical to begin our sketch of the Pacific Coast tribes with the most northern, the Tlinkit, which, although strictly an Alaskan tribe hardly touching the borders of Canada, greatly influenced the Tsimshian and Haida Indians to the south and the Athapaskan peoples of Canada immediately behind it.

---

[1] The word " tribe " is used loosely throughout this chapter as a synonym for the awkward expression " linguistic group." It must not be understood to imply any political unit larger than a village, or group of neighbouring villages. *See* Chapter x.

TLINKIT

The Tlinkit ("People") occupied all the coast-line of south-eastern Alaska from mount St. Elias to the Portland canal, with the exception of part of Prince of Wales island which had been colonized by the Haida Indians shortly before their discovery by European voyagers. In this rugged fiord region communication was entirely by sea, and the Indians made long voyages in their dug-out canoes to trade sea-otter skins, native copper from the Copper river, and Chilkat blankets manufactured from cedar bark and the wool of the wild mountain goat, for slaves and shell ornaments that came up to them from the south. About one-third of the population consisted of slaves, some of them members of neighbouring tribes kidnapped or taken prisoners by the Tlinkit themselves, the majority captive Salish Indians (or their slave descendants) from the south of British Columbia, who had passed in barter from one tribe to another. However exalted had been the rank of these slaves in their own land their lot among the Tlinkit was generally wretched in the extreme. They hunted and fished for their masters, manned (with some commoners) the war[1] and travelling canoes, and performed nearly all the drudgery around the villages. The erection of a new house, the launching of a new canoe, the funeral of a nobleman, or an insult offered to a chief might at any time demand their brutal sacrifice, for in the eyes of their masters they were only a form of property that could be destroyed like other property at a mere whim. The wealth of a nobleman, in fact, was largely reckoned by the number of slaves he could command, although it included also his hunting and fishing grounds, his houses and canoes, and the trade goods he possessed, especially the number of sea-otter skins.

The staple food of the Tlinkit, as of all the tribes along the north Pacific coast, was fish, principally halibut, salmon, and oolakan; but the flesh of seals, porpoises, and sea-otters, and abundant berries, roots, and seaweed, gave their diet a considerable measure of variety. The Indians normally laid by a sufficient store of food during the summer months to last them throughout the winter, but if their supplies became exhausted from any cause there were numberless clam beds that could tide them over a season of scarcity. Their dwell-

---

[1] An old woman of high rank usually steered the war canoe. Niblack, A. P.: "The Coast Indians of Southern Alaska and Northern British Columbia"; Ann. Rept., U.S. Nat. Mus., 1888, p. 253 (Washington, 1890).

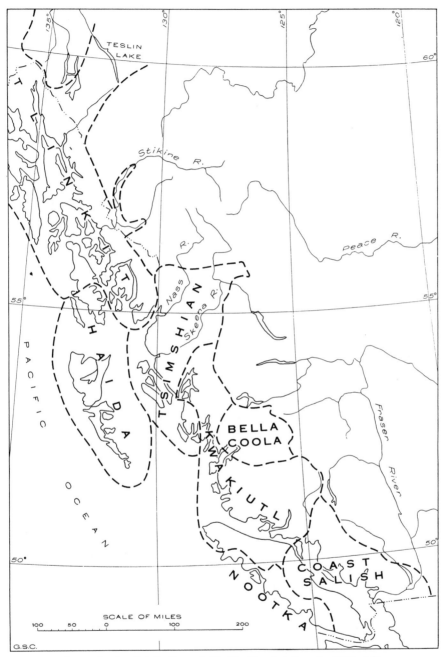

Approximate distribution of Pacific Coast tribes in 1725 A.D.

ings were the large, gabled, plank houses, typical of all the tribes north of Vancouver island, elaborately decorated on the outside with carved and painted designs, and spacious and comfortable within, judged by the native standards of living. These houses extended in a row along the water front except in villages that were subject to frequent attacks, when they were erected on almost inaccessible cliffs and fortified with palisades of trees and brushwood. The furniture consisted mainly of a number of cedar chests and boxes for storing food, clothing, and the paraphernalia used in dances; but there were also a few skins and cedar-bark mats strewn over the benches, and a miscellaneous assortment of baskets, cooking vessels, trays, horn spoons, and other articles stowed away in convenient recesses, or deposited on shelves beneath the rafters.

In addition to body armour composed of two or three thicknesses of hide, or of hide reinforced with wooden slats, the Tlinkit and other west coast tribes wore helmets of solid wood, and probably hideous masks to protect their faces and to inspire terror in their enemies. To the bows and arrows, clubs, and spears employed by nearly all Canadian tribes some Pacific natives seem to have added a stone dagger, which was copied and elaborated in steel after the first contacts with Europeans, and became for nearly a century a familiar weapon along the whole coast from Vancouver island to the gulf of Alaska.

The Tlinkit devoted all the summer months to hunting, fishing, and long journeys for war and trade. In winter they did carpentry of all kinds, and manufactured baskets and clothing. Most of their feasts and dances took place during the winter, although by no means confined to that season. Every stage in the career of a high-born Tlinkit was marked by a ceremony, in nearly all cases a pot-latch.[1] Several families often united to build a special house and hold an elaborate potlatch when their children received ancestral names and underwent the piercing of their ears and noses; for the expense of the ceremony, with its lavish distribution of presents to all invited guests, generally exceeded the means of a single household. There was another potlatch when a daughter became eligible for marriage, still another when a son came of age, assumed the name

---

[1] A potlatch was a feast, generally, but not always, accompanied by masked dances, in which presents were distributed to all the guests.

of an ancestor on his mother's side, erected a memorial column or totem-pole as a visible sign of his rank, and began the construction of a house. Every marriage involved much feasting, and the bestowal on the bride of a dowry equal to the price paid by the bridegroom and his kinsmen; and for every funeral there was a feast of mourning before the corpse was cremated, or deposited in a coffin and either buried in the ground or placed on top of a mortuary post.[1] To burnish their escutcheons ambitious men gave grand potlatches in honour of dead ancestors, and contributed lavishly to other men's potlatches to enhance their own prestige and dignity. No new house could be built without the aid of numerous workmen, owing to the size and weight of the posts and rafters; and the recognized payment for such services was a series of feasts and dances accompanied by the distribution of gifts. There were feasts of a similar character to welcome distinguished visitors; for the deadliest insult a man could sustain was to meet with a reception unbecoming his rank, and most of the wars between neighbouring villages and tribes had their origin in real or fancied slights and injuries. So, for one reason or another, feasts and ceremonies occurred constantly in all the Tlinkit villages, except when the people had scattered to their fishing-grounds or were busily engaged in storing away their food. It is worth remarking that in all these ceremonies the matrilineal system of the Tlinkit linked a man with his mother's kinsmen, not his father's, for it was through his mother that he inherited his rank and clan, and his legal successors were not his own children, who would belong to his wife's clan, but the children of his sister.

In 1835 the total number of the Tlinkit was estimated at 5,850, but many villages had already been depopulated by repeated epidemics of smallpox, which was introduced by Spanish navigators in 1775. The United States census of 1910 recorded a population of 4,426, to which should be added the 250 (approximately) living within the boundaries of Canada.

HAIDA

The dense forests, sparse in game, in the interior of the Queen Charlotte islands, and the deeply indented coast-line frequented by shoals of salmon and halibut, by sea-otters, sea-lions, and fur seals,

---

[1] The higher the rank of the dead man, the more elaborate, of course, was his funeral. Bodies of slaves who died of old age were simply cast out or thrown into the sea.

made the Haida ("People") almost wholly dependent on the sea for their livelihood. Their villages lay on the coast near halibut banks, and the forested hills behind them were little valued except so far as they provided timber for houses and canoes. Of land animals the

250

Skedans, a Haida Indian village on the Queen Charlotte islands.
(Photo by G. M. Dawson.)

Haida killed only a few black bears that came out to the coast to feed on berries and on the dead salmon along the edges of the streams. Yet they were mighty hunters on the sea, and captured more fur seals and sea-otters than any other tribe along the Pacific coast. Every nobleman kept a stock of the skins of these sea mammals to distribute at potlatches and to trade with the Tsimshian, so that when the fur traders of the late eighteenth century began to frequent the northwest coast it was from the Haida that they gathered their richest harvest.

The isolation of their home and their dependence on the sea made the Haida great voyagers, and, as is commonly the case with maritime peoples, keen imitators of the tribes with which they came into contact. In their dug-out canoes they raided the mainland as far as Sitka in the north, and to the lower end of Vancouver island in the south. Naturally they encountered most frequently the Tlinkit and the Tsimshian, and it was from these tribes that they borrowed most extensively. They copied with indifferent success the basketry of the Tlinkit, and derived from the same source most of their shamanistic paraphernalia and songs. Their phratries bore the same names as the Tlinkit phratries, Raven and Eagle,[1] and were similarly divided into a number of clans, with subdivisions into family groups or " houses " each governed by its own chief. From the Tsimshian, with whom they traded canoes and sea-otter skins for Chilkat blankets and the oil of the oolakan or candle-fish, they derived the majority of their dance songs, and the beginnings of a secret society that the Tsimshian had themselves taken over from the Kwakiutl.

The shamans or medicine-men of the Haida and other west coast Indian tribes, like medicine-men elsewhere in Canada, claimed to have received special powers from the supernatural world in answer to prayer and fasting; but the passion of the west coast people for ritualism made them elaborate the fasting process, and distinguish their medicine-men by certain peculiarities in appearance or dress. Diseases were treated in much the same way as· elsewhere, e.g., by massage, sucking over the afflicted part through a tube, application of herbs, etc., all to the accompaniment of much drumming, shaking of rattles, and the singing of medicine-songs. Peculiar to the medicine-men of the Haida, Tlinkit, and Tsimshian was the use of a special " soul-catcher," a bone tube, generally carved, for capturing the wandering souls of the sick and restoring them to their bodies. Since the souls of even healthy people often wander, especially when the body sleeps, every Haida war-party carried at least one medicine-man to capture and destroy the souls of enemies, whose bodies would then be slain in the approaching battle. Dread of the medicine-man afflicted the Haida Indians even after his death, impelling them to deposit his body in a special grave-house overlooking the water which none but other medicine-men had the courage to visit.

The secret society of the west coast Indians probably originated among the Kwakiutl. Its members were men and women who under-

---

[1] Some Tlinkit villages called the second phratry not Eagle, but **Wolf**.

went prolonged and usually arduous initiation rites in order to gain the favour and patronage of certain supernatural guardians. Those who had the same supernatural guardian sometimes formed a fraternity that acted as a separate unit within the society and held its own public ceremonies and dances. Among the Kwakiutl there were a number of these fraternities, and the society was so powerful that when it conducted its ceremonies during the winter months it suspended the normal organization of the communities and practically controlled the lives of the people. The chiefs of the Haida, however, would not tolerate such usurpation of their authority and prestige. When they borrowed (or bought) the institution from the Tsimshian they retained all rights to initiation in their own hands, restricted membership to near kinsmen, permitted the dances only at potlatches, and prevented any union of initiates into groups that might usurp the control of the villages. Strictly speaking, therefore, there was no secret society among the Haida, only an unorganized body of initiates who vaguely imitated the dramatic ceremonies of the secret society to the east and south in order to glorify their " houses " and clans.[1]

The dependence of the Haida on the sea reflected itself in their religion. They believed, like other Indians, that supernatural beings surrounded them on every side; and the more philosophic among them postulated a being on high, a " Power of the Shining Heavens," as the ultimate source of the power that resides in both the supernatural world and the world of the senses. Yet it was to the " Ocean-Beings " that they offered most of their prayers and sacrifices, because they considered that these beings could embody themselves in fish and sea mammals and, in consequence, affect the main food supply of the people. So the Haida offered them grease, tobacco,[2] and the feathers of the flicker, either by burning these objects in the fire (which released their souls), or by throwing them into the water.

The ceremonial life of the Haida closely paralleled that of the Tlinkit; in both there was a succession of feasts and potlatches to mark every event from childhood to the grave. The Haida, however, were more addicted to tattooing than any of the other west coast

---

[1] Cf. Swanton, J. R.: " The Haida"; Memoirs Am. Mus. Nat. Hist., vol. 8; Jesup Expedition, vol. 5 (New York, 1909).

[2] The Haida grew a tobacco-like plant, not for smoking, but to chew with lime obtained by burning shells. They abandoned its cultivation, however, as soon as they obtained smoking tobacco from Europeans.

tribes, and as the process was very painful, they performed it in three stages, each of which required the assumption of a new name and the holding of a potlatch. Cremation, common among the northern Tlinkit, was comparatively rare among the Haida, who sometimes deposited their dead in caves, but more frequently laid them in mortuary houses, three or four in a single structure, or else placed the coffin on the top of a carved post or in a niche in its side. Occasionally the body of a prominent chief lay in state within his house for a whole year before removal to its final resting place.

Contact with Europeans wrought a speedy change in the lives of these islanders. Potatoes, introduced by the early voyagers, took the place of the vanished sea-otter skins in purchasing oolakan oil from the Tsimshian. Steel tools gave a tremendous impetus to sculpture, for the Haida, though inferior to the Tlinkit in basket-making, far surpassed them and all the other west coast tribes in painting and wood-carving. Enormous totem-poles that only the highest chiefs could afford in the days of stone adzes now stood before every house, and Haida carvers found their services in demand up and down the coast of the mainland. A few turned their talents to metal-work, and from the large United States dollar wrought silver bracelets and brooches beautifully engraved with the highly conventionalized bird and animal designs so typical of west coast art. Potlatches became more frequent when money could purchase the Hudson's Bay blankets that replaced skins as the currency, and whole villages flocked to Victoria to gain quick wealth by lending their women to immoral white men. But smallpox at the end of the eighteenth century, and both smallpox and venereal diseases in the nineteenth, took their toll of the population, which rapidly dwindled from perhaps 8,400 in 1800[1] to less than 1,000 (including the Haida on Prince of Wales island) a century later. To-day there are but two inhabited villages on the Queen Charlotte islands, Skidegate and Massett, and their combined population numbers barely 650.

TSIMSHIAN

The third northern people along the Pacific coast, the Tsimshian ("people inside of the Skeena river"), were divided into three

---

[1] Newcombe, C. F.: "The Haida Indians"; International Congress of Americanists, XVth sess., 1906, p. 146 (Quebec, 1907). That Newcombe's estimate is not excessive appears from the census made between 1836 and 1841, which gave a total of 8,328. Dawson: "Report on the Queen Charlotte Islands." p. 173 B.

groups, the Tsimshian proper around the mouth of Skeena river, the Gitksan ("Skeena River people") farther up the same stream, and the Niska who inhabited the basin of Nass (Niska) river. Between these three groups there were slight differences in social organization and in customs, and rather more noticeable differences in speech,

62815

A Tsimshian maiden wearing a Chilkat blanket and carved
head-dress.

although they all spoke dialects of the Tsimshian language. Owing to their geographical positions, the Niska and the Gitksan devoted more time to the hunting of land animals, particularly mountain goats and bears, than the Tsimshian proper, who for their part directed their energies to halibut fishing, and the hunting of seals,

A Tsimshian Indian. (*Painting by Paul Coze.*
Reproduction rights reserved by the artist.)

sea-lions, and sea-otters among the islands off the coast. Neverthe-less all three groups depended mainly on the incredible numbers of salmon that migrated each year up the rivers, and all three gathered, towards the end of winter, at the various oolakan fishing stations along the Nass. One would have expected that the abundance of fish and game, and the quantities of berries and edible roots that could be gathered during the summer months, would have relieved the people from all anxiety concerning their food supply; yet occa-sionally they exhausted all their reserves in February, and suffered great privation until the oolakan appeared in the Nass river about the beginning of April.

Although there were only two exogamic phratries among the Haida and Tlinkit,[1] the Tsimshian had four, subdivided as usual into clans and "houses." The Tsimshian proper and the Gitksan, but not the Niska apparently, distinguished four strata in the popu-lation instead of three, viz., slaves, commoners, nobles, and, above the nobles, a class of ruling or "royal" families who strictly prohibited marriage outside of their own order. The Haida had the germs of this "royal" class in their social system, inasmuch as the heads of certain "houses" that ranked higher than others in their clans tended to intermarry in order to keep their property and rights within the same set of people.[2] But among the two sub-tribes of the Tsimshian, owing perhaps to the greater authority of the chiefs, such intermarriages became obligatory, so that noble and "royal" families were as sharply separated as nobles and commoners. In their customs and beliefs, however, the Tsimshian differed but little from the Haida. They held similar feasts and potlatches for every important event, such as the erection of a new house-post or the assumption of an ancestral name; and they had the same faith in a supreme sky-god whom they occasionally approached in prayer, but more often neglected in favour of lesser supernatural powers believed to influence the food supply, or to have rendered assistance to their forefathers in the past. Medicine-men practised their art in the same way, and acquired their status either by purification and fasting, as among the Haida, or else by sickness and subsequent recovery, their recovery being regarded as proof that they had power

---

[1] But *See* footnote p. 144.
[2] Thus a Haida chief, like the chiefs of the Tsimshian, commonly married his cousin, i.e., his father's sister's daughter, who belonged, of course, to another phratry.

to heal the same malady in others. The Tsimshian usually cremated their dead, but sometimes they buried them, or in special cases, practised a form of mummification. They adopted from the Kwakiutl not only the notion of a secret society, but several of the actual fraternities, among them the horrible " Cannibal Society " whose members tore to pieces human corpses and devoured portions of the flesh.[1]

716

A Kwakiutl woman. *(Photo by G. M. Dawson.)*

All the tribes bordering the north Pacific, and some of the interior natives, greatly relished the oil of the oolakan, and through their control of the Nass river the Tsimshian acquired almost a monopoly of this article along the northern portion of the coast. At the same time the mountains of their home supplied them with goat's

---

[1] Often, perhaps generally, they substituted the flesh of an animal, although the laity was not aware of the deception. An early missionary witnessed the rending of an actual corpse. Mayne, R. C.: " Four years in British Columbia and Vancouver Island," p. 285 ff (London, 1862).

wool for blankets, and goat- and sheep-horn for the manufacture of the highly prized carved spoons. Geographically, too, they held a strategic commercial position between the Tlinkit to the north, the source of all the native copper, and the Kwakiutl to the south, who supplied both slaves and dentalium shells, while right at their door dwelt the otter-hunting Haida. It was only natural, therefore, that they should become the great traders and middlemen of the region, importing with one hand and exporting with the other. They even carried their oolakan oil overland to exchange for furs with Gitksan and Athapaskan-speaking Indians who did not visit the sea.[1] All this interchange of material things was accompanied by an equal interchange of customs, ceremonies, and folk-tales that converted the entire coast, viewed from a larger standpoint, into a single cultural unit.

The Tsimshian population at the end of the eighteenth century is not known. Duncan, an early missionary, estimated their number at 10,000 during the second quarter of the nineteenth century,[2] but his figure seems much too high. Probably 6,000 would be nearer the mark. A census in 1924 gave a total population of 3,448.

BELLA COOLA

Immediately south of the Tsimshian, beginning at Douglas channel, were the Kwakiutl, the nearest of the southern tribes that did not favour exogamous phratries or the recognition of descent through the female line alone; and jutting into the Kwakiutl territory, almost dividing that people into two halves, were the Bella Coola,[3] a people that formerly occupied some two score villages on the Dean and Bella Coola rivers, and on the fiords into which these rivers flow. Each Bella Coola village contained from two to twenty or even thirty plank houses built in a row facing the water front; and each house sheltered from two to ten families. Although all the villages may not have been inhabited at the same time, yet the population when Alexander Mackenzie visited the region in 1793 must surely have numbered at least two or three thousand, of whom 30 per cent perhaps were slaves. To-day, owing to diseases intro-

---

[1] E.g., from the Nass to the village of Kuldo on the upper Skeena river, along what is still known as the "Grease" trail.
[2] Mayne: Op. cit., p. 249 f.
[3] A Kwakiutl word of unknown meaning.

duced by Europeans and the breaking down of the social life, the total population scarcely equals three hundred, all confined to a single village at the mouth of the Bella Coola.

The language spoken by this tribe and its position at the heads of the fiords and along the rivers that empty into them indicate that it broke off from the main body of the Salishan people to the south and pushed its way across the mountains into its present location on the coast.[1] Yet the Bella Coola have no tradition of such a migration, and until recently knew little of any other peoples except the Kwakiutl who bounded them on three sides and the Carrier and Chilcotin Indians who hemmed them in behind. Like the Kwakiutl, from whom they derived most of their customs and religious beliefs, they divided the year into two cycles, a winter season given over to potlatches and religious performances, and a summer when they gathered their food supplies. Their principal food, of course, was the salmon, but in April and May, before the commencement of the salmon run, they gathered in purse-like nets almost as rich a harvest of oolakan as the Tsimshian.[2] They killed, too, a few seals, bears, and porcupines, and a considerable number of wild goats, ducks, and geese. Although meat was never plentiful, the abundance of berries and edible roots compensated for its scarcity, and provided the natives with a rich and varied diet even in the months of mid-winter.

The Bella Coola had no phratries, but a number of what have been called "genealogical families", or what we have considered clans.[3] The members of each clan claimed descent from a mythical ancestor who in the beginning of time came down from the home of the sky-god Alkuntam and settled at some spot in the valley of the Bella Coola or Kimsquit river. The village he supposedly established there, and the surrounding territory he used for hunting and fishing, belonged to all the members of the clan through inheritance from their fathers or mothers. But as women went to live in their husbands' villages the rights of their descendants tended to lapse from disuse. Furthermore, since membership in a clan gave not only property rights, but authority to use certain names, to hold certain ceremonies, to wear certain masks at dances, to employ certain

---

[1] Less probably, it reached its present home by sea.

[2] Like the Tsimshian, they carried its oil over the mountains, along another "Grease Trail," to the Athapaskan Indians of the interior.

[3] Using "clan" in its unspecialized sense, without reference to the method of reckoning descent, to avoid the more unfamiliar terms gens and sept.

designs in the decoration of the house, and to enjoy other privileges of a similar character, there was naturally a strong disinclination to cheapen all these rights by opening too widely the door to membership; and the obvious way to restrict their diffusion was to discourage marriage outside the clan. Thus the same social features that gave rise to a class of "royal" families among the matrilineal Tsimshian who possessed rigidly exogamous phratries, created among the bilateral Bella Coola a shift towards endogamy and the stressing of descent through the male line rather than through the female.

In other ways, too, the Bella Coola differed from the Tsimshian. Tsimshian chiefs had more individual authority, and were more jealous of their positions. At feasts and potlatches they had definite seats according to their rank; a man who usurped the place of a superior, or of one who considered himself superior, immediately stirred up a feud. Bella Coola chiefs were not so carefully graded; they willingly moved aside at feasts to make room for fellow chiefs. Rank depended on the number of potlatches a man had given, and any one could give a potlatch who possessed the necessary wealth and could claim descent from one of the mythical founders of the clans. A man who gave four potlatches, and revived at each a new ancestral title (after a period of seclusion in the back of his house), became one of the society of chiefs who controlled all the activities in the villages. Such a potlatch was highly spectacular. Its giver, with the help of his kinsmen, dramatized the myth from which he derived his new title, and in most cases arranged also for a fictitious visit from the dead ancestor whose place he was resurrecting for himself in the community.

Most potlatches took place in the autumn, after the people had stored away their food and before the secret society began its winter dances. Among the Bella Coola the secret society was theoretically founded on the curious belief that every year, at the beginning of winter, all the miscellaneous host of supernatural beings who haunt this world returned to their real home in the sky[1] and held a series of dances or dramatic performances for the entertainment of the sky-god. The initiated Bella Coola claimed to reproduce these performances in their houses, under the direct patronage, the laity believed, of the supernatural beings themselves, some of whom tem-

---

[1] Thither go also, the Bella Coola believed, the souls of the dead, while their shadows depart to an underworld.

porarily descended to earth and stalked through the Indians' dwellings. An atmosphere of mystery pervaded the villages throughout the whole season, and even the children moved about with solemn faces, believing that the supernatural beings were constantly in their midst. Only those were initiated who could prove an inherited right to perform one of the special dances; but since the cost of initiation was much less than for a potlatch, and most of the Bella Coola could conjure up the right from their genealogical traditions, membership was open to most adults, commoners and nobles alike. A performance usually lasted four nights, and one succeeded another with little intermission (although in a different house) until the close of the season. Several men, or women, might have the same supernatural guardian (or, in other words, the prerogative for the same type of performance, e.g. the right to perform the cannibal dance); but the only bond among them was their common membership in the general society.

KWAKIUTL

The Kwakiutl (" Beach on the other side of the river ") occupied the northern corner of Vancouver island from Johnstone strait to cape Cook, and all the coast of the mainland from Douglas channel to Bute inlet, except the small portion controlled by the Bella Coola. Linguists distinguish three groups among them: the Haisla of Douglas channel and Gardner canal, the Heiltsuk from Gardner canal to Rivers inlet, and the Kwakiutl proper to the south of Rivers inlet.

It is possible that all the Kwakiutl were originally divided into a number of exogamous clans or " genealogical families " that reckoned descent either through the male line alone, or through both male and female. Under the influence of the matrilinear Tsimshian, however, the northern villages developed phratries in which property and rank descended through the mother, while the southern villages, without establishing phratries, modified the rules of inheritance so that property and rank passed through the women by subterfuge; they passed, that is, from a man to his daughter's husband, and from the daughter's husband to the grandchild. Families that had no daughters arranged fictitious marriages to keep the system working. Imitating the Tsimshian, again, the northern group sometimes cremated their dead, a practice that did not find favour with the southern

Kwakiutl, who generally deposited the dead in trees, in caves, or, in the case of special chiefs, in canoes.

Yet the borrowing was not all one-sided, for it was the Kwakiutl, apparently, who originated the secret society that spread over most of the coast-line. Fundamentally, this society seems to have evolved from the concept of the guardian spirit obtained by youths through

714
Koskimo, a Kwakiutl village on Quatsino sound, B.C. *(Photo by G. M. Dawson.)*

prayer and fasting. Throughout eastern and central Canada, as we saw earlier, every boy, and sometimes girls as well, solicited the aid and protection of one of the countless supernatural beings that the Indians postulated in the world around them. None of them knew which of these spirits would answer his prayer, and none of them conceived that he might hand on his " blessing " to a successor; it was a secret source of power that lapsed with the individual's death. The Blackfoot and Sarcee slightly modified the doctrine inasmuch as they believed that by resuscitating the conditions of the original " blessings," and by the correct repetition of the sacred songs, they could transfer certain medicine-bundles without losing the protection of which they were the symbols.

The Kwakiutl, followed by other tribes on the Pacific coast, changed the doctrine much more radically. From causes still obscure they selected a certain number of supernatural beings as the hereditary guardians of their clans, made the right of seeking their protection subject to the laws of descent in the same manner as names and real property, converted the actual acquisition of the " blessing " into a complicated ritual, and banded together into a powerful secret organization the men and women who took part in it. Thus came into being, apparently, the secret society of the Pacific coast, which then underwent much further elaboration, slightly different in different localities, through the incorporation of features that properly belonged to potlatches and other ceremonies. Even among the Kwakiutl it varied from district to district. In the southern villages the members grouped themselves into fraternities according to the supernatural being that had taken them under its protection, or, viewed from another angle, according to the type of dance and dramatic performance for which they had qualified; and all the inhabitants of a village separated themselves into two groups, initiated members or Seals, and uninitiated and superannuated individuals called Sparrows. In the main, however, the Kwakiutl society had almost the same organization, and performed much the same dramatic dances as the Bella Coola society just mentioned, which indeed had been derived from it.

Practically identical with that of other tribes, also, was the potlatch system of the Kwakiutl, except that there was more rivalry between the heads of clans, and, consequently, more extravagance and wanton destruction of both food and property for no other purpose than to enhance the prestige of the potlatch-giver. Another outcome of this rivalry was the development of a more or less fixed rate of interest on all " gifts "; for every recipient of a gift, unless of definitely lower status, had to return it later in double quantity—i.e. 100 skins if he had received 50—or else acknowledge his inferiority and either submit to the scornful taunts of his rival or blot out the disgrace by defeating him in war. Yet the potlatch, even as it existed among the Kwakiutl, was not an entirely harmful institution. It consolidated all the members of the clan, for only by the united efforts and contributions of every individual could the chief maintain his dignity and the clan its prestige; and it was a powerful spur to ambition, especially in post-European times after the abolition of slavery, because it provided a means whereby men of low standing, through industry and foresight, could win their way to the highest positions. In spite of all its abuses its prohibition by the government probably contributed not a little to that decline in the morale of the west coast tribes which, even more than the ravages of European diseases, is gradually bringing about their extinction.

We have no reliable estimate of the Kwakiutl population during the eighteenth and early nineteenth centuries. In 1924 it was slightly under 2,000. Considering the number of villages and even districts now deserted, and the general decline of the Indians all along the coast, we shall not be far wrong in estimating the population in 1750 at from 5,000 to 6,000.[1]

Interior of a Nootka house. *(Reproduced from "Cook's Third Voyage," London, 1785, Plate 42.)*

NOOTKA

The Nootka,[2] who inhabited the coast of Vancouver island from cape Cook to port San Juan, had the distinction of being the only whale hunters in British Columbia.[3] Like the Haida, whom they resembled in their partial dependence on sea mammals, they were

[1] Mooney estimates 7,200 in the year 1780. Mooney, J.: Op. cit., p. 28.
[2] The meaning of the name is unknown.
[3] Two or three tribes in the state of Washington, including a branch of the Nootka, the Makah, also hunted whales.

trained from childhood in the management of dug-out canoes, and did not hesitate to travel almost beyond sight of the stormy coast in pursuit of their ocean game. Only the chief of a clan was allowed to harpoon a whale, but any man might hunt the seals, sea-lions, and sea-otters that frequented the coast in large numbers before the days of the European fur trade. Fish, however, particularly salmon, halibut, and herring, furnished the main food supply, as it did everywhere along the British Columbia coast; and roots and berries provided the usual variety in the diet. If Nootka men won a deserved renown for their daring and skill in hunting sea mammals, their women earned equal praise for their basketry, which even to-day finds a ready market among Europeans, although specimens made for the tourist trade rarely maintain the quality of the earlier baskets that were woven for home use only.

The northern tribes of British Columbia exerted little influence on the Nootka. Their clans were nominally exogamous, but inheritance could pass through both the mother and the father,[1] and a man who in ordinary life was a member of his father's clan might even marry within it by affiliating himself temporarily with his mother's clan and enlisting the help of her kinsmen. Potlatches featured every important occasion in life, whatever the season of the year; but the Nootka reserved their most elaborate potlatches, not for marriages or accessions to chieftainship, but for the coming of age of their daughters. Various non-hereditary clubs, almost exclusively social, gave colour to these festivals with their dances and songs. Ambitious men secluded themselves in the woods at certain periods, and by mimicking the capture of seals and whales, by prayer and fasting, sought to increase their success in hunting.[2] In addition to individual medicine-men, who gained their status in the same way and adopted much the same practices as the medicine-men of other tribes, there was a medicine society and ritual for curing complaints that resisted all other forms of treatment. The shamans of the society dramatically cast their guardian spirits into the bodies of their patients, " cooked " them with the supernatural force, and initiated them as members. The highest families owned certain

---

[1] The eldest son was enrolled in his mother's clan, if that ranked higher than the father's; later children might belong to either. Privileges, e.g. the right to certain dances, descended through both parents.

[2] See illustration, p. 172.

caves in which they laid their dead, but the majority of the Nootka deposited them in trees, either enclosed in boxes or wrapped in cedar bark.

The chief deities of the Nootka were the sky-god, the thunder, and the supernatural wolves. Their superstitious awe of wolves found expression in a wolf ritual, which had many features in common with the secret society dances of the Kwakiutl and Bella Coola Indians. It lasted, however, only about eight days, and though it generally took place in winter, might be held at any season. During its performance the Nootka often killed a slave, practised self-torture, and ate dogs, just as the Kwakiutl did in their winter dances; but the main incidents were the carrying off of novices by fictitious wolves, their seclusion in the woods and subsequent recapture, the exorcism of the wolf spirits from their bodies, and a succession of imitative dances.

The Nootka have experienced the same decline in numbers as other west coast tribes. Their present population is slightly under 1,500, as compared with perhaps 6,000 at the end of the eighteenth century.[1]

COAST SALISH

The Coast Salish (" people ") inhabited all the coast of the mainland from Bute inlet to the mouth of Columbia river. and the portion of Vancouver island not occupied by the Kwakiutl and Nootka—from Johnstone strait, that is, to port San Juan. They were as skilful as the Nootka in making baskets, and from dog and goat hair, mingled with cedar bark, they wove excellent blankets which they decorated with simple geometric patterns quite different from the complex designs (derived from the peculiar style of painting) that were woven into the " Chilkat " blankets of the Tsimshian and Tlinkit. Clams and the meat of goats and deer were commoner foods than elsewhere along the coast, but they could not replace fish as the staple diet throughout the year. The houses, too, were unlike those of other tribes, having no gables, but long roofs with a gentle pitch that made admirable platforms at feasts and dances.[2]

The Coast Salish within Canada, excluding their kinsmen in the United States, spoke half a dozen dialects not mutually intelligible,

---

[1] As late as 1860 Sproat estimated that they could muster 1,700 warriors. Sproat: Op. cit., p. 18.
[2] See illustration, p. 93.

but the differences in culture call for two divisions only, the village groups north of the city of Vancouver, including those on Vancouver island, and the inhabitants of the Fraser River delta. Both these divisions separated the population into the usual three classes, slaves,

20518

Coast Salish dug-outs at Victoria, B.C. *(Photo by R. Maynard.)*

commoners, and nobles, and some villages even recognized a fourth class of "royal" families as among the Tsimshian. Both divisions, too, had exogamous clans with descent exclusively in the male line and with the chieftainship passing from father to eldest son. But the delta people separated their three classes much less rigidly than the rest of the Coast Salish, and often passed over the son of a chief if another relative seemed more worthy of the position. Furthermore, they seldom carved the crests of their clans on their house-posts, regarding ancestral crests as less important than the acquisition in youth of a guardian spirit; and their secret society was only a pale reflection of the Kwakiutl society, which the more northern Coast Salish closely imitated. Carving and painting became less frequent, less conventionalized, and less grotesque, the nearer one approached the United States boundary. Although ceremonial life remained fairly rich throughout the entire territory of the Coast Salish, there was a steady fading away of all those characteristic traits that distinguish the north Pacific Coast peoples from the other tribes of Canada, and indeed from all other tribes in America.

We have no estimate of the numbers of the Coast Salish before about the middle of the nineteenth century, when European diseases and demoralization due to liquor had already produced a serious decline. Mooney conjectured that they exceeded 15,000 when Captain James Cook explored the northwest coast in 1778.[1] Unless this

71405

Grave monument of the Coast Salish. *(Photo by Harlan I. Smith.)*

figure is unduly high, which seems improbable, they have suffered as greatly as the other tribes along the coast, for the population to-day does not exceed 4,000.

[1] Mooney: Op. cit., p. 28 f.

During the century and a half of their contact with Europeans all these west coast tribes have undergone less intermixture, indeed, but a far greater decline than the tribes of eastern Canada who have been subjected to similar influences for four centuries. For the Europeans who took possession of the Pacific coast were farther advanced in civilization than the primitive farmers and fur trappers who had settled in the east. Machinery and rapid transportation were ushering in a new age that the Indians could not comprehend and in which they found no place. Their complex social organization, so different from that of any European country, broke down completely. The grades in their society had no significance for the invading whites, and the potlatches that helped to give these grades stability fell under the ban of the law. Slavery was abolished, and the new individualism that gave even the ex-slave an equal opportunity with the noble destroyed the balance and order in the "houses" and clans. Reversion to the old conditions was impossible, and whither the new would lead no one could foresee. The Indians can still provide cheap labour in the fish canneries, but there they compete with more industrious and efficient labourers from China and Japan. The reserves to which they are confined contain fertile tracts of land, but Indians untrained to agriculture cannot rival either Europeans or Chinese in the cultivation of the soil or the marketing of their products. Socially they are outcasts, economically they are inefficient and an encumbrance. Their old world has fallen in ruins, and, helpless in the face of a catastrophe they cannot understand, they vainly seek refuge in its shattered foundations. The end of this century, it seems safe to predict, will see very few survivors.

CHAPTER XXII

TRIBES OF THE CORDILLERA

INTERIOR SALISH

The largest nation in the interior of British Columbia was the Interior Salish, who differed in customs, dialects, and even physical appearance from the Salishan-speaking Indians of the coast. They were divided into five tribes that were often hostile to one another.

(1) Lilloet ("Wild Onion") Indians, of the Lillooet River valley.
(2) Thompson Indians, in the Fraser River valley from about Yale to Lillooet, and on the Thompson river as far up as Ashcroft.
(3) Okanagan[1] Indians, of the Okanagan lake and river.
(4) Lake Indians, of the Arrow lakes and upper Columbia river.
(5) Shuswap[1] Indians, controlling the Fraser River valley from Lillooet to Alexandria, and all the country eastward to the summits of the Rocky mountains.

At the end of the eighteenth century there was a small Athapaskan-speaking tribe, wedged in among these five Salishan tribes, which occupied the valley of the Nicola river and part of the valley of the Similkameen. Early in the nineteenth century the Thompson River Indians absorbed it so completely that only a few legends, and a small vocabulary of names, bear witness to its former existence.

The Lilloet were the westernmost of the five Interior Salish tribes, and the chief intermediaries in the trade with the coast people; they bartered the berries, hemp bark, skins, and goat wool of the interior for shells, slaves, and, occasionally, dug-out canoes. Trading relations subjected them to other influences, and the Lilloet adopted the exogamous clan system of the Coast Salish (though without the division into castes), impersonated the hypothetical clan ancestors in masked dances, and imitated some of the rites of the secret society. Similarly the westernmost bands of the Shuswap, who lived in close contact with the Chilcotin and Carrier, borrowed from those tribes a division of the population into nobles, commoners, and slaves,[2]

---

1 The meanings of these words are unknown.
2 Slaves were few in number, however, and probably half the population ranked as nobles.

subdivided the nobles into exogamous clans, and, about the beginning of the nineteenth century, instituted a number of dance associations modelled on the secret society of the coast.

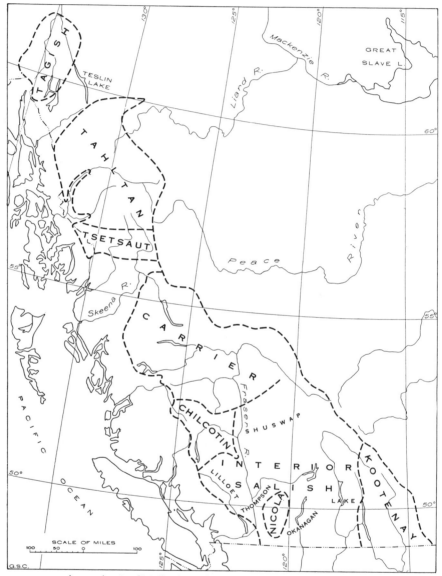

Approximate distribution of Cordilleran tribes in 1725 A.D.

Among the rest of the Interior Salish there were no clans, no trace of a secret society, and no restriction on marriage except nearness of kin. The foundations of society, like those of the hunting tribes in eastern Canada, were the family and the band, the latter a group of families more or less related by blood and marriage. Every band had a chief whose son generally succeeded him, but the

20830

Chiefs of the Thompson River Indians. *(Photo by James Teit.)*

real authority resided with an informal council of the elder men. The warriors elected a special chief to lead them in their war excursions, but his office terminated with the conclusion of the raid. Only women and children were taken prisoners, as a rule, and they soon married and became absorbed into the tribes of their captors. The hunting territory, and in fact all the land, belonged to the entire band, although a few families laid claim to certain fishing places, and to certain fences erected for deer hunting. The home and the furniture belonged to the wife, and descended to her daughters; the canoe,

Winter underground house of the Thompson River Indians. *(Photo by courtesy of the American Museum of Natural History.)*

weapons, and tools of the husband passed to the sons. Every family had a stock of hereditary names, and while fathers generally chose names for their children from their own family lists, not infrequently they selected them from the mothers'.

The dwellings themselves would have suggested a vast difference between these interior tribes and the Salishan people at the mouth of the Fraser. In place of the long, shed-like structures divided into stalls for twenty or thirty families, the winter home of the interior people was a circular, semi-subterranean house, not more than forty or forty-five feet in diameter, that was entered by a 'adder from the roof;[1] and the summer home was an oblong or conical lodge covered

---

[1] *See* the plan in part I, p. 92.

with rush mats.[1] The coast people stored their food in large boxes beneath the rafters or under the benches; the Interior Salish cached it outside the dwellings in boxes raised on posts, or, more often, in deep pits lined with bark. The dome-shaped sweat-house, infrequent on the coast of British Columbia, was as common in the interior as on the plains or in the eastern woodlands of Canada; it was the home of the youth during his period of fasting, and both men and women purified themselves in its steam before feasts and religious dances. Though the principal source of food remained the salmon, land animals—black-tailed deer, elk, bear, beaver, and marmot—took the place of sea mammals and were much more prominent in the diet. The Okanagan tribe even crossed the Rocky mountains, like their Kootenay neighbours, to hunt the buffalo on the prairies. Cooking vessels were not the neatly made boxes of red cedar employed by the tribes on the coast, but either vessels of birch bark or baskets woven so tightly that they held water. Often, however, the Indians preferred to roast their meat and fish on spits, or to bake them in the ashes.

Even in their dress the Interior Salish departed radically from the coast tribes and resembled the Indians east of the Rocky mountains. It is true that like the Coast Salish they made blankets of goat's wool, though without the admixture of dog's hair; but they also wove blankets from strips of rabbit fur, after the manner of tribes in northern and eastern Canada. Instead of the oblong cloaks, the capes, and the domed or conical hats woven from spruce-root, that were worn from Puget sound to the gulf of Alaska, they had robes of fur, and breech-cloths (men), tunics (women), leggings, and moccasins of dressed skin. Their transportation methods, again, were different. A few families had dug-out canoes like the river canoes used in the delta of the Fraser, but before the introduction of iron tools the great majority of the Interior Salish preferred the more easily made bark canoe, which generally projected under the water-line at bow and stern like the bark canoes of the Kootenay. So full of rapids, however, were the Fraser and Columbia rivers and their tributaries that the Indians performed most of their travelling on foot, and transported their weapons, trade goods, and household furniture on their backs or on the backs of dogs. A small, round-

---

[1] The Lilloet had at least one village fortified with a palisade, like some of the villages of the coast tribes. Journal of Simon Fraser; in Masson, i, p. 177.

headed snow-shoe, without cross-bars, and much inferior to the snow-shoe used by Indians farther north, was much in vogue for winter travel; the coast Indians, of course, were ignorant of its use.

30991

Interior Salish girl, wearing a feather head-dress and a blanket woven from the wool of the wild mountain goat. *(Photo by James Teit.)*

While the weapons and armour of the Interior Salish corresponded broadly with those that prevailed throughout the rest of the province, many warriors carried in addition small round shields similar to the shields of the plains' tribes,[1] and poisoned their arrow-heads with the flower of the ranunculus or with virus from the rattle-

---

[1] Simon Fraser saw a different type of shield among the Lilloet: "It was large enough to cover the whole body, composed of splinters of wood like the ribs of stays and neatly enclosed with twine made of hemp." Journal of Simon Fraser; in Masson, i, p. 179.

snake. Neither carving nor painting attained a high level, but all five tribes manufactured splendid baskets decorated externally, by the peculiar process known as imbrication, with geometric (and in modern times realistic) designs. The only other people in Canada who made comparable baskets were the Chilcotin and some bands of the Coast Salish, both of whom learned the art from the Interior Salish.[1]

For a period varying from one to four years after reaching maturity girls went into seclusion, and youths isolated themselves at

Summer tent of Shuswap Indians at Kamloops. *(Photo by courtesy of the American Museum of Natural History.)*

irregular intervals to obtain their guardian spirits. The marriage ceremony was a simple feast; men purchased their brides, and the women's kinsmen repaid the husbands later. The dead were buried in the ground or under a rock slide.[2] Most tribes had first-fruit ceremonies to celebrate the ripening of various berries, and the arrival of the first shoal of salmon each season. The clans of the Lillooet and western Shuswap held masked dances during the winter, and their chiefs gave potlatches after the manner of the coast tribes.

---

[1] Like the Haida, the Interior Salish (and also the Kootenay) cultivated tobacco, or a tobacco-like plant, but instead of chewing it they smoked it in tubular pipes carved from soapstone.
[2] The Shuswap "bury them in large tombs which are of a conical form, about 20 feet diameter and composed of coarse timber." Journal of Simon Fraser; in Masson, i, p. 167.

This potlatch system spread to the other Interior Salish tribes during the nineteenth century, but fell into abeyance again before its close.

The most notable festival was a ghost or circle dance, celebrated in summer or in winter whenever some member of a band claimed to have received a message from the land of ghosts. Then the people gave themselves over to a series of feasts and dances. On the morning of each dance day they fasted and washed; at noon they feasted and prayed the Chief of the Dead to preserve them from all ill; in the afternoon they danced; and at evening the men held a smoking ceremony. So greatly did they reverence this Chief of the Dead that at the coming of Europeans several bands elevated him to the rank of a sky-deity and identified him with the God of the Christian missionaries.

European diseases, and the complete overthrow of the old economic and social conditions, have produced a decline among the Interior Salish parallel to that of their kinsmen on the coast. Mooney estimates their number in 1780 at 15,500;[1] to-day it scarcely reaches 6,000.

KOOTENAY

The Kootenay,[2] who were taller than most of the Indians of British Columbia, inhabited in the second half of the eighteenth century the northern part of the state of Idaho, and the southeastern corner of British Columbia between the Rocky mountains and the Selkirks from about latitude 49 degrees north to 52 degrees north. Even at that time they seem to have been divided into two groups: the Upper Kootenay of the upper Columbia and upper Kootenay rivers, who continually crossed the mountains to hunt the buffalo on the prairies, and even attempted to reach the posts of the fur traders on the upper Saskatchewan;[3] and the lower Kootenay of the lower Kootenay river, who spoke a slightly variant dialect and, being farther removed from the mountains, seldom joined in the buffalo hunt but subsisted principally on fish. Both groups, as we know from their traditions and from the explicit statement of the explorer Thompson,[4] lived on the eastern side of the Rockies during the

---

[1] Mooney: Op. cit., p. 29 f.
[2] The meaning of the word is not known.
[3] Cf. Journal of Duncan McGillivray of the Northwest Company at Fort George on the Saskatchewan, 1794-5, with introduction, notes, and appendix by Arthur S. Morton, Toronto, 1929, p. 56.
[4] Thompson: Op. cit., p. 327 f.

earlier half of the century, but were driven westward by the Black-foot. In dress, customs, and religion they resembled the plains' tribes far more than they did the tribes of British Columbia, except perhaps certain bands of the Interior Salish. They had no clans or clan crests, no secret societies or masked dances, and no division into grades or castes. Their dress, like that of the plains' tribes, was entirely of skin, consisting of moccasins, leggings, a breech-cloth (for women a tunic), and a shirt or jacket; their dwellings were conical tents covered with buffalo hide or rush mats; and their cooking utensils were vessels of birch bark. The Lower Kootenay made also water-tight baskets of split roots, an art they probably learned from the neighbouring Salish, for the bark canoes and dug-outs of both the Lower and the Upper Kootenay were indistinguishable from Interior Salish craft. Wood-carving, however, was almost unknown among them, and the realistic figures which they painted on their garments, their tents, and even their persons, followed the style of painting among the plains' Indians, not the styles of the Pacific coast.

Society was as simple among the Kootenay as among the migratory tribes of eastern Canada. There was no chief governing the entire tribe, or either of its two divisions; but every band had its leader, who was supported by an informal council of the older men. One of his sons generally succeeded him, in spite of the fact that the Kootenay seem to have reckoned descent through the female line. For war, and for the annual buffalo hunt across the mountains, they followed the Salish custom of electing a special chief whose office terminated with the return of the expedition. Women and children captured in war (mainly from the Blackfoot) were kept as slaves, but treated mildly and sooner or later absorbed into the tribe.

Of the social and religious life of the Kootenay we have no detailed account. We know that they were inveterate gamblers, that they practised polygamy, securing their wives by purchase, and that the women carried their babies on their backs in highly ornamented wooden cradles not unlike those used by the women on the plains. Both boys and girls underwent the usual seclusion at adolescence, the boys, and often the girls also, seeking through dreams the protection of guardian spirits. Medicine-men, who exerted considerable influence in the different bands, and often occupied larger tents than the other Indians, derived their status from the customary visions gained during prolonged fasts and ratified, perhaps, by some public ceremony. The dead with their ornaments were buried in shallow holes amid rocks and boulders, sometimes so carelessly that the bodies

30607

A Kootenay chief. *(Photo by James Teit.)*

were exposed to the air. In the firm conviction that the dead would one day return to life at lake Pend-d'Oreille, all the Kootenay bands assembled at that lake in certain winters to hold a religious festival; and every night on their outward and homeward marches the Indians danced round fires in honour of the sun-god. They worshipped the sun above all the multitude of supernatural beings with which they peopled the universe. Before every war expedition they offered it prayers and tobacco smoke; and, to win its favour, some warriors even chopped off the joints of their first fingers, or, like certain plains' tribes, sacrificed pieces of flesh from their arms and breasts.

The Kootenay have adjusted themselves to European domination more successfully than any other tribe in British Columbia; for the isolation of their country prevented much settlement until the second half of the nineteenth century, when they had already taken to ranching and the raising of horses, an occupation that closely corresponded with their earlier pursuits. They have continued it ever since, although a certain number of the men find employment as guides for sportsmen and as labourers for white farmers and ranchers. To-day the Kootenay number around 1,050, of whom 501 were living in Canada in 1924, the remainder in the United States. Mooney estimated their number at about 1,200 before they came into contact with Europeans.[1]

CHILCOTIN

The Chilcotin (" Inhabitants of Young Man's River "), the southernmost of the Athapaskan-speaking tribes in British Columbia that survive to the present day, occupied the headwaters of the Chilcotin river and the Anahim Lake district from about latitude 51° 10′ to latitude 52° 40′, and from the Cascade mountains in the west to within measurable distance of the Fraser river in the east.[2] Like other Athapaskan tribes,[3] they clung tenaciously to their language, but derived the colour of their social and material life from neighbouring peoples—from their Carrier kinsmen in the north with whom they were frequently at enmity, from the Interior Salish tribes to the east and south, and from the Bella Coola and Kwakiutl Indians on the coast. Their country was rich in game—caribou, bears, goats, sheep, marmots, and rabbits—and yielded many edible roots and

---

[1] Mooney: Op. cit., p. 27.

[2] Simon Fraser met some of them in 1808 at the junction of Chilcotin and Fraser rivers; Masson, i, 165, 218. Cf. " The Talkotins, who inhabit the banks of Fraser's river in the vicinity of Alexandria were formerly on the most friendly terms with the Chilcotins, and when salmon failed among the latter they were always permitted to fish in Fraser's river " (Cox, Ross: " Adventures on the Columbia River"; vol. ii, p. 369 (London, 1831)).

[3] e.g., the Sarcee on the prairies, who adopted the culture of the Blackfoot, the Carrier, who copied the Tsimshian, and the Tahltan, who imitated the Tlinkit.

berries, but salmon ascended their rivers so irregularly that the Chilcotin bought much of their supply from the Shuswap of the Fraser river and from the Bella Coola Indians across the mountains. To the latter they sold dried service- and soap-berries, paints of different colours, the furs of various animals, and, in more modern times, snow-shoes; to the Shuswap a few furs, but mainly dentalia shells and woven blankets of goats' wool furnished them by the Bella Coola.

Trade naturally led to other interchanges until the culture of the Chilcotin became a blend of elements from several different sources. They learned from the Shuswap to weave rush mats and coiled baskets with imbricated decorations, even to carry their babies in osier hampers instead of in the birch-bark cradles used by many Athapaskan tribes to the northward. Some of them pointed the ends of their bark canoes to correspond with the " sturgeon-nosed " canoes of the Interior Salish and Kootenay, and spent the winter months in small, subterranean houses that differed only in size from the winter dwellings of the Shuswap. The Bella Coola supplied them with shell ornaments, head-bands of cedar bark to wear at dances, wooden boxes and trays for holding their food, and stone pestles for pounding their berries. Their clothing, however, resembled that of other Athapaskan tribes (moccasins, leggings, breech-cloth or skirt,[1] belt, robe, and cap); the majority preferred, even in the winter months, the Athapaskan rectangular, earth-covered lodge walled and roofed with bark or brush; and woven baskets were not more common than the birch-bark baskets and water-pails typical of northern and eastern Canada.

In their social organization the Chilcotin followed largely the Bella Coola. There were three or four bands in the tribe, each of which subdivided its members into the three classes, nobles, commoners, and slaves, and grouped the first two into clans. We know very little about these clans except that the most powerful was named the Raven, and that they reckoned descent through both the male and the female lines. Individuals obtained high rank by giving potlatches, but in one or two bands the chieftainship seems to have been hereditary. Boys and girls went into seclusion at adolescence, as usual, but the guardian spirits acquired by boys at this period were often determined by inheritance, owing to the influence of the Pacific

---

[1] It seems probable that, like the Carrier, they did not adopt the breech-cloth until the early years of the nineteenth century.

Coast customs. The clan held an elaborate potlatch at the funeral of a nobleman, distributed most of his possessions, and erected over his grave a wooden pillar carved to represent his crest. Yet the Chilcotin did not always bury their dead. Sometimes they cremated them, or left them on the surface of the ground under a pile of stones or brush.

Thompson remarked that the Chilcotin were bolder and more restless than their neighbours, the Carrier and the Shuswap, and during the first half of the nineteenth century the tribe had a bad reputation for turbulence. Smallpox decimated it about 1862, and the remnants of the population settled down to ranching. Some of them moved to the vicinity of Alexandria, on the Fraser river, where they have merged with the Shuswap and Carrier. The majority still occupy their old territory, and the westernmost band still crosses the mountains each summer to visit the Indians at Bella Coola. Their total number probably does not exceed 450, a serious reduction from the 2,500 estimated by Mooney as the pre-European population, or the 1,500 estimated by Teit.[1]

CARRIER

The Carrier lived directly north of the Chilcotin, in the valleys of the upper Fraser, Blackwater, Nechako, and Bulkley rivers, and around Stuart and Babine lakes up to the borders of Bear lake. Their name (English, Carrier; French, Porteur, said to be a translation of the term applied to them by their eastern neighbours, the Sekani) refers to their peculiar custom of compelling widows to carry on their backs the charred bones of their dead husbands. They had no common name for themselves, only names for the independent sub-tribes into which they were divided. In the nineteenth century, however, they adopted for themselves the obscure title Takulli, bestowed on them apparently by Europeans.

All the rivers in the Carrier country teemed with salmon during the summer months, and the lakes contained abundant carp and other fish that the Indians could capture under the ice during the winter. As with the coast tribes, therefore, fish was the staple food throughout the year. When the snow was off the ground the Carrier gathered many berries and roots, and hunted caribou, bears, beaver, marmots,

---

[1] Mooney: Op. cit., p. 27. Teit, J.: " The Shuswap "; Mem. Am. Mus. Nat. Hist., vol. 4; Jesup Expedition, vol. 2, p. 761 (New York).

and rabbits; but they rarely hunted in winter, lacking both snow-shoes and toboggans in pre-European times. Canoes and cooking vessels were made of birch bark. Some of the natives had, also, wooden cooking-boxes that filtered through in trade from the coast Indians, and woven baskets were current among the southern bands that traded with the Bella Coola, Chilcotin, and Shuswap.[1]

The dress of the Carrier resembled in the main that of other Indian tribes in the interior of British Columbia; it consisted of a robe, leggings, and moccasins, all of skin, with a cap and mittens for cold weather.[2] On ceremonial occasions the nobles in the western sub-tribes wore beautiful "Chilkat" blankets acquired from the Tsimshian, and their women disfigured their mouths with stone labrets from the same source, or with imitations of them made from maple. From the coast tribes, too, the Carrier obtained an abundance of shell ornaments and copper bracelets.

Houses, tools, and weapons all conformed closely to those of the surrounding tribes. Some of the Carrier who lived in the south passed the winter in underground houses similar to those of the Chilcotin and Shuswap; the winter lodges of the remainder were rectangular structures above ground, roofed with spruce bark and gabled at front and back by continuing the roof down to the ground on each side and omitting the upright walls.[3] Summer dwellings were constructed on a similar plan, but had low, plank walls and gabled roofs of planks or bark that made them almost identical with the winter dwellings of the Tsimshian and Bella Coola. Many noblemen carved their crests on the four pillars of their houses, but the carvings were very crude, for the Carrier lacked the artistic ability of the coast tribes. Warriors used the same weapons as their enemies, a bow and arrow, lance, club, and knife; and they wore "coats of mail" fashioned either from slats of wood or from a moosehide coated with fine pebbles like asphalt roofing. Some of them, however, carried oval shields and tipped their bows with stone points for stabbing at close quarters,

---

[1] Cf. Mackenzie: Op. cit., p. 299. Harmon, D. W.: " A Journal of Voyages and Travels in the Interior of North America," p. 219 (Andover, 1826).

[2] Men wore no breech-cloth, apparently, in pre-European times, but a few adopted the garment in the early nineteenth century. Many even discarded the robe in warm weather and went naked. Women, however, always added a short apron that reached to the knees. Harmon: Op. cit., p. 287.

[3] Morice (" Notes on the Western Denes," p. 188) states that there was no partition whatever in this house, but Ross Cox says that among the Carrier of the upper Fraser river " Several families generally club together and build a house, the size of which is proportioned to the number of inhabitants, and is partitioned off into several divisions." Cox: Op. cit., vol. ii, p. 347 f.

like the Sekani and Tahltan, their neighbours, and the Slave and perhaps other Indians in the valley of the Mackenzie.[1]

The influence of the coast tribes on the Carrier was not limited to the external culture; it permeated the whole fabric of the social and political life. The population was divided as usual into nobles, commoners, and slaves, but there was no "royal class" of rulers such as existed among the neighbouring Tsimshian. Slaves, too, were not

56923

Summer camp of a Carrier family. *(Photo by Harlan I. Smith)*

numerous, and, except on the border of the Tsimshian territory, a commoner who possessed sufficient energy, and gathered his friends to his support, could readily attain the rank of a nobleman by giving the requisite potlatches and assuming an appropriate title. The western sub-tribes around Stuart, Babine, and Fraser lakes (our information concerning the other Carrier groups is imperfect) were organized

---

[1] *Cf.* Mackenzie: Op. cit., p. 206. Emmons, G. T.: "The Tahltan Indians"; University of Pennsylvania, the Museum, Anthropological Publications, vol. iv, No. 1, p. 66. Masson: Op. cit., vol. 1, p. 91.

into exogamous phratries, clans, and houses, not two phratries only as among the Tlinkit and Haida, or even four as among the Tsimshian, but five.[1] Most of the details of this organization (e.g. the titles of the nobles, their crests and privileges) naturally came from the Tsimshian of the Skeena river, with whom many of these western Carrier intermarried; but the Kwakiutl of Kitimat, and the Salishan-speaking Bella Coola also contributed in varying degrees, depending on the strength of their contacts with the different sub-tribes. The system, therefore, differed slightly from one Carrier group to another. Thus, among the Indians of the Bulkley river, and of Stuart and Babine lakes, who rigidly adhered to the matrilineal organization of the Tsimshian, the son of a nobleman by a woman of the commoner class was a commoner, and only by the greatest exertions ever succeeded in raising himself above that class. But the Carrier around Fraser lake and Stony creek, who had frequent contact with the Bella Coola, placed more emphasis on the father's rank than on the mother's, and at Fraser lake counted a man among the nobles even if his father alone was noble.

The territory of each sub-tribe was divided among the phratries, and further subdivided among the clans. In consequence every district and every fishing place was claimed by some clan and considered the property of its chief, who supervised its use for the benefit of his fellow-clansmen and retainers. Yet the final ownership rested with the entire phratry, whose head man (i.e. the chief of the principal clan) could temporarily allot the area to some other clan and assign its usual possessors another district. Poaching by members of other phratries was a very serious offence certain to cause strife and bloodshed unless the chiefs of the phratries took up the issue and arranged for adequate compensation.

Nearly every community contained members of all the phratries, and the principal man in a village was the leading nobleman of the phratry most strongly represented. Although the phratries themselves were of equal rating, inequalities in their strength among the different sub-tribes affected the relative prestige of their chiefs. Even the most powerful chief, however, rarely dared to act without consulting the clan chiefs in his phratry, and generally also the chiefs of

---

[1] To-day their number has been reduced to four through the amalgamation of two phratries in the second half of the nineteenth century, after smallpox had decimated the people.

other phratries, so that the Carrier never possessed any unified government even within a single sub-tribe.

To buttress their social arrangement the Carrier adopted the potlatch system of the west coast tribes. Each event of importance— the erection of a large house, the return from a successful war raid. the coming of age of a son or daughter, a marriage, a funeral— demanded a feast and a distribution of presents. The funeral of a chief, indeed, and the installation of his successor, required not one potlatch only, but six, constituting a very heavy burden on the new incumbent and his clan.

To-day this old organization is disappearing rapidly. The population has dwindled to one-fourth of its former number, and individual homes replacing the large, semi-communal houses that were occupied by a chief and his kinsmen have broken down the solidarity of the clan. Where phratries and clans still persist, as on the borders of the Tsimshian country, phratric exogamy is no longer compulsory, individuals no longer insist on their rightful seats at dances, and shirk the expense of acquiring by potlatches, in defiance of the law, the titles, crests, and other privileges to which they are entitled by descent. European settlement, moreover, has completely changed the economic condition of the Carrier, and their adoption of Christianity has lessened their interest in the old social system, which in some districts is now almost forgotten.

The former religion of the Carrier was a blend of the beliefs current among neighbouring tribes. Like the Haida, they acknowledged rather vaguely a supreme sky-god (since interpreted as the God of the missionaries) to whom they occasionally offered sacrifices of food and prayed for help in times of famine. But they pinned most of their faith to a multitude of supernatural beings in nature around them, with whom they tried to gain contact through dreams, and whose aid they sought by the practice of various rituals. Men with special gifts, they claimed, gained closer contact than others with this supernatural world either through sickness, or by fasting and dreaming in special places; and through the power they derived from their visions, and the songs magically imparted to them, they could inflict and heal diseases,[1] capture the wandering souls of their fellow-

---

[1] Ross Cox remarks that the profession of a medicine-man was somewhat dangerous, because he was liable to suffer maltreatment and even death if his patient died. Cox, Ross: Op. cit., pp. 379, 388.

men, and perform other miracles that were beyond the power of the lay Indian. The sub-tribes that lived nearest the Tsimshian adopted the secret cannibal society of the coast tribes, and linked it with the superstition of an invisible, intangible force, dwelling in the mountains, that struck down its victims without warning and made them subject to periodic dementia. All the Carrier believed in reincarnation, and in an afterlife for the soul in a shadowy underworld, or in some far-away land in the west; but the doctrine was held too lightly to affect the daily current of their lives, and the average Indian felt that his career would come to a close with the burning of his body on the funeral pyre.[1]

Many epidemics, of European origin, have assailed the Carrier since the end of the eighteenth century, and the decline in population they initiated has continued to the present day. The tribe, reduced in numbers from 8,500[2] (in 1780) to about 2,000, has been confined to reserves within its old territory, which is now traversed by a transcontinental railway. European settlement has revolutionized the old mode of life. Fewer and smaller shoals of salmon ascend the rivers each year, and deer, caribou, and beaver have become much scarcer. With their fishing and hunting restricted, the Carrier have taken to petty farming, but they lack the farmer's love for the soil, and work without hope or energy. They lack, too, aptitude and training for the mechanical and clerical tasks that modern industry may require of them, and as labourers they are less patient and steady than European workmen. Some of the younger men cut railway ties in winter, or trap the fur-bearing animals that linger in the remoter and more mountainous districts. But the Carrier do not understand the complex civilization that has broken like a cataract over their heads, and they can neither ride the current nor escape it. The white settlers around them treat them with contempt,[3] and begrudge them even the narrow lands the government has set aside for them. So they will share the fate of all, or nearly all, the tribes in British Columbia and disappear unnoticed within three or four generations.

---

[1] For good descriptions of the peculiar funeral rites of the Carrier, and the sufferings of widows, *See* Cox: Op. cit., p. 387 ff, and Harmon: Op. cit., p. 216 ff.

[2] Mooney: Op. cit., p. 27.

[3] On the Skeena and Bulkley rivers, as in some other parts of British Columbia, a white man will not walk beside an Indian, but marches in front of him, unless, of course, the two men are hunting together.

TSETSAUT

Bordering both Tsimshian and Carrier on the north were the Tsetsaut Indians, who seem to have numbered about 500 at the beginning of the nineteenth century, but could reckon only three survivors at its close. They claimed the northwest shore of Portland inlet, perhaps also the eastern shore of Behm canal, thence north almost to the Iskut river, and east across the Nass and Skeena rivers to Bear lake. Although their territory touched the sea they were really an inland people, like all the Athapaskan tribes of Canada, for they lived on the land game and on the salmon in the rivers, and resorted to the salt water only for the oolakan run in the early spring.

Tsetsaut, "inland people," was a term applied by the Tsimshian to every Athapaskan tribe in the interior of British Columbia. The true name of what we know as the Tsetsaut tribe cannot now be recovered. The Tahltan called them Black Bear people, because, unlike the neighbouring peoples, they frequently wore clothing of black bear skin. They had many feuds with the Tahltan, particularly with an extinct branch of that tribe, the Lakuyip, that hunted around the headwaters of the Skeena and Stikine rivers. Their chief enemies, however, were the Tlinkit, and the Tsimshian of the Nass river; it was among the last-named people that the remnants of the tribe survived as slaves.

The culture of the Tsetsaut was a blend of Athapaskan and Pacific Coast traits. Their principal food, besides fish, was the meat of the marmot, their dwellings peculiar lean-tos, sheathed with bark on roof and sides, that bore a slight resemblance to the underground houses of the Interior Salish and Chilcotin. Their canoes were covered with bark—cedar bark instead of birch bark—probably because the latter was scarce; and they used cooking vessels and baskets of bark or of woven spruce roots. In all these features, and in part of their folk-lore, they resembled other Athapaskan tribes. Common among Athapaskan tribes, too, but rare or unknown on the Pacific coast, were the customs of a mother-in-law avoiding any meeting with her son-in-law, and of parents dropping their earlier names and calling themselves father or mother of such and such a child. Yet the social organization of the Tsetsaut, and about half of their folk-lore, were borrowed directly from the coast tribes. Like the

Tlinkit, for example, they divided their population into two exogamous phratries that reckoned descent through the female line.[1]

TAHLTAN

Very similar to the Carrier in their dress, their implements, and their general mode of life, were the Tahltan,[2] who occupied the country from about latitude 56° 30′ north to 60° north, and from the Cascade range of mountains to the Cassiar, thus controlling the entire drainage basin of the upper Stikine river, and the headwaters of some of the streams that fed the Taku, Nass, Skeena, Mackenzie, and Yukon rivers. The Stikine River valley below Telegraph Creek they shared with the Tlinkit, who caught salmon and gathered berries there during the summer months, whereas the Tahltan hunted over it during the winter after the Tlinkit had retreated to the coast.

The climate throughout all this interior country was rather dry,[3] and the snowfall in winter comparatively light. Grassland or stony ridges covered much of the area, and large timber was scarce except in the valleys near the coast. Yet it was a splendid game country, with abundance of caribou, moose, bear, and smaller animals;[4] and large shoals of salmon annually ascended the Stikine. The Tahltan regulated their lives to meet these conditions; they scattered to the hunting-grounds in the early winter, and gathered towards spring at the fishing-places to await the arrival of the salmon. In midsummer they moved to the mountains again to snare marmots. Some remained there until the hunting season, but the majority assembled on the Stikine river for the autumn trade with the Tlinkit and for the festivals that succeeded it.

Scarcity of timber allowed the Tahltan to make only a few spruce-bark canoes, and those small and of poor quality, little better than the temporary rafts that they sometimes constructed to cross

---

[1] All our information about the Tsetsaut comes from Boas, F.: " The Tinneh Tribe of the Portland Inlet, the Ts'ets'aut"; Fifth Report on the Indians of British Columbia, Rept. British Ass. Advancement of Sci., 1895 (London, 1895). I have consulted also a few notes left by James Teit.

[2] Two- or three meanings have been given for this name. The most probable is one given by Teit, a " basin-shaped hollow," from two Tlinkit words *tat*, " a basin or bowl," and *tan*, " to remain, to be." It seems to have been the Tlinkit name for the low flat at the mouth of the Tahltan river, on its west side, opposite the old village of Titcakhan from which the Tahltan derived their own name for themselves, *titcakhanotene*: " people of Titcakhan."

[3] It was the arid air of the interior that induced the Tlinkt to ascend the river, because they could dry fish there more easily than in the damp climate of the coast. After the Russians began to visit the northwest coast, about the middle of the eighteenth century, the Tlinkit kept a strict guard over the river to preserve their monopoly of the fur trade with the Tahltan, a monopoly that was not broken until the Cassiar gold rush of 1874.

[4] The Indians state that there were buffalo in pre-European times.

the numerous streams. Nearly all their travelling was done on foot, in winter without even snow-shoes, which neither they nor the Carrier acquired before the end of the eighteenth century. Sleds, too, were unknown; the only conveyance was a rude toboggan made from the leg-skins of the moose and dragged, not by the dogs, which served

19454

A Tahltan fishing village. *(Photo by James Teit.)*

only for hunting, but by the women. Travelling equipment was necessarily light—a few weapons and tools, spare clothing, hide thongs, bark cooking vessels, and material for sewing and netting— things for the most part readily transportable in the netted bags of babiche that the women fabricated in various shapes and sizes. For lodging the majority of the natives used lean-tos of poles laid closely together, roofed with bark, and packed with boughs and earth around the bottom; the more prosperous slung moosehides over a pole after the manner of a fly. Almost equally crude and comfortless were their permanent dwellings, erected in places to which they returned year after year; for at fishing sites they slept and dried their salmon in miserable bark-roofed huts with vertical walls, and elsewhere erected only double lean-tos, or A-shaped huts, long enough at times to shelter several families. In their principal village, on the Tahltan river, each of the six clans in the tribe owned a house of the latter type, 100 or more feet in length, that sheltered all the principal families of the clan, and provided a hall for potlatches and dances.

With two of their neighbours, the Taku branch of the Tlinkit, and the Nass River branch of the Tsimshian, the Tahltan had many petty wars that did not cease until the middle of the nineteenth century. Their weapons were bows and arrows, knives, and spears, occasionally also antler picks mounted on wooden handles; and for armour they wore cuirasses and helmets of thick goat skin. Like the plains' Indians they carried off the scalps of slain enemies, and held a scalp dance on their return home. Women captives became slaves unless they were ransomed by their kindred. To harden their bodies for the rigours of hunting and of war adult men up to the age of about forty used to whip each other's backs with willow switches and plunge naked into a snowbank or an ice-laden stream.

With two other neighbours, the Tlinkit at the mouth of the Stikine river and the Kaska of the Dease river, the Tahltan maintained unbroken friendship. From the former they obtained oolakan and salmon oil, dentalium and abalone shells and ornaments made from them, paraphernalia for potlatches, stone axes, woven baskets, and, not least important, slaves of Salishan or Kwakiutl stock whom the Tlinkit had themselves purchased from the Haida. In exchange they gave moose and caribou hides, sinew thread, babiche, leather bags, moccasins, and furs of various kinds, some of them purchased from the Kaska to whom they sold the treasures of the Tlinkit at about double price. One ornament of the coast tribes the Tahltan rejected, the labret, although the western Carrier had adopted it from the Tsimshian.

In the earliest times the Tahltan seem to have been divided into six loosely organized bands, each of which claimed a definite district as its hunting territory. Close contact with the Tlinkit, however, led to their adoption of the social organization of these neighbours, and long before the coming of Europeans the six bands had become six clans grouped into two exogamous phratries, Raven and Wolf. Descent then followed the female line, and succession to the chieftainship of each clan normally passed from a man to his sister's son. The three clans in each phratry still regarded themselves as local units in a sense, and claimed the ownership of definite districts, but in practice they pooled their hunting territories. The clans of the Raven phratry, on the strength of a rather fantastic myth, postulated a common descent for themselves, and their phratry consequently ranked a little higher than the Wolf, whose clans could claim no common origin. About 1750, or a little later, the Wolf phratry developed a fourth clan through the marriage of a Tahltan Indian with a Tlinkit woman of Wrangell who belonged to a clan not previously represented among the Tahltan. This new clan could count several families a century later, but it never built a long communal house beside the six communal houses erected by the other clans on the Tahltan river, and it recognized as its chief, not one of its own members, but the head man of the clan among the neighbouring Tlinkit.

Along with this coastal organization into phratries and clans, the Tahltan accepted also a division into nobles, commoners, and slaves. A slave remained a slave always; he might marry a slave woman, with the consent of his master, but their children still remained slaves, the property of the man who owned the mother. Any commoner, however, could attain high dignity and rank as a noble by amassing wealth and giving a series of potlatches. The Tahltan distinguished three kinds of potlatches, those given by parents to confer high rank on their children, those held at the conclusion of mourning for the dead, and those given by rival men to increase their personal prestige. In potlatches of the last kind the usual rivals of the Tahltan were Tlinkit Indians.

Tahltan women carried their babies, not in the birch-bark cradles used by Carrier mothers, but in leather bags fitted with legs for older children, without legs for infants. Adolescent girls, secluded ın a separate hut and subjected to many taboos, underwent intensive training for from one to two years. Outdoors they covered their heads with robes so that no men could see their faces, and they often carried little sacks into which they confessed their wrongdoings and prayed for deliverence from further sin. Boys in their teens fasted at frequent intervals to obtain guardian spirits, then sought the counterparts of the animals or birds that had appeared to them in their dreams and preserved the skins as tokens of their blessings. All the young, unmarried men in each band lived together in a special lodge or clubhouse, a custom rare among Canadian Indians, though common in other parts of the world. Whenever one of them discovered a maiden to his liking he accompanied his prospective parents-in-law for several months and delivered to them all the products of his hunting and fishing. His own parents then paid the bride-price, which was later returned to the young couple as a dower. If a man's wife died he could claim any unmarried sister she might have, without further payment; and when he himself died, his sister's son, being his legal successor, supported the widow and as a general rule married her.

The Tahltan cremated their dead and laid the charred bones on top of a post or within a small box raised a few feet above the ground. They sang chants over the dying to guide the souls on their journey to the land of sunrise; and other chants at the funeral pyre. One of their death chants ran as follows:

> Yana-a. This way is the trail.
> This way it goes. Don't miss it.
> The trail goes right to the east
> where the sun rises.[1]

Families of high rank, at the decease of one of their members, sometimes killed a slave and threw the corpse into the river, following a custom of the Tlinkit; at other times, on the contrary, they freed a favourite slave. Widows blackened their faces and wore mourning for about a year; though subjected to many restrictions they did not undergo such harsh usage as Carrier widows. The Tahltan believed in reincarnation, like all or nearly all Indian tribes, and at the funeral of a loved kinsman a woman often performed a peculiar ceremony to bring about the re-birth of his soul in her next child.

---

[1] The Tahltan were very fond of singing, and were always composing songs for their children. The death chant given above has been taken from the notes and phonograph records collected by James Teit and now deposited in the National Museum of Canada.

Two high deities received recognition, a sky-god and a sun-god, but the Tahltan paid little regard to either beyond occasionally burning a little food to the sun-god. Parents prayed to the day-dawn for the welfare of their children, and postulated the existence of a supernatural game-mother who controlled the supply of birds and animals. The guardian spirits that boys obtained in their dreams were nearly all animals. So also were most of the familiars

33112

A Tahltan sweat-house. *(Photo by James Teit.)*

of the medicine-men, which were usually gained through dreams in like manner, following instruction at times from older medicine-men. For the Tahltan, like other Indians, saw supernatural forces at work in everything around them, but gave most heed to those that most affected their food supply.

Game is still abundant in the basin of the Stikine river, and by trapping the fur-bearing animals in winter, fishing, freighting, and serving sportsmen as guides in summer, the Tahltan can live quite prosperously. But they do not thrive under the new conditions. They are wanting in initiative, like other Athapaskan peoples, and lack the capacity to strike out, each man for himself, without relying on the support and encouragement of his fellows. So, while a few of their women are marrying white men and dropping out of their ranks, the tribe as a whole is declining. Its population in pre-European times, although never estimated, must have been three or four times greater than it is to-day. The Department of Indian Affairs could register only 288 Tahltan at Telegraph Creek in 1924.

TAGISH

The Tagish[1] lived north of the Tahltan, in the valleys of the upper Lewes river above its junction with the Teslintoo, and of the Teslin as far as Teslin lake. We know nothing of their history before the second half of the nineteenth century, when they numbered only seventy or eighty individuals and had built two rough wooden houses on the river connecting Marsh and Tagish lakes.[2] In their general mode of life, and in their hunting and travelling equipment, they seem to have closely resembled the Tahltan and other Athapaskan tribes. Their language, however, was Tlinkit, so that originally they must either have been an offshoot of the coast people, who had adopted the customs of the interior tribes, or an Athapaskan tribe that had given up its native tongue. The latter seems the more probable, even though elsewhere the Athapaskan peoples seem to have been more tenacious of their language than of anything else;[3] for the Tagish were completely dominated by the Tlinkit, who compelled them to serve as agents in purchasing furs from the natives on the Pelly river.

---

[1] Meaning unknown.
[2] Dawson, G M.: " Report of an Exploration in the Yukon District, N.W.T., and Adjacent Northern Portion of British Columbia "; Ann. Rept., Geol. and Nat. Hist. Surv., Canada, 1887, pt. B, p. 204 (Montreal, 1888).
[3] e.g., the Sarcee.

CHAPTER XXIII

TRIBES OF THE MACKENZIE AND YUKON BASINS[1]

If we omit from consideration the tribes dwelling along the coast, and a small group of Eskimo who occupied the northeast corner of the continent, all the inhabitants of North America beyond about the 56th parallel spoke dialects of that Athapaskan tongue which Sapir suggests may be remotely connected with the Tibeto-Chinese-Siamese group of languages in eastern Asia. They were essentially woodland peoples like the Algonkians of eastern Canada; the treeless seacoast of the Arctic repelled them, and the " barren lands " with their herds of caribou and musk-oxen drew from most tribes only brief and hurried incursions. Winter was long and severe in their territory, and game, though generally plentiful, subject to wide seasonal variations both in numbers and in movements. Perhaps for these reasons, perhaps for others not so readily discernible, the Athapaskans appear to have been always pressing southward in the centuries preceding the coming of Europeans. To the southeast the Algonkian Cree blocked all passage; in that direction the northerners could make no headway. One tribe, the Sarcee, familiar perhaps with the hunting of buffalo in the Peace River area, drifted out into the open prairies and linked its fortunes with the Blackfoot; but none of its fellow-tribes ventured to follow in its footsteps. Some, keeping to the woodlands, crossed the Rocky mountains into British Columbia, or starting from the basin of the upper Yukon river, followed down the western flank of the mountains and established a line of " colonies " from Alaska to southern California. The majority, however, lingered in the northland, where they continue to occupy almost the entire basins of the Mackenzie and Yukon rivers.

SEKANI

The Sekani (" People of the Rocks," i.e. Rocky mountains) controlled the basins of the Parsnip and Finlay rivers, and the valley

---

[1] These tribes, like those of the preceding chapter, are given greater space than their historical importance would appear to warrant, because they are very little known even to professional students of the American Indians.

of the Peace as far down as the modern town of Peace River.[1]
Harassed by Cree and Beaver Indians on their eastern flank,
towards the end of the eighteenth century they expanded westward, occupied the country around Bear lake and the northern end
of Takla lake, and even established a village on Tachick river in
close proximity to the Carrier of Stuart lake. Southward they
occupied the territory round the junction of the Fraser and Willow
rivers, but were driven northward again by the combined Carrier

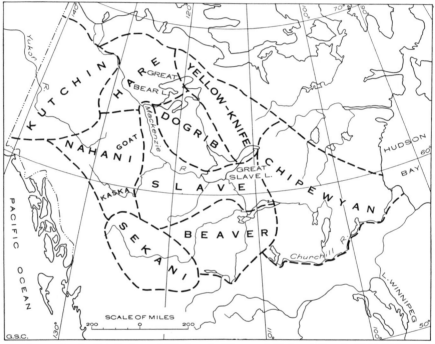

Approximate distribution of Mackenzie River and Yukon tribes in 1725 A.D.

and Shuswap. The establishment of trading-posts at Fort McLeod,
on McLeod lake, in 1805, and at Fort Connolly, on Bear lake, in 1826,
checked any further expansion, especially when the latter post was
moved to Fort Grahame, on the Finlay river. Alcohol and diseases
then demoralized the tribe, white trappers and miners invaded its
hunting territories, game became less plentiful, and the natives, constantly undernourished, rapidly diminished in numbers and are now
approaching extinction.

---

[1] *Cf.* Mackenzie: Op. cit., p. 140.

The Sekani were, first and foremost, hunters, living on moose, caribou, bear, porcupine, beaver, and smaller game. They employed the same weapons in hunting as in war, the bow and arrow, a club fashioned from the jawbone of a moose, and a spear which for beaver-hunting was fitted with a toggle head; but their weapons procured them less game than their snares of babiche, which they used for every animal from the marmot to the moose. Unlike the neighbouring Carrier, they hunted in winter and summer alike, and resorted to fishing only when driven by sheer necessity.[1] Then they used nets of willow bark or nettle-fibres, fish-hooks of bone set in a wooden shank, and tridents wielded from a canoe by the light of jackpine torches, or through the ice when the lakes were frozen over. Although the fish-baskets of more western tribes were unknown to them, they sometimes constructed weirs of brush near beaver-dams, broke the dams, and collected the stranded fish as the water drained away. Even to-day they retain the scorn of true hunters for fishermen, and speak contemptuously of the Carrier as " Fisheaters," because fish predominated so largely in their diet.

Like most Athapaskan tribes, the Sekani made far less use of stone than of wood, bone, horn, and antler. Indeed, their only stone implements seem to have been spear- and arrow-points, adze blades, and sometimes knives; in the last they often used beaver teeth. Their cooking vessels were made of spruce bark or woven spruce roots, their dishes of wood or bark, their spoons of goat horn or wood, and their bags of hide or babiche netting. Canoes and dwellings both had coverings of spruce bark. Living as they did by the chase, the Sekani had no permanent villages, but erected rough, conical lodges of poles covered with spruce-bark, or still cruder lean-tos overlaid with bark, skins, or brush. Food that they were unable to carry along with them they cached in trees (later, when they obtained steel axes, on specially built platforms) and carefully peeled the bark from the trunks to prevent the ascent of the crafty wolverine. All their clothing, like that of most Canadian tribes, was of skin. Men wore a sleeveless shirt, at times laced together between the legs in lieu of a breech-cloth (which they adopted only after contact with

---

[1] The Finlay and Parsnip rivers drain into the Arctic ocean, and, therefore, lack the salmon of the rivers that drain to the Pacific coast.

the Cree); leggings that reached to the thighs, and moccasins with in-soles of groundhog or rabbit fur. Women wore a similar costume, except that they either lengthened the shirt or added a short apron, and their leggings reached only to the knees. A robe, a rounded cap, and mittens, provided additional protection in winter. Shirt and moccasins were commonly embroidered with porcupine-quill work. Hunters wore necklets of grizzly-bear claws, and both men and women had bracelets of horn or bone; but only a few natives possessed ear pendants of dentalia shells, and none of them wore anklets. Rather exceptionally, too, the Sekani seem not to have practised tattooing, although they used paint freely enough on their persons and clothing.[1]

60675

A Sekani hut of poles and spruce bark. *(Photo by D. Jenness.)*

The political organization and social life were exceedingly simple. The tribe was divided into several independent bands,[2] each under the guidance of a leader who possessed little or no real authority. Common customs, a common language, and frequent intermarriage gave the bands a feeling of unity, but families of different

---

[1] Petitot, who is quoted in the Handbook of American Indians, art. Sekani, did not visit the Sekani, and wrote from hearsay only; his description of their appearance, dress, etc., is quite unreliable.
[2] There seem to have been four fairly well-defined bands at the end of the eighteenth century.

bands frequently quarrelled and started blood feuds. There was no name for the entire tribe; the term Sekani applied to one band only, the band that controlled McLeod lake and the headwaters of the Parsnip river. In the early nineteenth century this and a neighbouring band that controlled the lower Parsnip tried to adopt the phratric system of the Stuart Lake Carrier; but they abandoned the attempt as soon as they found that phratries did not aid them in the fur trade with Europeans. To-day they remember only that the strongest phratry was the Beaver, and that the Carrier of Stuart lake, who have not yet given up their phratries, still class as Beaver any McLeod Lake Sekani who happen to attend their feasts. Two other bands of the Sekani, which have made Fort Grahame their headquarters, attempted to establish phratries similar to those that prevailed among the Carrier of Babine lake and the Tsimshian of the upper Skeena river; but they too failed to assimilate the system fully, so that to-day it functions only at petty feasts. At no time did it affect the ownership of hunting territories, which remained the property of the bands, although in recent years families have been selecting and claiming individual hunting and trapping grounds after the fashion of white trappers.

The Sekani regulated marriage solely by the degree of consanguinity. They permitted polygamy, favouring especially marriage with two sisters; but they disclaim the wrestling for wives that occurred so frequently among the Beaver and Mackenzie River tribes, and assert that there were few instances of polyandry. The bridegroom had to hunt for his parents-in-law until the birth of his first child, or else for a period of from twelve to eighteen months, but he and his bride maintained the dignity of their new status by always building a separate lodge for themselves. Babies, who were carried in bags of groundhog or rabbit fur, received names associated with the dream guardians of their fathers or relatives, " Moose-antler," for example, if the dream guardian happened to be the moose. Girls underwent the usual period of seclusion to protect the community from harm, and boys of corresponding age fasted and dreamed for guardian spirits. Every boy obtained a guardian spirit, always from an animal or a bird, but he could count on its aid only in great emergencies. If he were fortunate, he might obtain through dreams in later life other guardian spirits, either from the animal world or from such forces as wind and thunder; and on their aid he could rely at all times. He then became one of the recognized medicine-men of the community, able to cause and cure diseases, and to deliver the people in times of famine. Real deities seem to have been lacking in the old Sekani religion; and if there were local spirits, supernatural beings that haunted special localities, the present generation of Indians has forgotten them. Yet they still believe that man and the animal world are linked together in some mysterious way, and that the animals possess special powers which they may grant the Indian if he seeks them in the proper manner.

Harmon states that in the early years of the nineteenth century the Sekani of the upper Parsnip basin burned their dead, following the custom of the Carrier, whereas at an earlier period they buried them in the ground.[1] The present-day Sekani have a clear remembrance of cremation, but not of burial in the ground. They assert that they discontinued cremation before the middle of the century, and reverted to an ancient custom, never entirely abandoned, of covering the dead with the brush huts that had sheltered them during their last days and then deserting the locality; but men of influence during that period they deposited in coffins raised on platforms or trees.[2] To-day, like all other Indians, they bury in the ground, following the Christian ritual.

The Sekani numbered 160 in 1923, 61 having their headquarters at Fort McLeod and 99 at Fort Grahame. In addition, there was a mixed Sekani-Kaska band, with an infusion of European blood, that roamed between the Finlay and Liard rivers, trading sometimes at Fort Grahame, sometimes at Dease lake; it numbered between 40 and 50. What the pre-European population must have been it is difficult to estimate, but, judging from the number of the Beaver Indians lower down the Peace river, it must have exceeded 1,000.

BEAVER

About the middle of the eighteenth century, according to Mackenzie, the Beaver occupied not only the entire basin of the Peace river below its junction with the Smoky, but the district around lake Claire and the valley of the Athabaska river as far south as the Clearwater and Methy portage. Probably the inhabitants of

---

[1] Harmon: Op. cit., p. 310.
[2] Cf. Morice, A. G.: " The Western Dénés"; Proc. Can. Inst., 3rd ser., vol. vii, p. 146 ('Toronto, 1888-9).

Lesser Slave lake, the "Slave" Indians mentioned by Mackenzie, were one of their bands, although this is by no means certain. Before 1760, however, bands of Cree, provided with firearms by the fur traders on Hudson bay, crossed over into the basin of the Mackenzie, drove out or destroyed the "Slave" Indians of Lesser Slave lake, and, sweeping the Beaver from the valley of the Athabaska, confined them to the basin of the Peace. The eastern Beaver then patched up a truce with the Cree, adopted their dress and many of their customs, and joined them for a few years in trading at Chipewyan; but they never attempted to regain their lost territories, since the fur posts established soon afterwards on the Peace river took care of all their needs. The western Beaver, however, moved farther up the Peace river, displaced the Sekani from the mouth of the Smoky river to Rocky Mountain canyon, and maintained their old customs for several decades.[1]

We know very little about the early customs of the Beaver, except that they did not differ greatly from those of the Sekani. Like the latter, the Beaver depended far more on hunting than on fishing, and employed snares at every possible opportunity. Moose, caribou, beaver,[2] and other game abounded, and there were numerous buffalo which the Indians drove into pounds after the manner of the plains' tribes. Yet they esteemed the buffalo less highly than the moose, which gave them not only meat, but skins for clothing and for the covers of their tents. These tents were the conical tipi-like structures, common throughout the basin of the Mackenzie, which the Sekani covered with spruce bark, but most of the tribes with caribou skins. The Beaver often discarded them during the dry summer months, using in their place either temporary shelters of brush roughly constructed in the same form, or simple lean-tos.

For transport the Beaver used toboggans drawn by the women, and canoes covered with spruce bark, which were apparently the commonest type of canoe among all the Athapaskan tribes previous to their contact with the Cree.[3] Their cooking vessels, also, were

---

[1] Mackenzie: Op. cit., pp. 123, 126, 139 f, 146. Mackenzie calls the western Beaver, who subsequently centred around Forts Dunvegan and St. John, Rocky Mountain Indians, the same name that he applies to the Sekani. The Indians who have their centre to-day at Hudson Hope are of mixed Beaver-Sekani parentage, save for some Cree, who hold themselves aloof from their neighbours.

[2] The Indian name for the Peace river was *Tsades*, "River of Beavers"; Petitot, E.: "En route pour la mer glaciale," p. 292 (Paris, 1887), whence the name Beaver given to the entire tribe and the term *Tsa'tcu*, "Beaver people," for the subdivision living around Fort St. John.

[3] The Chipewyan made small birch-bark canoes in Hearne's day (Hearne: Op. cit., p. 135). Mackenzie saw canoes of birch bark that would carry two persons only among the Slave and Dogrib, whereas other Slaves whom he met had spruce-bark canoes (Mackenzie: Op. cit., pp. 39, 106). Wentzel (1801) describes birch-bark canoes from 12 to 18 feet long among the Slaves (Wentzel, in Masson Op. cit., ser. i, p. 90).

probably of spruce bark or woven spruce roots, although in more recent times they used vessels of birch bark. They were skilful in treating hides, and packed all their possessions in bags made of moose or caribou skin, either solid or netted from babiche. Arrowheads and knives had blades of flint, but some knives were made of moose horn and others had beaver-tooth blades. The principal weapons were spears and bows and arrows; but whether the bows had stone points for stabbing, and whether the Beaver wore armour of any description, is not known. In fishing they used a bone hook attached to a line of babiche, fish-nets also made from babiche, and occasionally stone weirs with platforms of poles below on which the fish became stranded.

Like all the Athapaskan peoples of northern Canada, the Beaver had no real tribal unity, but were divided into a number of independent bands that roamed over separate hunting territories. Women underwent restrictions of the same character, and youths fasted for guardian spirits and served their parents-in-law in the same manner as the Sekani. The funeral rites, however, were more reminiscent of the plains' tribes. The Beaver deposited their dead in trees or on platforms, and relatives gave themselves over to an excessive display of grief, destroying or throwing away all their property. Men lacerated their bodies, put on their war caps and often set out on the war trail; women cut off their hair and severed a joint from the finger. There can be little doubt that the Beaver believed in a future life, but their religion, apart from the doctrine of guardian spirits, is unknown. Goddard describes a semi-annual sacrifice of food accompanied by public prayers for prosperity, but one strongly suspects that the ceremony was derived from the Cree.[1]

In 1924 the Beaver numbered about 600, scattered on several reserves along the Peace river. They were raising a number of horses, and trapping the fur-bearing animals during the winter months. Estimating from Mackenzie's statement that some 210 hunters traded at Vermilion and at the mouth of the Smoky river in 1790, we may presume a pre-European population of about 1,500.[2]

---

[1] Goddard, P. E.: "The Beaver Indians"; Anth. Papers, Am. Mus. Nat. Hist., vol. x. p. 228 (New York, 1912). Cf. Mackenzie: Op. cit., p. 148, "I never witnessed any ceremony of devotion which they had not borrowed from the Knisteneaux."

[2] Mooney: Op. cit., p. 26, estimates 1,250.

A Chipewyan Indian. (*Painting by Paul Coze.*
Reproduction rights reserved by the artist.)

CHIPEWYAN

The Chipewyan ("Pointed Skins," a Cree term referring to the form in which the Chipewyan dried their beaver skins[1]) was the most numerous Athapaskan tribe in northern Canada in the first half of the eighteenth century, and controlled the largest area. Although its exact boundaries are uncertain, and probably fluctuated at different periods, it seems to have claimed possession of the vast triangle enclosed by a line from Churchill to the height of land separating the headwaters of the Thelon and Back rivers,[2] another running south past the eastern ends of Great Slave and Athabaska lakes to the Churchill river, and a third east to the coast a little south of Churchill.[3] After the Hudson's Bay Company established its post at Churchill in 1717 the Chipewyan, well supplied with firearms, drove the coast Eskimo northward, and oppressed the two Athapaskan tribes in the northwest, the Yellowknife and the Dogrib, by denying them access to the trading post, forcing them to exchange their furs for a tithe of their value in European goods, and even robbing them outright of their possessions and women. With the Cree on their southern border they kept an uneasy peace after the Hudson's Bay Company established a truce between them in 1715, but with the section of the Cree that drove the Beaver and Slave Indians from the Athabaska and Slave rivers they fought intermittently until about 1760, when the two tribes concluded an armistice. In 1781 smallpox destroyed the majority of the Chipewyan (nine-tenths of them, according to Hearne), and when Fort Chipewyan was established on lake Athabaska in 1788 most of the remainder preferred to carry their furs to the new trading post rather than undertake the long and arduous journey to Churchill. Since then they have enjoyed unbroken peace, but have become entirely dependent on the trading posts, suffered from constant malnutrition, experienced epidemics of influenza and other diseases, and declined in numbers from an estimated 3,500[4] in pre-European times to little more than 1,000.

---

[1] Thompson: Op. cit., p. 128. The Handbook of American Indians, art. Chipewyan, follows Petitot (Monographie des Dènè-Dindjie, p. 24) in deriving the name from the shape of the shirts, pointed and ornamented with tails before and behind.

[2] The line curved in Hearne's day to embrace Yathkyed and Dubawnt lakes, but whether the Chipewyan controlled these lakes in the early eighteenth century, or drove back the Eskimo later, is unknown.

[3] The year before the establishment of the fort at Churchill a small party of Chipewyan visited York Factory. Eskimo as well as Chipewyan frequented Churchill at that time, the Eskimo in summer only in order to secure wood, apparently, for sleds, boats, and other needs (Captain Knight's Diary of York Factory, MS. copy in Dominion Archives, Ottawa).

[4] Mooney: Op. cit., p. 26.

The Chipewyan were an edge-of-the-woods people. They followed the movements of the caribou, spearing them in the lakes and rivers of the barren grounds during the summer, and snaring them in pounds or shooting them down with bows and arrows during the winter when they took shelter in the timber. Buffalo, musk-oxen, moose, and smaller game tided them over periods when caribou were lacking. They snared, too, numerous water-fowl, and caught many fish with spears, bone hooks, and nets of babiche. Some bands kept almost entirely to the timber, moving from one grove to another. Others spent the greater part of the summer on the barren grounds, carrying their tent-poles (which they converted into snow-shoes in the autumn), and pounding their dried meat into pemmican, or eating raw meat and raw fish like the Eskimo.

Life under these conditions was hard and uncertain. Moving about the country were many independent bands, some large, some small, whose leaders had no authority or power to keep their followers under control. Strong men plundered the weaklings, and forcibly carried off their women. The latter ranked lower than in any other tribe; separated from all boy companions at the age of eight or nine, married at adolescence, often to middle-aged men, and always subject to many restrictions, they were the first to perish in seasons of scarcity. In winter they were mere traction animals; unaided, they dragged the heavy toboggans. In summer they were pack animals, carrying all the household goods, food, and hides on their backs.[1] The aged and infirm of both sexes were abandoned by their companions and starved to death on the trail. A superstitious horror of bloodshed checked murder within the tribe, and though the Chipewyan massacred enemies from other tribes without respect to age or sex, they imposed on themselves afterwards many severe penalties and taboos. They seldom covered their dead, but left them to be devoured by birds and animals. Families destroyed their property on the death of kinsmen, widows cut off their hair and went into mourning for a year, but widowers suffered no restrictions.

It required from eight to eleven caribou skins to make a complete costume for one man (robe, shirt, leggings, moccasins,[2] breechcloth, cap, and mittens), and as many more to furnish him with a

---

[1] The Chipewyan did not employ dogs for hunting, and only rarely for dragging the toboggans; but they loaded them with the caribou-skin tents during the summer months.
[2] The Chipewyan, like several other northern tribes, joined the moccasin to the legging. Mackenzie: Op. cit., p. cxx.

tent, lines, nooses, and nets for fish and beaver. A skilful hunter enjoyed great prestige and could maintain several wives; he needed them indeed to pack all his hides. Men depended for success in the chase on dreams and visions in which they conceived, like other Indians, that they were communicating with a supernatural world.[1] Medicine-men claimed a similar derivation for their supposed powers; they could both cure and cause disease with the aid of familiar spirits, according to the judgment of their tribesmen, who employed no herbal remedies and ascribed all illness and death to witchcraft.

74880

A Chipewyan camp near Churchill, Hudson bay. *(Photo by R. Bell.)*

For the Chipewyan seem to have recognized no deities, offered up no public prayers, and possessed no real religion except this belief in guardian spirits. The souls of the dead, they thought, entered a stone boat and travelled along a river to a beautiful island abounding in game. Only the good reached the island in safety; when the evil came within sight of it the stone boat sank and they struggled in the water forever. A few souls, after remaining on the island for a time, might be born again, but the prospect of possible reincarnation left the Indians coldly indifferent.

---

[1] They painted the symbols of their visions on their shields before entering a fight. Hearne: Op. cit., p. 175 f.

Although the best known of all the northern Athapaskan tribes, the Chipewyan seem to have possessed the weakest culture, with the exception of their near relatives the Yellowknife. Some of their traits, indeed, they borrowed from their neighbours. They tattooed their faces in the same way as the Yellowknife and Dogrib, with three or four parallel bars across each cheek.[1] From the Yellowknife, probably, they learned to use copper for hatchets, ice-chisels, awls, knives, and arrow- and spear-heads;[2] from the Cree, perhaps, they acquired birch-bark vessels for boiling their food, since other tribes in the Mackenzie River basin used vessels of spruce bark or of woven spruce roots. They had no feasts or ceremonies of their own except the performances of medicine-men, but they imitated the feasts and dances of the Cree. Women did not use cradle-boards or bags, but carried their babies on their backs after the manner of Eskimo women; and some of the men used the Eskimo double-bladed paddle. Art was confined to some very crude painting on wood, and a little work in porcupine-quill and moosehair that was much inferior to the work of tribes along the Mackenzie river.

YELLOWKNIFE

The Yellowknife hunted over the country northeast of Great Slave and Great Bear lakes, having the Chipewyan on their south-eastern border, Eskimo to the east and north, Hare Indians to the northwest, and Dogrib and Slave to the west.[3] In dialect, appearance, and customs they were hardly distinguishable from the Chipewyan,[4] but politically they ranked as an independent tribe. Both were typically edge-of-the-woods people, living in skin-covered tipis and spending the summer on the barren grounds in pursuit of caribou and musk-oxen. Both were weak in ceremonial life; the Chipewyan borrowed their songs and dances from the Cree, the Yellowknife from the Dogrib. If the Chipewyan harassed and oppressed the

---

[1] See Hearne: Op. cit., p. 299. Mackenzie says "one to four straight lines on their cheeks or foreheads"; Op. cit., p. cxx.

[2] Copper implements have been found in ancient stone houses on Victoria island, which certainly date back several centuries, so that the Yellowknife themselves may have learned to use copper from the Eskimo.

[3] Early writers generally call them Copper Indians or Red Knives; all three names, of course, refer to their use of copper instead of stone and bone. According to Franklin (Journey, p. 287) they claimed to have lived originally on the south side of Great Slave lake; if true, this must have been before the eighteenth century.

[4] A tradition, current among the Yellowknife as late as 1914, averred that their dialect had once been very different from Chipewyan, but that they had adopted the Chipewyan dialect and customs before the arrival of Europeans.

Yellowknife, the latter meted out the same treatment to the unoffending Slave, Dogrib, and Hare. The Dogrib massacred some of them towards the end of the eighteenth century,[1] but the check was short-lived, for in 1789 Mackenzie and his co-traders met some Yellowknife Indians north of Great Slave lake within the territories of the Dogrib and Slave, and from 1800 onward a band that hunted north of Great Bear lake and traded at Old Fort Franklin was carrying off women from Slave, Dogrib, and Hare.[2] In 1823 the Dogrib turned again, and this time crushed the Yellowknife completely.[3] The remnant then retreated to the northeast corner of Great Slave lake and amalgamated with the Chipewyan.[4] To-day they trade at Resolution, but they number only about 150, and have so far lost their former pride and independence that they prefer to be included among the Chipewyan. Mooney estimates their original population at 430.[5]

SLAVE

If we may trust Mackenzie's account, the Slave[6] Indians were neighbours of the Beaver in the early eighteenth century, inhabiting Athabaska lake, Slave river, and the western half of Great Slave lake. When the Cree invaded this region they retreated down the Mackenzie river, and at the end of the century occupied a broad stretch of country behind both banks of that river from its outlet at Great Slave lake to Norman, the basin of the lower Liard and the west end of Great Slave lake. They had the reputation of being a peaceable, inoffensive people, although they treacherously massacred many Nahani Indians of the upper Liard and drove the remainder into the mountains, then, a little later, destroyed a trading post at Fort Nelson. Surrounding tribes seldom ventured to attack them, attributing to them great skill in witchcraft.

Unlike the Chipewyan, the Slave never ventured out on the barren grounds, but clung to the forests and the river banks, hunting the woodland caribou and the moose. They organized no communal drives and built no pounds, since the woodland caribou and the moose

---

[1] Hearne: Op. cit., p. 200.
[2] Keith, in Masson: Op. cit., ser. ii, p. 106 f.
[3] Back: Op. cit., p. 457 f; Richardson: Op. cit., vol. ii, p. 14 f.
[4] One or two families seem to have found refuge with the Hare. *Cf.* Franklin, Sir John: " Narrative of the Second Expedition to the Shores of the Polar Sea, in the Years 1825-26-27," p. 64 (London, 1828).
[5] Mooney: Op. cit., p. 26.
[6] This name, often modified to Slavey, was given to them out of contempt by the Cree.

do not wander in herds; but they ran these animals down on snow-shoes in the spring, and snared them with the help of dogs during the summer and winter. Snares served them for all animals except the beaver, which they captured in wooden traps in the autumn, and killed with spears and clubs in the winter, after breaking down the houses. Nearly half their diet consisted of fish, which were caught in nets of twisted willow bark, or with lines of the same material fitted with hooks of wood, bone, antler, or occasionally birds' claws; but the moose and the caribou, with the smaller fur-bearing animals, provided them also with clothing, bags, and babiche for snares and lines.

Their clothing was very similar to that of the Beaver and Chipewyan, but more heavily bordered with fringes and with more ornamentation in moose-hair and porcupine-quill. The moccasins were joined to the leggings; men wore a tassel instead of a breech-cloth; and, around the mouth of the Liard, where moose and caribou were less plentiful, the majority of the women had garments of woven hare-skin, a material they used also for cradle-bags. Both sexes wore belts, bracelets, and armlets of leather embroidered with porcupine-quills. Men added necklets of polished caribou antler, and sometimes passed a goose-quill or a plug of wood through the septum of the nose. On the warpath they wore head-dresses of bear-claws, or caps with upstanding feathers, and protected their bodies with wooden shields and cuirasses of willow twigs.

In summer the Slave lived in conical lodges covered with brush or spruce bark, for only a few hunters could afford coverings of caribou hides. Generally two families pitched their lodges together, facing in opposite directions so that they would have a common entrance and a common fireplace in the middle. Their winter dwelling was a low, oblong cabin of poles with walls chinked with moss and a roof of spruce boughs. They used stone adzes hafted on wooden handles for cutting down trees, and knives with beaver-tooth blades for whittling wood and bone. Their clubs were of caribou antler, and their spears, daggers, and arrowheads had bone or antler points; but a few hunters used arrowheads of copper acquired from the Dogrib or Yellowknife, and of flint or chert obtained on the upper Liard, whence they also secured pyrites for making fire. Women cooked in vessels of woven spruce roots by means of hot stones, but sometimes in vessels of bark, presumably spruce bark.[1]

Like all other Athapaskan tribes, the Slave were divided into several independent, semi-leaderless bands named generally from the territories over which they hunted.[2] Each band selected an experienced man to lead its war-parties, but disallowed him any authority when the fighting ended. An informal council of the hunters decided all local quarrels not immediately settled by offers of compensation. Youths paid for their brides by hunting for their parents-in-law twelve months or longer, and men wrestled occasionally for each other's wives. They imposed on the women those periodic restrictions customary among all the northern tribes, and considered it no crime to destroy female infants at birth. Yet, unlike the Chipewyan, they treated their wives with great kindness, and took upon themselves all the hardest work, even the preparation of the lodge and the procuring of firewood. Moreover, they never abandoned the aged and infirm, but carried them about with them, even when it entailed considerable hardship on the family and band.

The fundamental religious concept, as among all the northern Indians, was of a guardian spirit, acquired through dreams, that aided in times of crises. Like their neighbours, the Slave attributed sickness and death to sorcery, and, lacking herbal remedies, had recourse to medicine-men who pretended to extract from the patients' bodies, by massage and suction, splinters of bone and other objects that passed for the sorcerers' instruments. If death seemed imminent the patient confessed all his wrong-doings in the hope of delaying the fatal hour, a custom that prevailed perhaps among most of the northern tribes, since it has been reported also from the Dogrib and Yellowknife.[3] There were two methods of disposing of the dead. Sometimes the relatives deposited them on scaffolds; sometimes they covered them with leaves or snow, placed all their property beside them, and erected small huts over the remains to protect them from wild animals. Their theory of the afterlife

---

[1] *See* Mackenzie: Op. cit., pp. 35-39, and the letters of Wentzel and Keith in Masson: Op. cit.

[2] A band that lived about the junction of the Liard and Mackenzie rivers was called Beaver by the early fur traders, and Strongbow by Franklin. It should not be confused with the Beaver Indians of the Peace river.

[3] Keith, in Masson: Op. cit., ser. ii, 127. Petitot: Monographie des Dènè-Dindjie, p. 75, Autour du Grand lac des Esclaves, p. 216.

resembled the Chipewyan; for they thought that the souls of the dead, aided by otter and loon spirits to which their relatives entrusted them, passed through the earth, crossed a large lake, and began life anew in another world.

Mooney estimated the pre-European Slave population at about 1,250; to-day there are not more than 800.[1]

DOGRIB

At the end of the eighteenth century a western group of Dogrib[2] Indians seems to have shared with the Slave the country between lac la Martre and the Mackenzie river, and a band that derives its origin from both these tribes hunts in this territory to-day. Another band, a mixture, apparently, of Dogrib, Slave, and Hare, wanders around Great Bear lake, carrying its furs to Norman; while two small groups of families, part Dogrib and part Yellowknife, hunt with the Yellowknife to the northeast of Great Slave lake and trade at Resolution. The country between Great Slave and Great Bear lakes seems to have been the home of the Dogrib for at least two centuries. In the time of Hearne few, if any, of them ranged far to the east of the line of lakes between Rae and Great Bear lake through fear of the Yellowknife,[3] Chipewyan, and Cree. When the Cree and Chipewyan withdrew after the smallpox epidemic at the end of the eighteenth century the Dogrib were still oppressed by the Yellowknife; but in 1823 they massacred many of these enemies and effectively destroyed their power. Since that date they have been free to expand, and in 1919 a party even visited the mouth of the Coppermine river. For the last hundred years, however, the main body of the tribe has centred around Rae, on the north arm of Great Slave lake, and hunted over the territory to the northward.

The Dogrib were neither an edge-of-the-woods people entirely, like the Chipewyan, nor yet a purely woodland people like the Slave. In dialect they more closely resembled the latter, the differences in speech following a few regular phonetic laws. They were not very

---

[1] Mooney: Op. cit., p. 26.
[2] They derive their name from a legend recounting their descent from a dog. *See* Petitot: Autour du grand lac des Esclaves, ch. xiv.
[3] Petitot says that the boundary between the Dogrib and the Yellowknife was the mountain range about 65 degrees north and 116 degrees west (Autour du grand lac des Esclaves, p. 253).

partial to fish, and depended for their main supply of food on the herds of barren-ground caribou, which they snared in pounds and speared in lakes after the manner of the Chipewyan and Yellowknife. Unlike these tribes, however, they were afraid to spend more than a few days at a time on the treeless barrens because of the lack of fuel, and in their brief incursions generally carried a supply of fire-wood. The net they used for fishing was not made of babiche, like the Chipewyan fishnet, but of willow bark, like the net of the Slave and Hare; and though their usual dwelling was a conical, skin-covered tipi indistiguishable from the lodge of the Yellowknife or Chipewyan, for winter they occasionally built rectangular huts of poles and brush, after the manner of the tribes along the Mackenzie river. They wore the usual costume of shirt, breech-cloth, leggings, and moccasins, but followed the practice of the Hare in separating the leggings from the moccasins. Like the Hare and Slave, again, they treated their wives with kindness, regardless of whether or not they had seized them from other men by wrestling; but they showed less consideration than the Slave for the aged and infirm, whom they often abandoned quite pitilessly to perish.

In other Athapaskan tribes a man dropped his name only at the birth of his first child (being known henceforward as the " father of so and so "); the Dogrib seem to have changed their names with each successive child. They made petty offerings to local spirits, especially to spirits supposed to haunt lakes and rapids, placed their main reliance on guardian spirits acquired in dreams, and required their medicine-men to prophesy and to inflict and cure diseases—traits that were common to all the northern Athapaskans. The scaffolds on which they deposited their dead carried streamers to amuse the shades of the deceased and retain them near their resting places; mourners, as usual, destroyed all or most of their property, and the women gashed themselves in token of their grief. A year after the funeral they uncovered the remains, renewed their death chants, and held a memorial feast.

The present number of the Dogrib hardly exceeds 750. It may have reached 1,250 in pre-European times.[1]

---

[1] Mooney: Op. cit., p. 26. Petitot says that 1,200 Dogrib frequented Fort Rae in 1859, but a strange epidemic known as the " Fort Rae sickness " reduced their number to 788; Autour du grand lac des Esclaves, p. 189.

The Hare Indians lived west and northwest of Great Bear lake, extending in the east to a little beyond the Anderson river, and in the west to the first line of mountains west of the Mackenzie river. Although they hunted caribou in the vicinity of the Eskimo lakes, they did not descend the Mackenzie itself much below the Ramparts through fear of the Eskimo, who occasionally visited that place to obtain flinty slate for arrowheads and knives. Their nearest neighbours, the Kutchin, Eskimo, and Yellowknife, rather despised them on account of their timidity, for they often concealed their camps under fallen trees some distance back from the river and fled at the slightest indication of strangers.

Their mode of life did not differ greatly from that of the Dogrib and Slave. Woodland caribou, moose, and beaver were scarce in their territory, but a few musk-oxen and many herds of barren-ground caribou roamed the tundra north of Great Bear lake. The Hare hunted these caribou in April, and again in August and the early part of September; but they seem to have been less skilful in the chase than other Indians, and throughout the greater part of the year relied on fish, supplemented by hares during the winter months. In seasons when hares were scarce—every seventh year or thereabouts—they suffered great hardships, and generally some of them perished of starvation. It was, indeed, to their dependence on the hare that they owed their name. It furnished them not only food, but clothing, for though they preferred garments of caribou fur, not all families could secure enough hides, especially families that clung to the banks of the Mackenzie river and rarely wandered east into the barren grounds.

There was no originality in the costume of the Hare, which resembled that of the Slave and Dogrib except for the extensive use of rabbit fur and the rarity of ornamentation. In summer they wore a shirt, leggings, and moccasins, possibly also a breech-cloth; in winter they added a robe, and in lieu of a cap, attached a hood to the shirt after the manner of the Kutchin and Eskimo.

Neither did they display any originality in their implements and weapons. There was a stone-bladed adze, knives, daggers and ice-chisels of caribou antler, whittling knives with beaver-tooth blades, bows and arrows[1] and babiche snares for hunting, nets of willow bark, and probably spears for fishing. The dwelling was the usual rectangular hut of poles and brush with a gabled roof and covering of spruce boughs; during the summer they often contented themselves with simple lean-tos. In the nineteenth century many families possessed tipis covered with caribou hides, later replaced by cloth; but tipis were probably rare in pre-European times. Like all other northern Athapaskans, they made fire with pyrites, cooked in water-tight baskets of interwoven spruce roots and willow, and served up their food in dishes of wood or bark.

Their social life also contained very little that was remarkable. The tribe comprised several independent, semi-leaderless bands, each controlling a definite territory; there were five in the middle of the nineteenth century, but these may not have corresponded exactly to the pre-European alinement. The hardships of life caused frequent desertion of the aged and the destruction of female infants. Male prisoners taken in raids were staked to the ground, and their quivering hearts given to the women to devour, a custom that savoured more of the plains' tribes and the Iroquoians than of the Athapaskans. Alone of all the Canadian Indians, the Hare and the "Loucheux"[2] seem to have practised circumcision.[3] In these same two tribes medicine-men permitted themselves to be suspended in the air to facilitate communion with their guardian spirits. There were two ceremonial feasts; a memorial feast to the dead a year after burial, and a lunar feast on the occasion of each new moon. The latter was celebrated by most Athapaskan tribes, but at eclipses only. The memorial feast, and indeed all the burial customs of the Hare, were identical with the Dogrib rites. Some Hare death chants recorded by Petitot[4] greatly resemble the corresponding chants of the Tahltan.

The Hare have experienced all the epidemics that have ravaged the other tribes along the Mackenzie river. Their original popula-

---

[1] Their arrows were longer than those of neighbouring tribes, whence the name Long-Arrowed Indians applied to them by Keith (Masson: Op. cit., series ii, p. 117). *Cf.* Petitot: Monographie des Dènè-Dindjie, p. 37 f.

[2] Petitot: Monographie des Dènè-Dindjie, p. 78. By Loucheux he probably means the Bâtard-Loucheux, a band of mingled Hare and Kutchin that hunted between the Mackenzie river and the Eskimo lakes in the first half of the nineteenth century.

[3] Petitot: Monographie, p. 78: Traditions indiennes du Canada nord-ouest, p. 249 f, Paris, 1887. Mackenzie (op. cit., p. 36) states that the appearance of circumcision was general among some Slave and Dogrib Indians he encountered below Great Slave lake. Yet the restriction of the practice to this small area, and the lack of any references to it by other travellers, raises a suspicion that Mackenzie and Petitot may have been deceived.

[4] Petitot: Monographie des Dènè-Dindjie, p. 69 f.

tion has been estimated at 750[1]; to-day it approximates the same figure, if we include a considerable number of hybrid Indians who make Great Bear lake their centre.

NAHANI

Very little is known about the Nahani Indians who inhabited the mountainous area between the upper Liard river and the 64th parallel north latitude. They were divided into several tribes, or independent bands, some of which have now disappeared. From about McDame creek, on Dease river, to the Beaver river that joins the Liard above Liard, dwelt the two bands of the Kaska[2] Indians, the *Tsezotene*, "Mountain people," on the west and the *Titshotina*, "Big water people,"[3] on the east. In recent times the boundary line between these two bands has lain about the junction of the Kechika and Dease rivers. East and northeast of them, on the Beaver and South Nahanni rivers, were the Goat Indians (*Esbataottine*, often wrongly translated "Sheep Indians"), who included, or were closely allied to, a band at the headwaters of the Keele river; for the South Nahanni Indians used to cross over to the Keele and travel down that river to Norman, on the Mackenzie. The names of the tribes that formerly occupied the upper waters of the Big Salmon, Pelly, Mac-Millan, and Stewart rivers are uncertain[4]; but tradition states that about 1886 the original Pelly and Ross River Indians were destroyed by a band that crossed the Rocky mountains from the Mackenzie river—Hare Indians, probably, from the vicinity of Norman. One or two survivors found refuge with a portion of the Big Water band of the Kaska, who then moved northward and took possession of the Pelly river. Other Indians from Teslin lake, and from the Yukon about Dawson, moved into the same vacant area, so that the band that to-day calls itself "Pelly River Indians" is of recent and composite formation.[5]

In their mode of life, and in most of their social customs and religious beliefs, the Kaska differed but little from the Sekani to the

---

[1] Mooney: Op. cit., p. 26.
[2] A Tahltan word for which the Indians of Telegraph Creek give two interpretations: (1) rags wrapped round the feet in lieu of stockings, and (2) long moss hanging from a tree.
[3] i.e. the people who claimed possession of Frances lake.
[4] Cf. Dawson, G. M.: "Report on an Exploration in the Yukon District, N.W.T., and Adjacent Northern Portion of British Columbia"; Geol. and Nat. Hist. Surv., Canada, Ann. Rept., 1887, pt. B, pp. 201-203 (Montreal, 1888).
[5] MS. of Poole Field, National Museum of Canada.

south or from the tribes along the Mackenzie. They lived principally by the chase, using bows and arrows, spears, clubs (for beaver), and above all snares of babiche or twisted sinew. Buffalo were plentiful in pre-European times, according to Indian traditions,

69892

Salmon-weir of the Kutchin Indians, Upper Yukon river.
(Photo by W. E. Cockfield.)

and sheep and goats still exist in numbers on the mountain ranges; but the most important game animal was the caribou, which the Kaska, like their kinsmen to the east, south, and west, drove into pounds and captured with snares. Their dwellings were conical tipis covered with bark or brush, or, at times, rectangular huts of the same materials; in summer they were often satisfied with simple lean-tos. They used baskets of woven spruce roots for cooking, spoons of wood, or of goat or sheep horn, and dishes of wood or birch bark. Spruce-bark canoes[1] facilitated summer travelling; in winter the Indians wore snow-shoes and their women dragged crude toboggans made from the leg-skins of the caribou, for dogs served only for hunting. Of tools there were stone adzes and hammers, chisels of antler, awls of bone, and knives with blades of stone or beaver teeth.

In all these traits, and also in their dress, the Kaska closely resembled other Athapaskan tribes to the east and south. Men wore no breech-cloth, apparently, although in winter, like the Sekani, they sometimes tied the ends of the robe between the legs. Their usual costume was a skin shirt pointed in front and behind and fitted with a hood in cold weather, long leggings fastened into a belt above and sewn to the moccasins below, mittens, and a robe of caribou or woven rabbit skin. Shirts, leggings, and moccasins were often profusely ornamented with porcupine-quill embroidery. Women carried their babies in bags of beaver or other skins padded with moss and rabbit fur.

Typically Athapaskan, also, was much of the social life. Kaska girls passed a period in seclusion and submitted to the same restraints as girls in the Mackenzie basin. Whether boys of corresponding age fasted for guardian spirits has not been recorded, but is scarcely open to doubt because the tribe held the same beliefs about animals, and its medicine-men practised their art in much the same way as other Athapaskans. In the new Pelly River band, and probably among the Kaska also, the prospective bridegroom served the girl's parents for a season before the marriage feast, and thereafter he and his parents-in-law avoided all speech with one another. Women were treated kindly, but performed most of the drudgery inevitable in a life of constant movement from one hunting ground to another. The dead were wrapped in skins in early times, and left on the ground beneath a covering of brush.

---

[1] Moose, though plentiful to-day, seem to have been rare or absent in pre-European times, and the canoes covered with moosehide, now built occasionally by the Kaska, are modelled on the older spruce-bark canoes.

The geographical position of the Kaska, however, near the headwaters of the Stikine river, exposed them to influences coming from the Pacific coast. They learned to weave the hair of the wild mountain goat into ropes, game bags, and even robes ornamented with blue and green designs. From the Tahltan and Tlinkit they adopted cremation, later superseded by burial in the ground; and they copied the organization of the same two tribes just as their Sekani neighbours to the south copied the organization of the Carrier and Tsimshian. So they alined themselves into two exogamous phratries, Raven and Wolf, that reckoned descent through the female line alone, cremated each other's dead, and held reciprocal potlatches. Yet this phratric system never gained a very firm hold among them, and disappeared entirely before the end of the nineteenth century. It persisted a few years ago among the new band in the Pelly River district, but at no time has it affected the Goat Indians on the Beaver and South Nahanni.

Mooney estimated the pre-European Nahani population at 1,500;[1] to-day it is probably less than half that figure.

KUTCHIN[2]

The Kutchin or Loucheux group of tribes[3] inhabited the basin of the Peel river from its source to its junction with the Mackenzie. and the entire basin of the Yukon from the mouth of the Pelly river downward, except for a small strip of country around its delta at Bering sea. There were several distinct tribes within this area, some of them divided into bands; but the lists given by different authors by no means agree, band names being often confused with tribal names.[4] The dress and customs of the Kutchin in what is now Canadian territory varied but little, and the traveller would have encountered no marked change in the dialect until he reached Fort Yukon within the boundaries of Alaska. The Hare Indians of the lower Mackenzie could understand the speech of the Peel River Kutchin, but it was only partly intelligible to the more distant Chipewyan.

---

[1] Mooney: Op. cit., p. 26.

[2] Since this was written I have come to the conclusion that it would have been preferable to include the Kutchin among the Cordillera tribes rather than among those of the Mackenzie basin.

[3] *Kutchin*, "people," is the equivalent of the word *dene* or *tinne* by which the tribes of the Mackenzie River basin designate themselves. The name *Loucheux*, "squint-eyed," i.e., slant-eyed, came from the early French-Canadian voyageurs, and strictly applies only to the eastern tribes, those living on the Peel and Porcupine rivers, some of whom frequented also the lower Mackenzie.

[4] Some writers have included among the Kutchin the vanished bands or tribes of the Pelly River basin, and even the Nahani at the head of the Keele river.

72453

Kutchin chiefs. *(Reproduced from Richardson, Sir John: "Arctic Searching Expedition, London, 1851," vol. I, Pl. III.)*

To the north of the Kutchin were the Eskimo, with whom they alternately fought and traded; to the south the highly organized Tlinkit Indians of the gulf of Alaska, who were accessible by passes through the mountains. Both these neighbours influenced the culture of the Kutchin, although at basis it followed much the same pattern as the culture of the tribes in the basin of the Mackenzie.

The Canadian Kutchin devoted most of the summer to fishing, and the winter to hunting caribou, moose, hare, and other game. They used snares just as extensively as other tribes in northern Canada, and constructed the same kind of caribou-pound. Their fishing-gear included a rather peculiar hook, a spear (double-gaff) modelled on an Eskimo weapon, and a long dip-net and a fish basket of willow that they probably copied from Pacific Coast types. Seines of willow bark were made by some of the Alaskan Kutchin, but not by the Canadian, apparently, except by those who frequented the lower Mackenzie. The bow was almost identical with the Eskimo bow, being made of three pieces of wood jointed together and backed with a strong lashing of twisted sinew. One tribe, the Han, that lived where the towns of Dawson and Eagle now stand, attached a wooden hand-guard to the "grip" of the bow, but none of the others seems to have favoured this contrivance, although it was used by Indians frequenting Great Bear lake. All the Kutchin adopted the Eskimo sled instead of the usual Indian toboggan, and built their birch-bark canoes with flat bottoms and almost straight sides like the Eskimo umiak. They made wooden food-trays of Eskimo type, with bottoms inset as in a cask, although they also used birch-bark trays; and they cooked their food in woven baskets of spruce or tamarack roots, as did other Indians of northern Canada.

The dress of the Kutchin, too, reflected Eskimo influence. The caribou-skin shirt was short waisted and had long tails before and behind like the shirt of the Eskimo. The women sometimes enlarged it behind so that they could carry their babies against their naked backs after the manner of Eskimo women; but more often they used a peculiar birch-bark cradle shaped something like a Mexican saddle. The leggings, of one piece with the moccasins, were so full that they hardly differed from Eskimo trousers, and they carried embroidery of beads or porcupine-quills along the sides where

Eskimo trousers had bands of coloured skin. Common to both peoples were the long mittens necessitated by short shirt sleeves, and the hood replacing a cap that was worn by Eskimo of all ages, but among the Kutchin mainly by children. The Kutchin shirt was peculiar in one respect; it had long fringes decorated with seeds or with beads of dentalia shells, and bead or porcupine-quill embroidery on breast, shoulders, and back. Men wore head-bands, necklaces, and nose-pendants of the same shells (which constituted, indeed, a regular currency[1]), painted their faces with red ochre and black lead, and planted bright feathers in their hair, after plastering it with grease and red ochre. Their proud bearing and colourful dress called to mind the Indians of the plains rather than the sombre and depressed natives of the Mackenzie River valley who were more nearly akin. Women tattooed radiating lines from the lower lip to the chin similar to the lines on Eskimo women, but they never pretended to rival the men in the adornment of their persons.

The dwellings of the Kutchin showed a certain originality. They enlarged the domed sweat-house that was almost universal throughout the upper half of North America, left an opening in the roof for a smoke-hole, banked snow around the outside wall, and strewed the floor with fir boughs. With a small fire burning within, this novel home was fairly comfortable even in the coldest weather.[2] Most of the tribes used the same type of tent in summer also, but some bands of the Vunta tribe that frequented the lower Mackenzie at that season erected oblong huts of poles, brush, and bark to serve both for dwellings and for smoke-drying their fish.

The social organization was rather unusual, although it was obviously connected with the systems current along the Pacific coast. The Kutchin were divided into three exogamous phratries that counted descent in the female line; yet they recognized no distinctions of rank, knew nothing of crests or totems, and held no potlatches except those in honour of the dead. Chiefs were chosen for courage or wisdom alone, and possessed little more authority than the chiefs or leaders in the tribes along the Mackenzie. Men without relatives or friends found security only by attaching themselves to leading

---

[1] *See* part I, p. 114.
[2] Some inland Eskimo of northern Alaska used similar dwellings doubtless copied from the Kutchin.

families, a very mild form of servitude compared with the slavery of the Pacific coast. The Kutchin never purchased slaves, and never acquired any in their petty wars; for they massacred men, women, and children without mercy, sparing only some of the younger women to carry away for wives. Their own women received no gentle treatment; they performed nearly all the hard work in camp,[1] transported all the family possessions, ate only after the men had eaten, and had no voice in family or tribal affairs except the one prerogative of selecting husbands for their daughters. Mothers often killed their girl babies to spare them the hardships

73455

A Kutchin dance. *(Reproduced from Richardson, Sir John: "Arctic Searching Expedition, London, 1851," vol. I, Pl. IX.)*

they themselves had undergone; and old or infirm men and women who could no longer support themselves were strangled, sometimes at their own request. Yet life was not all hardships, even for the women. The Kutchin were passionately fond of games, and of singing and dancing; and young and old, women as well as men, took part in these diversions.

[1] Except the cooking. Murray, A. H.: "Journal of the Yukon, 1847-48"; edited by L. J. Burpee, Publications of the Canadian Archives, No. 4, Ottawa. 1910, p. 86. Jones, Strachan: "The Kutchin Tribes, Notes on the Tinneh or Chepewyan Indians of British and Russian America"; communicated by George Gibbs, Smithsonian Report, 1866, p. 326 (Washington, 1872). Hardisty's statement that the women cooked, if true, may have referred to some tribe that did not frequent Fort Yukon and was unknown to Murray and Jones; or the customs of the Kutchin may have been changing in his day. Hardisty: Op. cit., p. 312.

We know very little about the religion of the Kutchin. Their hunters often prayed to a moon-deity before starting out on their expeditions, and burned fat in the fire to obtain success in the chase. They had the same belief as other Indians in supernatural beings that haunted special localities, and they tried to propitiate them with offerings of beads. Every misfortune was attributed to witchcraft, and the Kutchin paid great deference to the medicine-men who claimed to acquire special powers from the unseen world through the usual fasting and dreaming. The dead were either burned immediately and their ashes suspended in bags from the tops of painted poles, or, if persons of note, deposited in trees within wooden coffins and burned several months later when the flesh had decayed; for the Kutchin dreaded burial in the ground. Relatives destroyed their property, lacerated their bodies, and made the same display of grief as the Mackenzie River Indians, but they also adopted from the Tlinkit the custom of holding a memorial feast or potlatch within a special enclosure, when the guests sang mournful songs, danced, and indulged in various games, and departed with gifts for which they subsequently made a partial return.

There are perhaps 700 Kutchin living within the borders of Canada to-day. A census made by the Hudson's Bay Company in 1858 gave a population of 1,179.[1] Seeing that even then the tribes had declined greatly through infanticide, wars, and European diseases, Mooney estimates a pre-European population of 3,000.[2]

---

[1] Dawson: " Report of an Exploration in the Yukon District," p. 206 B.
[2] Mooney: Op. cit., p. 26.

CHAPTER XXIV

THE ESKIMO

The last of our physiographic regions was the Arctic and sub-Arctic coasts of Canada from the Alaskan boundary to the strait of Belle Isle, excluding only the southern and western shores of James bay. This was the home of the Eskimo (a Cree word meaning "Eaters of raw meat"), a people distinct in physical appearance, in language, and in customs from all the Indian tribes of America. Yet just as their peculiar physical appearance masked but did not debar their partial derivation from the same division of mankind as the Indians—from the great Mongolian stock that predominates throughout eastern and northern Asia—so their peculiar customs and mode of life have so many links with the customs of many of our Indian tribes that one suspects not merely borrowing on both sides, but the derivation of their cultures from the same or kindred sources in past ages.

Canada was not the home of all the Eskimo, nor even of one-half their number, for they extended from the Siberian shore of Bering sea in the west to Greenland in the east. Alaska and Greenland each contains to-day twice as many Eskimo as there are in Canada,[1] where long stretches of coast-line have no inhabitants at all and the many large islands north of the mainland are deserted, though many of them bear the ruins of prehistoric dwellings and camp-sites. If we pry more closely into the distribution of our Eskimo at the time of their first contacts with Europeans we find them grouped in certain areas fringed by large tracts of territory that seldom felt their footsteps. What was the cause of this?

Except in two regions, the basins of the Colville and Noatak rivers in Alaska and the barren grounds between Hudson bay and Great Slave and Great Bear lakes, the Eskimo were everywhere a littoral people, who subsisted during the greater part of the year on the sea mammals frequenting the coast, and journeyed inland only

---

[1] Eskimo population of Alaska in 1910, 14,087: Indian Population in the United States and Alaska, 1910, p. 112, Washington, Government Printing Bureau, 1915; of Greenland in 1927, 15,634: Greenland, vol. iii, "The Colonization of Greenland and Its History Until 1929"; published by the Commission for the direction of the Geological and Geographical Investigations in Greenland, p. 404 (Copenhagen and London, 1929); of Canada in 1929, 7,103; of Labrador "not more than 1,000 on the Atlantic coast south of Cape Chidley": Encyclopaedia Britannica, 14th edition, article "Labrador."

for brief periods in summer to hunt caribou and musk-oxen and to fish in the lakes and rivers. It was the greater abundance of sea mammals and fish in the waters of Alaska and Greenland that occasioned the greater concentration of population in those regions. In Arctic Canada sea mammals were abundant in certain localities

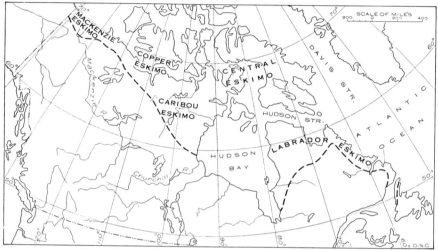

Approximate distribution of the Eskimo in 1525 A.D.

and scarce in others, owing largely to the conditions and movements of the sea-ice.[1] The Eskimo, therefore, made the localities of abundance their centres, and moved away from them only for special reasons—to fish and hunt inland, or to procure wood in distant forests for making boats, sleds, weapons, and the various requirements of their households.

We observed in our last chapter that the Chipewyan and Yellow-knife Indians at the eastern margins of Great Bear and Great Slave lakes trusted for their food supply, their clothing, and coverings for their tents to the enormous herds of barren-ground caribou; and we naturally ask why the Eskimo did not follow their example, why they clung to the seashore and devoted most of their energies to the capture of sea mammals. The reason was that the barren-ground caribou migrated seasonally; every spring they moved northward to their summer pasture grounds and fawning districts, and at the

[1] Hence the ruined houses in the Arctic archipelago lie mainly on the south sides of the islands, which were less blocked with ice than the northern coasts. The Eskimo abandoned this region several centuries ago, probably owing to a gradual uplift of the land that left the surrounding waters too shallow for the passage of the larger sea mammals.

approach of winter moved south again to the edge of the forests. The Indians, being themselves edge-of-the-woods people, kept in contact with them throughout the whole year, following them over the barren grounds in summer and snaring them in winter within the woods. A small minority of the Eskimo, the bands living inland from Hudson bay, also made the caribou their mainstay, and seldom

36972
The fuel-gatherer of a Copper Eskimo family.
(Photo by D. Jenness.)

or never visited the coast to hunt the sea mammals. But these barren-ground or "Caribou" Eskimo constantly suffered from famine during the winter months, for so few caribou remained within their territories, which did not extend to the forests, that they had to fall back on the fish in the lakes and rivers, and on a few musk-oxen, to tide them over the coldest and stormiest period of the year.[1] So the main body of the Eskimo made their homes on the coast where, given favourable weather, they could capture sea mammals both in winter and in summer, and in summer, moreover, could trap the shoals of salmon trout that migrated yearly up the creeks and rivers. Yet even they abandoned their sealing and fishing places when midsummer approached, and hunted the caribou while its fur was prime, and for a month or two afterwards when it assumed the long thick coat so valuable for winter garments and sleeping-robes. For the caribou was well-nigh indispensable to all Eskimo, because its fur offered the most suitable clothing for extremely cold weather, its sinew provided thread for sewing and lines for sealing and fishing gear, and its bones and antlers could be worked into numberless articles ranging from harpoons and arrow-heads to thimbles.[2]

For another reason, too, the Eskimo were better off on the sea-coast than following the movements of the caribou month by month. Inland, on the barren grounds, there was no fuel except scattered patches of heather, dwarf willow, and the creeping dryas. The Caribou Eskimo had to build separate kitchens of snow to cook with these fuels in winter,[3] and in their real dwellings, the snow-huts in which they worked and slept, kept only tiny lamps of burning caribou-fat that lacked even the warmth necessary to dry their clothing. The coast Eskimo, on the other hand, derived an excellent fuel from the blubber of the sea mammals, particularly the seals, and as long as they prospered in their seal-hunting lacked neither food for themselves nor light and warmth in their houses. Even if their hunting was not always successful, or without its dangers and hardships, yet, given territories that lay outside the limits of the forests, they endured fewer famines on the seacoast, and could render their homes more comfortable, than their kinsmen who roamed the barren lands of the interior.[4]

Many Indian tribes also hunted sea mammals—the Beothuk of Newfoundland, the Micmac of Nova Scotia, and all the tribes along

---

[1] Cf. Birket-Smith, Kaj.: " The Caribou Eskimos, Material and Social Life and their Cultural Position"; Report of the Fifth Thule Expedition 1921-24, vol. v, pt. i, pp. 101, 135 (Copenhagen, 1929).

[2] In northwest Greenland caribou were so scarce that the local " Polar" Eskimo, who inhabited that district, generally wore trousers of polar-bear fur and coats of seal, rabbit, or bird skin.

[3] Despite their name, " Eaters of raw meat," the Eskimo always preferred cooked food, or, for second choice, frozen. They ate raw meat and fish only when driven by necessity.

[4] It is much easier, of course, to find reasons why the Eskimo should have developed a different mode of life from the Indians, given an Arctic and sub-Arctic home, than to explain how they came to settle down in that home. No theory yet advanced seems to provide a satisfactory answer to the latter problem.

the Pacific coast. The Nootka of Vancouver island, like the Eskimo, attacked even the mighty whale. Both Indians and Eskimo employed fundamentally the same methods, which were indeed but adaptations of fishing devices and of the methods of hunting animals on land; but under the stress of a peculiar environment the Eskimo elaborated them in several ingenious ways. Let us consider first their methods of hunting seals.

In Alaska, and in the region of the Mackenzie delta, the Eskimo set nets under the ice to capture seals, although, unlike the Indians, they never employed fish-nets until they came into direct or indirect contact with Europeans. Fragments of sealing-nets, made of baleen, have been discovered in Hudson bay and northeastern Greenland, so that they may once have been used throughout most of the Arctic. The Greenland Eskimo, and those living near the Magnetic Pole in Canada, sometimes adopted another " fishing " device. Two men went out together; one, lying flat on the ice, peered through a hole from which he had brushed away all snow, thus enabling the light to shine through to the water beneath; and his companion stood above him, ready to strike with a long harpoon as soon as the watcher signalled the presence of a seal. Other Eskimo living on the Back river, and several Indian tribes, speared fish in the same way, but in fishing one man performed both functions—he both peered through the hole and plied the spear.[1]

The usual method of capturing seals in winter, one practised by every coastal group from Bering strait to Greenland, seems to have been evolved from this "peep-hole" method. Knowing that the seal must rise to the surface to breathe, and that it maintained several holes in the ice that covered the sea from October or November until May or June, the native searched out one of its breathing holes and harpooned the animal the moment it broke water. Only the trained eye of an Eskimo, or the keen scent of a dog, could detect the tiny hole concealed beneath a foot or more of snow; and even when the hunter discovered it, there was no certainty that the seal would visit this particular one for several hours, or, if it did rise there, that the harpoon, aimed blindly at the dark centre of the hole, would unerringly strike its mark. Most hunters used cunningly

---

[1] One may still see Tsimshian Indians spearing salmon by this method in the shallow Kispiox river during the months of February and March. But they now use a lure (often a piece of coloured cloth) to attract the fish, and do not trouble to brush away the snow from around the hole.

contrived "indicators" to warn them when the seal was approaching the surface; but no amount of human ingenuity could guarantee invariable success, or banish the hardships of a motionless watch, often for many hours, exposed to all the rigours of an Arctic winter.

In the mild days of spring the seals came out of their holes to bask in the sun on the surface of the ice, and the Eskimo stalked them like land game. They were more difficult to stalk than caribou, however, for there were usually no sheltering hillocks or ice-cakes behind which the hunter could take cover, and he had to approach much nearer to throw a harpoon than to launch an arrow. In the spring, too, and even during the winter in localities where a strong tide or current produced a lane of open water, the natives harpooned many seals from the ice edge and retrieved them in their skin-covered

A Labrador Eskimo hunter in his kayak. *(Photo by F. Johansen.)*

canoes or kayaks. The open sea of midsummer, of course, necessitated harpooning the animals from the kayak itself. Not all the coastal Eskimo, however, employed the kayak for sealing. Those who lived between Coronation gulf and the Magnetic Pole left the sea before the ice broke up and directed their energies to fishing and caribou hunting.

To describe the complicated sealing equipment of the Eskimo —the various types of harpoons, the throwing board that increased their range, the air-inflated skin or bladder poke sometimes attached to the shaft, and all the other appliances—would involve us in too much detail. It is unnecessary, also, to describe the hunting of the walrus and the whale, the beluga and the narwhal, by many eastern and western Eskimo during the spring and summer months, for it closely resembled the hunting of seals at those seasons.[1] What most concerns us here is that the dependence of the Eskimo on sea mammals, particularly seals, throughout the greater part of the year differentiated them from all the Indian tribes of America, but that their methods of hunting them, however ingenious, were after all only modifications of fishing methods, and of methods of hunting land animals, that were common to both peoples.

The Eskimo could not employ all the methods of fishing and hunting known to their Indian neighbours. They could organize community drives against the caribou, herding them into the water in order to spear them from their canoes, or between lanes of dummy enemies made of turf-capped stones that converged in a row of archers concealed in shallow pits; but, except in certain parts of Alaska,[2] where willow and other shrubs attained a considerable height, they could not snare them in pounds as was the practice of the Athapaskan Indians. Neither could they spear fish by torch-light after the manner of many Indian tribes, not so much from lack of bark for torches, as because there was no darkness during the summer when the lakes and rivers were free of ice. Weirs of stones took the place of brush weirs, and instead of basket traps, for which material would have been scanty, one or two groups used bags of skin.[3] Why no Eskimo ever employed fish-nets, however, is rather puzzling, for all their Indian neighbours used them, and their introduction in post-European times has been an unmixed blessing.[4] Their absence was the more surprising because of the remarkable ingenuity of the Eskimo in other ways, and because of the rapidity with which they have adopted all civilized appliances that can help them in their food-quest.[5]

We have mentioned their remarkable ingenuity, and have noticed some examples of it in their methods of hunting the sea mammals. It revealed itself also in their transportation methods, their dwellings, and even in their dress. Confronted with a similar environment other primitive peoples might have evolved a stable

---

[1] In whale hunting, they generally employed the large, open, skin boat with a complement of paddlers instead of the one-man kayak.

[2] e.g. the basin of Colville river.

[3] Birket-Smith: Op. cit., vol. 1, p. 120.

[4] Mathiassen (" Archæology of the Central Eskimos," vol. ii, p. 58 f) considers the evidence for the complete absence of the fish-net in pre-European times not altogether conclusive.

[5] We can understand more easily why they did not domesticate the caribou or American reindeer; for it is fairly certain that whatever north Asiatic tribe first domesticated that animal was already acquainted with domesticated horses and probably cattle.

skin-covered boat propelled by oars, comparable with the Eskimo *umiak*,[1] but very few could have invented so wonderful a hunting craft as the light and speedy *kayak*.[1] The dog-sled, which is superior to the Indian toboggan for travelling over the hard-packed snow of the Arctic and sub-Arctic coasts, was another invention of the Eskimo; and they developed the dog as a traction animal far more than any Indian tribe. Remembering their isolation and the meagre resources that nature supplied to them, it is hard to see what improvements were really possible on the sled for winter travel, the *kayak* for hunting and crossing small lakes and rivers, and the *umiak* for skirting the seacoast, except the use of a sail on the *umiak*: and even that was perhaps known to the Greenland Eskimo.[2]

Let us turn now to their dwellings. The universal dwelling in summer was a tent of seal or caribou-skin, ridged in the eastern Arctic and conical in the western, the two types overlapping from the central region westward. The Mackenzie River Eskimo, and some of their kinsmen in Alaska, strengthened the frame of the conical tent with a hoop that was lashed to the poles about 6 feet from the ground. There was, also, a third type of tent, the round or cupola type, which the inland Eskimo of Alaska adopted from the neighbouring Kutchin. Winter dwellings were equally varied, owing partly to environmental conditions. Where driftwood was plentiful, as in most of Alaska and in the delta of the Mackenzie, the Eskimo built rectangular, semi-subterranean, turf-covered houses of logs[3] that had long underground passageways and entrances in the floor.[4]

Typical of the Canadian Eskimo was the domed snow-hut, which seems to have been unknown in Alaska, and employed by the Mackenzie Delta natives, and by the natives of Greenland, only when travelling. The Greenland Eskimo lived in large log houses constructed on a different plan from the Alaskan ones, possibly through the influence of the early Norsemen.[5] Finally, on the Green-

---

[1] For brief descriptions of these craft *See* p. 109 f.

[2] *Cf.* Birket-Smith, Kaj.: "The Ethnography of the Egedesminde District"; Meddelelser om Grønland, vol. lxvi, p. 258 f. It seems not unlikely, however, that the Greenland Eskimo learned the use of sails from the Norsemen, for Mathiassen's excavation of a thirteenth (?) century Eskimo settlement near Upernivik shows that the Norsemen influenced them slightly in other ways. Mathiassen, T.: "An Old Eskimo Culture in West Greenland"; Geog. Rev., vol. xx, No. 4, p. 605 ff (October, 1930).

[3] Bones of the whale were substituted in districts where wood was scarce.

[4] The Mackenzie Delta Eskimo sometimes built their hut in the form of a cross so that it could house three families.

[5] *Cf.* Birket-Smith: "The Caribou Eskimos," vol. 2, p. 47.

land side of Smith sound, and on the Diomede islands in Bering strait, there were natives who still dwelt in stone huts, roofed with whalebones or driftwood and chinked with earth, similar to those erected many centuries ago from the Arctic archipelago to Labrador.

Whatever the nature of their winter dwellings, all Eskimo illuminated them in the same way, with a stone (from Bering strait southward a pottery) lamp burning oil from the blubber of the sea mammals, or, in the case of the Eskimo inland from Hudson bay, the fat of the caribou. The coastal natives used this lamp to cook their food, and fashioned their cooking-pots from the same

37016

A village of snow-huts. *(Photo by D. Jenness.)*

material, soapstone, or, in Alaska, pottery. Only during the summer months, from May to September, did they dispense with the lamp and cook outdoors with driftwood, or with the miserable fuels supplied by their treeless habitat—heather, dwarf willow, and the creeping dryas. There were two methods of making fire, by striking together two lumps of pyrites, and by friction with a thong drill. Both methods had a wide distribution in America, but the blubber lamp was the Eskimos' own creation; without it they could hardly have sustained the severity of their environment.

Their dress also was original, for the climate demanded fuller clothing than in other parts of America. The coat (or shirt, for it was closed down the front) was fitted with a hood that drew over the head, making caps so unnecessary that they were seldom worn except at dances. Among all the Canadian Eskimo the shirt was cut away at the sides like a European frock coat. Its length in front varied, but behind it had a very long tail that provided a useful appendage for fishermen and seal-hunters who sat on snow-blocks for several hours over holes in the ice. The women's shirt resembled the men's except that the shoulders were wider and the hood more expansive. Mothers enlarged the back to make room for their babies, who nestled snugly underneath, against the warm body; for neither cradle-boards nor moss-bags found favour in the Arctic. The rest of the costume was equally well devised. Both sexes wore breeks, the women's being a little shorter than the men's. The latter had stockings that just overlapped the breeks, and during the summer months boots of equal length that they replaced with low shoes during the winter. Women wore similar low shoes in winter. But their stockings were like very wide hip boots that tucked into the belt with straps, and, in Hudson bay, had a large pocket on each outer side; and their summer boots were cut to the same shape as the stockings.

All these garments were normally of caribou fur, except the shoes and boots, which were made of sealskin; and they were worn double during the winter, with the fur of the inner garment against the body. Since caribou hides lose their fur with dampness most men possessed sealskin shirts for rainy or misty weather, and summer seal-hunters used waterproof shirts of the same material, dehaired, which they lashed round the cockpits of their kayaks. The seal-skin boots required constant repairing when travelling over stony ground, and the women's hood, hip stockings, and boots were awk-ward and ungainly. Yet the complete costume, even in winter, weighed only about 5 pounds, and was warmer and more satisfactory than woollen clothing of twice its weight. Hence white men explor-ing the Arctic have frequently adopted it in preference to European dress.

If the Pacific Coast Indians excelled in carpentry, the Eskimo excelled in general artisanship. They were perhaps the most skilful of all Canadian aborigines in chipping glassy stones like flint and quartz into arrow- and spear-heads, knife blades, saws, drills, and skin scrapers. Where hard nephrite was available, as in Alaska, they shaped and polished it into adze-blades, whetstones, and even labrets. Their single- and double-edged hunting knives of ground slate, and the women's semi-lunar knives of the same material, were generally superior to Indian tools of this character; the semi-lunar knife, in fact, seems to have been copied by some Algonkian and Pacific Coast tribes. In Coronation gulf the Eskimo substituted local copper for flint and slate in all their cutting tools, and the Greenland natives sometimes used meteoric and telluric iron; but both these metals they treated simply as malleable stones.

It was in working antler, bone, and, particularly, ivory, however, that the Eskimo most excelled. Arctic explorers have been astonished at the variety of articles they manufactured from these materials. The majority, it is true, were small, but they were made with great care and skill and in most cases served some useful purpose. Merely to list them all would fill several pages, for they ranged from parts of harpoons and arrows, ice-chisels, sled-shoes, toggles, and handles of various shapes and sizes, to needles and needle-cases, thimbles and thimble-holders, and a wealth of miscellaneous objects for everyday use, besides numerous toys and amulets. Some were carved into animal and human forms, others carried incised decoration. The latter was always geometrical in prehistoric times, but in Alaska, after the natives acquired iron tools, it blossomed into vivid scenes of daily life.

There was very little basketry among the Eskimo except around the Yukon delta in Alaska and farther south, for its place was taken by bags of skin. Nor was there any embroidery in porcupine-quill or moose-hair, because neither the porcupine nor the moose extended into Eskimo territories. But needle-work was well developed; most of the ornamentation on clothing was produced by means of narrow bands of differently coloured skin or fur finely stitched together with sinew thread. We need not wonder that the Eskimo should be the only American people to devise a thimble, for after all thimbles were of little use to Indians who did not tailor their garments. But we cannot help admiring their resourcefulness in equipping themselves with so many serviceable articles from extremely limited means; and we marvel that a people subjected to all the hardships and uncertainties of life in the Arctic should foster a genuine love of art and display high talents in sculpture and engraving. We may recall that they possessed an equal gift for music, and that among the songs to which they danced on winter evenings there were some really beautiful melodies.

38571

Eskimo travelling by sled and dog-team. *(Photo by J. J. O'Neill.)*

In the spheres of social life and religious beliefs, however, the Eskimo ranked lower than most Indian tribes in Canada. Their small and, as a rule, widely separated communities recognized no chiefs of any kind. Men of unusual ability or personality, especially if they were shamans, wielded a certain amount of influence; but even they seldom thought of issuing commands to their communities, still less to the inhabitants of other communities in their neighbourhood. Rules of conduct that had arisen in various ways, and were generally sanctioned by long antiquity, regulated life within each group, and for anti-social practices such as theft and murder the penalty was death, either by sentence of the group or through the operation of the blood-feud. Like so many primitive races, the Eskimo lacked the independence of judgment and free initiative that characterize more civilized peoples. Hence discord seldom reared its head in their semi-communistic bands, and there was little need of any one in authority when each man's impulses unconsciously took the same direction as the impulses of his neighbours.

The nearest to public officials were the shamans, men and women who claimed, through the aid of their familiar spirits, to diagnose the causes of misfortune and sickness, to see what was happening far away, and to intervene between the lay Eskimo and the supernatural world. Some trained for this profession by apprenticing themselves to recognized practitioners who would transfer to them one or more of their familiars. Others adduced their authority from sudden calls or visitations that came to them unheralded when they were wandering alone over their hunting-grounds. Sometimes they performed juggling tricks similar to those of Indian medicine-men, and divined by "weighing" the head or foot of a patient; but their usual practice was to induce in themselves a kind of temporary dementia (Arctic hysteria, as the phenomenon is called in Siberia), and in that condition to give utterance to more or less incoherent ravings which the laity interpreted as oracles. Though all Eskimo could bandage a wound, and set in splints a fractured limb, they were as ignorant of herbal remedies as their Athapaskan neighbours. Like the latter, they ascribed all sickness and misfortune to magical causes, to the violation of a taboo, the enmity of a sorcerer, the ill-will of malevolent spirits, or the separation of the soul from the body. The shaman's methods of treatment corresponded with these diagnoses; they attempted to withdraw from the patients' bodies splinters of bone or wood that were presumably implanted there by sorcery, to propitiate or deter the malevolent spirits, and to capture and restore the errant souls. Not only were they the physicians of the communities, but its priests, for it was they who interceded with the supernatural world when caribou and fish seemed lacking, storms prevented the hunters from capturing seals, and the people were threatened with starvation.

The religion of the Eskimo brought them little comfort. They visioned a numberless host of supernatural beings around them, many of them harmless, perhaps, a few on rare occasions helpful, but all of them pregnant with power for ill. The being that the majority of the Eskimo dreaded most was a sea-goddess reputed to control the weather and to regulate the supply of seals. With unremitting care, too, they conciliated the souls of animals, which would surely take offence if the people failed to observe the time-honoured rituals and taboos, especially those that related to game.

Even the souls of the dead inspired them with fear, for they held unusually vague and contradictory notions concerning the after-life, and frequently attributed misfortune to the malicious souls of kinsmen recently deceased.[1] So gloomy, indeed, was their religion that it hindered more than it helped them in their hard struggle to exist. If the Eskimo had been morose or dispirited we might be tempted to conjecture that it was the very hardness of this struggle that made their religion gloomy; on the contrary, they were the most cheerful and laughter-loving people in America. We dare not assert that environment has absolutely no influence on temperament, and that temperament does not affect the religous beliefs, and yet the religion of the Eskimo and their temperament seem bewilderingly at variance.

Apart from the performances of the shamans there were very few public ceremonies to interrupt the normal current of life. In parts of the eastern Arctic, there was a festival every autumn to ensure an abundant supply of game;[2] it was known in some districts as the "darkening of lamps." The natives of northern Alaska performed certain rituals on the eve of the whale-hunting season in the early spring; and farther south, where there was closer contact with Athapaskan tribes, the Eskimo feebly imitated at second hand the potlatches of the Pacific Coast Indians. In this part of Alaska, around the deltas of the Yukon and Kuskokwim, performers at the winter "potlatches" frequently wore wooden masks, which were not common in other parts of the Arctic. Everywhere the long winter gave rise to almost nightly song-fests and dances, for darkness drove the seal-hunters home between three and four o'clock in the afternoon and favourable conditions for sled travelling permitted frequent visits to neighbouring villages.

Life, on the whole, was fairly orderly and peaceful in these Eskimo communities. Whether their dwellings were of logs, snow-blocks, or skins stretched round a framework of poles, each was almost identical with its neighbours, for no family could burden itself with more possessions than were strictly necessary. There were no distinctions of rich and poor. The successful hunter un-

---

[1] *Cf.* Rasmussen, Knud.: " Intellectual Culture of the Iglulik Eskimos"; Report of the Fifth Thule Expedition, 1921-1924, vol. vii, No. 1, p. 56 f (Copenhagen, 1929).
[2] *Cf.* Boas, F.: " The Central Eskimo," p. 604 ff: Sixth Ann. Rept., Bur. Am. Ethn. (Washington, 1888). " The Eskimos of Baffin Land and Hudson Bay"; Anth. Papers, Am. Mus. of Nat. Hist., vol. xx, p. 139 ff (1901).

hesitatingly shared his food with less fortunate comrades, partly because such had been the custom of his father and grandfather, partly because he knew that the day would come when he himself

39726

Copper Eskimo woman and child. *(Photo by J. R. Cox.)*

would be in need. In summer the families, scattered at different fishing and hunting grounds, were too busy gathering and storing away food for the months of early winter to give much thought to other pursuits. They had more leisure in winter, when they reassembled at the seashore, the daylight was short, and blizzards often kept the men from sealing and the entire community within doors. It was then, when food supplies were low and anxiety weighed on every heart, that quarrels were most apt to arise, that suspicions of sorcery found ready lodging, and hidden jealousies came to the surface. Even the certainty of blood-revenge did not always check a sudden knife-thrust that left its victim gasping in the snow. Generally the murderer and his family fled to some distant community, but the feud remained unforgotten and sooner or later a retaliatory murder kindled its flame afresh. These never-ending blood-feuds, to which innocent women and children fell victims as often as the murderers themselves, greatly increased the insecurity of life, and, combined with all the other hazards, produced in the Eskimo a profound fatalism only half concealed by their unfailing cheerfulness.

Other dark features in the social life were the frequency of infanticide, and the abandonment of the aged and infirm, customs that were perhaps unavoidable in many districts owing to the hard struggle for existence. The Eskimo were really very fond of their children, and treated them with great indulgence. Both boys and girls were subjected to a number of taboos that related for the most part to their diet, and women endured many restrictions, especially in times of childbirth; but the seclusion of adolescents, enforced by many Indian tribes, was unknown. Marriage took place without ceremony, although the son-in-law generally hunted with his wife's parents for a season or two. Either party could dissolve the union at will, and husbands even exchanged wives temporarily, for the Eskimo ranked friendship above chastity, and indeed held the latter in little esteem. Nevertheless, couples nearly always clung together after they had issue, and domestic quarrels occurred far less frequently than in more civilized homes. Women had a well-recognized position, less inferior to men's than among any Indian tribe except perhaps the Iroquoians; but whereas Iroquoian women derived their higher status mainly from the economic importance of their cornfields, Eskimo women owed their position largely to the indispensability of expert seamstresses for making the tailored clothing necessary to withstand an Arctic climate.

The Eskimo could not bury their dead in the ground, which was perpetually frozen a few inches below the surface. In the western and eastern Arctic they generally covered the corpse with logs or stones,[1] but over a large part of the central Arctic they left the body unprotected except by its covering of skins. Beside a man they laid his hunting equipment, beside a woman her sewing tools, that the souls of these objects might still serve their owners in the afterlife. Widows, widowers, and all who handled a corpse incurred a number of temporary taboos, but the mourners, unlike most Indians, neither mutilated themselves nor manifested their grief in other extravagant ways.

The Eskimo of eastern Canada and Labrador have been in contact with Europeans for more than two hundred years, and those of the Mackenzie delta for more than a hundred, whereas the bands that live along the Arctic coast between that delta and the Magnetic Pole remained almost uninfluenced until the twentieth century. To-day every inhabited region in the Arctic and sub-Arctic is exploited by European fur-traders. Bows and arrows have yielded to firearms; tools of bone, ivory, stone, and native copper to tools of steel; and clay or stone cooking pots to kettles and pots of iron or aluminium. The *kayak* and the *umiak* have disappeared completely from many districts, for the hunting of whales has ceased and sealing and walrus-hunting, except with rifles from the edge of the ice, are on the decline. Skin tents are rapidly giving way to cloth tents, not so much because the latter are lighter and easier to transport as because firearms have diminished the number of caribou, and trapping leaves the natives but a short period in which to hunt either caribou or seals. Partly for the same reasons, and partly from a misguided imitation of Europeans, many Eskimo now wear woollen underclothing and even the complete European costume, although their earlier garments of loosely fitting caribou fur were more picturesque and hygienic, and offered greater protection against the intense cold.

Very few Eskimo now hunt intensively during the winter months; instead they trap foxes, which are useless to them for either food or clothing. In order to maintain their families during that season they buy European food from the fur-traders, largely flour,

---

[1] The platform burial practised in parts of Alaska may be post-European.

sugar, and tea. Now a diet of straight seal-meat will keep a hunter or a trapper in good health, but a diet that consists mainly of bannock and tea is practically starvation. So, over large parts of the Arctic and sub-Arctic the Eskimo are now worse clad, and more ill-nourished, than in the days of their isolation.[1]

There seem to have been about 2,000 Eskimo living between the Alaska-Canada boundary and cape Bathurst when Sir John Franklin's expedition explored this coast in 1826. In 1929 there were less than 800, and of that number only about twelve were really native to the district, the remainder being immigrants from Alaska. The earlier inhabitants perished from diseases introduced by Europeans; as late as 1900 an epidemic of measles caused great mortality. In 1902 typhus carried off all the surviving inhabitants of Southampton island, Hudson bay. Other parts of Hudson bay, Baffin island, and the Labrador peninsula suffered great depletions in the eighteenth and nineteenth centuries, and during the last few years European diseases have been ravaging the newly accessible groups between Coronation gulf and the Magnetic Pole. So from a pre-European population estimated by Mooney at 22,500 the Canadian and Labrador Eskimo have been reduced to 8,000 (in 1929). Some decline was inevitable, perhaps, because even our mildest diseases are fatal to unimmunized natives, and the isolation of the Eskimo until the twentieth century deprived them of all medical services. To-day, however, many of the survivors have developed a partial immunity to the commonest diseases, and the government is establishing a chain of doctors across the Arctic to check the spread of epidemics and to combat the high mortality, particularly of infants. At the same time it is conserving the wild life throughout the Arctic and sub-Arctic, and introducing domesticated reindeer from Alaska to augment the supply of meat and prevent the recurring famines. Assuming that these measures are successful, the Eskimo should more than hold their own during the present century, and by gradual amalgamation with white trappers and traders produce the hardy and resourceful stock necessary for the development of Canada's Far North.

---

[1] The same conditions prevail among the Athapaskan Indians of northern Canada, and doubtless contribute not a little to lower their vitality and render them easy victims to influenza, tuberculosis, and other diseases.

INDEX

A

	PAGE
Abenaki confederacy	270
Adornment	76. *See* Ornaments
Adzes	34ff *et passim*
Illus.	37
Afterlife	165f, 167
Bella Coola	341 (note)
Carrier	368
Chipewyan	387
Eskimo	418
Kootenay	360
Ojibwa	281
Slave	391
Tahltan	374
Aged, abandonment of	163 *et passim*
Strangling of	403
Agriculture	29f, 40ff
Illus.	41
Alcohol, effect of	253
Aleutian islands, migration via	243
Algonkian language	14, 17, 18, 20–23, 26
Algonkian tribes, Eastern Woodlands	265–287
Art	209
Canoes	108ff
Distribution	266
Hunting methods	59
Maple sugar	14
Moose call	54
Myths	188, 191
Organization	119ff
Origin	246
Pottery	215, 223
Privations	48
Religion	171
Remains	220–223
Sacrifices	173
Seasonal movements	48
Toboggans	102f
Trade	105, 113
Warfare	1, 26, 126 (note)
Algonkins	274f
Agriculture	40
Amulets	176
Feast of dead	160
Snow-shoes	102 (note)
Illus.	275
Amulets	176f *et passim*
Archæological remains	87 (note), 216–232
Armour	75 (note)
Carrier	364
Iroquoians	298
Montagnais	272

	PAGE
Pacific coast	330
Plains' tribes	310
Salish, Interior	356
Slave	390
Tahltan	372
Art	208–215 *et passim*
Assiniboine	308–317
Buffalo-hunting	56ff, 128f
Cremation	165
Horses acquired	129 (note)
Language	19
Organization	127f
Sowing of wild rice	42
Tattooing	80
Travois	103
Illus.	311
Athapaskan language	14, 18–20, 22, 26, 246
Athapaskans, Mackenzie and Yukon	377–404
Antiquity in America	246
Distribution	378
Future outlook	263
Influence of civilization	422 (note)
Wrestling for wives	156
Atiwandaronk	*See* Neutrals
Axes	34ff, 298 (note) *et passim*

B

Bark, ash, for dwellings	90
Birch, for baskets	31 *et passim*
" canoes	38, 108ff *et passim*
" cradles	150
" dwellings	38, 87ff, *et passim*
" food caches	41 *et passim*
" moose-call	54
Cedar, for baskets and mats	38
" canoes	38, 369
" cord	38
" dress	67ff
" dwellings	38, 90
" ornaments	78
Elm, for bags	214
" canoes	37, 105, 108
" dwellings	90
Pine, for canoes	108
Spruce, for canoes	108
Basketry	213f *et passim*
In archæological remains	217
Illus.	213
Beaver Indians, Peace river	113, 118, 241, 382–384
Expelled by Cree	255
Liard river	391 (note)

PAGE

Bella Coola Indians..............339–342
Canoes....................... 104
Cloak......................69 (note)
Drama....................... 203
Festivals....................161, 180
Fish weirs.................... 64f
Method of catching water-fowl..
62 (note)
Moccasins.................... 69
Myths....................... 188
Origin....................... 228
Religion..................... 170
Seasonal movements.......... 47
Social organization........... 140ff
Illus.............44, 104, 186, 196, 202
Beothuk.......................265–267
Camping sites................. 86
Canoes....................108, 265
Graves....................217, 266
Language...................14, 266
Organization................. 121
Use of red ochre.............. 81
Bering strait, migrations via...... 243ff
Blackfoot.....................317–324
Camp circle.................129 (note)
Conception of afterlife.......... 166
Dwellings.................... 90
Horses acquired.............129 (note)
Language..................... 8, 19
Organization...............126ff, 319
Reaction to civilization.......... 261
Religion..................... 319
Societies.........128, 129, 194, 320–322
Sun-dance..................162, 322
Travois..................... 103
Wanderings.................. 112
Wars....................... 256
Illus.........130, 164, 190, 318, 321, 323
Blood Indians........319. See Blackfoot
Blood-feud....................51, 420
Bows.................31. See Weapons
Buffalo-hunting...........54ff et passim
Illus.....................55, 57, 311
Bull-boats.................... 310
Burial, methods of..........163–165, 217
Assiniboine................... 312–3
Beaver..................... 384
Blackfoot.................... 320
Carrier..................... 368
Chilcotin.................... 363
Chipewyan.................. 386
Cree....................... 286
Dogrib..................... 393
Eskimo..................... 421
Haida...................... 335
Hare...................... 395
Hurons....................293, 296
Iroquois..................302 (note)
Kootenay................... 360

Kutchin..................... 404
Kwakiutl.................... 342
Micmac..................... 269
Montagnais.................. 273
Nahani....................398, 399
Naskapi.................... 273
Neutrals.................... 296
Nootka..................... 347
Ojibwa..................... 281
Salish, Coast................. 349
Salish, Interior............... 357
Sekani..................... 382
Slave..................... 391
Tahltan.................... 374
Tlinkit..................... 331
Tsimshian.................. 338
Illus....................164, 297, 349

C

Caches................41, 50 et passim
Cairns, stone........217, 225, 226, 313
Cannibalism..............285, 305, 338
Canoes..104–110, 369, 383 (note) et passim
Beothuk..................... 265
Bull-boats.................. 310
Kutchin.................... 401
Micmac.................... 268
Illus...104, 105, 106, 107, 109, 282,
348, 410
Caribou-eaters............13 (note), 426
Carrier Indians................363–368
Dramatic dances.............. 201–2
Dwellings..................91, 364
Education.................. 152
Fasting of adolescents........... 175
Gambling game.............. 159
Myths....................189, 192
Ornaments.................78, 364
Reaction to civilization.......... 261
Religion............171, 173 (note), 367
Religious revival............. 184
Seasonal movements.......... 47
Skill in making deadfalls....... 59
Social organization........141,
142 (note), 365–367
Songs..................206, 207, 208
Trade....................112, 114
Illus....................39, 365
Cayuga..............133. See Iroquois
Chiefs.....120, 127–8, 135, 137, 147, et al
Chilcat blankets..........67–8, 116, 212
Illus....................77, 336
Chilcotin Indians...............361–363
Basketry..................213, 362
Illus..................... 262
Children, care and training.......149–154
Chinookan language............19, 117

PAGE

Chipewyan...............385–388
  Burial..................... 164
  Conception of afterlife.......166, 387
  Dogs......................55 (note)
  Hunting method.............. 54
  Oppression by.............254, 385
  Seasonal movements........... 47
  Toboggan.............104 (note)
  Trade..................... 111
  Illus...................385, 387
Chippewa.............277. See Ojibwa
Chronology of archæological remains
      218–220, 237–8
Circumcision.................. 395
Classification of Indians........... 7–15
Clothing..................See Dress
Colour of eyes................ 2
    "   hair.................. 2
    "   skin.................. 2
Colours used by Indians........... 80–1
Confession of sin...........174, 374, 391
Cooking vessels.............31 et passim
Copper, for tools and ornaments..
      33, 36, 78, 388, 415
Copper Indians.............388 (note)
Corn.............29–30, 40–42 et passim
Cradles...............149–150 et passim
  Illus.................150, 151, 419
Cree................283–287, 316–317
  Buffalo drives..............58 (note)
  Confederacy with Assiniboine.... 127
  Costume................... 72
  Cremation................. 165
  Designs................... 209
  Dwellings..............89, 90, 284
  Expansion..........32, 195, 254–5, 284
  Future outlook............. 286–7
  Language................. 17, 19
  Medicines................. 113
  Privations................. 48
  Religion...........172 (note), 173, 286
  Skill in hunting............. 53–4
  Snow-shoes................ 102
  Tattooing................. 79, 80
  Vegetable foods............. 44
  Illus...................18, 284
Culture areas................. 8–12

D

Dances.......159–160, 201–204 et passim
  Illus.................181, 202, 403
Deadfalls................... 59
Deformation, artificial.........150 (note)
  Illus..................... 13
Deities................170–172, 183
  Assiniboine................ 313
  Eskimo................... 417
  Haida................... 334

PAGE

Iroquois.................. 301–2
Kutchin.................. 404
Nootka.................. 347
Ojibwa.................. 281
Salish, Interior.............. 358
Tahltan.................. 375
Designs, ownership of........... 145
  Illus................... 208
Digging-sticks................ 30
Diseases...............163 et passim
  Introduced.....251–253, 422 et passim
Divination, methods of.........273, 417
Divorce................... 156
Dogrib.................. 392–3
  Canoes................... 108
  Dress................... 76
  Hunting methods...........54 (note)
Dogs, absent among Beothuk...... 265
  For clothing.............29, 67 (note)
  " food............29 (note) 316, 347
  " hunting.............. 29, 55
  " sacrifices.............174, 281, 301
  " traction..............9, 29, 103–4
Dolls.................... 273
Drama.......201–204. See also Dances
  Illus.................186, 196, 202
Dreams, significance of......175 et passim
Dress.................67–83 et passim
Dwellings................84–99 et passim
  Illus. Assiniboine............. 91
  " Blackfoot.............. 318
  " Carrier............... 365
  " Chipewyan............. 387
  " Cree................... 18
  " Eskimo................98, 413
  " Haida................96, 332
  " Iroquois..............291, 301
  " Kwakiutl.............182, 343
  " Naskapi................ 271
  " Nootka................ 345
  " Ojibwa.............18, 88, 278
  " Salish, Coast......23, 93, 140
  " Salish, Interior......92, 354, 357
  " Sarcee................ 177
  " Sekani................ 380
  " Tahltan............... 371

E

Economic conditions.......... 28–52
  Effect of Europeans...........254–257
Education of children............ 152–3
Embroidery, porcupine—quill and
    moose—hair...........76 et passim
Erie Indians.........133 (note), 224, 299
Eskimo.................405–422
  Amulets................. 176
  Archæology.............. 228–232
  Art.................... 212

Eskimo *(Cont'd.)*   PAGE

Basketry...................... 214
Beadwork.................... 214–5
Blood-grouping................ 247
Boats..........108 (note), 109–110, 412
Burial.......................164, 421
Caches..................50 (note), 51
Dances....................... 201
Dogs...................29 (note), 103
Dress............70, 73–76, 78, 83, 413–4
Dwellings............:.85–6, 97–9, 412–3
Effect of civilization............. 421–2
Fecundity.................... 51
Festivals....................161, 418
Fishing methods....61, 62 (note),
                              63, 64, 411
Folk-tales.................... 190
Football...................... 158
Frequented Churchill........385 (note)
Future outlook............... 263
Great Spirit.................183 (note)
Hair-dressing................. 82
Hunting methods.54, 58, 59, 60, 61,
                              409–410
Infanticide...................52, 420
Lack of herbal remedies......53 (note)
Language.........19, 20, 24, 25, 26, 246
Method of carrying babies...150
                            (note), 419
Nets.....................63, 409, 411
Organization............119–126, 416–7
Origin....................... 246–7
Physical characteristics..........6, 247
Privations.................... 48
Religion....................170, 417–8
Sacrifice.................... 173
Seasonal movements........... 47
Songs....................... 205
Tattooing.................... 80
Trade....................... 112
Travel...................... 104
Wrestling for wives............. 156
Illus..7, 31, 35, 62, 74, 98, 119, 122,
        205, 407, 410, 413, 416, 419
Eyes, colour and shape............ 2

F

Face, shape of.................. 2–3
Fasting, ceremonial.........154 *et passim*
Fecundity of Indians............. 51
Festivals...........160–1, 201–4 *et passim*
Illus.......................93, 146, 297
Fire, methods of making..........29, 413
Firearms, effect of................ 254–5
Fishing, methods of..61–65, 409 *et passim*
Illus....................62, 64, 66, 397
Five Nations..............*See Iroquois*
Folk-lore...................185–199
Food supply.................. 40–52
Division of..................65, 66, 162

Fortifications............290, 298, 330, 355
Illus....................... 291
Fuel............30 (note), 84, 86, 290, 408
Illus....................... 407
Fur-trade, effect of.............. 255

G

Gambling..................... 158–9
Illus....................... 294
Game supply.................. 45–50
Games.......................158–161
Illus....................... 294
Gitksan..................... 336
Goat Indians.................. 396
Goat's wool...................*See* Wool
Graves.....................*See* Burial
Remains in............217, 225, 227, 266
Grease, used as ointment......... 81
Trade in oolakan grease.114–5 *et passim*
Gros Ventre 318, 326
Guardian spirits..175–6, 187 (note),
        343–4, *et passim*

H

Haida.......................331–335
Art........................209–212
Canoes...................... 105–6
Dress....................69 (note), 78
Dwellings.................... 94–96
Feasts...................... 154
Hunting of sea-lions............. 60
Language.......8, 14, 18, 20, 144 (note)
Organization.................140–148
Religion.....................170, 334
Seasonal movements..........48 (note)
Tattooing.....................79, 334
Trade.....................113 (note)
Illus...................96, 143, 252, 332
Hair, colour and texture........... 2
Methods of dressing............. 82
Hare Indians..................394–396
Dwellings.................... 90
Hunting methods.............54 (note)
Seasonal movements........... 48
Harpoons...................60 *et passim*
Head, shape of.................. 4, 227
Hochelagans.................288 (note)
Hoes....................... 30
Horses, effect of.........129–132, 256, 311
Hunting, methods of....48, 54–61, 409–411
Community hunting....47, 55–8, 65, 411
Illus.....................55, 57, 311
Hunting-grounds, ownership of.124,
        138, 145, 354, 366, 373, 381

PAGE

Hurons...................289–299
   Dwellings.................... 88
   Immigration.................. 224
   Language..................... 19
   Maintenance of law............ 138
   Organization...........133, 134 (note)
   Origin of name................ 82
   Religion..................... 170–3
   Trade..................... 45, 113
   Illus. 289, 294, 297
Hygiene, lack of................ 99

I

Indians, antiquity...............233–248
   Causes of unequal culture among. 27
   Classification................. 6–12
   Contributions to civilization..... 250
   Destruction by alcohol and
    diseases................... 251–4
   Future outlook...........259–264, 350
   Origin of name................ 2
   Physical characteristics...2–6, 227,
                   235, 240
Infanticide..........52, 391, 395, 403, 420
Infants, death rate among.......51–2, 150
Inventions of Indians and Eskimo
           32 (note), 250, 412–3
Iroquoian tribes...........29–30, 288–307
   Adoption among.............. 51
   Agriculture among............ 40–42
   Barbed fish-hooks............61 (note)
   Bead currency................ 113
   Burial....................... 163
   Community hunting............ 56
   Division of labour............. 156
   Dug-outs.................... 104–5
   Dwellings.............84–5, 89–90
   Immigration..................224, 233
   Language..................19, 20, 23
   Metaphorical speech.......... 201
   Myths.....................188, 191
   Organization.........133–139, 142, 147
   Origin...................... 246
   Ossuaries................... 217
   Pottery..... .... 215, 223
   Property.................... 111
   Religion....................170–176
   Seasonal movements........... 48
   Smoking introduced by......... 222
   Tattooing................... 79, 80
   Toboggans.................. 102–3
   Trade.....................111, 113
   Village remains............... 223
   Village sites................. 87
   Wild fruits of................ 43
Iroquois.....300–307. *See also* Iroquoian
   Armour..................... 272
   Costume.................... 73
   Cradle-boards............... 208–9

PAGE

Dwellings.................... 88–9
Education of children.......... 152–3
Expansion....................195, 255
Festivals..................... 161
New religion.................. 183–4
Organization.................133–139
Position of women....52, 70 (note), 420
Sacerdotal officials........... 180
Sculpture.................... 208
Societies.................... 208
Use of shells.................. 79
   Illus. 23, 136, 291, 301

K

Kaska.......................396–399
Kinship, methods of reckoning..... 123
Knives....................... 34
   Illus. 37
Kootenay Indians...............358–361
   Canoes..................... 108
   Language.................15, 18, 20
   Organization................. 132
   Reaction to civilization......... 261
   Illus. 3, 360
Kutchin......................399–404
   Dress...................... 73
   Dwellings................... 89
   Fishing-methods............. 61
   Hair-dressing...............82 (note)
   Shell currency............... 114
   Sleds...................... 102
   Illus. 115, 397, 400, 403
Kwakiutl.....................342–345
   Art.......................209–211
   Basketry.................... 101
   Deformation, artificial.......150 (note)
   Dwellings................... 94–95
   Festivals...................161, 180
   Language................... 18
   Organization................140–148
   Weirs...................... 63–4
   Illus. 13, 182, 338, 343

L

Labour, division of......70, 104, 156–7, 292
Lake Indians....351. *See* Salish, Interior
Lamps.................97, 99, 408, 413
Languages...................... 17–27
   Value for classification.......... 8
Law, maintenance of............125, 128
Lilloet Indians..351. *See* Salish, Interior
Long-house, Iroquois 23
Looms......................212, 214
   Illus. 68
Loucheux....................395, 399

M

	PAGE
Maize.	29, 30, 40–42
Malecite.	270
Agriculture.	40
Art.	208 (note), 209
Clans.	123 (note)
Dress.	73
Football.	158
Marriage.	123, 154–158
Assiniboine.	312
Cree.	286
Eskimo.	420
Hurons.	296
Iroquois.	302
Micmac.	269
Montagnais.	273
Slave.	391
Tahltan.	374
Tlinkit.	330
Masks, carving of.	208, 212
Illus.	179, 181, 186, 196, 303
Medicine-bundles.	310 (note), 322–324 et passim
Illus.	177, 318
Medicine-men.	178–181 et passim
Illus.	179
Medicine societies, Iroquoian.	295, 302
Ojibwa.	160, 178, 280, 286
Melanesia, contacts of America with	240–243, 248
Micmac.	267–269
Art.	208 (note), 209
Clans.	123 (note)
Cremation.	165 (note)
Destroyed Beothuk.	32, 254, 266, 267
Destruction by typhoid.	253
Dress.	73
Football.	158
Language.	8
Method of catching water-fowl.	62 (note)
Organization.	122
Ownership of hunting grounds.	124 (note)
Pipes.	222
Pottery.	221
Seasonal movements.	47, 48
Illus.	267
Migrations, seasonal for food.	46–48
Missisauga Indians.	277. See Ojibwa
Agriculture.	40
Mohawk.	133, 304–5. See Iroquois
Immigration.	224
Montagnais.	126 (note), 270–274
Abandonment of aged.	163
Chiefs.	120
Dwellings.	90
Ownership of hunting grounds.	124
Religion.	170, 173
Seal-oil for ointment.	265 (note)
Transport.	101–2

	PAGE
Mortality of Indians.	51
Mosaics, stone.	225
Mother-in-law taboo.	369
Mourning, use of black for.	81
Rites.	See Burial
Music.	206–8
Musical instruments.	160, 205, 276
Illus.	205
Muskegon.	284

N

	PAGE
Nadene languages.	20
Nahani.	389, 396–9
Canoes.	109
Name.	427
Naming, ceremony at.	280, 303–4, 312, 330
Naskapi.	270–4
Dress.	73
Dwellings.	90
Tattooing.	79
Illus.	271
Nature, conception of.	167–171, 190
Nephrite, trade in.	111
Use of.	36
Nets, for fish.	63 et passim
For seals.	61 (note), 409
Neutrals.	289, 296, 299, 300
Language.	19
Organization.	133
Nicola Indians.	351
Niska Indians.	336
Nootka Indians.	345–347
Basketry.	213
Canoe.	105
Dances.	203–4
Deformation, artificial.	150 (note)
Dwellings.	93–5
Fishing methods.	63
Footwear.	69 (note)
Hunting methods.	58–9
Language.	18–24
Organization.	140–8
Ornaments.	78
Sea-otter robes.	70
Seasonal movements.	48
Sites of villages.	87
Stocking rivers with fish.	53
Illus.	69, 105, 146, 172, 345
Norsemen, influence in Canada.	219
Influence in Greenland.	239, 412 (note)

O

	PAGE
Obsidian, trade in.	112
Use of.	36
Ojibwa.	277–283
Bags.	214
Burial.	165, 281
Canoes.	104 (note), 109 (note)
Clans.	123 (note), 277

PAGE

Conception of nature....168 (note), 280
Designs........................ 209
Dwellings..................... 89
Expansion................255, 282
Future outlook............260, 283
Maple sugar................... 44
Medicine lodge..........160, 178, 280
Ownership of hunting grounds...
124 (note)
Trade with Hurons............. 45
Wild rice.................... 42–3
Illus............18, 42, 88, 109, 278, 282
Okanagan Indians......351. *See* Salish,
Interior
Oneida................300. *See* Iroquois
Cruelty...................305 (note)
Onondaga..............300. *See* Iroquois
Dances...................... 160
Immigration................. 224
Oolakan, trade in oil of..114–5 *et passim*
Oratory...................... 200–1
Ornaments.................... 76–9
Metal....................335, 364
Shell..................79 *et passim*
Stone......................36, 223
Illus.....................115, 143
Ottawa Indians.........277. *See* Ojibwa
Agriculture.................. 40

P

Painting...................209–212
On hats..................... 70, 76
On person.................. 80–1
On robes.................... 76
On tents.................... 318
On wood.................... 9, 80
Illus................69, 182, 211, 318
Parents-in-law, avoidance of....... 398
Pelly River Indians.............. 396
Pemmican.................43, 50, 386
Petroglyphs.................. 217
Illus...................... 218
Petuns.............*See* Tobacco Nation
Phratries.............134, 141 *et passim*
Physical characteristics of Indians.
2–6, 227, 235, 240
Of Eskimo................... 6, 247
Pictographs................. 217
Piegan..................*See* Blackfoot
Colours used by............... 80
Gambling................... 159
Proportion of sexes........... 75
Pipes.....36, 208, 222–225, 228, 357 (note)
Trade in.................... 112
Pleistocene man in America....234–8, 248
Polygamy.................... 156
Polynesia, contacts of America with
240–3, 248

PAGE

Population checks on.............. 51
Of Algonkins.................. 276
Assiniboine.................. 316
Beaver...................... 384
Bella Coola.................. 339
Beothuk..................... 266
Blackfoot.................... 324
Carrier...................... 368
Chilcotin.................... 363
Chipewyan................... 385
Cree........................ 286
Dogrib...................... 393
Dominion.................... 1
Eskimo................405 (note), 422
Haida....................... 335
Hare........................ 396
Hurons...................288, 299
Iroquois.................... 306
Kootenay.................... 361
Kutchin..................... 404
Kwakiutl.................... 345
Malecite.................... 270
Micmac...................... 269
Montagnais and Naskapi........ 274
Nahani...................... 399
Nootka...................... 347
Ojibwa...................... 277
Salish, Coast................ 349
Salish, Interior.............. 358
Sarcee...................325, 326
Sekani...................... 382
Slave....................... 392
Tagish...................... 376
Tahltan..................... 376
Tlinkit..................... 331
Tsetsaut.................... 369
Tsimshian................... 339
Yellowknife................. 389
Porcupine-quill work........214 *et passim*
Potawatomi.......277, 299. *See* Ojibwa
Potlatch..116, 330 (note), 344–5 *et passim*
Pottery, for cooking vessels......215, 279
Among Assiniboine............ 308
Among Blackfoot............319 (note)
For lamps................... 413
For pipes.................208, 222
In archæological remains.217, 221–5, 268
Origin of................... 224
Pounds for game.........56–58 *et passim*
Illus....................... 55
Prayer...................174 *et passim*
Prisoners, treatment of, by Hare.. 395
Iroquoians................298, 306
Kootenay.................... 359
Micmac...................... 268
Montagnais.................. 272
Ojibwa...................... 279
Pacific Coast tribes.......... 328
Salish, Interior.............. 353

PAGE

Property, inheritance of...124, 141–2, 145,
147 (note)
Puberty, rituals at..............154, 175
Illus..................81, 146, 153, 155

Q

Quarries.............112, 217, 265 (note)
Illus........................ 231

R

Red ochre, use of....222, 225, 265, 272, 286
Red Knives...................388 (note)
Red Paint people................. 222
Reincarnation, belief in.....165, 296 (note)
Ceremony to cause.............. 374
Religion................167–184, 258
Assiniboine.................. 313
Beaver...................... 384
Bella Coola................. 341–2
Blackfoot................... 322–4
Carrier..................... 367
Chipewyan.................. 387
Eskimo.................... 417–8
Haida...................... 334
Iroquois.................... 301
Kootenay................... 360
Kutchin.................... 404
Kwakiutl................... 343–4
Montagnais and Naskapi........ 273
Nootka..................... 347
Ojibwa..................... 280
Salish, Interior.............. 358
Slave...................... 391
Tahltan.................... 375
Remedies, herbal.............53, 280
Resources of Indians........... 29–52
Rice, wild............... 42–3, 279, 308
Illus........................ 42
Rocky Mountain Indians......383 (note)
Rush, lodges of...........23, 87, 89, 90
For smoothing wood........... 96
Illus........................ 23

S

Sacrifices........170, 172–4, 281, 301, 491
Human...............173, 305, 328
Sails, knowledge of.............110, 412
Salish, Coast...................347–350
Art.......................209–211
Basketry.................... 213
Deformation, artificial.......150 (note)
Dwellings.................... 93
Movements.................. 228
Organization...............140–148
Weaving of wool.............. 68, 212
Weirs...................... 63–4
Illus..50, 66, 68, 93, 140, 157, 181, 348, 349

PAGE

Salish, Interior................. 351–8
Basketry.................213–4, 357
Burial.....................165, 357
Canoes.....................108, 355
Community hunting........... 56
Conflicts with Blackfoot........ 256
Dwellings.............91–3, 99, 354
Early remains................ 228
Organization...............132, 351–4
Reaction to civilization........ 261
Religious revival............. 184
Illus...81, 92, 151, 213, 353, 354, 356, 357
Salishan language........14, 18, 20, 23, 26
Sarcee....................... 324–6
Education of children.......... 153
Language.................... 19
Organization................ 127
Reaction to civilization........ 261
Societies.................... 128
Sun-dance.................. 162
Travois.................... 103
Illus...................... 325
Saulteaux..................277 (note)
Sculpture, in bone and ivory.....212, 227
In stone.........38, 208, 223, 227
In wood................208–212
Illus.................186, 196, 303, 349
Sekani..............148 (note), 377–382
Dwellings................... 91
Myths.................191 (note)
Ownership of hunting grounds... 124
Religious revival............. 184
Illus....................257, 380
Seneca........133, 135, 304. See Iroquois
Immigration of................ 224
Illus....................... 291
Sewing, tools for................ 70
Sexes, differences in speech........ 26
Division of labour....70, 104, 156–7, 292
Separation after adolescence.... 154
Sheep Indians................. 396
Shell, uses of, for adzes......35 (note), 95
Currency.................79, 113–4, 139
Hoes...................... 30
Inlay...................... 77
Knives....................34 (note)
Ornaments...37, 78–9, 114, 139, 223, 225
Records.................... 136
Weapons................... 59
Shell-heaps....216, 217, 222 (note),
225–228, 243
Dating of................... 220
Shuswap Indians........351. See Salish,
Interior
Signals...................... 311–2
Siouan language.......15, 18, 20, 23, 24, 26
Sioux....................... 326
Conflicts with Ojibwa.........278, 282
Illus................frontispiece, 326

PAGE

Sites, location of village.......... 86–7
Skin, colour of.................... 2
Skins, for clothing...........74 et passim
  For tents. ....87 et passim
  Working of................... 37
  Illus........................ 39
Slave Indians, Lesser Slave lake.. 383
Slave Indians, Mackenzie river...
                               389–392
  Adornment....................76, 390
  Dress....................... 73
  Dwellings.................90, 91 (note)
  Expelled by Cree.............. 255
Slavery, effect on population of... 51
Slaves on Pacific coast..140–1, 164,
       258, 328, 331 (note), 373, 374
Slavey..........See Slave Indians,
  Mackenzie river
Sleds.....................102 et passim
  Illus.......................119, 416
Smallpox, ravages of......251–2 et passim
Smoking, introduction by Iroquoians
  of........................ 224
Snare Indians.................... 424
Snares, use of.........46, 48, 49, 58, 59, 285
Snow-shoes..............34, 102 et passim
Soapstone, use of...36, 285, 357 (note), 413
  Trade in.................... 112
Social organization........118–148, 257–8
  Algonkin..................... 276
  Assiniboine.................. 314
  Beaver...................... 384
  Bella Coola.................. 340
  Blackfoot.................... 319
  Carrier..................... 365–6
  Chilcotin.................... 362
  Chipewyan................... 386
  Cree.......................286, 317
  Eskimo..................... 416–7
  Haida....................... 333
  Hare........................ 395
  Kootenay.................... 359
  Kutchin..................... 402
  Kwakiutl.................... 342
  Micmac..................... 268
  Montagnais.................. 272
  Nahani..................... 399
  Nootka..................... 346
  Ojibwa..................... 277–8
  Salish, Coast................ 348
  Salish, Interior.............. 351–2
  Sekani..................... 380
  Tahltan.................... 373
  Tsetsaut.................... 369
  Tsimshian................... 337
Societies, Pacific coast, 161, 180, 181,
                333, 341–4, 346
  Dramatic performances....202–4,
                   341–2, 368
  Illus....................... 181

PAGE

Societies, plains' tribes.119, 128–130,
          194, 314–5, 317, 320–2
Songs........................ 205–7
  Ownership................... 145
  Supernatural origin........... 204
Sorcery...............150, 178 et passim
Soul, idea of....................150, 296
  Fate after death.165–6, 279 (note).
    See Afterlife
Stature........................ 4
Stones, used for boiling water.... 31
  Cooking vessels..............285, 413
  Dwellings................... 85–6
  Lamps......................36, 413
  Methods of working........... 36
  Tools...................... 33–38
Stonies.................See Assiniboine
Strangers, rights of..........125, 138, 144
Strongbow................391 (note)
Sugar, maple................... 44
Sun-dance..27, 127 (note), 161, 162,
          192, 315–6, 317, 322
Sunflower seeds, ointment from.... 41
Sweat-houses.................. 89, 355
  Illus....................... 375

T

Taboos...................152, 173–4, 286
Tagish Indians.................. 376
Tahltan...................... 370–6
  Dwellings................... 91
  Organization................ 141
  Tattooing................... 79
  Illus......................371, 375
Tattooing 79–80, 284, 388
Textiles....................32, 38, 67–8
Thompson Indians..351. See Salish,
  Interior
Tipi......................90 et passim
  Illus.....................91, 177, 318
Tlinkit......................328–331
  Dwellings................... 94–6
  Language........14, 18, 20, 144 (note)
  Moccasins.................. 69
  Occupied Stikine river.......370 (note)
  Organization................140–148
  Weaving............67, 70 (note), 212
Tobacco....41, 165 (note), 250, 288,
          322, 334 (note), 357
  As religious offering..173, 273, 281,
               313, 314, 317
Tobacco Nation....133 (note), 289,
          290, 297, 299, 300
  Language.................... 19
Toboggans..................34, 100–2
Tools.....................33–9, 95–6, 415
  Illus.....................35, 37, 39

432

	Page			Page
Totemic clans, among Algonkins..	276		**W**	
Cree.	286	Wakashan language.		14, 18, 20
Iroquoians.	133–139	Wampum.		*See* Shells
Micmac.	268	Warfare	100, 125–6, 129. 137–9,	
Ojibwa.	277		144–5, 256, 278, 297–8, 312	
Pacific Coast tribes.	141–7	Effect on population.		51
Totem-poles.	95, 241–2	Weapons.		32–5
Designs on.	210	Beaver.		384
Manner of erecting.	96, 145	Hare.		394
Trade	111–6, 328, 333, 351, 362	Iroquoians.		298
Routes.	87	Micmac.		268
Traditions.	185–199	Montagnais.		272
Trails.	100, 291	Nahani.		397
Transport, methods of	46–7, 100–110	Ojibwa.		278
Travel, methods of	100–110, 310	Pacific Coast tribes.		330
Travois.	103, 310 (note)	Plains' tribes.		310
Illus.	103	Salish, Interior.		356
Trephining.	227, 240	Sekani.		379
Tribal divisons, map showing Eastern		Slave.		390
Woodland tribes.	266	Tahltan.		372
Cordillera.	352	Weaving	67–8, 76, 213 (note)	
Iroquoians.	290	Cedar-bark.		68
Eskimo.	406	Rabbit fur.		68, 285
Mackenzie and Yukon.	378	Sage-brush.		68
Pacific coast.	329	Wool	67–8, 76–7, 212, 399	
Plains'.	309	Illus.		68, 157
Tsetsaut.	369–370	Weirs for fish	63–5, 145, 411	
Tsimshian.	335–9	Illus.	62, 66, 397	
Art.	209–12	Whaling.	59, 410–1	
Dress.	77–8	Wheel, absence of.		32
Dwellings.	94–6	Widows, treatment of	286, 363, 374	
Fishing method.	409 (note)	Women, position of	52, 104, 162	
Language.	18	Blackfoot.		319
Moccasins.	69	Eskimo.		420
Mummification.	165	Iroquois.		135–7
Organization.	140–8	Kutchin.		403
Seasonal movements.	47	Slave.		391
Tradition.	195–9	Wood-working	37–8, 157. *See also* Art	
Weaving.	67, 212	Wool, weaving of	67–8, 76–7, 212	
Tuscarora.	133 (note)	Illus.	77, 155, 157, 336, 356	
		Wyandot.		290
V		**Y**		
Villages, selection of sites for	86–7	Yellowknife	34, 111, 122, 125,	
			388–9, 392	